3/4/2025

Ann,

Just wanted to share
A little glimpse of my work
as I pray that it helps
Practioners Engage our
Students in order to improve
their Educational outcomes

Erik M. Hines

BLACK MALES IN SECONDARY AND POSTSECONDARY EDUCATION

ADVANCES IN RACE AND ETHNICITY IN EDUCATION

Series Editors: Chance W. Lewis and
James L. Moore III

Recent Volumes:

ADVANCES IN RACE AND ETHNICITY IN EDUCATION
VOLUME 9

BLACK MALES IN SECONDARY AND POSTSECONDARY EDUCATION: TEACHING, MENTORING, ADVISING AND COUNSELING

EDITED BY

ERIK M. HINES
George Mason University, USA

AND

EDWARD C. FLETCHER JR.
The Ohio State University, USA

United Kingdom – North America – Japan
India – Malaysia – China

Emerald Publishing Limited
Emerald Publishing, Floor 5, Northspring, 21-23 Wellington Street, Leeds LS1 4DL

First edition 2024

Editorial matter and selection © 2024 Erik M. Hines and Edward C. Fletcher Jr.
Individual chapters © 2024 The authors.
Published under exclusive licence by Emerald Publishing Limited.

Reprints and permissions service
Contact: www.copyright.com

British Library Cataloguing in Publication Data
A catalogue record for this book is available from the British Library

ISBN: 978-1-80455-579-8 (Print)
ISBN: 978-1-80455-578-1 (Online)
ISBN: 978-1-80455-580-4 (Epub)

ISSN: 2051-2317 (Series)

Printed and bound by CPI Group (UK) Ltd, Croydon, CR0 4YY

INVESTOR IN PEOPLE

First, I dedicate this book to my sons, Erik Michael and Harper. I continue to advocate and educate individuals and systems on their behalf to ensure they have an easier path than me. Second, I dedicate this book to every Black man and boy who has questioned whether they are good enough for life and whatever endeavor they choose to pursue. I say to them, you are fearfully and wonderfully made and that you are the envy of the world!

—Erik M. Hines

CONTENTS

ABOUT THE EDITORS

Erik M. Hines, PhD, is a Professor of School Counseling in the Division of Child, Family, and Community Engagement within the College of Education and Human Development at George Mason University. Dr Hines prepares graduate students to be professional school counselors. His research agenda focuses on: (a) college and career readiness for Black males; (b) parental involvement and its impact on academic achievement for students of color; and (c) improving and increasing postsecondary opportunities for first generation, low-income, and students of color, particularly Black males. Additionally, his research agenda includes topics related to career exploration in the fields of Science, Technology, Engineering, and Mathematics (STEM) for students of color. He is a proud American Counseling Association (ACA) Fellow and recipient of the Al Dye Award from the Association for Specialists in Group Work.

Edward C. Fletcher Jr., PhD, is currently an Education and Human Ecology Distinguished Professor in the Workforce Development and Education program. He serves as a Faculty Associate for the Center on Education and Training for Employment, Editor for the Journal of Career and Technical Education, and Editor for the Career and Technical Education Research journal. Dr Fletcher also serves as Director for Research and Grants for the Department of Educational Studies. His research agenda examines the role of high school STEM career academies on the experiences, college and career readiness, and postsecondary transitions of students, particularly ethnically and racially diverse learners from economically disadvantaged backgrounds. Dr Fletcher was an Assistant Professor at Illinois State University in 2009 and an Assistant Professor at the University of South Florida from 2010 to 2019.

ABOUT THE CONTRIBUTORS

LaNorris D. Alexander, MA, is an emerging scholar in adolescent, postsecondary and community literacies. His doctoral research addresses the issues faced by marginalized students attending secondary schools and collegiate, undergraduate studies. Research interests include: learning and instruction methodologies, leading students and educators, navigating and overcoming challenges resulting from internal and settler colonialism. LaNorris has worked in higher education for two decades supporting student growth and development for personal and academic success. His research in culturally relevant and sustaining pedagogies fosters environments where students' personal literacies connect with classroom literacies, stimulating creative contributions from students and educators alike in the learning environment.

Johnnie Allen Jr., MSEd, (he/him/his) is a doctoral student in the Higher Education program at Florida State University (FSU), where he is a Graduate Research and Teaching Assistant and Instructor in the Leadership Learning Research Center. Johnnie is a two-time alum of Indiana University (IU). He earned his BS in Community Health and Public Health and MSEd from the IU HESA program. His research interest examines how productive masculinity in Black male leadership affects leadership engagement through a cross-sectional approach/lens with Black men at Historically black colleges and universities (HBCUs) and Predominately white institutions (PWIs). Johnnie is a McKnight Doctoral Fellow.

Sophia L. Ángeles, PhD, is an Assistant Professor of Multilingual Education in the College of Education at the Pennsylvania State University. She graduated from the School of Education and Information Studies with a PhD in Education with an emphasis on Urban Schooling. Prior to that, she worked as a professional K-12 school counselor in North Carolina and California. Her research examines how immigration and language policies shape the educational trajectories of high school immigrant youth.

Brandon Ash, MA, is an exploratory advisor at George Mason University, where he assists students in navigating the college experience by aiding course major and course selection, as well as connecting them with campus resources. In his over five years of Higher Education experience, he has served in various roles in Student and Academic Affairs with both undergraduate and graduate populations. He is currently pursuing his PhD in Higher Education Administration at Morgan State University. His scholarship focus includes retention, the academic success of Black college students, HBCUs, and academic support.

Araya Baker, EdM, MPhilEd, is a doctoral candidate in the Counselor Education program at The Pennsylvania State University. Broadly, Baker's scholarship focuses on understanding the influence of ideological and institutional socialization on the emotional, ethical/spiritual, and sociopolitical development of individuals. Specifically, he is interested in how white supremacy culture shapes views of authority and power, and how such views affect attitudes about counseling, help-seeking, and activist identity development. Baker holds an MPhilEd. in Professional Counseling from the University of Pennsylvania Graduate School of Education and an EdM in Human Development and Psychology from the Harvard Graduate School of Education.

Cameron C. Beatty, PhD, (he/him) is an Associate Professor in the Educational Leadership and Policy Studies Department at FSU. Dr Beatty is the Program Coordinator for the higher education graduate program and teaches in the undergraduate leadership certificate and serves as the Associate Director of the Leadership Learning Research Center. Dr Beatty's research foci include exploring the intersections of gender and race in leadership education and the leadership learning of Students of Color on historically white college campuses. Dr Beatty is also the Coeditor of the recent text *Engaging Black Men in College Through Leadership Learning*.

Guy J. Beauduy Jr., MEd, is a doctoral candidate at Montclair State University. He received his Master's degree in Rehabilitation Counseling from Florida Atlantic University. He is a Certified Rehabilitation Counselor (CRC), a Licensed Professional Counselor (LPC), and has over 5 years of clinical experience working in various community settings that address the concerns of ex-offenders, those with mental health and dual diagnosis, and clients in the vocational rehabilitation counseling setting. He has previously copublished literature on various topics in counseling and has presented on numerous counseling related topics at regional and national counseling conferences. His current research foci include multicultural competence in counseling, the LGBTQ+ population, and mentorship among Black men in counseling and counselor education.

Le Shorn Benjamin, PhD, is an American Society of Engineering Education Engineering Postdoctoral Fellow and former New York City Teaching Fellow. She has amassed over a decade of experience in the field of education and has been bestowed the honor of "Outstanding Research," "Diversity Efforts," and "Faculty Endowed Recognition" awards. During this time, her career has spanned international borders and included roles in educational research, program administration, higher education accreditation, and K-12 teaching. Dr Benjamin's research agenda explores minoritized student experiences, doctoral education, and, presently, issues related to broadening participation among underrepresented groups in engineering education.

Ivory Berry, PhD, is the Assistant Dean for Student Affairs and Director of Student Services for the College of Engineering and Architecture (CEA) at

Howard University. In this role, he works collaboratively with faculty and staff to reduce barriers to student success and enhance the student experience from recruitment to career placement. Dr Berry has over 15 years of professional higher education, and student and academic affairs experience working in various educational settings and serving diverse populations. His scholarship focuses on Black college student retention, critical race theory, and educational equity within higher education.

Canaan Bethea, MS, is a PhD student in Education with concentrations in educational psychology and research methods in sports psychology at George Mason University. Canaan's research focuses on critical race theory and self-regulation from the social cognitive theoretical perspective. A lot of what sparks Canaan's research interest are questions regarding cultivating self-regulatory skills in academic settings and sports context. Implications from his research help students, educators, and coaches cultivate equitable environments and self-regulatory mindsets.

Darion N. Blalock, MA, is a student affairs professional and currently serves as a Transfer Student Recruiting Coordinator at the University of Michigan. His role is broadly focused on educating prospective transfer applicants about the transfer application process, transfer credits and policies, and ensuring students are aware of relevant resources. In his professional work, his central aim is to provide students with holistic support, with a specific focus on traditionally underrepresented and underserved populations like those of racially minoritized, first-generation college status, and working-class backgrounds. Previously, Blalock worked as a Student Advisor at Washtenaw Community College.

Brittany N. Brewster, PhD, is an independent business consultant who has over 10+ years of training and curriculum development expertise, including management of large-scale leadership portfolios, research and assessment, and people management experience. Let's chat about how my background can be an asset to your organization's mission and vision.

Derrick R. Brooms, PhD, is the Executive Director of the Black Men's Research Institute (BMRI) at Morehouse College, serves as a youth worker, and is an award-winning educator and scholar. His education research primarily centers on Black men's pathways to and through college and he also examines the collegiate experiences of Black and Latino men. He is author of *Stakes Is High: Trials, Lessons, and Triumphs in Young Black Men's Educational Journeys* (2021). Brooms has been acknowledged with a Community Spirit Award (2016), Presidential Exemplary Multicultural Teaching Award (2017), and Jacqueline Johnson Jackson Early Career Scholar Award from the Association of Black Sociologists (2019).

DeOnte Brown, PhD, is a seasoned higher education administrator with experience related to student success. His work includes guiding diversity, equity, and

xvi ABOUT THE CONTRIBUTORS

inclusion efforts and administering college access, retention, and success focused programs.

Janice Byrd, PhD, is an Assistant Professor in the Counselor Education Program at the Pennsylvania State University. She earned her PhD in Counselor Education and Supervision from the University of Iowa and an MEd in Counselor Education (K-12 school counseling) from South Carolina State University. Dr Byrd has previous experience as a school counselor, career counselor, and with teaching youth in secondary settings. Using critical epistemologies, Dr Byrd's scholarship has been nationally recognized/awarded and it explores the lived experiences of Black people across all stages of the educational pipeline to interrogate how facets of their development (i.e., personal, social, academic, and career) is influenced by policies (education and healthcare), relationships (school, familial, and community), and broader ecological circumstances (racism, sexism, and social determinants of health) which affect their ability to be the best version of themselves.

Dakota W. Cintron, PhD, is a postdoctoral research fellow at the Center for Integrative Developmental Science at Cornell University. He received his PhD in Educational Psychology with a concentration in research methods, measurement, and evaluation from the Neag School of Education at the University of Connecticut. Dakota also earned an EdM in Measurement and Evaluation and MS in Applied Statistics from Teachers College at Columbia.

Patrick D. Cunningham, PhD, is an Assistant Professor at Appalachian State University. He served as a School Counselor for several years, both in North Carolina and overseas, in Dubai and South Korea. His research is focused on school counseling outcomes, antiracist school counseling practices, and family engagement in education.

Louis L. Dilbert, MS, is the Director of the TRIO Educational Opportunity Center and Military and Veteran Affairs at Florida Agricultural and Mechanical University (FAMU) and Adjunct Instructor in the Behavioral, Social Sciences and Education Department at Tallahassee Community College. He earned his Bachelor's degree in Health Education and Master's degree in Educational Leadership/Administration from Florida State University and is currently a doctoral candidate in Educational Leadership at FAMU. His research focuses on the factors that influence college choice for African American males from rural communities. His 17-year tenure in higher education has been working with disadvantaged and special populations in areas ranging from academic advising to disability services to his current roles that serve first-generation adult learners and military-connected students.

Stephanie Smith-Durkin, PhD, is an Assistant Professor at Old Dominion University. There, she works to effectively prepare counselors for culturally affirming and antiracist professional practices and ethical behaviors. Stephanie is a former school counselor with nearly two decades of experience working with children and their caregivers. She is also a dedicated member of the Counselors for Social Justice (CSJ) School Counseling Task Force and secretary for the Association of Child and Adolescent Counseling. Stephanie researches and presents on topics surrounding student mental health, social justice, multiculturalism, antiracism, and multi-tiered systems of support (MTSS). She is also a National Certified Counselor.

Jordan Farmer, MEd, is an experienced higher education professional with 8 years of demonstrated history working to support diverse populations of students on college campuses. He has experience working at both private and public institutions in the functional areas of athletics, residence life, academic affairs, graduate admissions, leadership education, and case management. His personal passions are mentorship and building relationships with students and the community.

Marcus Folkes, PhD, is an Assistant Professor of Counseling, Internship Coordinator, Licensed Mental Health counselor (FL), Licensed professional counselor (TX), and qualified supervisor. He received his MS in Clinical Mental Health Counseling from Bethune-Cookman University and his PhD in Counselor Education and Supervision with a specialization in Advance Counseling from the University of the Cumberlands. He has worked with clients across life span, while focusing and specializing in counseling with adolescents and young adults with adjustment or traumatic stress who are involved in the child welfare system. Dr Folkes enjoys advocating for diversity, equity, and inclusion in collaboration with other professionals. He has presented at many state conferences and local conferences on topics such as mental health 101, resiliency in youth, trauma-informed Care, self-care, intergenerational and transgenerational trauma, and mental health stigma.

David Julius Ford Jr., PhD, is a Tenured Associate Professor and Department Chair in the Department of Professional Counseling at Monmouth University, West Long Branch, New Jersey. He also serves as the Past President of the New Jersey Counseling Association. He is a Licensed Counselor in North Carolina, Virginia, and New Jersey, is a Board-Certified Counselor (NCC), and a Board-Certified Supervisor (ACS). His research interests lie in supporting Black male students at PWIs, Black Greek-letter Organizations, counseling LGBTQ+ clients, the intersection of race/ethnicity and sexual/affectional orientation, the intersection of religion/spirituality, race/ethnicity, and sexual/affectional orientation, and those impacted by HIV/AIDS. He is a strong advocate for more Black men in Counseling and Counselor Education.

Donna Y. Ford, PhD, is a Distinguished Professor of Education and Human Ecology and Kirwan Institute Faculty Affiliate at The Ohio State University. She is in the Department of Educational Studies, Special Education Program. She earned all degrees from Cleveland State University. Ford focuses primarily on the underrepresentation of Black and Hispanic students in gifted education and advanced classes. She is a leader in urban education. Dr Ford has authored more than 400 publications and 14 books. She presents in school districts and organizations on opportunity gaps, equity, multicultural curriculum, antiracism, and cultural competence.

Jesse R. Ford, PhD, is an Assistant Professor of Higher Education in the Teacher Education and Higher Education department. As a former student affairs administrator, he uses a theory to practice approach to student learning. Dr Ford's research uses culturally responsive frameworks to explore the social and political influences of race and gender. More specifically, he employs qualitative methodologies to tackle inequity in education, particularly within the socialization experiences of underrepresented students, faculty, and administrators across the P-20 pipeline.

Jessica Fort, MA, is a former Secondary Education School Counselor and current full-time PhD student in Virginia Commonwealth's Counselor Education and Supervision Program. Jessica's research examines the barriers of academic achievement for Black males and focuses on determining interventions through a strength-based approach to create positive educational experiences and academic outcomes K-12 and beyond.

Rose-May Frazier, PhD, is an Executive Director of Student Services at Florida Atlantic University. Dr Frazier possesses over 20 years of experience related to college student success. Much of her experience and expertise is related to academic advising and coaching services.

Rickya S. F. Freeman is a senior attending Florida Agricultural and Mechanical University majoring in Psychology with a minor in Sociology. She is a 2022 Cohort Fellow of the PURPOSE Program. Her research is focused on the support of mental health awareness of African American undergraduate College students.

Monique N. Golden, holds a PhD in Leadership and Education Policy with a background in Higher Education and Student Affairs. Monique's research interests include college student development, leadership, and success.

Scott L. Graves Jr., PhD, is a Professor in the School Psychology program at Ohio State University and the Director of the Positive Youth Development Lab. His research agenda is focused on identifying strengths in African American children that lead to positive social emotional and academic outcomes.

Jerrod A. Henderson, PhD, ("Dr J") is an Assistant Professor in the William A. Brookshire Department of Chemical and Biomolecular Engineering at the University of Houston. Henderson's work focuses on the lived experiences of Black male engineering students and K-20 student engagement. He is a Cofounder of the St. Elmo Brady STEM Academy (SEBA), an intervention aimed at exposing underrepresented fourth- and fifth-grade students and their families to hands-on STEM experiences. Career Communications Group has most recently recognized him with a Black Engineer of the Year Award for college-level promotion of education.

Paul C. Harris, PhD, is the Founder of Integrity Matters, LLC, which exists to build a just world. He previously served as an Associate Professor of Education at The Pennsylvania State University and the University of Virginia, and as a High School Counselor in Newport News and Loudoun County, Virginia. Dr Harris' work focuses on enhancing the academic, emotional, and career development of Black youth and empowering the identity development of Black male student-athletes. His contributions have been acknowledged by the American School Counselor Association, American Educational Research Association, Southern Association of Counselor Education and Supervision, and Education Trust.

Christian M. Hines, PhD, is an Assistant Professor at Texas State University. She is a comics and young adult literature in education scholar-practitioner. Her research highlights the representation of Black youth and adolescence in litera-ture, particularly their visual narratives in comics and graphic novels. As self-proclaimed "Blerd" (Black nerd), and former high school English teacher, she is interested in visual narratives as a way for students and education practi-tioners to understand the lived experiences of Black youth and various ethnic groups to be re-storied as heroes in their own communities through the enacting resistance and highlighting inequity and injustice for students within society and schooling spaces.

Mia R. Hines, EdD, is the Associate Director of the Early Identification Program (E.I.P.) at George Mason University. She served as an Academic Advisor in the College of Education's Office of Academic Services and Intern Support for stu-dents enrolled in the Bachelor's/Master's Teacher Preparation Programs. In this role one of her priority goals is to increase the number of teachers of color going into the classroom. Prior to working at FSU, Mia worked in the Neag School of Education at the University of Connecticut where she participated on the American Association of Colleges for Teacher Education's (AACTE) Networked Improvement Committee for the recruitment and retention of Black and Latino males. Mia also worked as a high school counselor in Maryland and North Carolina where she gained an extensive background in developing college and career readiness programs that assist students with matriculating through college. In addition, Mia has her school administrator license and has worked on school administration teams in an effort to support classroom teachers.

Marcel Jacobs, MA, is a fourth-year doctoral student in the school psychology program at Ohio State University. His research interests include understanding how constructs such as motivation and academic self-efficacy improve outcomes for Black youth.

David H. Kenton, JD, EdD, is an experienced higher education administrator and student advocate with experiences at varying types of postsecondary institutions. His work has most notably improved education for former foster youth and first-generation students.

Hyunhee Kim, PhD, is an Assistant Professor in the counseling program. She has professional counseling experiences to work with children, adolescents, college students, and adults in different settings. Her primary research interest is the role of relationships in educational settings. As a school counselor educator, she is interested in facilitating students' positive development and creating a supportive environment where every student feels included and thrives.

Deepika Nantha Kumar (pronouns: she/her/hers) is in the second year of her Master's program in Counselor Education with an emphasis on Clinical Mental Health Counseling at The Pennsylvania State University. She is Indian by origin. She is passionate about her research interest of assessing systemic barriers and their impact on mental health in Black and Brown communities. She is also the Vice President of community development for the international honor society Chi Sigma Iota Rho Alpha Mu chapter and served as a Cochair for the chapter's multicultural committee in the past.

Chance W. Lewis, PhD, is the Carol Grotnes Belk Distinguished Professor of Urban Education and former Provost Faculty Fellow for Diversity, Inclusion, and Access at the University of North Carolina at Charlotte. Additionally, Dr Lewis is the Executive Director of the University of North Carolina at Charlotte's Urban Education Collaborative which is publishing a new generation of research on improving urban schools.

Clifford H. Mack, Jr., PhD, has been a High School Counselor in the private school sector since 2007. He has served on the Florida School Counselor Board (FSCA) and North American Christian College Admissions Professionals (NACCAP) board. Dr Mack completed his undergraduate studies at Washington Bible College (Maryland), Master's in Counseling Psychology at Trinity International University (Florida), and PhD in Counselor Education at Florida Atlantic University. Currently he serves as a School Counselor at Calvary Christian Academy (Fort Lauderdale, FL). In addition to his practitioner role, Dr Mack serves as an Adjunct Professor for Florida Atlantic University, FSU, Lancaster Bible College, and Trinity International University.

Renae D. Mayes, PhD, is an Associate Professor in the Department of Disability and Psychoeducational Studies. She is a licensed school counselor and national certified counselor with experience in K-12 schools along with specialized educational settings. Informed by Critical Race Theory, Critical Race Feminism, DisCrit, and bioecological systems theories, her research agenda centers around the academic success and college readiness for gifted Black students with dis/abilities and Black girls. Mayes' research details the experience of students and families navigating schools, while also providing recommendations for dismantling systems of oppression through policy and practice.

Alagammai Meyyappan is a second year MEd student in Counselor Education at The Pennsylvania State University. Her emphasis is secondary school counseling. Alagammai is currently interning at the State College Area High School.

Dejanell C. Mittman, MS/EdS, is a doctoral student in the Counseling and Counselor Education Program at North Carolina State University. She has also been a practicing school counselor for 9 years and serves on the Guilford County (North Carolina) School Counseling Leadership Team. Dejanell's research is focused on the lived experiences of school counselors, school counselor advocacy, and school-based practicum experiences.

James L. Moore, III, PhD, is the Executive Director for the Todd Anthony Bell National Resource Center on the African American Male and the EHE Distinguished Professor of Urban Education in the Department of Education Studies at The Ohio State University. His research agenda focuses on *school counseling, gifted education, urban education, higher education, multicultural education/ counseling, and STEM education*, and Dr Moore is often quoted, featured, and mentioned in popular publications, such as the *New York Magazine, New York Times, St. Louis Post-Dispatch, Columbus Dispatch, Spartanburg Herald, Cincinnati Enquirer, Journal of Blacks in Higher Education, Chronicle of Higher Education*, and *Diverse: Issues in Higher Education*. Since 2018, he has been cited annually by *Education Week* as one of the 200 most influential scholars and researchers in the United States.

Tia Nickens is a second year MEd student in School Counseling at The Pennsylvania State University. She earned her BS in Secondary Education at the University of South Alabama. Tia has a passion for education, working to create adequate resources for all students. She is an active volunteer for the international honor society of Chi Sigma Iota and is currently serving as the President for the Rho Alpha Mu chapter. Tia hopes to continue this necessary research to help bring applicable information forward about marginalized identities.

Ezekiel Peebles, III, MS, is a Licensed Professional Clinical Counselor supervisor by the state of Ohio since 2011. Ezekiel is a National Certified Counselor by the National Board of Certified Counselors. He is the Founder and Clinical Director of Key Counseling & Consultation LLC, which is a private practice in Gahanna, Ohio. He specializes in psychotherapy that focuses on the wellness of the whole individual, not just sustaining mental/emotional health, but also managing their life and relationships. Additionally, he is a third-year doctoral student in the college of Education and Human Ecology, Counselor Education and Supervision program at The Ohio State University. His current research interests include *masculinity, men's issues, mental health, counselor identity, cultural competence, and social justice.*

Derrick Pollock, PhD, has higher education experience in foreign language instruction and support of international students. In addition to foreign language education, Dr Pollock's research interests include Black student motivation.

Michael Reid, Jr., MA, is a second year doctoral student in the Educational Policy and Planning program at the University of Texas at Austin. He is a Graduate Research Assistant at The Center for Community College Student

Engagement. Michael's research interests include income segregation, education philosophy, poverty and education policy, basic needs insecurity, and educational opportunity on P-16 levels.

Darius A. Robinson, EdM, (he/him/his) is a doctoral student in the Higher Education program at FSU. He also is a graduate teaching assistant at the Leadership Learning Research Center. His research interests revolve around the examination of leadership experiences of students of color, with a focus on Black males. Additionally, he is also a teaching associate with the Program of Instructional Excellence, using his experience to help other graduate teaching assistants at FSU. Prior to his doctoral journey, Darius has had professional experiences working in residential life, K-12 education and service activism with disaster rebuilding projects.

Miray D. Seward, PhD, is a research scientist at Search Institute. Her research primarily focuses on the identity development, socialization, and schooling experiences of Black women and girls.

E. Mackenzie (Ken) Shell, PhD, LPC, CPCS, CAADC, is an Assistant Professor of Counselor Education. He is a Licensed Professional Counselor (LPC) in Georgia, a Certified Professional Counselor Supervisor (CPCS) in Georgia, and a Certified Advanced Alcohol and Drug Counselor (CAADC). Prior to working at Central Connecticut State University, Ken worked at Clark Atlanta University where he served as a counselor educator and clinical mental health program coordinator. Dr Shell has worked in many counseling settings, such as school-based mental health, high school counseling, college career centers, and private agencies. He has worked with children, adolescents, and adults.

Paul Singleton, II, PhD, serves as a school counselor and DEI coordinator at The Potomac School in McLean, Virginia. His research interests surround African American male academic achievement, social and emotional well-being, and college and career readiness for African American males. Paul has had various educational experiences in low-income, culturally diverse communities (Hartford, Connecticut; Philadelphia, Pennsylvania; Washington, D.C.; Orangeburg, South Carolina; Abington, Pennsylvania) and schools identified as being at high levels of risk or underserved.

Tyron Slack, MSW, LCSW, is a fourth-year doctoral candidate in the Combined Counseling Psychology and School Psychology program at FSU. His clinical and research interests focus on the impact of racial microaggressions on Black and other underrepresented students, their academic success, resilience, and mental health.

Christopher L. Small, PhD, is a Teaching Faculty Professor in the Educational Leadership and Policy Studies Department at Florida State University. Dr Small serves as the Director of the Educational Leadership and Administration Master's/Specialist Program and teaches courses toward Florida Educational Leadership certification. Dr Small has over 11 years of Title I school principalship experience and conducts research on leadership preparation. Dr Small's research foci includes exploring the intersections of gender and race in leadership preparation programs, leadership learning for justice, equity, diversity and inclusion on K-12 campuses, and implications of leading for literacy instruction for Black male students.

Marcus L. Smith, MS, is a graduate student at the University of Cincinnati. His research and teachings focus on the intersection of Black masculinities, sports, and social and academic achievement. More specifically, his current research analyzes how the racial mindsets of college basketball coaches impact the mentoring they provide to Black student-athletes and the holistic development of Black student-athletes. Prior to this role, Smith worked as a high school and college basketball coach where he supported the social, academic, and athletic development of Black male student-athletes.

Jasmin Spain, MEd, has two decades of higher education experience, currently serving as the Assistant Vice President of Student Support at Pitt Community College (North Carolina). Jasmin serves as an Equity Coach for the Lumina Foundation associated R.E.A.C.H. Collaborative (Racial Equity for Adult Credentials in Higher Education). Jasmin is the Founder and Chief Visionary Officer of the consulting agency, The M.A.I.N. Initiative LLC, as well as the Founder and President of the registered nonprofit, U Good Bro, Incorporated. Jasmin is an active member of Alpha Phi Alpha Fraternity, Inc. and is also a Campaign for Black Male Achievement American Express Leadership Fellow.

Sam Steen, PhD, is a Professor, Licensed Professional School Counselor, and Director of the Diversity Research Action Consortium, who specializes in school counseling, group work and cultivating Black students' academic identity development. He was a school counselor for 10 years. Two objectives guide his scholarship: (1) to further develop creative and culturally sustaining school-based counseling interventions that improve student achievement including The Achieving Success Everyday Group Model (ASE Group Model) designed to promote social emotional and academic development for students of color and (2) to explore issues related to the training and preparation of preservice counselors and school counselors.

Nicholas T. Vick, EdD, is the current Associate Dean of Communications and Humanities and Director of the Honors Program at Tallahassee Community College. He is a seasoned administrator and instructor dedicated to student success. Nick has received numerous awards for his work in academic support including the North Carolina Tutoring and Learning Association Center of the Year, the Frank L. Christ Outstanding Center recognition from the National College Learning Center Association, and, most recently, the Association of Florida Colleges' Technology Commission Award.

Bobbi-Jo Wathen, PhD, serves as Director of School Counseling for Middleton Public Schools. She has also been a practicing school counselor for 11 years and is currently serving Middletown High School in Connecticut as Director of School Counseling. Bobbi-Jo is researching counselors' readiness to offer comprehensive career counseling to Black Boys and postsecondary transitions for Black Boys. She is also an education consultant for the National Center for Women in Information Technology, where she works with Counselors for Computing (C4C) to expand computer science access to women and people of color.

Ryan Wright, MEd, is a current doctoral student in Western Michigan's Counseling Psychology program. Prior to pursuing his doctoral degree Ryan obtained his Master's degree in rehabilitation counseling from the University of the District of Columbia. As a native of Washington, DC Ryan has served as a community mental health therapist and student support staff in Washington, DC schools prior to pursuing training as a therapist.

FOREWORD

There are times in history when certain books must be written! *Black Males in Secondary and Postsecondary Education: Teaching, Mentoring, Advising and Counseling* is one of these books! The famous words of W. E. B. DuBois (1903) are still relevant today where he noted, "how does it feel to be a problem?" Given the current state of our nation's political and educational climate, Black male students in our nation's educational system have been relegated to a substandard system where they have garnered media attention and a national spotlight not for the positive attributes they bring to the educational setting but for negative stories and headlines that are oftentimes manufactured to get likes and clicks.

I want to be crystal clear. Many Black male students are facing an academic death in our nation's secondary and postsecondary educational environments. Unfortunately, educators continue to make excuses why it is not their fault that Black male students are not achieving academically. However, they never discuss what is in their power to change when Black males students enter secondary and postsecondary schools in this great nation. As a result, this book is a welcome addition to the education knowledge base as it provides a new and fresh perspective on how to effectively serve Black male students via teaching, mentoring, advising, and counseling.

It is my hope that this book reaches the educators, counselors, and other stakeholders that it needs to reach to make a positive difference for Black male students to achieve academically in the most affluent country in the world. We can no longer, in this age of educational accountability, continue to stand by and watch the achievement levels of this student population be at or near the bottom of every major academic barometer and be comfortable with our work as education professionals. Once the education profession chooses to fully embrace the educational potential of Black male students, we will see transformation happen for Black male students that want to achieve at a high level but are in educational environments that do not develop their full potential.

This book, *Black Males in Secondary and Postsecondary Education: Teaching, Mentoring, Advising and Counseling* is also for Black parents who send their Black males to school expecting something great to happen only to be met with disappointment at the door of the school building or the postsecondary institution. The greatness they expect for their Black males is why many work one, two, or even three jobs to make sure these young Black males have food on the table and a roof over their head just so they can make it to school! Unfortunately, when their Black males matriculate through our nation's schools, they are met with "educational rhetoric." This educational rhetoric tells the parents all that is perceived to be wrong with their Black male child(ren) rather than how the schooling experience will put them in the best position to have a positive impact on their lives.

Finally, this book embraces the voices, hopes, and dreams of scholars who embody the faith that Black students to have a right to a quality education in this country. We thank you for valuable contributions so that one day the education profession can reach its full potential by serving the educational needs of Black male students. I have come to learn that we have to continue to push until this change happens. This is why I commend Dr Hines and Dr Fletcher for this valuable contribution to the education profession. An intentional focus on Black Males in Secondary and Postsecondary Education is exactly what we need at this moment. It is my hope that this book will spark a new movement of Black male academic success!

Chance W. Lewis, PhD
Carol Grotnes Belk Distinguished Professor of Urban Education
Director, The Urban Education Collaborative
University of North Carolina at Charlotte

REFERENCE

DuBois, W. E. B. (1903). *The souls of Black folk*. Random House.

PART I

PRIMARY AND SECONDARY SETTINGS

CHAPTER 1

GETTING GRAPHIC: RESISTING ANTI-BLACKNESS VIA THE VISUAL NARRATIVES OF BLACK BOYS

Christian M. Hines and LaNorris D. Alexander

ABSTRACT

Comics and graphic novels can disrupt traditional texts by challenging the "worship of the written word" (Torres, 2019), a feature of white supremacy that perpetuates textual hierarchies within educational spaces. Giving all of our students access to contemporary literature that centers Black youth perspectives is not only important in decolonizing literature education but also in presenting a holistic view of Black childhood. They can be used in the classroom as subjects to challenge stereotypical depictions by centering experiences, ideas, and concepts that are often marginalized in traditional curriculum. Within this chapter, we focus on comics and graphic novels as tools to enact students' multiliteracies and to analyze visual stories depicting BlackBoy adolescence, using the frameworks of BlackBoy Crit Pedagogy (Bryan, 2022), an equity framework that interrogates the interdisciplinary ways that Black boy students' literacy learning can be formed through the teaching and learning of Blackness, maleness, and the schooling experiences of Black boys. We utilize this framework to analyze the use of diverse comics and graphic novels to facilitate critical conversations of bringing inclusive visual texts into the classroom. We invite practitioners to reimagine curricular ideas and content centered on empowerment and Black boy adolescence and how those ideas are presented to youth through a variety of visual narratives.

Keywords: Comics; Black boys; literature; literacy; classroom; pedagogy

Black Males in Secondary and Postsecondary Education
Advances in Race and Ethnicity in Education, Volume 9, 3–23
Copyright © 2024 Christian M. Hines and LaNorris D. Alexander
Published under exclusive licence by Emerald Publishing Limited
ISSN: 2051-2317/doi:10.1108/S2051-231720230000009001

Literature creates avenues for students to question and challenge the societal and cultural infrastructure that exists around them. Students are able to make connections, understand commonalities, and appreciate cultural differences as opposed to engaging in "othering" of cultures and ethnicities that differ from their own. The notion of "othering" can be combatted by counter storytelling and including silenced stories that give voice and agency to a demographic that is typically marginalized and misrepresented. These untold counter stories are being written and told, but they are just rarely amplified.

Literature can be used as a tool that perpetuates colonialism by enacting the teaching of canonical texts that prominently center whiteness and the white gaze. Usually within these texts, Black boys are either nonexistent or only secondary to the white characters and subjected to stereotypes or some form of racial violence. To shift the focus of the centering of Black boys' perspectives and lived experiences, teachers should steer away from only teaching and reading narratives that perpetuate damaging and oppressive beliefs (Young et al., 2018) and move toward promoting more inclusive books within their classroom that promote equity of voice and liberation of racist ideologies. Providing students with literature that center Black boys and the multilayered ways they exist aids in the work of (re)shaping societal views and fighting against adultification bias – when Black children are seen as more adult than their white counterparts (Morris, 2018). "In children's books, seeing themselves portrayed visually and textually as realistically human was essential to letting them know that they are valued in the social context in which they are growing up" (Bishop, 2012, p. 9). Giving our students access to diverse texts, specifically texts that center Black boys, challenges them to think critically and holistically about the everyday lives of those around them.

In children's and young adult literature, the need for representation has become apparent so that adolescents may see themselves and their world reflected on the pages that they are consuming. There has been an outcry for diverse literature in the form of popular hashtags such as (Dávila, 2015) and (Whaley, n.d.). Representation matters in all media forms. Visual images are a commodity; they are bought, sold, valued, and traded. There is a lot to be said of seeing yourself within the confines of your own story, "images have the power to make something more real, more visceral, and more representational," (Moeller & Becnel, 2018, p. 8). Within a predominantly white publishing industry, it is important that children and young adults see themselves within the pages of the literature they are reading.

Research shows that children of color begin to discover their racial identity and focus on their ethnic development around middle school. Having characters that reflect their diverse cultural and ethnic background can aid in their racial development and challenge stereotypes. However, when considering diverse stories, one must look at who chooses the story, and how those diverse stories being told? "Stereotyping, caricature, and marginalization of people of color, poor and working-class children and families, gender and sexual minorities, immigrants, and other minoritized groups have been persistent problems in children's literature," (Thomas, 2019, p. 5). Even though there are diverse books being advertised and celebrated, statistics gathered by the Cooperative Children's

Book Center (CCBC) states that in 2018, the percentage of books depicting diverse characters were as follows: 50% white, 27% animals/other, 10% African American, 7% Asian Pacific Islander/Asian Pacific American, 5% Latinx, and 1% American Indians/First Nations. When considering that there is scarcity in representation, one must also consider who is authoring these diverse stories, the "#OwnVoices movement that calls for more youth literature written by people of color about their experiences" (Moeller & Becnel, 2018). Providing adolescents with not only compelling literature but also literature that authentically represents the world around them helps to create what Rudine Sims Bishop called "sliding glass doors," where the reader uses their imagination to walk through into an author's created world. Some of those worlds are visualized on the pages of graphic novels and comics.

GRAPHIC NOVELS AND COMICS IN THE CLASSROOM

Reading is a transactional process where the reader is an active participant within the spatial and sequential time progression of words and visual images (Freire, 1983; Iser, 1972; Rosenblatt, 1978). Graphic novels are becoming more commonly used in the classroom (Sheehan, 2018) and are increasingly the most checked out books in school libraries (Botzakis et al., 2017). Adolescents of all ages enjoy comics and graphic novels because the form combines both visual images and text, and youth can be immersed in an illustrated story within this medium (Yang, 2008). Comics usually refer to serialized issues that are distributed weekly and sometimes monthly. Graphic novels tend to be one cohesive story bound together in a 100 plus page book. Within publishing, serialized comic stories are now being combined in trade paperback form and they also are considered a type of graphic novels (Botzakis et al., 2017; Brenner, 2011). Graphic novels aid in formulating adolescent ideas of what is given prominence in terms of societal standards and influence. It provides navigational guidance to make sense of their everyday lived experiences (Moeller & Becnel, 2018), "The combination of image, text, and story that graphic novels employ makes their influence a visceral and powerful one" (p. 2). What adolescents see on the page leaves an impression on them about the world at large. The stories that are told should be accurate and racially authentic.

When presenting literature in the classroom, teachers can integrate text that evokes engaging in critical literacy. Critical literacy is "focused on the uses of literacy for social justice in marginalized and disenfranchised communities" (Moore & Begoray, 2017, p. 173); educators can promote critical literacy in the classroom using comics and graphic novels to cultivate a space that encourages discussion and promotes socioemotional learning. The reading of these visual texts engages the reader in varied levels of critical analysis, "reading comic books requires an active, though largely subconscious, participation on the part of the reader" (Versaci, 2001, p. 63). Engagement in visual literacy is a sensory experience (Parker, 2021) and an embodied practice (Snowber, 2012); the placement of text to images allot for nonlinear ways to comprehend time, space, and creates "visual permeance" (Yang, 2008) where control of the information and processes are held completely by the reader (p. 187). Comics and graphic novels captivate the interests of a wide range of diverse learners.

Adolescents in the 21st century interact and learn across multiple visual mediums and platforms (i.e., gaming, social media, streaming services etc.); the incorporation of this visual medium enhances the quality of the reading and comprehension process. Through visual representation, students can interact with text and see not only themselves reflected on the page but other ethnicities they may not be familiar with. "Graphic novels are helping to shape children's ideas of what is normal, acceptable, and powerful in a society they are just learning to navigate on their own." Using critical literacy while reading diverse comics and graphic novels allows the reader to question how the character of color is being represented in the story, and is that representation accurate and authentic?

BLACKBOY CRIT PEDAGOGY

Education when operating at its full capacity should provide opportunities for growth and the nurturing of knowledge for all students. Students should thrive in educational spaces that are framed around equity and access (Minor, 2018). Black and brown communities seek educational justice, however, because educational systems were not designed for marginalized communities to be successful; those systems need to be abolished and reimagined for all students to thrive and be successful. To work toward the establishment of education as a liberatory space for Black and brown students, educators have to be intentional and conscious in their efforts to not homogenize the identities, cultures, and experiences of their students. This transformation is possible by shifting away from harmful and racist practices and creating educational enclaves where students feel safe, supported, and are able to thrive. Abolitionist educator Bettina Love's (2019) work highlights the ramifications of the "education survival complex" (p. 27) where students are taught harmful practices such as policing of their bodies, exclusionary curricula, standardized testing, etc., that prepares them for learning how to "just get by," where they are always surviving and living on the cusp of regularly having to find a way through difficult learning and living experiences. It is essential for educators to take up resistance against educational inequities that are harmful to Black and Brown students and create educational spaces where students can thrive and not constantly fight to survive.

Bryan's (2022) conceptual framework of *BlackBoy Crit Pedagogy* interrogates and provides practical teaching strategies for acknowledging and affirming the educational experiences of Black boys. His research builds off the work of critical race theory (CRT) and how it is utilized in education (Ladson-Billings & Tate, 1995), Black Male Studies (Curry, 2017), and Black Critical Theory (Dumas & Ross, 2016), otherwise known as BlackCrit. BlackCrit was created under the premise that CRT covered race broadly and did not specifically address the "Black experience" and issues and structures that surround and promote anti-Blackness. BlackCrit explicates a need for theorizing surrounding Blackness to be specifically named and located alongside CRT. BlackBoy Crit Pedagogy centralizes pedagogical empowerment that is rooted four specific framings:

(1) Combating *anti-Black misandry*, which is the derision of Black boys/males that permeates social structures, policies, government, institutions, education, etc.
(2) The centering of the lived experiences and educational practices of Blackness, Black males including teachers and students.
(3) A healing counter culture pedagogy for Black boys.
(4) Family and community centered as collaborative partners in education.

Bryan also homes in on the impact educators have on influencing the types of texts that students have access to. He brings attention to what he calls *pedagogical malfeasance* – teaching and learning centered around whiteness as a dominant way of existing while simultaneously othering Black boys (Bryan, 2022, p. 46). He implores that educator(s) must work to dismantle acts of pedagogical malfeasance in schooling spaces. Within his own schooling experience, Bryans' elementary teacher affectionately named "Mr. C" provided books that were diverse in representation and worked toward the dismantling of anti-Blackness by providing varied constructions of Blackness free from white supremacy (Bryan, 2022, p. 5). This form of critical literacy (Freire, 1983) allows students to read the world through the word.

While Bryans work focuses on the early formative years of Black boy education, we believe his research is applicable in varied educational stages. Utilizing this framework in ELA classrooms centers Black literacies and voices in texts, art, media, etc., and provides students a foundation to develop their sociopolitical consciousness and critique the historical and contemporary positioning of Black boys within the structural dynamics of society. We utilize the BlackBoy Crit Pedagogy to interrogate several comics and graphic novels; *Quincredible: Quest to be the Best* by Rodney Barnes, *Miles Morales: The Ultimate Spiderman* by Brian Michael Bendis, *New Kid* and *Class Act* by Jerry Craft, *Long Way Down* by Jason Reynolds, *The Crossover* by Kwame Alexander, and *Monster: A graphic novel* by Walter Dean Myers and adapted by Guy A. Sims, that challenge perspectives and biases of Black boys via counter storytelling and visualizations that depict nuanced ways of being for Black boys. We selected these texts as they share important principles and details paramount to inclusive learning as well as social, emotional, and behavioral development.

EXPLORING BLACK BOYHOOD IN COMICS AND GRAPHIC NOVELS

Quincredible, Vol 1: Quest to Be the Best

Written by Black screenwriter Rodney Barnes, within this story, the reader is introduced to Quinton West who resides with his family in New Orleans,

Louisiana. Quin's life is forever changed when a meteor shower hits his parish, and he is left with the power of invulnerability. Quin is a loner who spends the majority of his time making electronics and discovering ways to keep his home and his parents safe. Quin is very in tune with the needs of his community and the sociopolitical structures of being Black in his world. Quin is a normal teenager who is trying to find his place in his world; he has a crush on a popular girl, trying his hand at activism and wondering what is the meaning of it all. Through a series of events, Quin discovers what it means to become a hero and protect the ones you love and even the ones you don't care for.

Quincredible tackles various social justice and racial issues such as displacement of Black communities' post Hurricane Katrina, police brutality, gang violence, and manipulation of marginalized communities. This text offers the readers ways to analyze visually the depictions of these social justice issues. Reading this text via the framings of BlackBoy Crit Pedagogy showcases to the reader the value of family and community. The main point of contention in this narrative is the increased violence and access to advanced weaponry in Quin's neighborhood. Quin and his team of enhanced humans seek to discover the reasons why they are being targeted and who is infiltrating and supplying the local people with weapons. Quin explains to his team that although it is important that they track down who is distributing the weapons, it is even more important that the locals aren't punished for that crime. He states that the people in the community are already still recovering from a natural disaster and a government that is not aiding and supporting them in the ways that are most needed, their issues are systemic, and the community needs to know that their local heroes support them even when their government does not. It is within these panels that the communal practice of Black culture is evident. As superheroes, Quin and his team want to do more than "police" their neighborhood. They want to give back and create a way forward. It is in this vein they are embracing the framing of family and community as collaborators in educating the community in safe noncriminalistic ways to better the neighborhood.

Quin himself embodies a healing pedagogy for Black boys. He starts out as a loner but ends up with a group of people that support him and want the best for him. His parents are a strong support system for him; they encourage his inventing while still allowing him time to find his place in the world and letting him know his home will always be a safe haven for him. This story can disrupt negative stereotypes of nonsupportive Black homes, while also adding that Black boys too need the space to discover who they are as they navigate their own adolescence. Quin has a deep need to protect his family by wanting to create an alarm system to keep them safe, but that need to protect also manifests when he decides to use his power and his intellect to protect his neighborhood. Quin has obstacles in his way that come in the form of local bullies, police, and villains. Yet his passion for the people, his people, Black people never wanes.

Quincredible provides Black boys with a chance to see the development of an everyday hero. Written by a Black man, Quin's narrative shows the authentic multiplicity of Black males and their nuanced journey to identity formation. Within this graphic text, they are given depictions and nuances of Black boyhood, and they can immerse themselves in Quin's quest to be the best, while figuring out what their own personal narrative will be.

Miles Morales: The Ultimate Spider-Man

Miles Morales' origin story offers a bit of a departure from the previous story as he is a Black character that was created by a white writer, created in 2011 by Brian Michael Bendis when the original *Spider-Man*, Peter Parker, died. Miles is Afro-Latino and has similar spider powers along with a few new ones such as the ability to camouflage and an electric venom strike that causes paralysis. Miles's origin story finds him navigating becoming a superhero and also winning the lottery to get into a highly elite charter school called Visions Academy.

Miles, though figuring out his super powers on his own, still has three different Black male figures that contribute to how he moves through life with these new changes. The first is his father Jefferson Davis who works alongside his wife to provide for his family and right the wrongs of his past. He tells Miles that when he was younger, he did not always make the best choices, and he had to make a way out of no way which differs from his brother Miles' uncle Aaron. Aaron takes a different approach to life where he is determined to take all he can while can. His advice often comes as a paradox for Miles because he encourages Miles to find himself and master his abilities to reach his full potential while also using Miles' new found abilities to further his own criminal activity.

It is within the scenes that Black boys can engage in criticality in observing the duality of Miles's father and uncle. Both want the best for Miles but at different costs. Jefferson understands that Black men don't always get a second chance to make an impression or to create the life that they want, so he is very strict and regimented in the way he instructs Miles to show up in life. Miles's uncle Aaron has opted to live a seedier life and wants Miles to help him gain the upper hand over his enemies and eventually run the city. Miles has to navigate family alliances and the vulnerability of whether or not to tell his father that he is *Spider-Man* – even though his father despises mutants and superheroes, and the toxic masculinity of his uncle Aaron who holds the truth of Miles' identity metaphorically in his hands. This creates a paradox that is highlighted by Curry (2017), where Black males historically are caught between societal constraints of vulnerability and hypermasculinity. Black boys may relate to the struggles Miles has at wanting to please and not disappoint either male figure in his life but at what cost?

BlackBoy Crit Pedagogy via this particular comic's text illustrates Miles maneuvering across his new identities. His story highlights different instances of Blackness; the spider that initially bites Miles and gives him his spider powers is engraved with the #42, along with the lottery number that is called when Miles is accepted to vision is the #42. Both of the numbers are symbolic for baseball player Jackie Robinson, the first African American to play in the major leagues. It is with this number that the writer is paying homage to Black culture and acknowledging that Miles is the first Black male *Spider-Man* (Low, 2017). Miles's story also emphasizes the school lottery system and the ways in which marginalized people have to gamble their future or their children on a system that should provide for them but only offers them limited chances at quality education. Miles is also biracial, and this allows for Black boys to understand the interplay of the heritages that Miles encompasses and how he chooses to honor them while still being a superhero.

Both Miles and Quinton's stories offer a view of what Black boys could be as superheroes of their own world and how that heroism can uplift and change their respective communities. The next two texts interrogate everyday lives of two ordinary middle school Black boys, whose stories are equally important even without the super powers.

New Kid and Class Act

The graphic texts *New Kid* and *Class Act* were written and drawn by Black creator Jerry Craft. These two stories introduce the reader to Jordan Banks and Drew Ellis, two middle schoolers who attend Riverdale Academy Day School affectionately called "RAD" by the students. In *New Kid*, the narrative centers on Jordan who is beginning seventh grade. Jordan is an artist, and throughout the graphic novel his drawings are depicted to show his understanding of the world around him and his meaning making of social systems. Jordan has three Black male figures in his life that affirm him and help to navigate his schooling and Blackness. These figures also fit within the BlackBoy Crit Pedagogy framings.

The first is Jordan's father Mr. Banks. His father is the manager at a local community center and is the main source of support for Jordan outside of his mother. His father advocates for Jordan several times throughout the book. Jordan is interested in going to an art school instead of the preparatory academy that he was accepted into. His father makes a deal that if he tries the school out until ninth grade, if he doesn't like it he can go to an art school. His father also takes time to help Jordan understand perceptions he may encounter as a young Black male and how to combat those perceptions. Mr. Banks gives Jordan tips for giving various types of handshakes (p. 8); Jordan illustrates through his drawings that people will remember you by your hand shake whether it's strong, weak, wet, dirty, etc., and those impressions will have implications for their assessment of a person. It is through this visual that the constructs of Blackness and BlackBoy Crit are apparent. Jordan's handshake lesson is similar to "the talk" that most Black families have with their children. It is how to be presentable in white spaces. This is reified in the texts because Jordan's hand shake interactions are typically with his white teachers and white classmates' parents. Mr. Banks as a stabilizing and affirming force in Jordan life allows him the chance to question society and learn who he is and how he shows up in the world.

The next representation of the significance of Black males in Jordan's life comes from his prealgebra teacher Mr. Garnier. Mr. Garnier has been a teacher at RAD for 14 years and is the authoritative intervener for both Jordan and Drew. When following up with Jordan on his experiences at RAD, Jordan tells Mr. Garnier that while he is getting used to the school, there are issues with people calling him and Drew the wrong name. They are often called the names of other Black students and lumped together as the same person. Jordan and Drew make a game out of this by calling each other the wrong names, but they are both upset that their teachers don't take the time to truly get to know them. Mr. Garnier offers a listening ear and offers encouragement to Jordan that things will get better. The name issue is one of many microaggressions that both characters face. Another prevalent one that many Black boys face comes in the form of literary assumptions. At the school book fair, Jordan and Drew are excited to purchase books about fantasy and heroes; however, their older white teacher instead hands them books she thinks they would like and relate to. The texts are books with Black characters, but they are struggle and trauma narratives that only showcase "urban grit" as a way for Black people to make it through life. This particular illustration offers readers a chance to pushback on why trauma narratives are the only narratives associated with Black people. Jordan and Drew pushback and explain that Black people are far more than poverty stories.

New Kid provides glimpses into Blackness and the Black experience through Jordan's eyes. He learns how Black socialization works in society (p. 96). He sits in on a conversation his parents are having on what it looks like to be the only person of color in a white space. While his mother advocates for "playing the game" and assimilating to certain roles until you make it to the top, his father advocates for being true to who you are and creating your own space to thrive in. Both views offer readers into conversations that shape the ideologies of Black people globally. Mr. Banks also decides to introduce Kwanzaa to Jordan in order to keep him in-tune to his Blackness. Jordan is an endearing character that is reflective of the everyday Black boy. His wants and needs are to hang out with his friends, have fun, and find his place in the world. He exists in the mundane and stays true to his culture and himself.

Class Act

Class Act works as a companion novel to *New Kid* and tells the story of Drew Ellis. Drew who also attends RAD brings a different perspective of being Black at a white institution. He is treated differently because he has a darker complexion than Jordan, and his hair is different. Jordan illustrates Drew's frustration with comics that illustrate to the reader the complexities of what Drew has to endure. The comics range from issues of his hair being touched, to skin color, etc. Drew lives with his grandmother in a less affluent side of town. He has community with Jordan and the other Black kids at school who can relate and understand his shared experiences.

The male influences in Drew's life that illustrate BlackBoy Crit Pedagogy in action come in the form of Jordan's Dad Mr. Banks and Liam's house manager Mr. Pierre. Mr. Pierre is from Haiti; he works for Liam's family and sends money back home to provide for his family. Drew's relationship with Mr. Pierre steers him toward not judging people based on what they have and what he doesn't. He also imparts on him the notion of doing what you have to do now in order to do what you want to do later. These communal relationships ultimately aid in shaping Drew and his ideologies. These various dynamics illustrate to readers a glimpse into Black boyhood.

Black boys have to juggle the identities of race and gender while navigating their way through life. By reading these perspectives, students and teachers alike can interrogate what it means to be a Black boy in society. These texts promote empathy and offer a varied way of being for Black boys. It also creates an avenue to disrupt anti-Black misandry by opening a discussion for the ways in which Black boys and children have to navigate whiteness. Drew struggles with the wealth of his friend Liam, because even though Liam is nice and welcoming, Drew understands that their lives are very different, and they both will be viewed by society in completely different ways. He contemplates what his friendship with Liam really is and even what interracial dating would look like for him. His white classmate Ashley affectionately bakes him treats and shows up to his games, and it makes Drew uncomfortable. Although he is friends with Ashley, he knows that the world will not always agree with them being together. It is within this moment the reader can fully grasp how adult thinking and decision-making is placed on this middle school character. Drew often questions whether he and his friends are just wearing masks and being performative. Are they really allowed to be themselves or are they just getting by?

Another criticality of viewing this text through the framework of BlackBoy Cit Pedagogy is when the school chooses Drew as one of the faces of diversity for the sister school Cardi De Academy. This school visit brings a group of Black students to tour RAD in hopes of convincing them to attend there the following school year. In a series of mishaps, the diversity teacher Mr. Roche struggles to pronounce their names, suggests they can come to the school on sporting scholarships, and proceeds to make the students feel bad about their current school in comparison to lavish and excessive wealth and access that RAD has. This brings into question the educational practices of well-meaning white teachers who in an effort to extend equality actually harm students of color by showing them what they think the students lack instead of honoring what the students can bring to the table.

Long Way Down

Author Jason Reynolds has written, *Long Way Down*, pinning the story of a Black boy on a journey in one day that spans across lifetimes. This is what life is often like for Black boys/young Black men. What occurs in a day can have a ripple effect that can extend across lifetimes. Reynolds introduces readers to the story focused on grappling with identity. Reynolds' protagonist, Will, is the omniscient narrator, who invites the reader to understand who he is and feel the journey on which Will finds himself on that encompasses one long day. The narrator begins his introduction with "My name is Will. William. William Holloman. But my friends and people who know me know me, just will." (paras. 1–3) The story rests heavily on who knows Will and how well they know him. These are important tenants paving the path to the protagonist's self-introspection. This introspection illuminates the story in a more in-depth and illustrative manner for readers. Will shares the personal connections attached to his names noting, "I'm only William to my mother," (para. 1) her youngest son, the baby boy. To his friends in the neighborhood, on the basketball court, traversing the streets, Will is a different person from William. Will is challenged with navigating the personae attached to his name. Readers of Reynolds' graphic novel are invited to visualize the evolution of William to Will to... just who else is he?

Will, the young Black boy, grows up in a neighborhood that entraps its residents and forces them to recognize life and death. Thus, Will is forced by his society, and his own impressionable nature, to accept the advice that finds him, makes him a victim and forces him to devote his life to it. Will is a knowledgeable and contemplative teenager who considers just what is the best choice for himself, his family, and those who are close to him. He is pushed to define and understand the value of life. He is also exhibiting thoughts and actions which illustrate just how he perceives life and how to defend it, if it becomes necessary. The story gives way for the protagonist and his supporting characters to exhibit their emotional intelligence or the need for help in mental support. Will is put in a position to share his emotional intelligence as he makes major decisions. There are several rules Will must adhere to navigate the allegiance in his daily life. The author puts to paper unwritten rules that show up for Black boys, asking for blind devotion and obedience without a promise or guarantee of benefits. The rules per Will to avenge a loved one done wrong in his neighborhood are: there's no crying, no snitching, and the person must get revenge. As the author pins, these are never to be broken; you *just don't no matter what*. Will is pushed to weigh his emotional intelligence and display of emotion and weigh his allegiance to keeping an unspoken and unwritten oath secrecy among his circle of friends and associates in the neighborhood. Finally, there is the rule of revenge. These rules are some of the same rules and decisions that Black boys often grapple with in day-to-day life between home, school, and family.

Reynolds' story illustrates Black boys, Black men, and one young Black girl in conversation debating these rules as well as their validity and application in life. Black boys and men in this story show up for one another in a number of ways. The goal of the text is to illuminate how Black boys show up in life, with the aim of fostering a teaching and learning environment that exhibits Black Boy Crit Pedagogy. Black boys show up as leaders as well as influencers in their communities. Bryan (2022) notes for learners and those understanding BlackBoy Crit, "The language and literacy practices found most often in schools do not mirror those practices in which many Black children engage at home. This is the experience of many Black boys in schools, who are misconstrued as struggling readers, but are able to read in a multiplicity of ways that are neither valued nor assessed in schools" (p. 8). Will's experience in this story shines a light on Black boys and their influence on one another's lives.

At key, developmental points in the lives of Black boys they encounter – as Will did – moments of realization in which they see themselves in the lives of others. Will sees himself in the life of his brother. Will sees himself in the life of his neighborhood mentor. Will sees himself and the decisions he is required to make through his uncle. Will also sees himself through the life of his father. The author writes this story allowing Will to see himself in the Black, male characters he engages. The conversations illustrate the cognitive work necessary for healthy social development among Black boys. This story illustrates Black boys as heavy thinkers and young men who expostulate intense societal issues inclusive of personal views laden with sadness, anxiety, anger grief, and other issues that Black boys bury deep inside of their cognitive and emotional wells. Fostering a healthy learning environment filled with opportunities for growth requires educators to recognize the triggers of these buried traumas and identify the signs of the sadness and anxiety and anger and worry for Black boys. These signs may be interwoven with what can be viewed as normal teenage experiences: growth spurts filled with significant changes in hunger, navigating the road into manhood by definition and experience or lack thereof. Bryan (2022) speaks to leaders and influential participants in the learning environments of the Black boys about whom these writers are speaking. He says, "Educating means that teachers provide Black children the tools to see the brilliance and ingenuity that lie in themselves and their own culture. Educating also means that educators must learn to recognize when actions, curriculum, and attitudes stymie Black boys' abilities to see their own brilliance and ingenuity" (p. 28).

Adultification of Black boys is a societal challenge which robs Black boys of their innocence. Will's life shifts from a regular day on the basketball court in his neighborhood to the martyr of his family and close circle responsible for following the rules. Adultification exists for Black boys in their worlds when society refuses to see their childhood innocence. It exists when teachers, educators, parents, and others in the circle of intimacy of Black boys neglect to honor Black boys' place to witness safety, hope, and a right to learn from those around them in a productive and healthy manner in society. Bryan (2022) describes this as spirit murdering and defines this for readers and learners of BlackBoy Crit as, "spirit murder is the psychological harm done to Black children because they are Black in America" (p. 46). Will's lived experience brings him swiftly to the point of being forced into early adulthood. Will can choose to redefine the person that the world around him attempts to script for him. Will should not be expected to do this alone. This choice exhibits his opportunity to resist society's adultification of a young Black boy being forced out of his childhood by his local society, family, friends, or circle of intimacy. Spirit rejuvenation asks educators, family, and intimate circles of Black boys to speak positively of the opportunities available to them. Share opportunities that will render a positive outcome. Spirit rejuvenation requires these people to become a solid wall of defense against those policies and people who are procreators and enactors of spirit murder.

Within this graphic novel Black men show up as interrupters. These same men in this story illustrate the unseen side of the victimhood associated with the rules in which Will demonstrates some understanding. In this one day journey, these Black men show up for Will, to put the critical analysis in front of the eyes of the reader. Yes, this graphic novel introduces critical inquiry from one Black boy to another, from one Black man to a Black boy to be a spirit rejuvenator. This graphic novel invites the readers to analyze whether these rules really work if the evidence shared exhibits otherwise. In this text Black men show up as confessors and comforters. There is immense value in this graphic novel for all students and not only for Black boys but certainly for the endeavor of strengthening the personhood, livelihood, and learning potential of Black boys. Black boys in this text attempt to fill the voids left by early elimination through death, incarceration, or otherwise constructed methods of extinction which Black boys experience in their day-to-day lives.

The questions of who I am, how I see myself are significant contributions to who and what black boys bring to the classroom or my learning environment. Nathan Bryan, reflects that one of his teachers had books that affirmed Black boys in their classroom this scholar also shares about BlackBoy Crit Pedagogy. Bryan (2022) admonishes educators to introduce scholar identity beginning with, "... the ability to see themselves" (p. 29). Black boys seeing themselves is paramount to the necessary sense of belonging. Belonging is a major tenant to Reynolds' description of the protagonist. Will takes the readers on a journey through who he is through self-discovery on a day of reckoning as a young, Black boy in traversing through his neighborhood. His encounters illustrate moments of maturity, understanding of self and how he learned what he believes and what he knows. The pivots in Will's maturity emerge for the reader as Will questions what he's learned in his 15 years and attempts to practice spirit rejuvenation. He asks his family and those in his social circle what he should do. He testifies of his understanding of those who followed the rules. Those with whom he converses on this journey include his father, his older brother, a neighborhood mentor, his uncle, and a childhood friend. However, Reynolds implies and embeds a critical interrogation of the readers who see these rules. Are they valid? Do they demonstrate any success for the lives of those who practice and hold these rules in high regard? Do they really work for those who follow them? For whom does following these rules that Will shares bring a benefit? Why is crying not seen as a benefit for Black boys when it is natural? Why doesn't the refusal of snitching (or becoming a corroborating witness) appear to work for Black boys and their families, especially in this novel?

The Crossover

This graphic novel is an adaptation of the verse novel *The Crossover*, by author Kwame Alexander, that speaks to the healthy learning potential and characteristics that can foster positive and successful social and cognitive development in youth, particularly Black boys. Author Alexander and illustrator Dawud Anyabwile offer a portrayal of the life of a family of young, Black, 12-year-old, twin brothers Josh and Jordan Bell. The twins come from a two-parent home and currently attend middle school where their mother is the assistant principal. This particular tale provides an insider perspective of the experience of living in a world that encapsulates a supportive and optimistic environment for two healthy Black boys navigating their world through educational dedication as well as athletic discipline. Alexander tells the story through the protagonist, Josh Bell, who shares his and his family's identity through verse and vibrant illustrations in limited color – black, orange, and shades of gray. Readers are able to be immersed in this experience through the eyes and voice of a preteenage boy's outlook on his present and future.

This graphic novel is relevant for Black boys because it directly connects with the experiences boys will have, school responsibilities administered by parents and educators, sports facilitated by a parent or school coach staff, as well as the mundane day-to-day life in school sharing interactions with male friends and romantic interests, which present opportunities for challenges and development. Josh is the more extroverted and expressive of the brothers whose athletic prowess on the basketball court supersedes his athletic interests. Jordan's, his twin brother, skills appear to be equally distributed between the basketball court and the classroom. Readers are able to follow the day-to-day mentality and emotions of young Black boys seeing Josh's experiences ebb and flow more clearly between three direct passions: excelling and dominating in basketball, doing well in school because it permits him to play basketball as much as he desires and a new, budding romantic interest in a girl who attends school with him and his brother.

Identity is depicted for readers by Josh sharing how he got his name and a personal physical description of characteristics that are particularly important to a 12-year-old. He has a nickname, Filthy McNasty, given to him by his father and, ironically, quite different from characteristics readers may presume the name is referent to in a teenager. The name belies history for his father as it came from famed jazz pianist Horace Silver. The nickname provides Black cultural and historical relevance that connects the current story to the greatness and dedication of other Black men that have passed on. Josh connects readers with his family, exhibiting his father as a devoted, retired professional basketball player and lover of jazz music, who has traveled the world and secured the family's financial status. His father connects Josh's active athletic prowess to the musical and rhythmic feel of a song. Josh's passion for basketball connects him with professional NBA greats. Josh exhibits the ability to see his future success in sports by mimicking the prowess of other successful Black athletes like Kevin Durant, Lebron James (who also champions educational success), and Chris Paul.

Alexander identifies for readers, particularly Black boys, the steppingstones that are necessary to become as great as what they see on television, hear in music, as well as see on social media. Illustrator Anyabwile captures images of Josh on the page with these musical and athletic successors, and his father, to exhibit for readers the propensity for Black boys to visualize themselves in the same frame as greatness, dedication, and discipline. Josh has a twin brother Jordan, named after basketball phenom Michael Jordan. Jordan also has a nickname, JB. The nicknames are utilized with their friends in school and on the basketball court. Alexander positions Josh through the words of his mother to deliver golden nuggets of educational advice to teen readers as well as sharing confirmation for adult readers (who may include other parents and educators) that children do receive and reciprocate the salient advice administered while they are growing and developing.

Alexander and Anyabwile connect the minds of preteenagers with a world that is very relevant to present day children. In this graphic novel, Black boys and men bond with one another. Josh bonds with his father and his love of basketball, as well as the success and skills of basketball professionals. The bond between the brothers, Filthy McNasty and JB, with their father challenges societal stereotypes of the Black family that Black fathers abandon the mothers and children of their families. This allows readers to see the family of a Black family as loving, successful, hopeful, diligent, and disciplined. The author and illustrator eliminate the negative associations purported frequently in news and media by illustrating this in the visuals of this graphic novel.

MONSTER

This graphic novel is also an adaptation, this time of a Walter Dean Myers classic by the same name. The story centers on Steve Harmon, a 16-year-old aspiring filmmaker charged with a crime. Steve Harmon is incarcerated for a crime that the court is trying to prove that he was an accessory to. It is important to note that this graphic novel is illustrated completely in black and white to centralize the harsh realities that Black men face within the justice system. A key scene in the texts is in the ways in which the illustrator provides a backdrop of a small child, Steve, at the interrogation room table with his parents, wrapped in his mother's arms (p. 59). Teenage Steve looks into the reflection window at himself. He begins a period of self-reflection. Who is Steve Harmon? Is he a good person? Is he a monster like the defense is making him out to be? Or is he a victim of his circumstance? This graphic novel much like Reynold's *Long Way Down* has a darker tone as it depicts the various ways that young Black boys are preyed upon by members of their own community.

It is necessary to point to the view of influences as it relates to traditional and nontraditional schooling. The texts illustrate the adversarial relationships between Black boys and their peers and older men in the neighborhood inclusive of what is popularly understood as toxic masculinity. Steve is accused of being a look out for a convenience store robbery gone wrong. The main accomplices of the robbery are two men "Bobo" and James King, men who have had a carceral history of breaking the law. As the story progresses, the reader is shown how bullying and intimidation tactics led to Steve making a choice that was detrimental to all of those involved. In this vein, Bobo and James instead of building up a young man in their neighborhood choose to ensnare and entrap him into the same lifestyle that has made them outcasts. The juxtaposition of this comes from Steve's film teacher Mr. Sawicki. Sawicki testifies on behalf of Steve that he has known him through his film club, and that Steve is an honest upstanding teen, with deep moral character who makes films that capture the humanity of his neighborhood. Mr. Sawicki becomes an ally as he is disrupting the prosecutions' notion that Steve is a monster who only cares for himself and disregards the welfare of others. Sawicki works toward dismantling the adultification of Steve through the eyes of the prosecution. It is in this example that educators can examine what it looks like to actively put the needs of Black boys above all else and understand that Black boys are often victim to a system that was never intended to serve and protect them. Bryan includes a quote to this experience stating:

> As my own experiences attest, the academic and social outcomes of many Black boys stand on a shaky foundation; most teachers fail to recognize their strengths, buy into and perpetuate long-held anti-Black misandric stereotypes and biases as foundational to their perceptions of Black boys, and neglect the academic and social needs of Black boys in and beyond early childhood education. As such Black boys' schooling experiences are often negatively impacted ty the types of anti-Black violence (e.g., physical, symbolic, curricular, linguistic, and systemic). (p. 26)

The author and illustrator of this adaption utilize the courtroom trial to exhibit one of the most negative experiences Black boys may fall victim to without clear self-identity, spirit rejuvenators, and powerful advocates to redirect their paths. Bryant notes the necessity of scholarly identity and fostering positive identity. He first defines scholarly identity for readers and later instructs readers how to utilize it saying, "Scholarly identity – the ability [for Black boys] to see themselves as scholars in schools,...Black Boy Crit Pedagogy requires a reversal in stance to acknowledge what is broken in our teaching, attitudes, literacy practices, and systems that govern the teaching of Black boys; (p. 29), [and being] intentional about centering the voices and experiences of Black boys" (p. 31). How would Steve Harmon's world function, and how would the story of this graphic novel change with other Black boys like Josh and Jordan and Will? Imagine the type of champion he would have been had he not followed the negative instructions of his neighborhood spirit murderers. What great fortune might he have had with a teacher like Bryan's Mrs. C, a Black parent as a school administrator like Josh and Jordan or growing up with parents like the Bells? Examining this story provides multilayered complexity to the ways in which Black boys have to make adult decisions that can have dire consequences. Steve Harmon's scenario extends far beyond possibly being an accessory to a crime; it delves into survival tactics, institutional racism, and structural reforms needed in the ways of creating and implementing culturally responsive policies and prac- tices in marginalized communities.

All of these stories show visual depictions of Black boyhood. These characters are navigating life in a society that does not always honor and affirm their Blackness. It within the pages of these stories that Black boys can see themselves illustrated in various ways from a boy who loves musicians and instruments, an artisan that paints his own world in colorful ways, athletes who dominate on and off the court, or even superheroes who not only want to save the world, but more importantly they want to give back to their communities. The message that is present in the stories, is an affirmation that Black boyhood is appreciated and invaluable. Students deserve to read these stories, and teachers can not only learn from them, but bring these texts into their classrooms to enact a transformative learning experience. What we provide students access to in ways of knowing through reading, are the ways we teach them how to know themselves.

INCORPORATING BLACKBOY CRIT PEDAGOGY IN THE CLASSROOM

As educators, we understand that reading and analyzing the text is only the beginning. To truly work toward enacting change the curriculum and pedagogy must be inclusive of practices that honor Black boyhood and create spaces for Black boys to read, learn, and explore with criticality in schooling spaces. Listed below are suggested applicable classroom practices that align with the tenants of BlackBoy Crit Pedagogy.

Tenant #1: Combating anti-Black misandry, which is the derision of Black boys/ males that permeates social structures, policies, government, institutions, education, etc.

Within each of the texts described in this chapter, the Black boys depicted disrupt or attempt to disrupt the stereotypical and hegemonic ideologies of what it is like to exist within a racialized society. Activities in the classroom that focus on naming the harmful policies that promote anti-Blackness can aid in the understanding and dismantling harmful and racist systems. An activity to consider would be having students read discuss one of the graphic novels, and then pair it with the reading and annotating of a classroom or school policy document. For example policies that cover dress code, attendance, codes of conduct, or disciplinary actions. The students can then discuss where these policies may target or exemplify anti-Blackness and suggestions to make them more equitable for all students. This promotes criticality in understanding policy inequities and makes room for opportunities for students to develop equitable solutions to be presented to the administration or school board.

Tenant #2: The centering of the lived experiences and educational practices of Blackness, Black males including teachers and students.

Weaving in Black culture and celebrating Blackness aids in enhancing students' cultural competencies. In *New Kid, Class Act*, and *Long Way Down*, Jordan, Drew, and Will each discuss variations of the "unwritten rules of being Black in society;" these rules are founded in cultural awareness of living in a racialized society. Having students create their own "How To" manuals that highlight different rules of engagement for their individual cultures and ethnicities and discussing them in class can cultivate a space of empathy, understanding, and cultural competency among their peers.

Tenant #3: A healing counter culture pedagogy for Black boys.

Utilizing these visual texts in the classrooms allows students to not only read about the experiences of Black boys but also to be privy to them via the illustrations. The visuals offer a realm of possibility of what can be and what is, in Black boyhood. To foster a healing counter culture pedagogy by having students take ownership of their narratives allows them the chance to center and shape the way they are presented and seen to the world. Having students create their own mini-comics, zines, or playlists that exemplify their lived experiences provides them with the opportunity to address any misconceptions and harm they may have experienced by re-storying themselves in a way that honors their culture and personhood.

Tenant #4: Family and community centered as collaborative partners in education.

Working with family or collaborating with community partners can elicit a sense of pride in students and develop positive relationships with those who are also invested in the students' academic and personal successes. Some suggestions on fostering these collaborations can look like having students create a campaign to address a need in their school or community. They may also work with local businesses on service learning projects where they learn the history of the business and its contributions to their local community. Students can also create a digital family tree and be allotted the opportunity to delve into their family history and explore how they came to be. This can also be explored through the creation of a map of their community, where they would consider the history of their neighborhood and identify personal and historical markers or people that make up their community.

MOVING FORWARD

Reading is a fundamental part of life. Using words, shapes, images, etc., we come to understand who we are and the world around us. In Table 1.1, we share some resources for your classrooms, homes, and learning environments that are beneficial for Black boys and all students. These comics and graphic novels speak to identity, race, coming of age, building community, etc. They share important factors of learning and development such as: creating healthy boundaries, making tough decisions, meeting high expectations, and applying what they learn to their academic and personal life.

Classrooms today should be reflective of the expansive and diverse representation of society; an accurate depiction of that expansion should reflect the multiplicity of Black boyhood and Black characters. In order for students to effectively grapple with the world at large, they should actively engage in reading about a variety of characters and experiences they can relate to and/or the experiences of those who differ from them to offer them a space to learn and foster empathy from. It is critical to not just have representative and inclusive books but to also use those books as a vehicle to prompt discussion and enact change. This creates an avenue to teach from a place of equity and engagement. The books and the curriculum that are brought into the classroom should promote liberation and work toward the decolonization of white centered texts. BlackBoy Crit Pedagogy offers practical ways to incorporate stories about Black boys and Black males that affirm identity and disrupt stereotypes and biases.

Colonized curriculum cannot be changed overnight, but access to diverse literature especially for those that center the lived experiences of Black boys is a start. Without culturally relevant reading materials and critical ways to engage with texts, students continue to develop narrow ideas about groups and cultures

Table 1.1. Suggested Black Boyhood Novels.

Title and Author	Grade Level	Themes and Topics
Stuntboy, in the Meantime by Jason Reynolds (Reynolds, 2021)	6–8	• Family • Self-esteem • Self-discovery
When Stars Are Scattered by Victoria Jamieson (Jamieson, 2020)	6–8	• Acceptance • African culture • Coming of age
Mister Miracle: The Great Escape by Varian Johnson (Johnson, 2022)	6–8	• Identity • Mystery • Self-discovery
Booked by Kwame Alexander (Alexander, 2022)	6–8	• Fitting in • Friendship • Sports
Miles Morales: Shock Waves by Justin A. Reynolds (Reynolds, 2021)	6–8	• Family • Friendship • Fundraising
Static: Season One by Vita Ayala	9–12	• Community • Cultural expectations • Familial relationships
Quincredible Vol. 2: The Hero Within by Rodney Barnes (Barnes, 2021b)	9–12	• Black boys in STEM • Local histories • Teen superhero
You Brought Me The Ocean by Alex Sanchez (Sanchez, 2020)	9–12	• Coming of age • Queerness • Superheroes
Black Mage by Daniel Barnes (Barnes, 2019)	9–12	• Coming of age • Community • Southern Black culture
Black by Kwanza Osajyefo (Osajyefo, 2017)	9–12	• Blackness • Police brutality • Rites of Passage

that differ from their own. This leaves them ill prepared to live in and work in an increasingly diverse and global society (Brooks & Cueto, 2018). The use of diverse literature in the classroom specifically comics and graphic novels is a microcosm of the world that exists around them and allows students a chance to interact and engage in critical thinking about their society; the way it was shaped and how it operates based on its current foundations by analyzing the visual narratives across panels. Incorporating comics and graphic novels that highlight the narratives of Black boyhood and that are inclusive, representative, and equitable is a chance to create equitable and affirming spaces for not just Black boys but for all students. These books work as tools of promoting advocacy and empathy in the classroom. How much more impactful would our learning environments be if we allow Black boys and young Black men to flourish if we heard their voices as exercises in freedom and liberation. Imagine how much more valuable these young learners would feel among their peers and be positioned to thrive in a world, in schools and in classrooms that welcome them and value their presence, listen to their voice, and guide their development with care.

REFERENCES

Alexander, K. (2019). *The crossover graphic novel*. Clarion Books.
Alexander, K. (2022). *Booked graphic novel*. Clarion Books.
Ayala, V. (2021). *Static: Season one*. DC Comics.
Barnes, D. (2019). *The black mage*. Oni Press.
Barnes, R. (2021a). *Quincredible, volume one: Quest to be the best*. Oni Press.
Barnes, R. (2021b). *Quincredible, volume two: The hero within*. Oni Press.
Bendis, M. (2018). *Miles morales: The ultimate Spider-Man*. Marvel.
Bishop, R. S. (2012). Reflections on the development of African American children's literature. *Journal of Children's Literature, 38*(2), 5–13.
Botzakis, S., Savitz, R., & Low, D. E. (2017). Adolescents reading graphic novels and comics: What we know from research. In K. A. Hinchman & D. A. Applemann (Eds.), *Adolescent literacies: A handbook of practice-based research* (pp. 310–322). The Guilford Press.
Brenner, R. (2011). Comics and graphic novels. In *Handbook of research on children's and young adult literature* (pp. 256–267). Routledge.
Brooks, W., & Cueto, D. (2018). Contemplating and extending the scholarship on children's and young adult literature. *Journal of Literacy Research, 50*(1), 9–30.
Bryan, N. (2022). *Toward a BlackBoyCrit pedagogy: Black boys, male teachers, and early childhood classroom practices*. NCTE-Routledge Research Series.
Craft, J. (2019). *New kid*. Harper.
Craft, J. (2020). *Class act*. Quill Tree Books.
Curry, T. (2017). *Man-not: Race, class, genre and the dilemmas of black manhood*. Temple University Press.
Dávila, D. (2015). #WhoNeedsDiverseBooks?: Preservice teachers and religious neutrality with children's literature. *Research in the Teaching of English, 50*(1), 60–83.
Dumas, M. J., & Ross, K. M. (2016). "Be real black for me": Imaging BlackCrit in education. *Urban Education, 51*(4), 415–442.
Freire, P. (1983). The importance of the act of reading. *The Journal of Education*, 5–11.
Iser, W. (1972). The reading process: A phenomenological approach. *New Literary History, 3*(2), 279–299.
Jamieson, V. (2020). *When stars are scattered*. Dial Books.
Johnson, V. (2022). *Mister miracle: The great escape*. DC Comics.
Ladson-Billings, G., & Tate, W. F. (1995). Toward a critical race theory of education. *Teachers College Record, 97*(1), 47–68.
Love, B. (2019). *We want to do more than survive: Abolitionist teaching and the pursuit of educational freedom*. Beacon Press.
Low, D. (2017). Waiting for Spider-Man: Representations of urban school 'reform' in Marvel Comics' Miles Morales series. In M. A. Abate & G. A. Tarbox (Eds.), *Graphic novels for children and young adults: A collection of critical essays* (pp. 278–297). University Press of Mississippi.
Minor, C. (2018). *We got this: Equity, access, and the quest to be who our students need us to be*. Heinemann.
Moeller, R. A., & Becnel, K. (2018). Drawing diversity: Representations of race in graphic novels for young adults. *School Library Research, 21*, 1–17.
Moore, A., & Begoray, D. (2017). "The last block of ice": Trauma literature in the high school classroom. *Journal of Adolescent & Adult Literacy, 61*(2), 173–181.

Morris, M. (2018). *Pushout: The criminalization of Black girls in schools*. New Press.

Myers, W. D. (2015). *Monster: A graphic novel*. Harperalley.

Osajyefo, K. (2017). *Black*. Black Mask Studios.

Parker, M. (2021). *Teaching artfully*. Clover Press.

Reynolds, J. (2021). *Stuntboy, in the meantime*. Atheneum/Caitlyn Dlouhy Books.

Reynolds, J. A. (2021). *Miles morales: Shock waves*. Graphix.

Rosenblatt, L. (1978). *The reader the text the poem: The transactional theory of the literary work*. Southern Illinois Press.

Sanchez, A. (2020). *You brought me the ocean*. DC Comics.

Sheehan, K. (2018). Graphics are novel. *Voices from the Middle, 26*(2), 59–62.

Snowber, C. N. (2012). Dancing a curriculum of hope: Cultivating passion as an embodied inquiry. *Journal of Curriculum Theorizing, 28*(2).

Thomas, E. E. (2019). *The dark fantastic: Race and the imagination from Harry Potter to the Hunger Games*. New York University Press.

Torres, J. E. (2019, June 14). *CHAT: Disrupting genre*. #Disrupttexts. https://disrupttexts.org/2019/06/14/disrupting-genre/

Versaci, R. (2001). How comic books can change the way our students see literature: One teacher's perspective. *English Journal, 91*(2), 61–67.

Whaley, K. (n.d.). #Ownvoices: Why we need diverse authors in children's literature. https://www.readbrightly.com/why-we-need-diverse-authors-in-kids-ya-lit/

Yang, G. (2008). Graphic novels in the classroom. *Language Arts, 85*(3), 185–192.

Young, J. L., Foster, M. D., & Hines, D. (2018). Even Cinderella is White: (Re)Centering Black girls' voices as literacies of resistance. *English Journal, 107*(6), 102–108.

CHAPTER 2

THE CAREER ACADEMY AS A VEHICLE TO PROMOTE BLACK MALE STUDENT INTEREST IN STEM COLLEGE AND CAREER PATHWAYS

Edward C. Fletcher Jr., Erik M. Hines, Donna Y. Ford and James L. Moore III

ABSTRACT

The purpose of this study was to examine the learning experiences of high school Black males participating in an academy of engineering that was configured as a magnet school. We followed a qualitative case study design to explore the experiences of 16 Black male academies of engineering students. We identified three recurring themes from the interviews with the Black male academy of engineering students: Promoting Interests in STEM, Drawing Connections to Core Academic Concepts, *and* An Affinity for Hands-on Learning through the Engineering Curriculum. *The results of our study helped us to better understand how academies provide a platform for Black male students' interest in engineering as a viable college and career pathway.*

Keywords: Black males; high school students; career academy; engineering education; STEM; magnet school

Researchers have exposed the negative academic experiences and lack of engagement of Black male students in schools, especially urban ones (Brown et al., 2019; Wright, 2019). Compared to Black females and all other ethnic and racial groups, Black males have the lowest academic achievement (Hernandez-Gantes & Fletcher, 2013; Moore et al., 2008), academic engagement,

Black Males in Secondary and Postsecondary Education
Advances in Race and Ethnicity in Education, Volume 9, 25–44
Copyright © 2024 Edward C. Fletcher Jr., Erik M. Hines, Donna Y. Ford and James L. Moore III
Published under exclusive licence by Emerald Publishing Limited
ISSN: 2051-2317/doi:10.1108/S2051-231720230000009002

graduation rates (Ford, 2010; Jackson & Moore, 2008), and college and career readiness skills (Fletcher & Cox, 2012; Whaley & Noel, 2012). These challenges are based on multiple factors associated with systemic racism in the United States (Danforth & Miller, 2018), which further reveals that educational systems are microcosms of the larger society. To that end, many Black students have had negative educational experiences based on a myriad of issues, including: attending schools that have a lack of resources; being targets of disproportionate disciplinary actions; not having access to highly qualified teachers; and experiencing negative interactions with school staff members (84% of whom are white) who do not provide culturally responsive instruction (Brown et al., 2019; Wright, 2019). Thus, many issues emerge based on a cultural disconnect or mismatch between school stakeholders and their ethnically and racially diverse learners (Achinstein & Aguirre, 2008). For example, white teachers often have inherent biases and, consequently, provide preferential treatment to white students in which they share cultural backgrounds, identities, languages, and norms (Danforth & Miller, 2018; Johnson & Sondergeld, 2020). However, there are few studies that have examined the educational experiences of Black students who are schooled in settings with school stakeholders that match their backgrounds, identities, and cultures.

Even further, there are reports in the literature that in some cases, white urban school stakeholders restrict access and opportunities to participate in science, technology, engineering, and mathematics (STEM)-related career-themed curricula to underserved students, particularly Black males (Johnson & Sondergeld, 2020). The same holds true in gifted and talented education where Black students are underrepresented by as much as 50%; Black males are the most underrepresented at 65% (Ford, 2010). The lack of culturally responsive approaches in urban schools contribute to a troubling and quite problematic issue of a low participation rate of Black male students in high school STEM-themed programs and schools (Brown, 2019). Notably, these STEM related-programs provide pathways to high-wage, high-demand, and high-skilled occupations (Collins, 2018). The sense of urgency and concern to address the underrepresentation of Black males in STEM is shared by educators, employers, government agencies, and researchers alike. Thus, research is needed to examine the intersection of gender and race to discover ways to engage students from underserved groups in STEM college and career pathways (McGee & Robinson, 2019).

Given that only 5% of Blacks obtain science and engineering occupations (even though they make up 12% of the workforce, National Science Board, 2018), there has been a concerted effort to broaden the participation of Black students in the STEM pipeline, beginning at the K-12 level (National Science Board, 2018). One increasingly popular strategy designed to expand such opportunities is the development of high school magnet career academies in which STEM learning is the focus. Researchers have noted promising findings in regard to the academic success of Black male students taught within some public magnet high school contexts across the country (Kumah-Abiwah, 2019). The mission of these types of programs is to recruit STEM-interested learners to urban schools within a county, and offer rigorously intense core academics, college preparatory coursework (e.g., accelerated courses), and work-based learning opportunities to participate in a wide array of STEM content and experiences. Another component of the mission of STEM-focused high schools stemmed from the 1954 *Brown v. Board of Education* Supreme Court case. In response, various school districts across the country attempted to desegregate and improve the racial balance of students by establishing magnet programs and schools to recruit students from across an entire county and provide them with transportation (Metz, 2003); yet, Black and Latinx students are oftentimes still underrepresented in these contexts (Kaser, 2006). According to Nasir and Vakil (2017):

> Although districts often tout the success and rigor of such programs, less attention has been paid to which students within the school have access to these spaces and how students are racialized and gendered within them. (p. 378)

Hence, it is critical that we better understand how academies provide a platform for Black male students' interest in engineering as a viable college and career pathway. STEM courses at the high school level help students discover their interests, enable them to be more competitive in applying to colleges and universities, and prepare them for the rigor and challenges of majoring in STEM during college (Bottia et al., 2015).

PURPOSE AND RESEARCH QUESTION

The purpose of this study was to examine the learning experiences of high school Black males participating in an academy of engineering that was configured as a magnet school. In this particular case study, the school stakeholders, in many cases, matched the cultural identities of the students within the academy and school. In this chapter, we intend to provide a clear understanding of how equitable STEM spaces within urban schools can facilitate possibilities for supporting the talent development of Black male high school students in socially transformative learning spaces. Our study was undergirded by the following research question:

(1) What are the learning experiences of high school Black males participating in an academy of engineering?

REVIEW OF LITERATURE

The Schooling Experiences of Black Males

Researchers have demonstrated that Black males frequently experience negative schooling outcomes, often more than other student groups (Ford & Moore, 2013; Hines et al., 2020; Jackson & Moore, 2008). Black males are overrepresented and misidentified for special education, the least or last to be referred and identified for gifted and honors/advanced placement courses (Ford & Moore, 2013; Hines et al., 2020). Moreover, Black males are more likely to be suspended, expelled, and receive harsher disciplinary infractions than their peers (Aud et al., 2011; Gregory, 1995; Skiba et al., 2011; Yeager et al., 2017). Parental involvement and high teacher expectations play a role in positive school outcomes for Black males (Hines et al., 2019; Hines & Holcomb-McCoy, 2013). Further, there is evidence that certain school environments and programs (e.g., high school STEM-themed career academies) are more effective at engaging Black students because of the hands-on nature of the curricula and the increased interpersonal supports of the small learning community (Fletcher & Cox, 2012).

Career academies are programs of study featuring small learning communities found within high schools (Stern et al., 2010). They focus on providing students with a college-preparatory curriculum integrated within a career theme. Thus, curricula in career academies feature the integration of academic and technical content to increase rigor and relevancy to students' career interests. The academy model also emphasizes partnerships with employers and postsecondary institutions (Castellano et al., 2007; Kemple & Snipes, 2000). The aims of career academies align both with the provisions of the Perkins V legislation – related to establishing programs of study – as well as Stone and Lewis' (2012) three-part definition of college and career readiness. First, academic knowledge in and of itself is not sufficient. Instead, high school graduates need to be able to apply what they learn through the occupational expression of academic knowledge. In essence, "graduates should know how to use mathematics or science to solve real workplace problems (Stone & Lewis, 2012, p. 15)." Second, many refer to employability skills as "21st century skills" or "soft skills." These skills include capabilities such as responsibility, collaboration, and critical thinking/ problem-solving. Third, technical skills are specific competencies needed for each occupational area.

With the growing popularity of the career academy concept, the quality of implementation has varied greatly as schools and districts have rushed to join the bandwagon. To this end, there have been efforts to inform related implementation with the development of standards of practice by school networks such as National Academy Foundation (NAF). NAF has supported the implementation of the career academy model beginning in 1982 (Stern et al., 2010). NAF provides curricular support, professional development, and technical assistance to a national network of high school career academies in five career themes: Engineering, Finance, Health Sciences, Hospitality and Tourism, and Information Technology (NAF, 2014). For nearly 40 years, NAF has refined a model that provides youth access to industry-specific curricula, work-based learning experiences, and relationships with professionals. Over 5,000 business professionals serve as mentors, engage NAF students in paid internships, and serve on local advisory boards. During the 2019–2020 school year, over 120,000 students attended 620 NAF academies across 38 states, including D.C., Puerto Rico, and the US Virgin Islands. NAF academies reported that 97% of seniors graduated on time. In terms of student selection, NAF academies operate under an open enrollment policy. Therefore, any student may enroll and participate in an NAF academy. While some schools require that students apply to gain entry, students are not selected based on prior academic achievement. However, in the case of some magnet schools that are oversubscribed, students may enter a lottery system and then may be selected at random.

The NAF model has grown into a fully developed school reform initiative used to support the expansion of academies across 38 states, but little is known about which specific indicators of participation contribute to student success. In fact, the Career and Technical Education Research Network funded by IES has determined that NAF is an organization that is ready for rigorous research based on their evaluability assessment conducted in 2020 (Hughes et al., 2020). Within the proposed project, we will target specific elements (e.g., academy development and structure, integrated curricula and instruction, and work-based learning) of the NAF model – informed by literature demonstrating how the aforementioned factors contribute to student outcomes. Understanding specific elements that contribute to student success are critical, and our abilities to understand them have implications for future researchers in terms of examining the causal impact of the factors on long-term longitudinal student outcomes.

Research on Career Academies

The career academy model represents a promising approach for promoting college and career readiness. The career academy model is widely used in high schools as it has been found to positively promote student success factors (Kemple, 2008; Kemple & Snipes, 2000). In general, researchers have documented that career academies have a role in reducing dropout rates, improving attendance, increasing academic course taking, and producing positive employment outcomes (Kemple, 2008). Using experimental research designs, prior researchers have found positive effects of participation in career academies on the attendance, on time graduation (Hemelt et al., 2019; Kemple, 2008), academic course-taking, dropout rates, and various labor market outcomes (Kemple, 2008; Kemple & Snipes, 2000) of high school career academy students compared to nonacademy students. However, researchers have also found that the standardized mathematics and reading scores (Kemple & Snipes, 2000), ACT scores (Hemelt et al., 2019), college matriculation (Hemelt et al., 2019), and degree attainment (Kemple & Snipes, 2000) of academy students were not significantly different from their nonacademy counterparts.

Related to learners from diverse backgrounds, Moore (2006) found that (a) having a strong interest in STEM; (b) participating in high school career and technical education (CTE) programs that emphasize STEM; (c) acquiring high aptitudes in science and mathematics; (d) gaining the support from parents and family members; and (e) fostering meaningful experiences and relationships with school personnel were all inspirational aspects motivating Black males to major in STEM areas in college. Moreover, Fletcher and Cox (2012) found that Black students believed participation in career academies was the most meaningful aspect of their schooling experiences and provided them an opportunity to gain a sense of community/belonging, acquire hands-on training, and explore their own individual interests. Thus, it is quite plausible that career academies have a positive impact on Black students.

The NAF academy model features three core elements – academy development and structure, integrated curriculum and structure, and work-based learning experiences. The first element of the NAF academy model that we will study is the academy development and structure component, which focuses on small learning communities using student cohorts, career-themed and sequenced coursework, and career-themed guidance. Academies are either organized as small school-within-schools or as whole school/wall-to-wall (where all students in the school participate) programs and emphasize block scheduling for students. The idea is to break down larger high schools into a small family-like atmosphere where students are assigned to the same teachers for four years – enabling students to form a community of learners as well as a close knit and caring environment (Stern et al., 2010). Researchers have found that the use of small learning communities is a contributing factor promoting a positive school culture (Fletcher et al., 2019). Related research has revealed the challenges of building positive and supportive cultures in large, comprehensive, urban high schools – particularly those that serve low-income and ethnically and racially diverse youth (Letgers et al., 2002; Murphy, 2010). The difficulty of establishing a positive culture in comprehensive high schools typically stems from their relatively large student populations and fixed departmental silos. Hence, one major recommendation that addresses the issue of large schools is the idea of establishing small learning communities. The term "small learning communities" denotes a variety of school structures and configurations – including schools within a school and magnet programs that are wall-to-wall (where all students participate in a given career theme) (Kuo, 2010). Researchers have found that students in small learning communities experience an increased sense of personalization and belonging, and lower levels of school vandalism (Page et al., 2002). Based on related evidence, Kuo (2010) recommended that: "policymakers and practitioners should continue to find opportunities to reduce the size of large high schools and increase the sense of personalization, belonging, and safety among students, teachers, and staff" (p. 395). In NAF academies, teachers receive instructional supports and technical assistance using industry validated curricula provided by NAF. Through this structured support, teachers form deep relationships with their students and make stronger connections between their teaching practice and real-world applications. The structure of each academy is designed such that students interact with teachers and peers in a small learning community who share interests in a given occupational area and are situated within a cohort. Thus, students have the same peers and teachers throughout their four years in high school – thus, forming a community. This allows for interdependent learning by which students learn from each other while simultaneously learning to work collaboratively. Between improved teacher relationships, enhanced relevance, and using problem-based learning, students are likely to have higher engagement in school – a relationship that we propose to investigate in this chapter – and a positive student experience – which we will also examine by interviewing academy and nonacademy students (Fletcher et al., 2020). We further will examine the organizational/contextual elements that contribute to the academy development and structure of each school/academy.

The second component is the integrated curriculum and instruction, which promotes career and academic learning around a relevant career theme (e.g., Business and Finance, Engineering, Health Sciences, Hospitality and Tourism, and Information Technology) through project-based activities involving core academic content. Career academies integrate career-themed curricula with college preparatory coursework to encourage students to learn core academic subjects in an applied career-oriented fashion. The term "curriculum integration" is referred to in a variety of ways – as a method or process to connect skills, themes, concepts, and topics across disciplines and between academic and technical education (Pierce & Hernández-Gantes, 2015). Teachers that integrate curriculum connect multiple content areas to breakdown overarching theories, concepts, and big ideas that help students and enhance learning from one subject to another (Klein & Cornell, 2010). Curriculum integration may be implemented around an occupational theme such as IT or may involve concept connections within single subjects such as arithmetic, algebra, geometry, or across two or more subjects, such as mathematics and CTE (Pierce & Hernández-Gantes, 2015). The purposeful integration of academic and technical education is a signature feature of successful programs bringing meaning and relevance to curriculum and instruction (Castellano et al., 2012). The occupational context serves as the source of relevant learning tasks and applications involving authentic representations of what employees do in the world of work (Hernández-Gantes & Brendefur, 2003). Findings from the Math-in-CTE experimental study demonstrated that the integration of mathematical concepts in CTE courses – teaching mathematics in an occupational context – resulted in statistically significant higher scores for students on two of three mathematical assessments. However, the assessment scores within the third examination did not produce significantly different achievement compared to the control group (Stone & Lewis, 2012; Stone et al., 2008). Thus, it is expected that – based on the quality of such learning experiences – academy students will have enhanced college and career readiness engagement, academy students will take more rigorous course taking, and academy students will benefit from gains in academic achievement. In our project, we examined perceived learning experiences by interviewing students and determining the academic achievement, on time graduation, and their acceptance into college through administrative data. We further examined the integrated curricular nature of the academies/schools by examining the organizational/contextual elements through classroom observations and interviews of school personnel (including teachers).

The third component is providing students with work-based learning experiences. Career academy students engage in successively progressive work-based learning experiences from ninth through 12th grades that are developmentally and age-appropriate. It has been well-documented that students often find learning as void of meaning and are prone to question the relevance of instructional tasks (Castellano et al., 2012; Hernández-Gantes & Brendefur, 2003). To address this disconnect in teaching and learning, career academies emphasize learning in specific occupational contexts to enhance the relevance of student experiences. The premise is that the authenticity of occupational contexts provides opportunities to make learning more meaningful for students (Newmann & Wehlage, 1995; Stipanovic et al., 2012). Through providing a range of work-based learning experiences, NAF academies address this call to encourage authentic learning in real-world contexts. Under the NAF model, work-based learning includes career awareness and exploration activities in ninth (e.g., field trips) and 10th (e.g., job shadowing) grades, and experiential opportunities (e.g., industry certifications and paid internships) in 11th and 12th grades. Kuh (2015) argued that students who participate in high-impact, work-based learning practices "invest substantial time and energy to educationally purposeful tasks, interact frequently with their teachers and peers, get feedback often, and apply what they are learning" (p. xi). That is, work-based learning enables students to apply what they know in real-world settings, while building exposure to, preparation for, and experience in their interested career path (Papadimitriou, 2014). In this regard, work-based learning experiences should help students acquire both the employability and technical skills needed to be college and career ready (Hernández-Gantes, 2016; Stone & Lewis, 2012). We will investigate this in our proposed study by collecting survey data from students regarding their participation in both college and career readiness activities (including work-based learning experiences) as well as their perceptions of the 21st century skills they attain through their school experiences.

METHOD

Research Design

We followed a qualitative case study design to explore the experiences of 16 Black male academies of engineering students (Stake, 2006; Yin, 1994). Our research approach was interpretivist in nature and attempted to capture the meaning of participants' experiences and their sense-making regarding participation. During discussions with the participants, we were able to understand and interpret the meanings of their decisions to engage in the academy of engineering. We used pseudonyms throughout our discussions to replace participant and school names as well as locations.

We studied a NAF (formerly known as the National Academy Foundation) academy of engineering (the case) operating within unique contexts (e.g., community and school district) at a distinguished level according to the NAF standards of practice. NAF continuously evaluate their high school academies to assess their level of implementation based on standards of practice. They rate academies on three levels of implementation, using the following hierarchy from highest to lowest: distinguished, model, and certified. NAF's educational design is based on these elements: academy development and structure, curriculum and instruction, advisory board, and work-based learning. In our case study, we relied on indirect (interviewing participants) data-gathering methods, which were conducted virtually using Zoom due to the COVID-19 pandemic (Stake, 2006; Yin, 1994).

Selection Criteria

We purposely selected Stanton Academy (pseudonym) because it was a distinguished NAF academy of engineering and its demographics – 99% African American and 95% economically disadvantaged student population. We believed Stanton Academy would help us uncover how a high-fidelity NAF academy helps to broaden participation of Black male engineering students. Hence, the richness of the academy context and students' experiences helped us to answer our research question.

The Case: Stanton Academy

Demographics. Stanton Academy is located in the city of Stanton (population of approximately 124,000) which is 55% white, 37% African American/Black, 4% Latinx, and 3% Asian. The median income was approximately $42,000, and 19% of the community members lived below the poverty line. The city of Stanton was home to a historically black college and university.

The Stanton Engineering Academy was a public school with a distinguished (whole school magnet) NAF academy (one of several career-themed programs) embedded within the school. It was located in an urban area within the Southeastern region of the United States. Stanton Academy was comprised of approximately 1,263 students and 71 teachers (who were majority Black). In terms of gender, 51% of students were female and 49% were male. Concerning ethnic and racial background, 99% of students were Black and 1% were Latinx. Ninety-five percent of students qualified for free and/or reduced lunch. The graduation rate was 81%. Stanton Academy relied on an application system for student admission to the academy of engineering and several other career-themed academies within the school.

Researchers' Positionalities

It is helpful to acknowledge our own inherent biases, perspectives, and frames of reference as researchers, which most likely influenced and shaped research encounters, processes, and findings. All authors are faculty (three Black men and one Black woman). We have professional backgrounds in the field of career and technical/workforce education, special education (with an emphasis in gifted education), and counselor education. All three of us have studied issues related to the impact of student participation in high school STEM-themed career academies as well as inequities in access to academically rigorous programs in schools, particularly for ethnically and racially diverse as well as students who come from economically disadvantaged backgrounds.

Data Collection

We conducted three virtual group interviews with 16 Black male academies of engineering students. The content of the interviews were related experiences of Black male academy of engineering students. Each interview lasted for 30–60 minutes in duration. The university's IRB approved all components of this study.

We relied on the knowledge of an insider informant – a school administrative assistant – to provide us with a list of participants to interview.

Data Analyses

All interviews were audio-recorded and transcribed verbatim. We used constant comparison analysis to capture the experiences of Black male academy of engineering students (Leech & Onwuegbuzie, 2007). We first read the entire dataset of transcripts. After doing so, we divided the dataset into smaller meaningful segments. We then labeled each segment with a code. Afterward, we compared each component and collapsed those with similar codes. Last, we developed themes for each code group. For example, in arriving at a theme, the entire research team first read every transcript individually. We then individually reread each transcript to search for patterns/codes related to the experiences of Black male academy of engineering students. We met as a research team to discuss the codes that emerged. We then went back to the transcripts to select quotes that match the codes – those that accurately depicted the experiences of Black male academy of engineering students. We finally were able to discuss and agree on possible phrases/statements that represent the codes, which became our themes. We relied on analytical triangulation by engaging in the collective reading and analyses of transcripts.

DATA INTERPRETATIONS

We identified three recurring themes from the interviews with the Black male academy of engineering students. The first theme is *Promoting Interest in STEM* which reflects the students' investment in engineering as a result of engaging in the engineering curriculum. The second theme is *An Affinity for Hands-on Learning through the Engineering Curriculum* which denotes the students' preference for engaging in hands-on engineering projects. The third theme is *Drawing Connections to Core Academic Concepts* which highlights the students' understanding of the integrated nature of the engineering curriculum and demonstrates their understanding of core academic concepts through engineering lessons.

Promoting Interest in STEM

The Black male academy of engineering students shared with us that the career academy served as a motivator for pursuing their interests in STEM college and career pathways. The students shared that the most memorable component of their academy experience was the work-based learning activities they engaged in, which provided them with a good understanding of the engineering profession as well as inspired them to pursue engineering as a college and career pathway. For example, Javon noted:

> It's given us a good view of what to expect in the engineering world and helped push us further along the path.

They specifically noted a variety of work-based learning opportunities that they participated in, which helped them discover whether engineering was the right field for them. These work-based learning experiences included resume development, mock interviews, discussions with STEM professionals, and internships. The experiences, especially the internships, helped to demonstrate what their roles and responsibilities would be in an engineering career, helped them to cultivate their employability skills, and assisted in their preparation for majoring in engineering in college. Derek talked to us about his academy experience and the work-based learning experiences that he found meaningful. He said:

> I would say the mock interviews; it actually got you ready for how competitive the real-world engineering interviews are. Like I had to compete with some of my classmates for interview spots, and I had to build a resume. That's probably the most memorable thing, and if we're able to be accepted into one of those prestigious institutions. It's amazing. The academy's prepared us quite a bit. We've done a lot of, like I said, mock interviews, professional development. We just learned how to best present ourselves to companies and institutions, put our best foot forward, and show what experiences we've had. It's just all around just been a great experience...The academy has provided us a lot of opportunities to see what the world has to offer...how many opportunities there are out there, and how to reach them. They've also provided us with a lot of experiences that will help us later on in life. We've done a bit of professional development, we've done internships, we've done interviews. We've just all around just got a good view of what the engineering world has to offer. I would say we got like a head start into what our futures will look like...Well, I've taken advantage of any opportunity given to me. Currently, I'm in the works of trying to make it back into my Exxon internship that I had last year. I'm just trying to move my way into the engineering world.

Samuel described to us how the academy prepared him for the world of work in engineering and inspired him to major in engineering in college. The students shared with us that the academy provided the impetus for career exploration in determining whether engineering was a viable career pathway for them as well as what type of engineering (e.g., chemical, civil, electrical, and mechanical) they were interested in pursuing.

Even further, the students talked to us about how the academy provided learning experiences related to establishing an engineering identity. In that regard, Samuel noted:

> Really they taught us really how to be engineers. Like how to think like one, how engineers should be, and how to be really professional in the engineering field too.

An Affinity for Hands-on Learning Through the Engineering Curriculum

Many of the students we interviewed told us that they had an interest in engineering because it is a profession that involves building things and that they enjoyed the hands-on learning activities they engaged in within the academy. The Black male academy of engineering students told us that they enjoyed the projects they completed in the academy because they were tasked to build things and enjoyed working with their peers in groups.

The experience that I had it was something that I always wanted. 'Cause I always wanted to go to a school where we're doing hands-on learning. We're building stuff and all that. Then when we first came and I saw how classes working with engineering, and how we had groups, we had to do this project, complete this, I felt that it really was something that I enjoyed doing. It was a great experience.

Samuel echoed the sentiment about him enjoying working with his hands. He went on to say:

Me, personally, I always liked to work with my hands, like especially for the degree I'm trying to get, which is mechanical engineering. It's really like working with your hands and trying to solve a problem. That's something that I really enjoy doing ever since younger. That's why I pursued the engineering field.

Similarly, Leroy stated:

Agreeing with [Kevin], like participating – I'm a hands-on learner as well, so participating, it helps me understand more and remember more than just listening.

The students further noted that through the hands-on experiences they were gaining in the academy, they also had to problem-solve, collaborate, and develop their critical thinking skills. In addition, the students enjoyed the competitive nature of the engineering competitions they participated in within the academy of engineering. Derek shared with us that:

Furthermore, to build off of what [Samuel] said, it causes you to think out of the box and be innovative in order to be able to think creatively and solve problems that we might see around the school, like [Samuel] said. For example, in civil engineering...we had to pick a geotechnical problem that we had to do on campus and solve what the most cost-available thing to solve the problem. Also, well, last year when I was in eleventh grade, we had an engineering symposium, where we had to compete against each other to see how we could move some balls down to the other end. That was pretty challenging. Everybody had really good ideas. Some ideas worked, and some ideas didn't work. It was just fun to see everybody be competitive. It really was challenging since everybody, like I said, was competitive.

Thus, students shared with us the enjoyment they received from the challenging nature of the engineering field as well as the competitions they participated in. In fact, the students' most memorable experiences in the academy of engineering were typically related to projects they completed in their engineering classes. More specifically, they enjoyed the innovative thinking needed to complete the projects as well as the experimental (trial and error) nature of problem-solving within their engineering classes. For example, Joshua shared with us his most memorable experience as:

In the academy, it's both visual learning and hands-on learning. You will sit in class, write notes, understand the notes, and they'll teach you about notes. Then you will get a project on how to come up with a solution or how to build it. This one project we had was to build a bridge, and we only could use straw and tape...Paper clips. You couldn't use a certain amount of tape. You couldn't use too much tape. You had to come up with a different idea. To see if your bridge was able to work, we put a book on top, and if it held the book for longer than a minute, you passed. You had to come up with a solution on how to solve that. That's what I liked.

Similarly, Joshua said:

> To me, failure is what leads up to success. Let's say I have a problem I'm doing. I will keep trying and failing at it until I succeed and get it right. Let's say we're doing a project, and my project isn't working. I will keep trying different ways and then failing, it will keep edging out the wrong ways, and I will eventually find the right ways. That's how participation works out for me 'cause, if I keep failing, I'll eventually find the right way, which is what leads to success.

Jamal emphasized the high level of engagement the engineering classes offered which contributed to his motivation and investment in learning. He described how the hands-on projects in the academy of engineering motivated him to pursue engineering. He stated:

> My experiences with the program, I'm more of a hands-on person. I don't really like the – like sitting down, doing notes the whole time in class, which is why I like the program because...all right. I'm more of a hands-on person. I don't like writing down notes the whole time in class. That's why I like the program because there's a lot of projects that you do throughout the year, which not only it makes it fun, but it makes you want – it makes you more invested into engineering. It makes you want to do it more.

Similarly, Kevin articulated his interest in the academy of engineering because of the competitive and hands-on nature of the projects:

> Participating in this academy helps me because I'm a competitive person, so building these structures and catapults, cars and stuff, I always want to be the person that wins, so it teaches me to be competitive in a safe way.

The students were clear in their passion for the engineering classes and the engagement they had from building things, the hands-on nature of the projects, and the employability skills (e.g., collaboration, critical thinking, problem-solving, and creative thinking) they employed within the academy of engineering.

Drawing Connections to Core Academy Content

The Black male academy of engineering students also shared that engaging in the engineering academy helped them draw connections to core academic content (e.g., mathematics and science) as well as better understand concepts within their core academic classes through the applied nature of the engineering classes. For example, Cameron noted:

> My experience, it gave me, like, a first-time view of takin' knowledge and actually applyin' it to what you tryin' to do. Like learnin' somethin', and after that, seein' if you can recreate what you learned in a physical way. Then, like I said before, if you workin' with team and partners, try and be the person that make sure everybody do what they supposed to do. Make sure ain't nobody like [unintelligible 38:18] their havin' problems. 'Cause if a lot of people on the team don't like each other, they not gonna work together, and you can't build a whole house by yourself. Ya'll gonna have to do somethin' together, so that's it.

The students acknowledged that their engineering classes not only helped them within their own personal lives in the context of problem-solving but also helped them better understand their core academic subjects by applying core academic concepts to a real-world engineering context.

Thus, the engineering classes helped the students understand concepts in their core academic content areas. Darius explained the relevancy of the engineering concepts he learned to his personal life and the connections he made with other subject matter. He noted:

> Like what [Kevin] said, it helps us from our day-to-day lives. It's bigger than engineering. It helps us solve problems with family, friends, any of that. Just for academically, it helps also because it helps us with math, science, even sometimes English and reading sometimes. 'Cause it gives us different ways to think about how to go for a certain problem that presents itself. It all ties into one another.

James concurred with Darius and indicated how the engineering classes helped him in improving his performance in his core academic subjects. He stated:

> The [engineering] academy is academically challenging to me because I'm not really good at math, so the equations, they helped me better in math. For example, we take geometry, so we do some equations dealing with geometry, and it really helped me. It helped me boost my grades.

Kevin described the integrated nature of the engineering curriculum. He shared:

> My experience at this engineering academy at [Stanton Academy], it's a good experience. Teachers, they not only use visual learning, like on the board, but hands-on learning. We also use mathematic equations to determine what we're building, like what levers and stuff like that. A project that we did, we had to create a catapult out of popsicle sticks. We could only use a certain amount of, and we had to see which person in class's catapult shot the furthest.

Leroy described how he learns mathematic concepts in his engineering classes. He commented:

> My experience with the program is very good because it's fun, it's hands-on, and you learn a lot of things with calculations, with weight, grams. One time, one of the projects, we had to make a boat out of cardboard, and we had to calculate how big the boat could be without making it sink on water.

The students were unified in sharing the positive learning experiences they gained from the academy of engineering. They believed that the integrated nature of the engineering curriculum (e.g., using core academic concepts within their engineering projects) enabled them to perform better in their core academic courses.

DISCUSSION

The results of our study helped us to better understand how academies provide a platform for Black male students' interest in engineering as a viable college and career pathway. The academy of engineering at Stanton Academy was a positive learning space for Black male students as they appreciated the hands-on nature of the curriculum and participation in it reinforced core academic concepts as they were able to contextualize their learning in an applied setting (Bottia et al., 2015;

Fletcher & Cox, 2012; Fletcher et al., 2019, 2020). Thus, we found that the academy did indeed help Black male students connect academic and technical content to increase rigor and relevancy to students' career interests.

The career academy model represents a promising approach for promoting college and career readiness. The academy facilitated Black male students' preparedness for college and careers as it fostered their abilities to apply what they learned through the occupational expression of academic knowledge (Stone & Lewis, 2012). The academy also helped students increase their employability skills (e.g., collaboration, critical thinking, and problem-solving). Even further, the students were able to hone in on technical skills related to engineering.

Our findings challenge what we consider possible within urban schools that serve Black male students, and can inform how we utilize high school STEM curricular programs to broaden the pipeline of talent for STEM career pathways. Black male students at Stanton Academy benefitted from having STEM curricular programs that aligned with their learning preferences and promoted their academic success. Thus, Black male students in the academy of engineering were engaged in the academic learning environment as a function of having a shared culture (e.g., ethnic and racial background), common experiences, and heightened interests in connecting with each other. This case study enabled us to recognize that career academies have the potential to promote academically beneficial relationships with Black male students that address their needs as future engineers.

Recommendations for Practice

Based on our findings, we recommend that school personnel provide students with a robust set of STEM programs that provide students opportunities to select customized career pathways to pursue; career academies are one way to establish college and career pathways for students with their focus on work-based learning, college preparatory activities and curricula, and small learning communities around a career theme. We also recommend that school personnel work with their feeder middle schools in providing vertical integration programming by establishing a pipeline for students interested in various career pathways (e.g., STEM). Further, we recommend that school personnel provide students with rigorous curricular programs (e.g., advanced placement [AP] and dual enrollment options) in conjunction with work-based learning experiences (e.g., internships, job shadowing, and mock interviews) and college tours. These types of rigorous activities can assist Black male students in seeing beyond their zip codes and envisioning a pathway to high-demand, high-skilled, and high-wage college and career opportunities.

Further, it is important for Black male students to get access to mentoring from other Black male professionals in the school (e.g., school administration, school counselors, and teachers) as well as within their community (e.g., advisory board members, alumni, business and industry partners, community members, and parents). The cultural matching of school personnel helps with ensuring Black male students receive culturally responsive support and high expectations for success. These efforts are likely to lead to Black male students who are inspired to pursue STEM in college and for their careers.

Recommendations for Policy

Our findings emphasize the potential of career academies to promote college and career readiness for high school students as a comprehensive school reform initiative. Career academies may be aligned with the Perkins V provision in regard to preparing students for both further education and careers in emerging professions that are high-skill, high-wage, and in-demand (The Strengthening Career and Technical Education for the 21st Century Act, 2018). Based on findings in this study, students at Stanton Academy (a high fidelity academy) are likely to benefit from a higher engagement with work-based learning opportunities as well as college readiness activities. Student preparation for STEM careers, work-based learning, and dual enrollment all meet the objectives of the current Perkins V legislation. As such, this study suggests that career academies might be meeting the needs of students in preparing them to transition into college and careers.

We also believe this study has implications for reforming and improving current Perkins V legislation. Policymakers might take into consideration – when reauthorizing the legislation – the need to delineate more clearly the specific components and what types of activities (e.g., curricular integration, advisory board, and particular work-based learning experiences) are needed to implement an academy at a high fidelity that is associated with preparing students to be college and career ready. We recommend that schools have a strategic plan for implementing work-based learning to ensure students gain awareness, exposure, and experience in their chosen program of study – that is age appropriate and progressively intensifies as students advance grade levels. Students should begin by examining career pathways within a career cluster and culminate their experiences by participating in internships to learn what it is like to be an employee of a job within their chosen career fields. For college preparatory experiences, we believe that a reauthorization of Perkins should detail what types of activities are most appropriate – from dual enrollment to college tours. This would enable schools and school districts to ensure that all students have access to the same types of college and career preparatory activities and enable the federal government, states, school districts, and schools to monitor their progress. It would also be helpful for the legislation to set participation rate targets for schools to ensure that all students have access to college and career preparatory activities, and that a large percentage of students participate.

Recommendations for Further Research

We recommend that future studies include longitudinal analyses to follow up with high school Black male students who participated in academies of engineering to examine their post high-school outcomes, particularly as it relates to pursuing STEM college majors and/or careers. We also recommend that researchers examine Black male academy of engineering students' engagement in other important college readiness activities such as AP, honors, and international baccalaureate programs. Further, we recommend examining how participation in academies influences their achievement (e.g., ACT/SAT scores, grades, and GPAs).

LIMITATIONS

We also recognize the limitations inherent in our study. First, the generalizability of this study rests in our analytic interpretations regarding Stanton Academy as a case study. Generalizing to other schools and academies is based on similarities in institutional contexts as well as particular student demographics. Second, we relied on the assistance of an insider informant to provide us with participant information to recruit the Black male academy of engineering students to interview for this study.

CONCLUSION

Findings from our case study demonstrate that the career academy has the potential to provide a transformative learning experience for Black male students interested in pursuing engineering as a college and/or career pathway. Students in this academy benefitted from the hands-on learning nature of the curriculum. They were able to draw connections to core academic concepts to strengthen their understanding. In addition, the academy promoted their interests in pursuing STEM as a viable option post-high school. Within that context, this case study highlights ways in which the academy can serve as a pipeline of talent for Black male students interested in STEM.

ACKNOWLEDGMENT

Funding for this research was provided by the National Science Foundation's EHR Core Research program (Award # 2000472).

REFERENCES

Achinstein, B., & Aguirre, J. (2008). Cultural match or culturally suspect: How new teachers of color negotiate sociocultural challenges in the classroom. *Teachers College Record, 110*(8), 1505–1540.

Aud, S., KewalRamani, A., & Frohlich, L. (2011). *America's youth: Transitions to adulthood*. National Center for Education Statistics. NCES 2012-026.

Bottia, M. C., Stearns, E., Mickelson, R. A., Moller, S., & Parker, A. D. (2015). The relationships among high school STEM learning experiences and students' intent to declare and declaration of a STEM major in college. *Teachers College Record, 17*(3), 1–46.

Brown, B. A. (2019). *Science in the city: Culturally relevant STEM education*. Harvard Education Press.

Brown, B. A., Boda, P., Lemmi, C., & Monroe, X. (2019). Moving culturally relevant pedagogy from theory to practice: Exploring teachers' application of culturally relevant education in science and mathematics. *Urban Education, 54*(6), 775–803.

Castellano, M., Stone, J. R., III, Stringfield, S. C., Farley-Ripple, E. N., Overman, L. T., & Hussain, R. (2007). *Career-based comprehensive school reform: Serving disadvantaged youth in minority communities.* National Research Center for Career and Technical Education. http://www. nrccte.org/

Castellano, M., Sundell, K., Overman, L. T., & Aliaga, O. A. (2012). Do career and technical education programs of study improve student achievement? Preliminary analyses from a rigorous longitudinal study. *International Journal of Educational Reform, 21,* 98–118.

Collins, K. (2018). Confronting color-blind STEM talent development: Toward a contextual model for Black student STEM identity. *Journal of Advanced Academics, 29*(2), 143–168. https://doi.org/ 10.1177/1932202X18757958

Danforth, L., & Miller, J. (2018). African American males from female-headed households: Using family resilience to navigate their way to college. *Journal of Family Social Work, 21*(1), 63–79. https://doi.org/10.1080/10522158.2017.1321604

Fletcher, E. C., & Cox, E. (2012). Exploring the meaning African American students ascribe to their participation in high school career academies and the challenges they experience. *The High School Journal, 96*(1), 4–19. https://doi.org/10.1353/hsj.2012.0017

Fletcher, E., Dumford, A., Hernandez-Gantes, V., & Minar, N. (2020). Examining the engagement of career academy and comprehensive high school students in the United States. *The Journal of Educational Research,* 1–15. https://doi.org/10.1080/00220671.2020.1787314

Fletcher, E., Warren, N., & Hernandez-Gantes, V. (2019). The high school academy as a laboratory of equity, inclusion, and safety. *Computer Science Education, 29*(4), 382–406. https://doi.org/10. 1080/08993408.2019.1616457

Ford, D. (2010). *Reversing underachievement among gifted Black students* (2nd ed.). Prufrock Press.

Ford, D. Y., & Moore, J. L., III. (2013). Understanding and reversing underachievement and achievement gaps among high-ability African American males in urban school contexts. *The Urban Review, 45*(4), 400–415.

Gregory, J. F. (1995). The crime of punishment: Racial and gender disparities in the use of corporal punishment in US public schools. *The Journal of Negro Education, 64,* 454–462.

Hemelt, S., Lenard, M., & Paeplow, C. (2019). Building bridges to life after high school: Contemporary career academies and student outcomes. *Economics of Education Review, 68,* 161–178.

Hernández-Gantes, V. M. (2016). College and career readiness for all: The role of career and technical education in the US. In D. Wyse, L. Hayward, & J. Pandya (Eds.), *Sage handbook of curriculum, pedagogy and assessment* (Vol. 2, pp. 674–689). Sage.

Hernández-Gantes, V. M., & Brendefur, J. (2003). Developing authentic, integrated, standards-based mathematics curriculum: [More than just] an interdisciplinary collaborative approach. *Journal of Vocational Education Research, 28*(3), 259–284.

Hernandez-Gantes, V., & Fletcher, E. (2013). The need for integrated workforce development systems to broaden the participation of underrepresented students in STEM-related fields. In R. Palmer & J. Wood (Eds.), *Community College and STEM* (pp. 57–76). Routledge.

Hines, E. M., Cooper, J. N., & Corral, M. D. (2019). Overcoming the odds: First generation Black and Latino male collegians' perspectives on pre-college barriers and facilitators. *Journal for Multicultural Education, 13*(1), 51–69. https://doi.org/10.1108/JME-11-2017-0064

Hines, E. M., Hines, M. R., Moore, J. L., III, Steen, S., Singleton, P., Cintron, D., II, Traverso, K., Golden, M. N., Wathen, B., & Henderson, J. A. (2020). Preparing African American males for college: A group counseling approach. *Journal for Specialist in Group Work, 4*(2), 129–145.

Hines, E. M., & Holcomb-McCoy, C. C. (2013). Parental characteristics, ecological factors, and the academic achievement of African American males. *Journal of Counseling and Development, 91*(1), 68–77.

Hughes, K., Miller, T., & Reese, K. (2020). *Ready for causal research: A national evaluability assessment of career and technical education programs (preliminary report).* Career and Technical Education Research Network.

Jackson, J. F. L., & Moore, J. L., III. (2008). The African American male crisis in education: A popular media infatuation or needed public policy response? *American Behavioral Scientist, 51*, 847–853.

Johnson, C., & Sondergeld, T. (2020). Outcomes of an integrated STEM high school: Enabling access and achievement for all students. *Urban Education*, 1–27. https://doi.org/10.1177/0042085920914368

Kaser, J. S. (2006). *Mathematics and science specialty high schools service a diverse student body: What's different?* Learning Research and Development Center, University of Pittsburgh.

Kemple, J. J. (2008). *Career academies: Long-term impacts on labor market outcomes, educational attainment, and transitions to adulthood.* MDRC.

Kemple, J. J., & Snipes, J. C. (2000). *Career academies: Impacts on students' engagement and performance in high school.* Manpower Demonstration Research Corporation. http://www.mdrc.org/publications/41/full.pdf

Klein, J., & Cornell, D. (2010). Is the link between large high schools and student victimization an illusion? *Journal of Educational Psychology, 102*, 933–946. https://doi.org/10.1037/a0019896

Kuh, G. D. (2015). Foreword. In S. J. Quaye & S. R. Harper (Eds.), *Student engagement in higher education* (pp. ix–xiii). Routledge.

Kumah-Abiwah, F. (2019). Urban education and academic success: The case of higher achieving black males. *Urban Education*, 1–27. https://doi.org/10.1177/0042085919835284

Kuo, V. (2010). Transforming American high schools: Possibilities for the next phase of high school reform. *Peabody Journal of Education, 85*(3), 389–401. https://doi.org/10.1080/0161956X.2010.491709

Leech, N. L., & Onwuegbuzie, A. J. (2007). An array of qualitative data analysis tools: A call for qualitative data analysis triangulation. *School Psychology Quarterly, 22*, 557–584. https://doi.org/10.1037/1045-3830.22.4.557

Letgers, N., Balfanz, R., & McPartland, J. (2002). *Solutions for failing high schools: Converging visions and promising models.* Office of Vocational and Adult Education.

McGee, E. O., & Robinson, W. H. (2019). *Diversifying STEM.* Rutgers University Press.

Metz, M. H. (2003). *Different by design: The contact and character of three magnet schools.* Teachers College Press.

Moore, J. (2006). A qualitative investigation of African American males' career trajectory in engineering: Implications for teachers, school counselors, and parents. *Teachers College Record, 108*(2), 246–266.

Moore, J. L., III, Henfield, M. S., & Owens, D. (2008). African American males in special education: Their attitudes and perceptions toward high school counselors and school counseling services. *American Behavioral Scientist, 51*, 907–927.

Murphy, J. (2010). *The educator's handbook for understanding and closing achievement gaps.* Sage.

NAF. (2014). *Statistics and research: 2013–2014.* Retrieved at http://naf.org/statistics-and-research

Nasir, N., & Vakil, S. (2017). STEM-focused academies in urban schools: Tensions and possibilities. *The Journal of the Learning Sciences, 26*(3), 376–406. https://doi.org/10.1080/10508406.2017.1314215

National Science Board. (2018). *Science and engineering indicators 2018* (NSB-2018-1). National Science Foundation.

Newmann, F. M., & Wehlage, G. G. (1995). *Successful school restructuring: A report to the public and educators.* Center on Organization and Restructuring of Schools.

Page, L., Layzer, C., Schimmenti, J., Bernstein, L., & Horst, L. (2002). *National evaluation of smaller learning communities literature review.* Abt Associates.

Papadimitriou, M. (2014). High school students' perceptions of their internship experiences and related impact on career choices and changes. *Online Journal for Workforce Education & Development, 7*(1), 1–27.

Pierce, K., & Hernández-Gantes, V. M. (2015). Do mathematics and reading competencies integrated into career and technical education courses improve high school student scores? *Career and Technical Education Research, 39*(3), 213–229.

Skiba, R. J., Horner, R. H., Chunch, C. G., Rausch, M. K., May, S. L., & Tobin, T. (2011). Race is not neutral: A national investigation of African American and Latino disproportionality in school discipline. *School Psychology Review, 40*, 85–107.

Stake, R. (2006). *Multiple case study analysis.* Guilford.

Stern, D., Dayton, C., & Raby, M. (2010). *Career academies: A proven strategy to prepare high school students for college and careers.* University of California Berkeley Career Academy Support Network.

Stipanovic, N., Lewis, M. V., & Stringfield, S. (2012). Situating programs of study within current and historical career and technical educational reform efforts. *International Journal of Educational Reform, 21*, 80–97.

Stone, J. R., III, Alfeld, C., & Pearson, D. (2008). Rigor and relevance: Testing a model of enhanced math learning in career and technical education. *American Educational Research Journal, 45*(3), 767–795.

Stone, J. R., III, & Lewis, M. V. (2012). *College and career ready in the 21st century: Making high school matter.* Teacher's College Press.

Strengthening Career and Technical Education for the 21st Century Act 20 U.S.C. § 2301. (2018).

Whaley, A., & Noel, L. (2012). Sociocultural theories, academic achievement, and African American adolescents in a multicultural context: A review of the cultural compatibility perspective. *The Journal of Negro Education, 81*(1), 25–38.

Wright, C. G. (2019). Constructing a collaborative critique-learning environment for exploring science through improvisational performance. *Peabody Journal of Education, 54*(4), 1319–1348. https://doi.org/10.1177/0042085916646626

Yeager, D. S., Purdie-Vaughns, V., Hooper, S. Y., & Cohen, G. L. (2017). Loss of institutional trust among racial and ethnic minority adolescents: A consequence of procedural injustice and a cause of life-span outcomes. *Child Development, 88*, 658–676.

Yin, R. (1994). *Case study research: Design and methods* (2nd ed.). Sage.

CHAPTER 3

A PERFECT STORM: EDUCATIONAL FACTORS THAT CONTRIBUTE TO MISEDUCATION AND UNDERACHIEVEMENT AMONG BLACK STUDENTS

Donna Y. Ford, James L. Moore III and Ezekiel Peebles III

ABSTRACT

This chapter focuses on two aspects of the achievement gap – underachievement and low achievement among Black males in urban school contexts. More specifically, the authors explain several problems/issues confronting Black male students in P-12 gifted and talented, advanced placement, and special education programs, along with the school-to-prison pipeline – inequitable discipline in the form of suspensions and expulsions. We parse underrepresentation and overrepresentation for this student group. A central part of this discussion is grounded in the achievement gap literature on Black students in general with implications for Black males in particular. Another fundamental aspect of this discussion is the need for educators to adopt an anti-racist (social justice or civil rights) and cultural competence approach to their work, which means being equity-based and culturally responsive in philosophy and action. Suggestions for closing the achievement gap and otherwise improving the achievement of Black males are provided for educators. We also compel educators to go beyond talking about equity by setting quantifiable equity goals for minimum and maximum percentages (and numbers).

Keywords: Black males; achievement gap; urban schools; cultural competence; equity; anti-racists

Black Males in Secondary and Postsecondary Education
Advances in Race and Ethnicity in Education, Volume 9, 45–66
Copyright © 2024 Donna Y. Ford, James L. Moore III and Ezekiel Peebles III
Published under exclusive licence by Emerald Publishing Limited
ISSN: 2051-2317/doi:10.1108/S2051-231720230000009003

When my son, now an adult, was a second grader, he was so disengaged in school, disillusioned by school that the grades of this advanced Black boy were plummeting from A's and B's to failing. More drastically and unexpected was that he threatened to drop out of school – not high school, not college, but elementary school! I was stunned, frustrated, desperate, afraid, and angry. My family has a lineage of high achievement, in spite of our race, zip code, and low-income status. Like me, my son was identified as gifted and talented. Like me, he became a temporary underachiever. Years later, I based my dissertation on our combined experiences and almost 150 Black students of being gifted Black high achievers who were pushed into underachievement by educators' low and negative expectations of us. Our formal school experiences affected our college and university experiences (Donna Y. Ford).

The experiences of the first author are all too common for Black males in P-12 settings. The prevalence is so common that Black males from all socioeconomic statuses are achieving far below their potential. They are underachievers and low achievers who have been denied the opportunity to develop their potential. This academic discrepancy between potential and performance in their formal schooling flows over into their college academic performance, persistence, and motivation. This waste of potential and promises must be addressed with pre-vention, early intervention, and intervention efforts. In this chapter, the coau-thors share their professional experiences with Black males who lose their motivation and passion for learning, who become disengaged and disillusioned based on their school-based experiences. Gifted and talented and special educa-tion Black males are the focus of this chapter because both, for similar reasons, become underachievers and low achievers at all levels of education, regardless of abilities, skills, and family income and education. We discuss psychological, social, and cultural factors that contribute to Black male underachievement in formal schooling; with implications for higher education attainment and achievement. We emphasize the need to *prevent* underachievement and low achievement to eliminate or decrease emotional exhaustion, frustration, time, effort, and resources on intervention. Building on the motto of the United Negro College Fund – A Mind is a Terrible Thing to Waste – we contend that "A Mind is a Terrible Thing to Erase."

THE STATUS OF P-12 BLACK MALE STUDENTS

A massive volume of data, reports, theoretical, and conceptual scholarship expose the abysmal status of Black males in P-12 educational settings. Fueling Black male underachievement is racial prejudice and discrimination by educators, who are overwhelmingly White and high income. Black males are placed in double jeopardy by virtue of being culturally different from their teachers by race and/or gender. Subsequently, they are being miseducated, which results in underachievement at all ability levels – with and without special education needs; with and without gifted and talented needs; and with and without behavioral challenges. We discuss underachievement first followed by these discriminatory problems.

Black males in our nation's school system are disproportionately experiencing negative school outcomes, including academic failure, high dropout rates, low graduation rates. We attribute these subpar academic performances to racial prejudice and discrimination among educators (e.g., teachers, administrators, counselors, psychologists). To the point, keeping in mind the perfect storm analogy, Black males' low achievement and underachievement are disparately impacted by:

(1) *Inequitable underrepresentation in gifted and talented education (GATE) and Advanced Placement (AP) classes* (Ford, 2010, 2013; Ford & Moore, 2013). The US Department of Education Civil Rights Data Collection (CRCD) (www.ocrdata.ed.gov) for every year indicates that Black males are the least likely of all students to be in GATE and AP (Ford, 2013; Ford & Moore, 2013). Black males comprise about 9% of US schools but less than 4% of GATE. They are underrepresented by about 60%.[1] The percentages are similar for AP overall, and individual classes (e.g., AP math, science). Ford (2013) reported that educator *under-referral* is the number one reason that this student group is denied access to both programs for advanced learners, followed by traditional intelligence test (Naglieri & Ford, 2015; Sternberg et al., 2021). Grissom and Redding (2006) reported that even when Black students match White students in grades, test scores, and family characteristics (e.g., income, educational attainment), *teachers still under-refer* Black students. Undeniably, racial, gender, and economic prejudices are operating with significant impact;

(2) *Inequitably high participation rates in special education* (SPED) (Donovan & Cross, 2002; Fletcher et al., 2022; Hines et al., 2022) males are over-referred for services in the high-incidence areas, such as specific learning disabilities (LD), attention-deficit/hyperactivity disorder (ADHD), and emotional and behavioral disorders (EBD). They are two to three times more likely to be in these SPED categories than White students. These high-incidence disabilities require intelligence tests and teacher input, such as completing a checklist. Noteworthy is that intelligence tests continue to be biased against Black students (Ford & Moore, 2013). Ford and Moore provide a comprehensive exploration of tests and other measurements, concluding that traditional intelligence tests and subjective checklists disadvantage Black students, and they caution educators about making high-stakes decisions with these students.

At this point, it is important to mention that some professionals do not believe that tests are biased against Blacks and in favor of Whites. We will not devote time to such assertions and debates. Why? Because the American Psychological Association (APA) *finally* issued a formal apology to minoritized people in late 2021 for past and current racism in testing and evaluation. The apology was titled: "Apology to People of Color for APA's Role in

Promoting, Perpetuating, and Failing to Challenge Racism, Racial Discrimination, and Human Hierarchy in U.S." (https://www.apa.org/about/policy/racism-apology). The first two authors critiqued the apology, being mindful of the focus of this chapter and our decades of scholarly foci on equity, diversity, and inclusion which consists of anti-racist and cultural competence among educators in beliefs and attitudes, words, and deeds (https://www.diverseeducation.com/opinion/article/15286201/time-will-tell-three-black-scholars-ponder-apas-apology-for-silence-and-complicity-in-perpetuating-racism).

When it comes to low-incidence disabilities (e.g., vision, hearing, physical) overrepresentation is less likely. The Office for Civil Rights, Civil Rights Data Collection (CRDC) indicates that little to no overrepresentation in these categories. In effect, racial, gender, and economic prejudices and discrimination are operating; and

(3) *Unjust overrepresentation for disciplinary infraction (suspension and expulsion)* – often called the school-to-prison pipeline. Per the Office for Civil Rights CRDC (www.ocrdata.ed.gov), Blacks are consistently two to three times more likely to be suspended (more than once, in school and out of school) and expelled than White students. J Luke Wood and Paul Harris, along with the Schott Foundation, have conducted several studies about students by states and districts; their findings mirror those of the Office for Civil Rights CRDC. Teachers' negative expectations are the primary, most influential reason for these dismal outcomes. Preschool-aged Black boys represent *over half* of suspensions, despite being about 10% of these young students. The percentages change little as they advance in grade levels. Regardless of age, Black males are inequitably educated; they are convicted in the womb (Upchurch, 1997).

Concretely stated, educators' deficit thinking is the common denominator for under-referrals to GATE and AP, over-referrals to SPED, and over-referrals for discipline. Considering culpability, educators are the common denominator for the achievement gap, underachievement, and low achievement. The result of these adverse and discriminatory school outcomes are low academic motivation, engagement, and interest among too many Black males of all ages, income levels, and academic statuses (Harris & Wood https://www.cos.edu/en-us/Research/Documents/Black%20Minds%20Matter.pdf; Schott Foundation, 2012; Wood et al., 2018).

Underachievement, low achievement, and other adverse/negative school performances/outcomes are often discussed under the "achievement gap" and associated terms, such as the opportunity gap, access gap, experience gap, resource gap, expectation gap, and teacher quality gap, to name but a few. However, we note that the achievement gap and underachievement are not synonymous. The achievement gap juxtaposes the performance of Blacks compared to Whites, who are deemed to be the norm to which all minoritized students are compared and, subsequently, (mis)labeled and educated accordingly with GATE, SPED, or general education placement, programs, and services. While it is not popular to speak this truth, the education students receive is based on these three labels and becomes more complicated when behavior is added. Regardless of their ability and potential, Black males are the most mislabeled and miseducated students (Woodson, 1933). Nationally, data indicate that Black high school students, on average, perform 4 years behind White students in reading and math (e.g., Barton, 2003; Barton & Coley, 2009). This is especially true for Black males in urban settings (Jackson & Moore, 2006, 2008; Moore & Lewis, 2012).

The achievement gap does not focus on potential or what the student may be capable of, academically. However, a guiding assumption or principle we profess is that there should not be a significant or stubborn disparity in performance, most often measured by test scores, between White and Black students, regardless of gender. No racial and/or low-income group is genetically or culturally superior (or inferior) to another; as such, high achievement and giftedness exist in *every* demographic group, including urban Black males. To this end, the initial step to begin reversing low achievement and underachievement, as well as closing the achievement gap, is situated in finding and rectifying causal and correlational factors.

Student underachievement (i.e., a discrepancy between potential and performance) and low achievement (i.e., performance is below average) are two major concerns of families and anti-racist and culturally competent educators, including those working with GATE and high-potential students. Rightfully and necessarily so, many scholars and organizations have spent decades unraveling the complex and entrenched issue of Black males' pervasive and abysmal social and educational experiences (e.g., Schott Foundation). Conversely, advocacy for and scholarship on GATE males is miniscule. In this chapter, we seek to fill this massive void by shedding much-needed light on this underperforming and underestimated group of Black students. We begin with attention to the achievement gap between Black and White students. We recognize that the information provided is seldom directly tailored to Black males; however, the scholarly information presented next is indeed relevant to Black males in general, those who should be in GATE, who should *not* be receiving SPED services, and who are unnecessarily disciplined. Pictorially, the conceptual model we operate from is a Venn diagram whereby we examine the three problems separately and intersectionally.

We use the term "low achievement" to define or describe Black males who are performing below average, which is often less than a "C" average in school/academic settings. Using the statistical Bell Curve, half of all students will automatically be low achievers given that they fall below the 50th percentile or average (Ford, 1996, 2010). Low achievement indicates nothing about what a student is capable of; this designation tells us only that the student is performing below average in terms of grades and/or test scores. When seeking to raise the performance of low-achieving males, the overarching question is: "What can be done to raise their performance so that they are not below average?"

Low achievement and underachievement are not synonymous. Highly capable Black males can be both an underachiever and high achiever, even with high grades and/or test scores (Ford, 1996, 2010). For example, if a Black male (or any student) puts forth little effort in school but gets high grades or test scores, then he is not working to his potential and, thus, is a high-performing underachiever. The student may not be failing, but he/she is not performing at an expected level based on test scores, teacher beliefs, and/or caregiver views. Albeit, subjective when a teacher or caregiver believes a student making A's and/or B's can do better, the student is likely an underachiever (and gifted).

Note that a GATE or high potential Black male can be both a low achiever and underachiever (e.g., he has a D average but is able to perform at a higher level). At the heart of the notion, definition, and reality of underachievement is a discrepancy between ability or potential (e.g., perceived and/or tested) and predicted performance. A student can be an underachiever because of a discrepancy between (a) intelligence test scores and achievement test scores; (b) intelligence test scores and grades/grade point average (GPA); (c) achievement test scores and grades/GPA; and (d) expectations of educators and/or caregivers for the student and some measure of his/her predicted performance (e.g., grades/GPA, achievement test score). Thus, there are both objective and subjective ways to define and measure potential-performance discrepancies. When seeking to raise the performance of Black male underachievers, the overarching question is: "What can be done to help urban, highly capable Black males reach their academic potential?"

No one variable or factor is responsible for the stubborn and pervasive achievement gap(s) between Black students and White students. Differences in achievement and education outcomes must be discussed within the context of social, cultural/familial, school, and individual factors, given that no one variable contributes to or causes underachievement and low achievement (Ford, 2010; Hébert & Schreiber, 2010; Henfield et al., 2008; Moore & Owens, 2008; Siegle, 2012; Vega et al., 2012). As discussed later, when urban, highly capable Black males do not achieve their academic potential, there are no quick answers or easy fixes. Poor achievement, if not temporary or situational (e.g., moving to a new school, parental/caregiver divorce, personal or family illness, teacher disinterest, etc.), is a function of many intricate and interactive factors that collectively take their toll on the educational experiences and subsequent performance of Black students (Barton & Coley, 2009; Cohen & Lotan, 2004; Ford & Moore, 2013), including those who are GATE and high potential (e.g., Ford, 1996, 1998, 2010, 2013; Henfield et al., 2008; Moore & Owens, 2008).

Five guiding premises frame this chapter and our assertion that poor achievement (be it the achievement gap, underachievement, or low achievement) among Black males with all the labels and associated needs can be both prevented and reversed:

Premise 1: *Poor achievement is learned, and it can (and must) be unlearned* (Ford, 1996, 2010). In essence, Black males are not born underachieving or low achieving. There is no underachievement gene; no one is born an academic underachiever;

Premise 2: *Gifts and talents exist in all racial, cultural, gender, and economic groups.* Thus, Black male underrepresentation in GATE, overrepresentation in

SPED and discipline, and their underachievement and low achievement should not exist to the magnitude that they do;

Premise 3: *Deficit thinking – prejudice and discrimination – is a central factor that influences Black males' underachievement.* Black males' low achievement is often a function of what takes place in schools relative to policies, practices, and belief systems (Toldson, 2019) (e.g., low educator expectations, racism, sexism, irrelevant curricula, poor quality and culturally incompetent educators, few or no resources, etc.);

Premise 4: *Terminology matters and often describes educators' thinking and expectations of Black males.* The term "urban," for example, is riddled with negative connotations and expectations. It frequently conjures up notions of "poverty," "apathy," "crime," "violence," and an entrenched and debilitating stereotypical belief that Black males (including those with high potential) have a disregard or disdain for self-improvement or self-advancement. When this deficit-oriented view is held among school personnel, it is difficult and nearly impossible for Black male students to muster up the commitment, energy, and resources to challenge those in authority and to make changes to succeed in school (Ford et al., 2006; Moore & Owens, 2008); and

Premise 5: *Educators need to adopt and practice a social justice or civil rights policy and stance.* Ladson-Billings (2006) coined the term "education debt" which she considers to be more accurate than the achievement gap. She states: "This debt comprises historical, economic, sociopolitical, and moral components" (p. 3). When this debt is paid, Black males will receive the education to which they are legally and morally entitled.

While this article focuses on gloomy issues or topics that are difficult for some educators to discuss, admit to, accept, and share responsibility for, it is also optimistic in its underlying premise that underachievement and low achievement can be prevented and corrected among Black males in all school settings. Of course, improvement requires political, professional, and personal will and commitment from educators (e.g., teachers, school counselors, administrators, etc.) and Black families. It is, therefore, critical that these educators work individually and collectively to improve Black male achievement and outcomes in urban and all other school settings.

MORE ATTENTION TO THE PERFECT STORM

In 1996, Ford proposed that at least four major overlapping factors contribute to poor student performance, be it the achievement gap, low achievement, and/or underachievement. These influential factors (social, school, family, and individual) are briefly described next.

Rings of Influence: Factors Contributing to Underachievement

One or more social, school, cultural/familial/community, and individual factors play a key role in influencing all students' performance, but this chapter focuses specifically on Black males.

The social factor is the broadest and most encompassing of the four variables; this factor focuses on salient issues, such as racism, biases, prejudice, and discrimination (Ford, 2010; Henfield et al., 2008; Vega et al., 2012). Social factors include, but are not limited to, negative stereotypical attitudes about and behaviors toward Black males – regardless of academic performance and potential. Deficit thinking fuels and feeds such prejudicial and often unfounded beliefs, feelings, and behaviors, which is the belief that Black males are genetically and/or culturally inferior to Whites (Allport, 1954; Ford, 2010; Ford et al., 2002; Merton, 1936). In the research and conceptual or theoretical literature, numerous writers (e.g., Menchaca, 1997; Steele, 2010; Valencia, 2010) have concluded that substantial consequence of this negative perception is low expectations and the attendant denial of access to educational opportunities that could drastically improve the educational, economic, vocational, and social status of Black males, such as greater access to GATE and AP, as previously noted. Scholars have found this denial of access and deficit thinking to be particularly evident in urban school contexts (Lewis et al., 2008; Lewis & Moore, 2008a, 2008b; Moore & Lewis, 2012).

Cultural factors, the second ring of influence, focus on context-specific issues, such as those pertaining to families, communities, and peers. The focal point is on what takes place in the cultural, lived experiences of students. Questions relate to the quality of life for Black males in their neighborhoods, and with family and friends. Do Black males in urban and nonurban schools and settings have access to equitable, culturally responsive and rigorous resources, academic and emotional supports, role models, and mentors at home and in their community? How involved are parents, caregivers, and families in their children's lives? To what degree do adults in the lives of Black males promote learning and education, and have the social, cultural, and economic capital to open locked academic doors for them? How supportive are friends/peers regarding school, high achievement, and participation in GATE and AP classes? Do Blacks accuse Black males who do well in school of "acting White"?

When families or caregivers, community members, and/or peers adhere to an anti-achievement ethic, Black males face significant and greater challenges to achieving in school settings. This is commonly evident when families or caregivers do not support education, when they fail to promote learning and education in the home environment, and when they are not involved in their sons' education at home and/or school (Barton, 2003; Barton & Coley, 2009). We must stress that Black families or caregivers are quite concerned about their sons' education, but they frequently have little social, cultural, educational, and fiscal capital. In turn, these families/caregivers find themselves challenged, relative to more privileged families, to effectively support their sons' education and expose them to pivotal educational experiences (e.g., Grantham et al., 2005; McAdoo & Younge, 2009;

Olszewski et al., 1987; Wright et al., 2022). Further, as discussed later, when school achievement is disparaged among peers, some or many Black males become discouraged and less motivated (Ford, 2010; Ford et al., 2008; Fordham, 1988; Fordham & Ogbu, 1986; Whiting, 2009).

As discussed above, school and educational factors also contribute, in formidable ways, to poor academic outcomes for students. For instance, teachers who are not culturally competent and/or who are biased against Black males contribute to their poor achievement and educational outcomes (Ford, 2011; Gay, 2010; Ladson-Billings, 2006, 2009). In addition to negative, stereotypical, and prejudicial attitudes (Ford et al., 2002; Haycock & Crawford, 2008; Valencia, 1997, 2010), poor teacher quality (Barton, 2003; Barton & Coley, 2009), and limited resources (Lewis & Moore, 2008a, 2008b; Moore & Lewis, 2012), also hinder, without question, the achievement of capable Black males in schools. Placement with students by teacher quality and experience, for example, is seldom accidental or coincidental (Lankford et al., 2002). As Haycock and Crawford lamented:

> Year after year, decade after decade, countless studies told us that on these measures, we didn't have a fair distribution of teacher talent... Minority and poor students in particular were typically taught by significantly more than their fair share of unlicensed, out-of-field, and inexperienced teachers who often didn't have records of strong academic performance themselves. (p. 14)

The aforementioned three set of factors address external variables. We now turn to internal variables. At the individual or personal level, educators must consider personality, motivation, self-perception (e.g., self-esteem, self-concept, and racial development identity and pride), need for achievement, need for affiliation, and other variables that commonly influence achievement among Black males. Those with low motivation, poor self-perceptions, and/or a strong need for affiliation are less likely to engage and excel in schools and academics (Whiting, 2006, 2009). These and other social, familial/community, school, and personal/individual factors, as just discussed, thwart many highly capable Black males from reaching their potential (i.e., underachievement, low achievement) and performing at comparable levels to White students and Black females (i.e., achievement gap). Specifically, the chances of such Black males achieving at higher levels are diminished under the aforementioned conditions. However, change is not only necessary but also possible.

THE ACHIEVEMENT GAP: A MORE COMPREHENSIVE REVIEW AND DISCUSSION

It is impossible to discuss underachievement and low achievement without discussing the achievement gap. In the previous sections, some of the factors contributing to the achievement gap were discussed. In this section, we present a more direct discussion of the gap, relying on the comprehensive works of Barton (2003), Barton and Coley (2009), and Hodgkinson (2007). They all present an overview of the primary correlates of the achievement gap between Black and

White students. While gender by race differences was not noted, we nonetheless believe the findings hold true. Further, based on our collective works and reviews of scholarship, the findings may actually underestimate how grave the correlates are when disaggregated by race and gender. Thus, we feel confident that the information that follows is more than appropriate at shedding light on the achievement gap among Black males compared to others.

The comprehensive work of Barton and Coley (2009), grounded in meta-analysis procedures, identified 16 variables that consistently and substantively contribute to the Black–White achievement gap. The 16 variables are categorized into three major factors and subfactors or correlates – home, school, and health and nutrition. Specific attention is devoted to differences by income and race. As noted by Barton and Coley (2009), "most of the risk factors are related to poverty and all poor children, regardless of race/ethnicity, are at risk of not fulfilling their potential" (p. 10). Essentially, race and income should be interrogated and deconstructed; educators must not assume or presume that these two variables (alone or combined) completely determine student achievement. Even if poverty were to disappear, racism would still exist.

School Factors

Seven correlates found in school settings contribute most to the math and reading achievement gaps between Black and White students.

Curriculum rigor. Regardless of the term used to describe academic rigor (e.g., expectations, challenging curriculum, academic environment, academic press, access to gifted, and/or advanced placement classes [see Barton & Coley, 2009]), volumes of research demonstrate that students' academic achievement depends extensively upon the academic rigor of the curriculum. Inequitably, the curriculum is frequently less rigorous for Black males and females than for other students, particularly in urban and low-income schools. Instructional rigor includes teachers' expectations of students, as has been learned from research on teacher expectation–student achievement. When expectations are low, negative, or deficit-oriented, teachers often neither challenge nor expect much from Black students (Patton et al., 2003; Ford et al., 2011, 2018).

Academic rigor is also defined as high-level instruction and access to challenging programs, such as GATE and AP classes (Barton, 2003; Barton & Coley, 2009). Black males are less likely than *all* other students to participate in honors, AP and GATE classes. To repeat, Ford (2010, 2013), using data from the Office of Civil Rights, CRDC reported that Black males are under-represented by almost 60% in GATE. Putting a face on the percentages, over 150,000 Black males are under-referred, under-identified, and under-educated (Ford, 2013). The percentages and discrepancies are equally appalling in AP classes for Black students in general and Black males in particular.

Teacher preparation. The crucial importance of teacher preparation and quality on student achievement cannot be underestimated or trivialized. Black males and their urban peers are more often taught by teachers who are unqualified, or poorly prepared, including teachers who lack certification, out-of-field teachers, teachers with the fewest credentials, and teachers with the lowest college grades and test scores (Barton & Coley, 2009; Moore & Lewis, 2012). In schools with large Black enrollments, some 30% of teachers do not even have a minor in the subject area in which they teach. In mostly White schools (e.g., suburban schools), the percentage drops to 20% (Barton, 2003). Relating teacher quality to the issue of academic rigor, ill-qualified teachers have difficulty teaching and challenging Black males, including those who are gifted and highly capable; these teachers are also less likely to raise Black male students' achievement because they do not have adequate academic training to do so; that is, cultural competence is lacking (e.g., Ford, 2011; Irvine, 2010; Ladson-Billings, 2010; Saracho & Gerstl, 1992; Shade et al., 1997). We are of the belief that definitions and descriptors of teacher quality must include cultural competence.

Teacher experience. Inexperienced or novice teachers, those with less than five years of classroom experience, are more likely to teach in urban than suburban settings (Barton & Coley, 2009; Lewis et al., 2012). In schools with high percentages of Black students, which are often located and segregated in urban settings, one in five of the teachers have less than three years of experience; conversely, in schools with low Black enrollment, 10% of teachers have less than three years of teaching (Barton, 2003). To state the obvious, teacher inexperience, except in rare circumstances, adversely affects the quality of instruction given to and received by Black males, which contributes to their underachievement, low achievement, and poorer school achievement.

Teacher absence and turnover. Further complicating the above issues on teacher quality and experience, studies indicate that teachers working in urban, high-minority schools often have low attendance rates and high turnover rates, which results in classes being taught by less prepared (and ill-qualified) substitute teachers. Most Black students are likelier to attend schools with high levels of teacher absence and turnover. For instance, 5% of Black students, compared to 28% of White students, had a teacher who left their teaching position before the school year ended (Barton & Coley, 2009). In 2007, 8% of White eighth graders attended schools where more than 6% of the teachers were absent on an average day; this percentage was almost double (11%) for Black students. Being taught by different teachers, being taught by substitute teachers – essentially, having inconsistent instruction – hinders and compromises the learning opportunity and achievement of Black students in general and Black males in particular.

Class size. In schools where there are high percentages of Black students, class sizes are larger (Barton & Coley, 2009). When these students represent 50% or more of the school population, the class size averages 23 students; however, in schools where Black students are less than 15% of the school population, class sizes average 14 students (Barton & Coley, 2009). Essentially, larger classes are more difficult to manage; more time is spent on behavior than teaching, resulting in Black students being denied the opportunity to learn at the same rates as White students.

Instructional technology. This achievement gap correlates with the digital divide, which includes access/availability, teachers' skills, and students' use of technology to augment instruction. Inadequate access to and/or underutilization of instructional technology impedes students' learning. Schools with higher percentages of Black students are less likely to have computers in the classrooms, internet access, and updated high-quality software (Barton & Coley, 2009). In addition, data indicate that 77% of teachers in predominantly White schools versus 52% of teachers in predominantly minoritized schools were at the intermediate or advanced skill level (Barton & Coley, 2009). A further problem concerns how and whether teachers use technology in the classroom; 61% of students in low-minority schools are given assignments to conduct research on the internet, compared to 35% for students in high-minority schools (Barton, 2003). As a result, Black males, even those with high potential, are ill-qualified to compete in situations where technological skills are essential, which is clear in many cases.

Fear and safety. As Maslow's (1943, 1954) *Hierarchy of Needs* illustrates, engagement, performance, learning, and achievement are significantly compromised when students feel unwelcome, unsafe, and threatened. Classroom discipline, disruptions, and negative peer pressures (including gangs, bullying, and fears about fights at school) are reported more often by Black males than other students (Barton & Coley, 2009). Students have difficulty concentrating and staying focused or engaged under such duress. As a result, they may have poor attendance and/or high dropout rates to avoid such threats and stresses, or they may not put forth effort in school to avoid negative attention from peers who may accuse them of "acting White" (Ford et al., 2008; Fordham & Ogbu, 1986). In essence, educators contribute to the achievement gap between Black and White students in meaningful ways.

Home Factors

Six additional correlates of the achievement gap, based outside of school, meaning in the home, should be addressed as we seek to understand and support Black males; many of these correlates are tied directly to poverty, which is a "universal handicap" as Hodgkinson (2007) has posited.

Parent–Pupil ratio. The extent to which parents or primary caregivers are available to and spend *quality* time with their Black sons or children varies by family income, and family structure or composition. A larger percentage of Black students (compared to White students) live in single-parent homes (Barton & Coley, 2009; Moore & Lewis, 2012), and many are low income. Among all students living in homes with mothers only, the rates are 17% for White children, compared to 49% for Black children (Barton, 2003). Hodgkinson (2007) reported that "regardless of race, the children in married couple families are much less likely to be poor (about 8%), while 29% of White children and 52% of Black and Hispanic children who live with a single mother are likely to be poor" (p. 10).

When parental or caregiver presence is low to nonexistent, all Black males are left to make choices and fend for themselves. The lack of supervision frequently results in less structure and discipline for these students; they seldom spend their unsupervised time studying and/or participating in school-related activities, causing them to fall behind academically and further behind their White male counterparts.

Parent participation. The degree to which Black parents/caregivers are involved in their sons' education influences their children's academic achievement and school behavior. Urban Black families or caregivers tend to participate less in their children's education than others (Barton & Coley, 2009). Specifically, 44% of urban parents and 20% of suburban parents report feeling unwelcome in schools; therefore, student achievement is jeopardized (Barton, 2003). Given these statistics, it seems reasonable to assume that Black family members' feelings of being disenfranchised and discounted by school personnel contributes to their low participation rates as opposed to a lack of care or desire for the best for their children.

Student mobility. Hodgkinson (2007) raised several key concerns about student mobility. Yearly, 22% of children under the age of five move to a different house with low-income families moving more than higher-income families. Another sobering reality is that this trend is more common in urban than suburban schools. Sadly, "large numbers of teachers may start and end the year with 24 students, but 22 of those 24 are different from the students they welcomed the first day of school" (Hodgkinson, p. 9). During COVID-19, it was revealed again that Black males, mainly those who live in poverty, have the highest rates of changing schools. Further, two out of five students who change schools frequently are below grade level in reading, and one third of these students are below grade level in math (Barton, 2003). Clearly, numerous negative and far-reaching consequences accompany changing schools.

Language – talking, vocabulary, and reading. Reading is strongly and positively correlated with language acquisition, literacy development, test scores, and achievement. An early longitudinal study, from 1993 to 2001, found that 3- to 5-year-old White preschoolers were read to more often than Black ones (Barton, 2003; Hart & Risley, 2003; Lee & Burkham, 2002). The consequences of poor reading skills are serious, and the effects are long-term. These Black students eventually perform poorly on intelligence and achievement tests, and struggle in school subjects. Much potential is lost among Black males who are not encouraged to pursue reading opportunities at school and at home.

Excessive TV watching. Black students watch more television than their classmates. For example, 42% of Black and 13% of White fourth graders were found to watch 6 hours or more of television each day (Barton, 2003). Excessive and unsupervised television watching negatively affects students' achievement. In such cases, Black students do less homework and reading, and participate in fewer after-school programs and intellectually stimulating activities. This absence or shortage of such activities contributes to the achievement gap between Black males and other demographic groups (e.g., White males, Black females).

Summer achievement gains/loss. Urban Black students often experience more loss academically over the summer than do their higher-income classmates and suburban Black and White counterparts. While trend data were not reported by Barton and Coley (2009), it is quite likely that Black males are less likely to perform to their potential as a function of low participation in rigorous academic summer opportunities. This problem now extends to COVID-19 loss since 2019. As a way of ensuring that Black males sustain their academic gains from schooling, families and school systems must partner with communities and multiple agencies to offer summer supplemental, enrichment, and/or remedial programs (Fletcher et al., 2022; Ford, 2011; Hines et al., 2022; Whiting, 2006).

Health Factors

Food Insecurity – hunger and nutrition. At the base of Maslow's (1943, 1954) hierarchy of needs theory is deficiency needs – those that humans cannot live without. Hunger and nutrition are strongly and significantly related to income level and racial status. The development and nurturance of the mind and body is jeopardized when Black males are hungry and in poor health (e.g., underweight, overweight, sick, lack of vitamins). Food insecurity, a term used by the US Department of Agriculture, reveals that, in 2005, about 30% of Black children and 10% of White children were food insecure (Barton & Coley, 2009). As one way to ensure that Black males are given every opportunity to reach their academic potential, it is critical that their nutritional and food needs be met. In many urban communities around the country, including during COVID-19, schools are forced to fill the gaps in students' homes, such as offering special meal programs for students and caregivers. Such programs are vital when substantial populations of families or caregivers are struggling to make ends meet (e.g., paying billings, buying food, etc.), which is undeniable among Black families because of employment discrimination – underemployment and unemployment – that result in wage and income gaps and inequities.

Low birthweight. According to Hodgkinson (2007), approximately 7% of babies are of low birthweight. However, for infants born to Black mothers, the proportion doubles. Note that even well-educated, middle-class Black mothers have more low birth babies than the norm for all demographic groups. Income alone does not guarantee quality access to medical and health services. Race still matters, which continues to be revealed during the COVID-19 pandemic.

Low birthweight can produce significant health problems that also increase being in one or more risk categories that impede educational achievement, and some special educational needs (e.g., developmental delay). In far too many cases, Black families are unable to access medical care because they lack health care benefits and cannot afford to pay such costs. Therefore, having access to proper, equitable health care is essential as we focus on efforts to close achievement gaps.

Environmental damage. Research on the dangers and harmfulness of lead poisoning is well established, with most work focused on Black and/or low-income communities. In this area, more attention is devoted to the academic effects of lead and mercury poisoning. To be blunt, environmental damage is based on racism, with Flint, Michigan being one well-known example. Black students are disproportionately exposed to both. Lead that exceeds governmental standards cause reductions in IQ and attention span, increases in reading and learning disabilities, as well as more behavior problems (Barton & Coley, 2009).

Black students are at the highest risk of exposure to lead from living in old homes and/or being around old industrial areas with contaminated buildings and soil; thus, Blacks have higher elevated levels of lead than other students. The effects of mercury are also severe and have long-term permanent effects. For example, mercury negatively affects intelligence, cognitive thinking, attention, language, fine motor skills, walking, muscles, visual spatial skills, hearing, speech, and more.

Given the aforementioned problems regarding underachievement, low achievement, and the achievement gap or gaps, what are the recommendations for Black males in academic settings? We now turn to recommendations for change grounded in equity, anti-racism, and cultural competence to address the perfect storm discusses herein. Our recommendations are also framed by the motto shared earlier – *a mind is a terrible thing to not just waste but also to erase.* We want to prevent and disrupt low achievement and underachievement (wasting minds); we want to prevent and disrupt underrepresentation and over-representation (erasing minds).

FROM VERBALIZING EQUITY TO SETTING QUANTIFIABLE EQUITY GOALS

In our individual and collective lived experiences as Black family members and scholars modeling, demonstrating, and demanding racial, gender, and economic equity in the larger society, and its microcosm – schools – we now turn to showing how educators and turn equity mottos, mantras, and philosophies into *visible* equity. When we observe GATE and SPED classrooms and other settings, and disciplinary data, we want to *see* equity whereby underrepresentation and overrepresentation are minimal and, ideally, nonexistent. We know that racial quotas are currently illegal. What we share now are not quotas; instead, these are minimum and maximum representation ranges that equitable. The formula was adopted by the first author in a GATE court case where the Equal Employment Opportunity Commission's (EEOC) 80% rule was adopted to set representation goals by race. States and districts have adopted what is known as "Ford's 20% Allowance" for underrepresentation and overrepresentation. An extensive explanation of the equity formula can be found in Ford (2013) and several other publications (e.g., Ford et al., 2018, 2020, 2021; Ford & Russo, 2015, 2016; Russo & Ford, 2015).

To set *minimum* underrepresentation percentages, begin with the percentage of each group in the nation, state, district, and/or building. The questions asked is: (a) What must be the *minimum* racial representation percentage for the nation, state, district, and building to be equitable? Multiply that percentage by 80% (0.8) for each group.

Likewise, what must be the *maximum* racial representation percentage for the nation, state, district, and building to be equitable? To set *maximum* over-representation goals, begin again with the percentage of each group in the setting. Multiply that percentage by 120% (1.2) for every group.

The equity ranges are presented in Table 3.1. It is important to understand that the percentages can be applied to the nation, state, district, and school building. Students not only have different experiences in school by race and by gender, therefore, we must not homogenize students between and within groups. We recommend that educators disaggregate their data by race x gender (e.g., Black males, Black females, Hispanic males, etc.), and by race x gender x income (e.g., Black males on free or reduced lunch, Black males not on free or reduced lunch, etc.). Importantly, in addition to calculating percentages, educators need to translate them into numbers. Depending on the number of students in particular educational setting, Black males can comprise 25%; that can be 500, 250,000, or more Black males.

RECOMMENDATIONS

The problems we have are a function of our thinking. We cannot change things until we change our thinking. (Albert Einstein)

The recommendations we now share are comprehensive but not exhaustive given the page limitations. There is no quick fix or panacea for reversing underachievement and low achievement among Black males, and closing racial achievement gaps has proven to be challenging, but not impossible. Educators must be vigilant, assertive, proactive, and unapologetic about improving the achievement of Black male students; this includes not caving into the divisive, racist status quo (such as those who are against Critical Race Theory, who abuse GATE by insisting that their child is gifted and talented when they do not require such services, who personify White flight – take steps to avoid having their child in diverse schools and classes). Also necessary is that justice and equity-minded educators hold leaders and decision-makers accountable for addressing prejudice and discrimination by being what Merton (1936) calls an all-weather liberal – individual who is not prejudiced and does not discriminate.

Table 3.1. Equity Ranges for US Students by Race for Gifted and Talented Education (GATE), Special Education (SPED), and Discipline.

US Student Group for 2020	School %	GATE *Minimum* Equity %	SPED and Discipline *Maximum* Equity %
Asian	5.42	4.34	6.50
Black	14.99	11.99	17.99
Hispanic	28.01	22.41	33.61
Native American	0.93	0.74	1.12
White	45.76	33.61	54.91

Note: Also calculate the number of students based on the percentages. Source from the US school demographics, *Condition of Education 2022* (https://nces.ed.gov/pubsearch/pubsinfo.asp?pubid=2022144).

One key recommendation lies in the unwavering need for efforts to directly, aggressively, proactively, and consistently address contributing social, educational, and familial factors, many of which were just discussed. In other words, the comprehensive strategies (e.g., prevention, early intervention, and intervention) must be tailored to the problems and needs specific to Black males. And the problems should not be thought to reside exclusively within Black male students, nor their family, culture, or community. Referring to Einstein's quote, deficit thinking – prejudice – has helped to create and maintain the achievement gap, underachievement, and low achievement, which result from miseducation – underrepresentation in GATE, and overrepresentation in SPED and discipline. Anti-racist, social justice, equity-oriented thinking recognizes that all students' problems also result from social/societal factors inside and outside of school. More specifically, educators must share the responsibility for the achievement gap in all of its manifestations and they cannot justifiably exonerate themselves from this role. The works of Ibram Kendi on being an anti-racist are highly recommended. Also important is being familiar with theories of prejudice and discrimination by Gordon Allport, Robert Merton, along microaggressions, and implicit and explicit biases.

Guaranteeing that Black males reach their potential requires a social justice philosophy in which school leaders and educators fight for and advocate for the rights of these males – without excuses. A social justice and humane stance is guided by the belief that all students are equal and entitled to a free, appropriate, equitable, anti-racist, culturally responsive education. This belief builds upon *Brown v. Board of Education of 1954* condoning racial equity due to the reality that circumstances and opportunities are not equal. From a social perspective, it is a sad reality that racism is not likely to decrease or even disappear in the near future. At the time of this writing, racism was on the rise. Black males not only contend with the COVID-19 pandemic, they also have to battle the racist pandemic. Racism is both present and pervasive in all types of school settings. However, with substantive preparation and understanding of Critical Race Theory and Social Justice Theory, school personnel can become more aware of and self-reflective about their own views of Black males. Further, this culturally responsive preparation must include discussions about theories and research on expectations, prejudice, stereotypes, and White privilege, along with attention to attendant discriminatory behaviors, policies, and practices.

At the higher education level, it is essential that professors improve or revamp their programs and curricula so that preservice and in-service educators (e.g., teachers, counselors, psychologists, and administrators) graduate from their programs being culturally competent – interested in and prepared to work with Black males. Cultural competence includes knowledge, dispositions, and skills that render educators effective and efficacious at working with culturally different males (and females). More specifically, higher education courses and field experiences (and professional development workshops) must have a multicultural focus (Fletcher et al., in press; Ford, 2011; Gay, 2010; Ladson-Billings, 2009). This recommendation will go far in combating underachievement, low achievement, and achievement gaps, GATE and SPED disparities, and the school-to-prison pipeline (i.e., discipline, hyper-policing, profiling) by improving teacher/educator quality and effectiveness, as well as multicultural efficacy with Black males. In *Black boys are lit: Engaging PreK-3 gifted and talented lack boys using Multicultural literature and Ford's Bloom-Banks Matrix*, Wright et al. (2022) created matrices that are rigorous (Bloom's Taxonomy) and relevant (James Banks' levels of multicultural infusion) with the main focus on promoting and nurturing achievement, motivation, and academic self-efficacy, plus racial and gender pride *early* among Black males. Education must invest in prevention and early intervention to be most effective with these students.

In addition to addressing the belief systems and cultural competency of school personnel, educators also need to learn how to effectively work with, support, and advocate for Black families (Davis, 2022; Henfield et al., 2008; Moore & Owens, 2008). When Black families are supported, informed, and empowered, they have a positive influence on their son's school outcomes. We support Epstein's (2010) family involvement framework. Clearly, a collaborative partnership between school personnel and families is a win-win for Black males.

From social and cultural perspectives, educators and families need to take deliberate, measured steps to help Black males to resist negative peer pressures and other external influences. It is well-documented that an anti-achievement ethic is a pervasive problem in urban schools (Ford, 1996, 2010; Ford et al., 2011). Therefore, schools and homes need to set a tone and standard of high expectations and stand ready to help Black males cope with their unsupportive peers. From a personal or individual perspective, school personnel must implement initiatives that build on Black males' academic and motivational assets and strengths. Academically, tutoring, study skills, test taking skills, and time management and organizational skills are necessary soft skills. Also, mentoring and role modeling are important for increasing exposure and coping skills for this student group.

SUMMARY AND CONCLUSIONS

Black males in all school levels (e.g., elementary, secondary, and postsecondary) and settings (urban, suburban, rural) can do so but seldom perform as well as other student populations (e.g., White males, Black females, etc.). Too many are underachievers and low achievers, and too many are not expected to perform at high(er) levels. More than any other group, these males face deficit thinking ad nauseum. This is a complex, multifaceted conundrum – one that begs for understanding and solutions. Social, familial, and cultural factors work independently and interactively to contribute to these problems. A litany of variables or correlates hinders Black males' achievement in educational settings, which were previously discussed.

Despite the poor or negative outcomes of these otherwise capable Black males, this situation is neither permanent, unchangeable, nor hopeless. These students are certainly capable of high levels of achievement; so many more can and must excel in academic settings. In closing, this higher level of achievement is possible when educators are formally prepared to be equity-oriented, anti-racist, and culturally competent, when families are supported and empowered, and when efforts focus on improving Black males' academic potential and identities. Doing this necessary and long overdue work means that Black males will have a much-needed sense of belongingness, of feeling valued. *A mind is a wonderful thing to embrace.*

AUTHOR NOTE

This chapter revisits and expands upon Ford & Moore III (2013). Understanding and reversing underachievement and achievement gaps among high-ability African American males in urban school contexts. Urban Review, 45(4), 400–415.

NOTE

1. Hispanic students are also underrepresented in GATE and AP. Asian and White students are overrepresented. The representation of Native American students in the programs mirrors the national representation.

REFERENCES

Allport, G. W. (1955). *The nature of prejudice.* Addison-Wesley Publishing Co.

Barton, P. E. (2003). *Parsing the achievement gap: Baselines for tracking progress. Policy information report.* https://eric.ed.gov/?id=ED482932

Barton, P. E., & Coley, R. J. (2009). *Parsing the achievement gap II. Policy information report.* Educational Testing Service.

Cohen, E. G., & Lotan, R. A. (2004). Equity in heterogeneous classrooms. In J. A. Banks & C. A. M. Banks (Eds.), *Handbook of research on multicultural education* (2nd ed., pp. 736–750). Jossey-Bass.

Davis, J. L. (2022). *Bright, talented, & Black: A guide for families of African American gifted learners* (2nd ed.). Gifted Unlimited.

Donovan, M. S., & Cross, C. T. (Eds.). (2002). *Minority students in special and gifted education.* National Academy Press.

Epstein, J. L. (2010). School/Family/Community partnerships: Caring for the children we share. *Phi Delta Kappan, 92*(3), 81–96. https://doi.org/10.1177/003172171009200326

Fletcher, E. C., Jr., Ford, D. Y., & Moore, J. L., III. (in press). Career academies as an exemplary model of preparing students of color to be college and career ready. In E. Hines & L. Owens (Eds.), *Equity-based career development and postsecondary transitions: An American imperative.* Information Science Reference.

Fletcher, E. C., Jr., Ford, D. Y., & Moore, J. L., III. (2022). From a bag lunch to a buffet: A case study of a low-income African American academy's vision of promoting college and career readiness in the United States. *College Access Journal, 7*(1), 10–33. https://scholarworks.wmich.edu/jca/vol7/iss1/4

Ford, D. Y. (1996). *Reversing underachievement among gifted Black students: Promising practices and programs.* Teachers College Press.

Ford, D. Y. (1998). The under-representation of minority students in gifted education: Problems and promises in recruitment and retention. *The Journal of Special Education, 32,* 4–14.

Ford, D. Y. (2010). *Reversing underachievement among gifted Black students* (2nd ed.). Prufrock Press.

Ford, D. Y. (2011). *Multicultural gifted education* (2nd ed.). Prufrock Press.

Ford, D. Y. (2013). *Recruiting and retaining culturally different students in gifted education.* Prufrock Press.

Ford, D. Y., Dickson, K. T., Lawson Davis, J., Trotman Scott, M., Grantham, T. C., & Taradash, G. (2018). A culturally responsive equity-based Bill of Rights for gifted students of color. *Gifted Child Today, 41*(3), 125–129.

Fordham, S. (1988). Racelessness as a strategy in Black students' school success: Pragmatic strategy or pyrrhic victory? *Harvard Educational Review, 58,* 54–84.

Fordham, S., & Ogbu, J. (1986). Black students' school success: Coping with the "burden of 'acting white'". *The Urban Review, 18,* 176–203.

Ford, D. Y., Davis, J. L., Whiting, G. W., & Moore, J. L. (2021). Going beyond lip service when it comes to equity: Characteristics of equity-minded, culturally responsive allies in gifted and talented education. *Gifted Child Today, 44*(3), 174–178. https://doi.org/10.1177/107621752 11011210

Ford, D. Y., Grantham, T. C., & Whiting, G. W. (2008). Culturally and linguistically diverse students in gifted education: Recruitment and retention issues. *Exceptional Children, 74*(3), 289–308.

Ford, D. Y., Harris, J. J., III, Tyson, C. A., & Frazier Trotman, M. (2002). Beyond deficit thinking: Providing access for gifted African American students. *Roeper Review, 24,* 52–58.

Ford, D. Y., Lawson Davis, J., Dickson, K. T., Frazier Trotman Scott, M., Grantham, T. C., Moore, J. L., III, & Taradash, G. D. (2020). Evaluating gifted education programs using an equity-based and culturally responsive checklist to recruit and retain under-represented students of color. *Journal of Minority Achievement, Creativity, and Leadership, 1*(1), 119–146.

Ford, D. Y., & Moore, J. L., III. (2013). Understanding and reversing underachievement and achievement gaps among high-ability African American males in urban school contexts. *The Urban Review, 45*(4), 400–415. https://doi.org/10.1007/s11256-013-0256-3

Ford, D. Y., Moore, J. L., III, & Scott Trotman, M. (2011). Key theories and frameworks for improving recruitment and retention of African American students in gifted education. *The Journal of Negro Education, 80,* 239–253.

Ford, D. Y., Moore, J. L., III, & Whiting, G. W. (2006). Eliminating deficit orientations: Creating classrooms and curriculums for gifted students from diverse cultural backgrounds. In M. G. Constantine & D. W. Sue (Eds.), *Addressing racism: Facilitating cultural competence in mental health and educational settings* (pp. 173–193). Wiley.

Ford, D. Y., & Russo, C. J. (2015). No child left behind, unless a student is gifted and of color: Reflections on the need to meet the educational needs of the gifted. *Journal of Law in Society, 15,* 213–239.

Ford, D. Y., & Russo, C. J. (2016). Legal issues impacting racially and culturally different gifted learners. *Excellence and Diversity in Gifted Education, 2*(1), 1–7.

Gay, G. (2010). *Culturally responsive teaching: Theory, research, and practice* (2nd ed.). Teachers College Press.

Grantham, T. C., Frasier, M. M, Roberts, A. C., & Bridges, E. M. (2005). Parent advocacy for culturally diverse gifted. *Theory Into Practice, 4*(20), 138–147.

Grissom, J. A., & Redding, C. (2016). Discretion and disproportionality: Explaining the underrepresentation of high-achieving students of color in gifted programs. *AERA Open, 2*(1). https://doi.org/10.1177/2332858415622175

Hart, T. R., & Risley, B. (2003). *Meaningful differences in the everyday experiences of young American children.* Brooke.

Haycock, K., & Crawford, C. (2008). Closing the teacher quality gap. *Poverty and Learning, 65*(7), 14–19.

Hébert, T. P., & Schreiber, C. A. (2010). An examination of selective achievement in gifted males. *Journal for the Education of the Gifted, 33*(4), 570–605. https://doi.org/10.1177/016235321003300406

Henfield, M. S., Moore, J. L., III, & Wood, C. (2008). Inside and outside gifted education programming: Hidden challenges for African American students. *Exceptional Children, 74*(4), 433–450.

Hines, E. M., Fletcher, E. C., Jr., Moore, J. L., III, & Ford, D. Y. (2022). Culturally responsive postsecondary readiness practices for Black males: Practice and policy recommendations for school counselors. *Journal of School-Based Counseling Policy and Evaluation, 4*(1), 11–25. https://doi.org/10.25774/teyc-zk40

Hodgkinson, H. (2007). Leaving too many children behind. In J. VanTassel-Baska & T. Stambaugh (Eds.), *Overlooked gems: A national perspective on low-income promising learners.* National Association for Gifted Children.

Irvine, J. J. (2020). Culturally relevant pedagogy. *Education Digest: Essential Readings Condensed for Quick Review, 75*(8), 57–61. https://eric.ed.gov/?id=EJ880896

Jackson, J. F. L., & Moore, J. L., III. (2006). African American males in education: Endangered or ignored? *Teachers College Record, 108,* 201–205.

Jackson, J. F. L., & Moore, J. L., III. (2008). The African American male crisis in education: A popular media infatuation or needed public policy response? *American Behavioral Scientist, 51,* 847–853.

Jackson, J. F. L., Moore, J. L., III, & Leon, R. L. (2010). Male underachievement in education across the globe: A shift in paradigm for gender disparities regarding academic achievement. In B. McGaw, E. Baker, & P. L. Peterson (Eds.), *International encyclopedia of education* (pp. 838–844). Elsevier.

Ladson-Billings, G. J. (2006). *From the achievement gap to the education debt: Understanding achievement in U.S. Schools.* Presidential Address at the American Educational Research Association Annual Meeting.

Ladson-Billings, G. (2009). *The dreamkeepers: Successful teachers for African-American children* (2nd ed.). Jossey-Bass.

Larson-Billings, G. (2010). *New directions in multicultural education complexities, boundaries, and critical race theory.* Semantic Scholar. https://www.semanticscholar.org/paper/New-Directions-in-Multicultural-Education-%2C-%2C-and-Ladson-Billings/83f46d93e3b83d0d698842d785a9185f363f42df

Lankford, H., Loeb, S., & Wyckoff, J. (2002). Teaching sorting and the plight of urban schools: A descriptive analysis. *Educational Evaluation and Policy Analysis, 24*(1), 37–62.

Lee, V. E., & Burkham, D. (2002). *Inequality at the starting gate: Social background differences in achievement as children begin school.* Economic Policy Institute.

Lewis, C. W., James, M., Hancock, S., & Hill-Jackson, V. (2008). Framing African American students' success and failure in urban settings: A typology for change. *Urban Education, 43,* 127–153.

Lewis, C. W., & Moore, J. L., III. (2008a). African American students in K–12 urban educational settings. *Urban Education, 43,* 123–126.

Lewis, C. W., & Moore, J. L., III. (2008b). Urban public schools for African American students: Critical issues for educational stakeholders. *The Journal of Educational Foundations, 22,* 3–10.

Lewis, C. C., Perry, R. R., Friedkin, S., & Roth, J. R. (2012). Improving teaching does improve teachers: Evidence from lesson study. *Journal of Teacher Education, 63*(5), 368–375. https://doi.org/10.1177/0022487112446633

Maslow, A. H. (1943). A theory of human motivation. *Psychological Review, 50*(4), 370–396.

Maslow, A. H. (1954). *Motivation and personality.* Harper and Row.

McAdoo, H. P., & Younge, S. N. (2009). Black families. In H. A. Neville, B. M. Tyes, & S. O. Utsey (Eds.), *Handbook of African American psychology* (pp. 103–125). Sage.

Menchaca, M. (1997). Early racist discourses: The Roots of deficit thinking. In R. Valencia (Ed.), *The evolution of deficit thinking* (pp. 13–40). Routledge.

Merton, R. K. (1936). The unanticipated consequences of purposive social action. *American Sociological Review, 1*(6), 894–904. https://doi.org/10.2307/2084615

Moore, J. L., III, & Lewis, C. W. (Eds.). (2012). *African American students in urban schools: Critical issues and solutions for achievement.* Peter Lang Publishers.

Moore, J. L., III, & Owens, D. (2008). Educating and counseling African American students: Recommendations for teachers and school counselors. In L. Tillman (Ed.), *Handbook for African American education* (pp. 351–366). Sage.

Naglieri, J., & Ford, D. Y. (2015). Misconceptions about the Naglieri Nonverbal Ability Test: A commentary of concerns and disagreements. *Roeper Review, 37*(4), 234–240.

Olszewski, P. M., Kulieke, M., & Buescher, T. (1987). The influence of the family environment on the development of talent: A literature review. *Journal for the Education of the Gifted, 2,* 6–28.

Patton, L. D, Bridges, B. K, & Flowers, L. A (2011). Effects of Greek affiliation on African American students' engagement differences by college racial composition. *College Student Affairs Journal, 29*(2), 113–123.

"Perfect storm" Merriam-Webster.com Dictionary, Merriam-Webster. https://www.merriam-webster. com/dictionary/perfect%20storm. Accessed on July 17, 2022.

Russo, C. J., & Ford, D. Y. (2015). Education for gifted students in the United States: An area in need of improvement. *Education and Law Journal, 16*(3), 188–196.

Saracho, O. N., & Gerstl, C. K. (1992). Learning differences among at-risk minority students. In H. C. Waxman, J. Walker de Felix, J. E. Anderson, & H. P. Baptiste (Eds.), *Students at risk in at-risk schools: Improving environments for learning* (pp. 105–136). Corwin.

Schott Foundation. (2012). *The urgency of now: The Schott 50 state report on public education and black males.* Schott Foundation for Public Education.

Shade, B. J., Kelly, C., & Oberg, M. (1997). *Creating culturally responsive classrooms.* American Psychological Association.

Siegle, D. (2012). *The underachieving gifted child.* Routledge.

Steele, C. M. (2010). *Whistling Vivaldi: How stereotypes affect us and what we can do.* W W Norton & Co.

Sternberg, R. J., Desmet, O. A., Ford, D. Y., Gentry, M. L., Grantham, T. C., & Karami, S. (2021). The legacy: Coming to terms with the origins and development of the gifted-child movement. *Roeper Review, 43*(4), 227–241. https://doi.org/10.1080/02783193.2021.1967544

Toldson, I. C. (2019). *No BS (Bad Stats): Black people need people who believe in Black people enough not to believe every bad thing they hear about Black people.* Brille/Sense.

Upchurch, C. (1997). *Convicted in the womb: One man's journey from prisoner to peacemaker.* Penguin Books.

Valencia, R. R (Ed.). (1997). *The evolution of deficit thinking: Educational thought and practice.* The Falmer Press/Taylor & Francis.

Valencia, R. R. (2010). *Dismantling contemporary deficit thinking: Educational thought and practice.* Routledge.

Vega, D., Moore, J. L., III, Baker, C. A., Bowen, N. V., Hines, E. M., & O'Neal, B. O. (2012). Salient factors affecting urban African American students' achievement: Recommendations for teachers, school counselors, and school psychologists. In J. L. Moore III & C. W. Lewis (Eds.), *African American students in urban schools: Critical issues and solutions for achievement.* Peter Lang Publishers.

Whiting, G. W. (2006). Enhancing culturally diverse males' scholar identity: Suggestions for educators of gifted students. *Gifted Child Today, 39*, 46–50.

Whiting, G. W. (2009). The scholar identity institute: Guiding Darnel and other Black males. *Gifted Child Today, 32*, 53–58.

Wood, J. L., Harris, F., III, & Howard, T. C. (2018). *Get out! Black male suspensions in California public schools.* Community College Equity.

Woodson, C. G. (1933). *The mis-education of the Negro.* The Associated Publishers.

Wright, B. L., Ford, D. Y., & Moore, J. L., III. (2022). *Black boys are lit: Engaging PreK-3 gifted and talented lack boys using multicultural literature and Ford's Bloom-Banks Matrix.* IAP Publishers.

CHAPTER 4

EXPLORING GROUP COUNSELING INTERVENTIONS FOR BLACK BOYS IN MIDDLE SCHOOL: USING THE ACHIEVING SUCCESS EVERYDAY (ASE) GROUP MODEL FOR RACIAL AND MATHEMATICAL IDENTITY DEVELOPMENT

Sam Steen and Canaan Bethea

ABSTRACT

In this chapter, we explore group counseling interventions for Black males and explain the Achieving Success Everyday (ASE) group model for racial and mathematical development. We use critical race theory (CRT) as a framework to analyze school counseling (SC) and mathematics literature that focuses on Black male students to inform the reconceptualization of the ASE group model for school counselors. We examine the programs and interventions that have been published with Black male participants in school settings within the SC literature. We also examine programs and interventions that have been specially designed to improve Black males' mathematics skills. We specifically focus on gathering findings that provide successful outcomes for Black males in public schools. We examine literature that reflects the role school counselors (SCs) take when supporting Black male students' academic, social, emotional, college, and career identity development. We believe uncovering ideas to capture Black males' experiences in school settings could shed light on how to foster Black excellence. Gaining an understanding of programs and interventions for Black male students

Black Males in Secondary and Postsecondary Education
Advances in Race and Ethnicity in Education, Volume 9, 67–85
Copyright © 2024 Sam Steen and Canaan Bethea
Published under exclusive licence by Emerald Publishing Limited
ISSN: 2051-2317/doi:10.1108/S2051-231720230000009004

through a CRT lens could inform future research, policy, and practice in SC while combating ongoing racism that continues to persist.

Keywords: Black males; group counseling; mathematics; racial identity; racism; CRT

INTRODUCTION

In this chapter, we begin by reviewing school counseling (SC) literature that attends to Black males in school settings. Next, the mathematics intervention literature for Black males that [intersects with SC literature] is reviewed, and we describe samples of the literature that we discovered. Critical race theory (CRT) is discussed as a framework to critique the corpus of literature as a way to build on the strengths and areas of growth. Scholars are challenged to dismantle a deficit-focused research agenda that stems from the plethora of literature that focuses on Black males from a perspective of lack and scarcity as a way to fuel the efforts to sustain meaningful and long-term successful academic and career outcomes of Black males. We describe an evidenced-based group counseling model that is being studied to promote Black males' racial and mathematical identity as a form of resistance to the systems of racism and oppression that is rampant within US public school settings. We conclude this chapter by providing recommendations for research, practice, and policy.

School Counseling for Black Males

Generally speaking, the role of the school counselor is to listen to students, help them understand decision-making, goal setting, and, when necessary, develop coping strategies. School counselors help students create and take advantage of opportunities for success while promoting equity in academic spaces. School counselors use their positions in schools to build relationships with students, school staff, and families (Appling & Robinson, 2021). These relationships offer great potential for enhancing the academic enrichment and experiences of middle school students. School counselors can enhance the academic experiences of middle school Black males in particular, by a number of SC strategies; however, the literature is often lacking an emphasis on the strengths and potential of Black males. Centering the experience of Black male students in SC research can offset the white racial hierarchy currently rampant within the literature (Appling & Robinson, 2021). And group counseling is emerging as one of the most promising interventions for Black youth, but the focus on Black males has room for growth (Appling & Robinson, 2021).

We attempt to capture and review programs and interventions that have been published with Black youth (both male and female) in school settings within the SC literature. Along the way, we examine this literature that reflects the role school counselors take when supporting Black students' development within public schools. This emerging understanding of programs and interventions will set up platforms to inform future research and practice targeted for Black males in particular while combating ongoing racism that continues to persist and offer creative opportunities to bolster potential for the pursuit of science, technology, engineering, and mathematical (STEM)-related careers.

Group Counseling Interventions in School Settings

School-based counseling research can change lives for the better, especially when aiming to foster spaces of equity, inclusive excellence, and social justice (Steen, 2020). Group counseling, a powerful yet underutilized resource in school settings, has implications for policy within counselor education and preparation, school-based practice, and research. In particular, furthering the development of ongoing research to demonstrate how SCs can ensure their work impacts the lives of students and academic achievement is an important endeavor (Griffith et al., 2019). School counselors have the requisite educational background and skill set to design and facilitate culturally sustaining group counseling interventions for Black males within school settings to meet an array of student developmental needs along with academic achievement (Ieva et al., 2021). While the ASCA (2014) position statement on group counseling suggests that groups in school settings promote academic achievement and personal growth, more research is warranted concerning using this modality to promote success across academic, social–emotional, and career development domains (Zyromski et al., 2018) and particularly for minoritized students (Steen et al., 2022).

There inarguably are a limited number of intervention studies to draw upon in the SC literature (Liu et al., 2020). And, the literature that has a primary focus on Black males is so scarce, that it becomes necessary to use as many articles as possible to explore all aspects of research and apply the findings accordingly. For this present intervention presented in this chapter, three seminal pieces and one recent article provide a backdrop for SC interventions (Liu et al., 2020; Whiston & Quinby, 2009; Whiston et al., 1998, 2011). These comprehensive articles provided ideas to develop better SC intervention studies. Furthermore, two systematic literature reviews of research on groups in schools that target achievement and therapeutic factors (e.g., socio-emotional) were used to offer ideas for better group counseling interventions (Steen et al., 2021, 2022). The innovative contribution in this chapter is an articulation of a model for conducting a group counseling intervention targeting Black youth's racial and mathematical identity that can be facilitated by school counselors.

Selected Group Counseling Interventions

Counseling interventions from previous research attempt to improve the academic performance of Black students, but often without an intentionality. For instance, Campbell and Brigman's (2005) SC intervention ($N = 240$ students) attempted to shed some light on the positive role that counseling can exert on improving students' academic success skills and performance. There were 12 students from each of the 20 schools that were involved in this research with only

9% of the students identifying as Black/African American. Students were randomly selected to be in either the treatment group or the comparison group. Two instruments were utilized to measure the impact of counseling interventions: The Florida Comprehensive Achievement Test (FCAT) and the School Social Behavior Scales (SSBS). A pretest and posttest design were utilized in this study. The study sought to understand the impact of explaining strategies in bigger classrooms (e.g., classroom guidance and curriculum delivery) before furthering students' learning in small counseling groups. The results of the study showed that students in the intervention group had significantly larger gains in reading and mathematics than students in the control groups. However, no explicit discussions of Blackness were provided.

A study by Appling and Robinson (2021) sought to explain the role that racial identity plays in Black students' academic performance. This research explains that Black males are often viewed as disengaged and disinterested (Appling & Robinson, 2021). One factor that this research study found potentially impacting Black students' academic achievement is their racial identity. Specifically, the interaction between race (racial identity development) and gender (ability to articulate clearly how one sees themselves) seems to impact the potential for academic success of Black males. Contrarily, more often messages infused with deficit labels, social injustices, and negative self-perceptions negatively impact Black males' performance (Appling & Robinson, 2021).

Next, Webb and Brigman (2007) designed an 8-session plus "booster" small counseling intervention to improve students' academic success. The term "booster" described group counseling sessions that reinforced coping strategies and focused on how changes in strategies positively impacted students' skills and grades. Directions for the Student Success Skills (SSS) group sessions explained exactly how much time the counselor should spend with students on each task in each section. However, the study omitted specific racial and cultural identity issues for Black students. For example, the first session begins with an introduction of the program, the importance of personalizing communication, group expectations, and introductions. In the middle of session 1, students learn the purpose of the group and five steps to help them focus on setting goals, building strengths, sharing successes and improvements, and ways of challenging themselves. The link to specific racial considerations either for students of color (e.g., Blackness) or students from the majority for that matter (e.g., whiteness) is not mentioned at all. Furthermore, even when more potentially culturally relevant and sustaining ideas are provided to students (i.e., students are given strategies to focus on social emotional or academic improvements) including using positive lyrics in music to "keep Kool" (Webb & Brigman, 2007), race is omitted. More recently SC scholars (e.g., Washington, 2021) conceptualized in a special issue for SC research, policy, and practice that an intentional use of hip-hop music could foster empowerment, stimulate motivation, and provide a platform to focus one's Blackness, this intervention as it currently stands fails to make this intentional effort (Washington, 2018). To offer another example of how hip-hop music and culture in particular could be used to combat systemic racism and offer ideas,

Washington (2021) posits that hip-hop can be used to provide positive, motivational, and culturally relevant messages to students.

In Webb and Brigman's (2007) work, all of the sessions end with students completing a progress rating and monitoring tool, completing seven keys to course mastery worksheet, and setting a goal for improvement. The next seven sections are similar and provide modifications for students to learn about managing anger (session 2), solving social problems (sessions 3 and 7), and discussing their group experience (session 8). The first eight sessions are held once a week. Booster sessions are recommended to be at least one month apart. In the supplemental sessions, students are asked to rate themselves on seven keys to course mastery. Participants are also instructed to find their strengths and areas for improvement and share these with their peers in the counseling session.

In a few cases, there are studies that focused solely on Black youth. For instance, a study by Steen (2009) used group counseling to support academic achievement and ethnic identity development for Black elementary students. The purpose of this study was to increase students' ethnic identity, learning behaviors, and grade point average (GPA) in Language Arts. Ethnic identity was a construct used that describes perceptions about one's race, while considering how race impacts their development. It is important to note that prior research by Phinney and colleagues found for upper elementary students that positive ethnic identity leads to positive attitude and belongingness in one's ethnic group (Phinney et al., 2007). Building on Phinney's work, the study by Steen included 20 African American elementary school students. A total of 15 students (five per group) were in the intervention groups, and five students were in the control group. Sessions were weekly and lasted for approximately 45 minutes. The sessions utilized the "4R" group model – review, revelation, reinforcement, and reflection. Findings discovered in the Steen study illustrated that there were no significant differences between the control group and intervention groups in GPA and learning behaviors; however, there was a statistically significant difference found in concerning students' racial identity. Using the multiethnic identity measure (MEIM) (Phinney, 2013), students who participated in the group intervention had higher score postintervention than the control group. In other words, the group counseling intervention was successful at improving the MEIM scores for the participants which could be used to surmise this intervention positively impacted students' social emotional development and their perceptions of themselves in particular. It is important to note that the researcher who was also the group facilitator identified as a Black male and explicit discussions about what it means to be Black within school settings took place within the study and were detailed and examined within the article.

Next, an evidenced-based group counseling intervention that was designed for Black youth within urban environments was called Coping Power in the City (CPIC) (Thomas et al., 2021). This program initially developed for young adults was modified for adolescents. Uniquely, this intervention included parent, teacher, and police officer components. For parents, the same coleaders who led the sessions for students provided parents with a space to learn and process their experiences navigating their community environments while raising their children. The teacher and police officer components focused more on professional development for these staff respectively. Although parent attendance was low, these sessions provided information congruent with the information provided in the 16 student sessions. Furthermore, the teacher sessions offered training to teachers on the principles of coping power and instructed teachers in how to enhance students' socioemotional well-being. The school police component was designed to promote knowledge and skills regarding working well with adolescent youth.

The overall focus of the CPIC program was to use the group modality and the other additional programs to decrease violence, negative behavior, and mental health concerns for Black adolescent students within their community contexts (Thomas et al., 2021). Of the 514 students who participated in the study, 46% were males, the rest female, and they all attended one of 10 urban high schools. Specifically, the intervention sessions ranged from 45 minutes to 60 minutes, and occurred once a week. A total of 16 sessions in this intervention focus on "goal setting, organizational and study skills, awareness of emotional arousal and anger, self-regulation of emotional arousal and anger, perspective taking, social problem solving, and contextual risk factors in relationships with deviant peers and associated school and neighborhood influences" (Thomas et al., 2021, p. 4). The one limitation is that while the program focused on Black youth in particular, there seemed to be a deficit focus, whereby the violence, demise, and danger was discussed. While this may be common, it is time to make intentional efforts at infusing the positive aspects of Black culture, the strengths of Black youth, and the capacity for brilliance for these populations in particular despite the odds.

Proposed Counseling Intervention With Implications for Groups
Some researchers have yet to complete interventions, but have already proposed strategies for counseling interventions to improve Black males' mathematics performance. Rap therapy and bibliotherapy are two intervention strategies for Black males that appear in counseling literature (Byrd et al., 2021; Washington, 2021).

Hip-hop therapy counseling interventions utilize hip-hop artifacts to highlight how anti-Black ideologies contribute in different ways to our society. Washington (2021) proposed that a critical hip-hop school counseling (CHHSC) framework can increase consciousness among Black males, resulting in increased academic performance. The author suggests that dehumanizing educational practices such as violent educational environments and whitewashed academic content has led to Black Males' disassociating with their educational experiences (Washington, 2021). Critical hip-pop counseling can be utilized to reconnect Black males with their educational experiences.

Critical consciousness is necessary for social action and social justice. Hip-pop themes such as impoverished cities, underfunded school systems, and social hierarchies provide a framework for discussing issues in Black neighborhoods. There are connections between hip-pop, social justice, and counseling. Hip-pop scholarship "represents the mobilizing of critical knowledge derived from the lived experiences of predominantly Black, Brown, and urban communities that reflect political desires and projects of liberation" (Tinson & McBride, 2013, p. 7). This approach can socialize the experience of learning history for Black males in middle school and secondary school. Rather than learning in ways that encourage conserving what is, students can learn to deconstruct social order. Instead of using hip-hop to explore and trivialize Black peoples' experiences, hip-hop can be utilized to explain Black history and develop historical consciousness.

Counseling psychology literature indicates that bibliotherapy can be utilized to improve the academic performance of Black males as well (Byrd et al., 2021). Bibliotherapy is a counseling intervention that utilizes books, stories, and narratives to teach students how to navigate difficult situations. It is recommended as a counseling intervention specifically for Black males because positive narratives can be utilized to dismantle negative stereotypes about Black males (Byrd et al., 2021). Anti-Black narratives that portray Black people as violent and ignorant have consistently been displayed in schools, and negative experiences and negative stereotypes could lead to Black male students having destructive beliefs about themselves (Challenger et al., 2020). Culturally relevant pedagogy and stories that showcase Black people's success can empower Black males' identity development and combat negative narratives about Black people (Byrd et al., 2021). The tenets of CRT are proposed to guide narratives in bibliotherapy sessions for Black boys. This can help Black boys grow knowledgeable about potentially detrimental situations that they are likely to face and be empowered to pursue academic excellence.

In summary, well-designed group counseling interventions can positively impact Black youth, and we make the case that this could be possible for Black male students' success explicitly. The work reviewed here included a variety of key factors for student outcome improvement beyond just Black males because the literature is still in its nascent stage (Steen et al., 2022). In sum, the articles selected for this sample of literature provide ideas that include but are not limited to exploring germane topics for Black males in particular, while also infusing Black culture. When offering interventions in school settings, identity development along the lines of race is an under explored prospect. Challenging and eliminating deficit labels and negative perceptions is imperative. Specific executive functioning skills, including student goal setting, planning, performance monitoring, and problem-solving, are applicable to Black males in school settings, and using their unique lens when tailoring these typical activities to their unique interests seems reasonable. For example, various counseling interventions used reflection, review, and self-evaluation toward the end of the session or during the last session. These reflective activities could include sentence stems like "as a Black male youth. . ." "for someone with your unique intelligence, gifts, and talents who navigates primarily white dominated environments" or "for you who is growing into Black manhood in this school and society." In addition to these skill development and reflective activities, domain-specific course mastery strategies were touched on, but could be more fully developed, especially for Black males (e.g., Steen, 2009; Webb & Brigman, 2007). Simply put, this area for research would make sense as programs become more intentional at integrating both academic and social emotional development.

Finally, it is important to note that successful small group interventions might include a multisystemic orientation that include the concerns of parents/caregivers, school staff, police, and school board members. We also believe that moving forward group counseling interventions might do well when targeting Black male youth to utilize CRT to ensure the work offers a form of resistance to the ongoing pernicious nature of racism while offering a hope for a brighter future (Steen et al., 2022).

MATHEMATICS INTERVENTIONS

In an effort to contribute directly to broadening the capacity for STEM-related postsecondary opportunities for Black males, we summarize interventions that are specifically designed for these youth and attempt to glean useful information that can help strengthen SC interventions. Some of the literature we found related to Black males focused on contributing factors for the lack of success in mathematics classes, strategies to promote academic success, mathematics interventions for urban schools, as well as mathematical interventions for urban teachers. We include a couple of examples that were not focused on deficits.

For example, some research suggests that mentoring can improve the academic success of Black male middle school students (Gordon et al., 2010). Similar to some of the SC literature, Black males have been cited as lacking identification with academic achievement and racial identity development which could be the result of internalized racial oppression and discrimination (Gordon et al., 2010) or simply school staff and systems that overlook or do not see Black students' value. However, meaningful and intentional mentoring is one way to mitigate issues of isolation and invisibility while fostering connection within schools. Mentoring is defined as providing support, guidance, and modeling through a positive relationship (Gordon et al., 2010). To illustrate the impact of research, Gordon et al.'s study included 61 students of which 83% were African American, and the other 17% of the participants were Latino. Students started the program in the fall of their seventh grade year with 29 students in the intervention (the Benjamin E. Mays Institute [BEMI]) program group and 31 students in the control group. Measures on the Racial Identity Attitude Scale (RIAS), Identification with Academics Scale (IAS), GPA, and Connecticut Mastery Test (CMT) were administered to both groups. Students involved in the BEMI program had more improvement in their academic performance than students in a control group. Also, students with higher racial identity attitudes scored higher in the mathematics section of the CMT. Results indicated that students completing self-evaluation along with academic performance can increase achievement for African American males. Some specific suggestions stemming from this study include assigning African American male mentors that can share and teach personal stories about African Americans that have reached the highest levels of academic success. Furthermore, infusing the positive aspects of Blackness within mentoring relationships for Black males has been found to improve academic outcomes. Mentors who are assigned to connect with Black male students can use an Afrocentric framework or worldview to help students to understand their history and roots. This need not be focused on only historical difficulties but rather on the strengths and accomplishments of Black folks from many different angles.

Another approach to elevate Black students' academic outcomes was explored in Brougham and Kashubeck-West's (2017) growth mindset study. They implemented an intervention aimed at improving participants' growth mindset and academic performance. One aspect of this study was a focus on cognitive orientation and/or internal changes such as strategy and effort. These researchers assert that students who possess a growth mindset believe that they can improve their abilities in a variety of dimensions which often leads to enhanced academic success. To illustrate, this study included 69 freshmen (49% identified as Black) who were drawn from an urban high school. They participated in a three-session intervention whereby participants in the treatment group read about how the brain learns in the first session. During the second session, students read about a student that struggled before improving from high levels of effort. In the final meeting, students wrote a letter to encourage another student based on what they had learned. The control group watched anatomy and physiology lessons during each of the three sessions. The results of the study showed an increase in students' growth mindset but did not show an increase in students' academic performance. The results of the study were presented to school staff including the school counselor, and as a result, growth mindset activities were infused into the counseling sessions. One limitation from this study was the lack of explicit discussion of Blackness within the intervention.

Varelas et al. (2012) presented a theoretical framework for Black males' mathematics achievement that focuses on content learning (CL) and Identity Construction (IC). CL is defined as the process of learning strategies and norms of practice for a specific academic discipline. However, building content knowledge is necessary but not sufficient for Black students' learning and academic success. IC is defined as the conceptualization of identifying as Black within the context of one's community. Three aspects of IC – disciplinary identity, racial identity, and academic identity – are impactful to Black males' performance in mathematics and science classes. Essentially, Black identity can intersect with STEM-related concepts as true student learning is a process that involves environmental and cultural factors. A person, the environment, and one's culture all impact each other during the learning process, and this applies for Black students as well. For example, Black male students' racial identity and mathematical identity are interconnected, and both can impact Black students' self-concept. Moreover, racial identity and mathematical identity are constructed during adolescent students' learning process. For Black students, positive or negative regard toward their race impacts their academic performance. To illustrate, middle school students share that their racial identity impacts the way they see themselves academically. Educators should help students create spaces for them to examine who they are as Black male students and who they are becoming.

For Black males in particular, schools have failed. Students who do gain access to advanced courses (e.g., mathematics) in public schools overcome and continue to experience systemic, structural, and ideological barriers inequality in school systems and treatment from teachers (Battey & Leyva, 2016; Berry et al., 2014). There are numerous cases of injustice within mathematical spaces, which remain centered on white school leaders, teachers, students; however, a more explicit understanding of Black students' success and the role school counselors play, when applicable, is needed.

The sample of findings presented from this limited corpus of an emerging body of research provides school counselors with ideas to create culturally sustaining interventions. We believe that group counseling can offer school counselors the platform to help Black middle school students access advanced level mathematics courses. The group intervention can integrate racial and mathematical exploration, resiliency, and anything that is pertinent to the students from their perspectives as Black male youth within their unique school environments. The integration of racial and mathematical exploration allows students to examine developmental milestones that are important to them along with important school-related material.

In summary, a number of pertinent intervention strategies are recommended for Black male students. One focus for mathematics interventions was mentoring. Another focus for mathematics interventions is racial identity development. Growth mindset intervention was also recommended. Next, we briefly discuss CRT, its application to SC, group counseling, and a reconceptualized evidence-based group counseling model developed for Black male middle school students pursuing Algebra 1 in the eighth grade as a gateway to advanced level mathematics courses in high school and beyond. This simple initiative is monumental in providing the platform to STEM opportunities following high school graduation.

CRITICAL RACE THEORY

Research in CRT began in legal studies with Derrick Bell. It grew out of a legal framework utilized in the critical legal studies movement (Cobb & Russell, 2015). However, the aim and tenants of CRT apply well in education research. Schools are a byproduct of the issues in society. If this framework rightfully addresses the civil rights issues in society, then it is likely to be a good framework to explain what is happening in schools in our society (Cobb & Russell, 2015). A hallmark of the tenets of critical theories is that they consider the perspective of a nondominant group and seek to empower society to social justice and inclusive excellence. CRT is a framework utilized by academic researchers to help consider the impact that race and racism have had on society. Five tenets guide CRT: "(a) Racism is ordinary and pervasive in society (b) the idea of an interest convergence (the notion that whites will support racial justice to the extent they will benefit from it or that there is a 'convergence' between Whites and non-Whites), (c) the social construction of race to the detriment of people of color, (d) the use of storytelling and counter-storytelling, and (e) whites have been recipients of civil rights legislation" (Delgado & Stefancic, 2001). CRT and its tenets are utilized to explain how education helps reproduce inequalities (Ladson-Billings, 1994).

CRT has been utilized many times in research regarding Black students' mathematical performance. CRT can be used to address structural inequalities that contribute to differences in mathematic test performance (Cobb & Russell, 2015), to highlight the brilliance of Black students (Jett, 2012), to teach social justice from a critical race perspective (Larnell et al., 2016), to develop a counter story of Black students' mathematics experiences (Terry, 2011), and to consider the mathematical socialization experiences of Black students (Martin, 2009).

Strategies to address setbacks in Black students' mathematics education and each of these studies utilized CRT to suggest strategies to eliminate differences in Black and white students' mathematics performance. Addressing structural inequalities in mathematics, highlighting black brilliance in mathematics, seeking social justice in mathematics, developing counter stories in mathematics, and supporting mathematics socialization are the strategies offered to narrow the mathematics achievement gap between Black and white students.

Looking critically at the mathematical experiences and achievements of Black students allows researchers to discover contributing factors and potential solutions to Black students' underperformance in mathematics. Structural inequalities and negative racial identities are some of the contributing factors of lower mathematic performance for Black students. Creating positive racial identities and providing equitable resources are potentially helpful strategies for Black students. CRT helps show researchers, educators, and education administrators how race plays a role in and explains academic success and failure in the United States. Educators, and school counselors in this case, have a responsibility to prepare students to resist racism (Hines & Hooks, 1994).

When Black students are compared to white students there is often a "gap" that is mentioned. There are so-called gaps in opportunity, achievement, intellectual, testing, and so forth. When discussing the "achievement gap" in particular, it is clear the comparisons are less likely comparing Asians, Latinx, or Southeast Asians but most likely Black students with their white peers (Pasque et al., 2022). We aim to present Black males without comparison to other "groups" as a way to counter any anti-Blackness that is often reflected within the scholarship for Black males in schools.

While anti-Blackness has been understood as the dehumanization of Black people to uphold white supremacist views, we situate this work by drawing upon Mustafa's definition of Black life-making (Mustaffa, 2021) which emphasizes the fostering of Black excellence in academics and scholarship. The current literature emphasizing deficits has led to inaccurate representation of Black students' true capacity for brilliance. As such, we reframe the conversation in a way that promotes Black students as generative (Mustaffa, 2021). In order to do this, we name racism broadly and anti-Blackness in particular as important areas to target within research, policy, and practice (Prasath et al., in press).

IMPLICATIONS FOR PRACTICE

This section provides practical applications of this research for school counselors, school counselor educators, and policymakers. Based on the literature explored, we assert that an intervention for Black males can be created that targets mathematics achievement and mathematics identity development; however, this intervention must be created within the context in which students see themselves. The following components are based on the literature explored in the current study and prior studies specifically related to group counseling in schools. For example, a group intervention developed for Black males in a school setting ideally will have a group facilitator that shares aspects of their racial identity. In addition to racial match, ideally a protocol would be used, and the leader will have received training in the use of these materials (e.g., definitions of mathematics and African American identity) (Steen et al., 2022).

The goals and outcomes for an intervention developed for Black males in schools were to strive to create spaces to foster positive experiences in school. School climate has been found to impact Black male students' mathematics identity and performance in mathematics class (Jackson et al., 2021), and the relationship between Black male students and school staff members plays an important role. The learning that occurs within the group intervention can be transferred to other aspects of their lives. In fact, there's evidence that groups in schools with children facilitated by school counselors will commonly produce the following therapeutic factors when targeting achievement such as imparting information, instillation of hope, universality, and when focusing on social/emotional development, imparting information, group cohesion, and interpersonal learning (Harris et al., 2021; Steen et al., 2021, 2022). It can be surmised that a group intervention like this will help Black male youth see role models, learn from others, provide support to one another, challenge one another, and navigate school environments with the necessary tools to achieve success. Intentional conceptualization of a group intervention for Black males that is based on the limited yet salient research offers opportunities to generate ongoing improvement as a form of resistance to the status quo.

Achieving Success Everyday Model

We take this opportunity to describe a small group intervention that was developed based on prior research studies conducted by the first author (Rose & Steen, 2014; Steen et al., 2018) and recommendations specified within the published literature about groups in schools (Steen et al., 2021, 2022) and group interventions/programs created and/or implemented with Black males published within the broader SC literature (Steen et al., 2022). In addition, the aim is to propose how to support mathematics achievement due to its significance and connection to broad secondary and postsecondary options. This added emphasis on mathematics for Black males in school settings offers a unique opportunity for SCs to show the impact that groups can have on student measures of success. The small group intervention is designed to help school counselors foster positive school experiences by supporting Black male middle school students who are navigating the ongoing pandemic, racial unrest, gun violence, depression, online learning and so forth, and systemic and institutional racism in school environments experienced by marginalized youth in mathematic spaces (Battey & Leyva, 2016). The more school counselors demonstrate the development and implementation of successful group counseling interventions that make a significant impact on academic achievement, social–emotional learning, college and career trajectory, decision-makers could endorse the use of more group counseling interventions in schools. As a result, more Black male students would have access to services that may address a myriad of important concerns that intersect their racial backgrounds, school experiences, and pathways to success.

The ASE group model is a school-counselor-led group counseling intervention that aims to draw upon the students' cultural backgrounds to improve their racial identity, mathematics identity, and resiliency outcomes. In order to more fully explore the impact of group counseling on Black male student success within the literature, a unique and targeted group intervention is described below and will be tested in the future.

As mentioned above, there inarguably are a limited number of intervention studies to draw upon in the SC literature (Liu et al., 2020). And, the literature that has a primary focus on Black males is so scarce, that it becomes necessary to use as many articles as possible to explore all aspects of research and apply the findings accordingly. For this present intervention presented in this chapter, three seminal pieces and one recent article provide a backdrop for SC interventions (Liu et al., 2020; Whiston & Quinby, 2009; Whiston et al., 1998, 2011). These comprehensive articles provided ideas to develop better SC intervention studies. Furthermore, two systematic literature reviews of research on groups in schools that target achievement and therapeutic factors (e.g., socio-emotional) were used to offer ideas for better group counseling interventions (Steen et al., 2021, 2022). The innovative contribution in this chapter is to synthesize this information and offer a model for conducting a group counseling intervention targeting Black youth that can be facilitated by school counselors.

Based on prior research (e.g., Steen et al., 2022), preliminary data suggest the use of protocols with group intervention studies in schools yield the highest effect sizes. Further, culturally sustaining group interventions provides opportunities to infuse race and culture (e.g., African American culture), role models, positive identity focus, confidence, and sense of belonging. The number of group sessions needed to produce optimal outcomes ranges from 10 to 20 sessions. In terms of the leader and participant race and gender match, it is reported that years of experience – more experience combined with the race/gender match – yielded higher effect sizes than racial mismatch. Next, when measuring academic outcomes in groups, it is recommended that longitudinal data are collected after the intervention ends. Finally, researchers need to consider more proximal outcomes (e.g., resiliency or leadership skills) in conjunction with achievement to make stronger claims. Below we present Table 4.1 offering the phases, tasks, and group stages of the ASE model for greater understanding. These details are based on this growing body of research and the ideas generated within this chapter.

Table 4.1. Overview of Achieving Success Everyday (ASE) Model Phases.

ASE Model Phases	Group Leaders' Goals/Tasks	Group Stages
Assessment	Gather preprogram data from students and parents. School staff can help identify students, their strengths, and areas for improvement. Assessments include Multi Ethnic Identity Measure, The Math Identity Scale, Math Self-Efficacy[a]. Attendance and GPA are examined. Students, parents, and school staff can provide ideas. These voices are critical to establishing a strong foundation. Parental consent and student assent is secured	This usually occurs before the group begins. Typically, this stage occurs while the program is being developed and students are being recruited
Review	Identify and review the purpose of the group, the ground rules, students' individual goals (academic and social–emotional), and any group goals; review feedback (e.g., perceptions) provided by the participants; collectively explore how the group sessions will start and end; discuss expectations during the sessions such as student and facilitator responses; define Blackness; explore community, engagement, and visions for the future	This likely occurs during the first session. This is typically the early stage of the group
Acquaintance	Work to establish group cohesion by discussing students' experiences in school and in relation to their race, class, and gender. Discuss students' identity development; model appropriate behaviors, interactions, and communication skills applicable in group and in the classroom; discuss ways to express emotions verbally and/or in their journals; discuss ways to establish safety in the group sessions. Discuss Blackness throughout this process	This can occur during and after session 2. Typically, this is considered the transition stage
Challenge	Provide Black males the opportunity to give and receive feedback; identify any barriers that they might be experiencing to being successful in their school experiences; discuss positive and encouraging language; facilitate activities that challenge students to gain greater personal insight	This occurs during the middle sessions. This is considered the transition and working stage
Empowerment	Allow the students to teach each other what it means to be a Black male youth; provide information, strategies, and skills to resist and build on their strengths; identify and acknowledge their personal strengths, assets, resiliency, and racial identity; process ways to use these strengths to thrive and flourish based on their unique experiences as Black male youth. Encourage (e.g., realistic and current)	This occurs during the middle sessions. This is considered the transition and working stage

Support/ *Assessment*	Celebrate the students' goal accomplishment; help them identify Black people as well as those outside of their race within their families, schools, and communities who could support them in their racial identity development; program participants (e.g., students, parents, school staff) will be interviewed and students will complete post assessments (e.g., Math Identity, Math Self Efficacy, and MEIM and GPA and attendance is reviewed). Celebrate the groups' accomplishments	The final sessions are the closing and evaluation stages. The last few sessions are used to discuss how to stay engaged after the program ends. Evaluation can be short term or during a booster session that could occur months after the group intervention ends

[a]To request any of these materials, please contact the first author.

IMPLICATIONS FOR RESEARCH AND POLICY

The goal of this ongoing line of research is to advance a group counseling intervention, increase knowledge, and skills targeting Black male middle school students so that they can gain access to, and be successful in, Algebra 1. This chapter sets the stage for a pending study that will be among the first to use a triangulated explanatory mixed method design to explore both Black students' experiences, their teachers, school counselors, and caretakers' perceptions, and the integration of these findings. Practical applications of this research will be provided for school counselors, school counselor educators, and policymakers.

In particular, recommendations for group counseling practice and research are evident. School counselors must use evidence-based interventions to target Black males. School counselors must also be intentional about infusing Black culture within the interventions. Student voice is often left out of the equation, and there is a great need to find ways to provide students with a platform to share their perspective of what works for them and what is less helpful. As the research continues to emerge, it will inform both the past research studies as well as future research studies. The evidence culminating from this research and the reflections generated by the researcher(s) are critical to ensuring that Black students are afforded the best chance for success within the academic enterprise. Policy is informed by research. We will continue to use mixed method research designs to enhance the value of the knowledge created for these youth.

In summary, small group interventions can be created in a way that could support building a strong identity as a Black male and scholar. Mathematics is connected to all aspects of our society, and significant connections can be made to the experiences of Black male students. In order to increase chances for success throughout one's academic journey in secondary and postsecondary schools, it is important that a strong mathematical identity is established early in one's academic career. This small group intervention is designed to help school counselors foster positive school experiences by supporting Black male middle school students who are navigating the ongoing pandemic, racial unrest, gun violence, depression, online learning and so forth, and systemic and institutional racism in many school environments and mathematics spaces within these schools (Battey & Leyva, 2016). The more school counselors demonstrate the development and implementation of successful group counseling interventions that make a significant impact on academic achievement, social–emotional learning, and college and career trajectory, the more likely these environments will fuel inclusive excellence. Group counseling programs and interventions in schools are very promising.

CONCLUSION

This chapter attempts to explain counseling interventions for Black males, strategies to improve Black males' academic performance, racial identity development, and the impact school counselors can have when using evidence-based group counseling models. In particular the ASE group model is highlighted as having the potential to help Black male middle schoolers improve both their mathematics performance and feelings about being Black and male within this society. The ASE group model is also proposed to be used to help school counselors provide a space for these youth to explore potential road blacks within school and strategies to resist and overcome these societal ills. It is important to note that as we write this chapter, the devastating impact of COVID-19 is undeniable and remains. The disease that causes the coronavirus is responsible for impacting the health of millions of Americans and contributing to the deaths of over one million Americans. COVID-19 has also contributed to close closures and virtual learning environments in countless school districts around the country and the impact of this continues. For example, there continues to be a tremendous impact on the academic experiences of students across the academic spectrum, and this disease does not discriminate. For all races and genders, the rates of students' depression and mental health disease increased (Wang et al., 2020). However, there are some data documenting the impact of COVID-19 on Black students in particular (Millett et al., 2020).

School counselors are positioned to help students, and group counseling can mitigate the impact of COVID-19. To reiterate, group counseling research and practice that focuses solely on Black male youth is reasonable based on the evidence culminating from this research and the reflections generated by the researcher. Specifically, a number of strategies were discussed for school counselors to utilize to support Black male students. Group counseling, for example, is identified consistently in the literature as being beneficial for students, and the first author is providing evidence that this is also the case when focusing on Black males. Group counseling interventions increase knowledge and provide strategies and skills for Black male children and adolescents (Steen & Hines, 2020). Furthermore, group interventions provide opportunities to infuse race and culture (e.g., African American culture), role models, positive identity focus, confidence, and sense of belonging (Steen et al., in press). Next, the authors begin to explore how strategies to support the learning of mathematics within the intervention give school counselors another strategy when they work with Black males. The goal need not be to teach Black male youth more strategies to do mathematics (although this is helpful), but how to think about learning and how to creatively problem-solve while infusing ideas to help them value their capacity for mathematics. School counselors and other school-based mental health professionals can be well prepared to make a significant impact on Black male students' academic success. In future studies, the ASE group model will be used with Black male youth to build on this ongoing line of research and scholarship.

AUTHOR NOTE

This material is based upon work primarily supported by the National Science Foundation (NSF) under NSF Award Number #2126056. Any opinions, findings and conclusions, or recommendations expressed in this material are those of the author(s) and do not necessarily reflect those of the NSF.

REFERENCES

American School Counselor Association. (2014). *ASCA mindsets & behaviors for student success: K–12 college- and career-readiness standards for every student*. American School Counselor Association.

Appling, B., & Robinson, S. (2021). K–12 school counselors utilizing critical race theory to support the racial identity development and academic achievement of African American males. *Professional School Counseling, 25*(1_part_4). https://doi.org/10.1177/2156759X211040043

Battey, D., & Leyva, L. A. (2016). A framework for understanding whiteness in mathematics education. *Journal of Urban Mathematics Education, 9*(2), 49–80.

Berry, R. Q., III, Ellis, M., & Hughes, S. (2014). Examining a history of failed reforms and recent stories of success: Mathematics education and Black learners of mathematics in the United States. *Race, Ethnicity and Education, 17*(4), 540–568.

Brougham, L., & Kashubeck-West, S. (2017). Impact of a growth mindset intervention on academic performance of students at two urban high schools. *Professional School Counseling, 21*(1). https://doi.org/10.1177/2156759X18764934

Byrd, J. A., Washington, A. R., Williams, J. M., & Lloyd, C. (2021). Reading woke: Exploring how school counselors may use bibliotherapy with adolescent Black boys. *Professional School Counseling, 25*(1_part_4). https://doi.org/10.1177/2156759X211040031

Campbell, C. A., & Brigman, G. (2005). Closing the achievement gap: A structured approach to group counseling. *The Journal for Specialists in Group Work, 30*(1), 67–82.

Challenger, C. D., Duquette, K., & Pascascio, D. (2020). "Black boys: Invisible to visible": A psychoeducational group fostering self-efficacy, empowerment, and sense of belonging for African American boys. *The Journal for Specialists in Group Work, 45*(3), 257–271.

Cobb, F., & Russell, N. M. (2015). Meritocracy or complexity: Problematizing racial disparities in mathematics assessment within the context of curricular structures, practices, and discourse. *Journal of Education Policy, 30*(5), 631–649.

Delgado, R., & Stefancic, J. (2001). *Critical race theory: An introduction*. New York University Press.

Gordon, D. M., Iwamoto, D., Ward, N., Potts, R., & Boyd, E. (2010). Mentoring urban Black middle-school male students: Implications for academic achievement. *The Journal of Negro Education, 78*(3), 277.

Griffith, A. N., Hurd, N. M., & Hussain, S. B. (2019). "I didn't come to school for this": A qualitative examination of experiences with race-related stressors and coping responses among Black students attending a predominantly White institution. *Journal of Adolescent Research, 34*(2), 115–139.

Harris, P. C., Seward, M. D., Mayes, R. D., Elopre, L., & Wengert, E. (2021). "We got to do better": Interactions between school counselors and Black male student-athletes. *Professional School Counseling, 25*(1_part_4). https://doi.org/10.1177/2156759X211040037

Hines, E. M., & Hooks, B. (1994). *Teaching to transgress: Education as the practice of freedom.* Routledge.

Ieva, K. P., Beasley, J., & Steen, S. (2021). Equipping school counselors for antiracist healing centered groups: A critical examination of preparation, connected curricula, professional practice and oversight. *Teaching and Supervision in Counseling, 3*(2), 7.

Jackson, L., Ford, J., Randolph, C., Schleiden, C., Harris-McKoy, D., & McWey, L. (2021). School climate as a link between high school Black males' math identity and outcomes. *Education and Urban Society, 53*(4), 469–487.

Jett, C. C. (2012). Let's produce culturally responsive pedagogues on deck. A response to "There is no culturally responsive teaching spoken here: A critical race perspective". *Democracy and Education, 20*(2), 16.

Ladson-Billings, G. (1994). What we can learn from multicultural education research. *Educational Leadership, 51*(8), 22–26.

Larnell, G. V., Bullock, E. C., & Jett, C. C. (2016). Rethinking teaching and learning mathematics for social justice from a critical race perspective. *Journal of Education, 196*(1), 19–29.

Liu, Y., Cochrane, W. S., Fox, D., & Sanetti, L. M. H. (2020). Treatment integrity of intervention studies in professional school counseling from 1997 to 2018: A systematic review. *Professional School Counseling, 23*(1). https://doi.org/10.1177/2156759X20907068

Martin, D. B. (2009). Researching race in mathematics education. *Teachers College Record, 111*(2), 295–338.

Millett, G. A., Jones, A. T., Benkeser, D., Baral, S., Mercer, L., Beyrer, C., Honermann, B., Lankiewicz, E., Mena, L., Crowley, J. S., Sherwood, J., & Sullivan, P. S. (2020). Assessing differential impacts of COVID-19 on black communities. *Annals of Epidemiology, 47,* 37–44.

Mustaffa, J. B. (2021). Can we write about Black life? Refusing the unquenchable thirst for Black death in education. *Educational Foundations, 34*(1), 68–84.

Pasque, P. A., Patton, L. D., Gayles, J. G., Gooden, M. A., Henfield, M. S., Milner, H. R., IV, Peters, A., & Stewart, D. L. (2022). Unapologetic educational research: Addressing anti-Blackness, racism, and white supremacy. *Cultural Studies↔ Critical Methodologies, 22*(1), 3–17.

Phinney, J. S. (2013). Multigroup Ethnic Identity Measure (MEIM) 1992. *Journal of Counseling Psychology.* https://doi.org/10.1037/a0034749

Phinney, J. S., Jacoby, B., & Silva, C. (2007). Positive intergroup attitudes: The role of ethnic identity. *International Journal of Behavioral Development, 31*(5), 478–490.

Prasath, P. R., Steen, S., & McVay, K. (in press). A creative strengths-based group counseling intervention for African American Boys. *Journal of Creativity in Mental Health.*

Rose, J., & Steen, S. (2014). The achieving success everyday group counseling model: Fostering resiliency in middle school students. *Professional School Counseling, 18*(1). https://doi.org/10.1177/2156759X0001800116

Steen, S. (2009). Group counseling for African American elementary students: An exploratory study. *The Journal for Specialists in Group Work, 34*(2), 101–117.

Steen, S. (2020). Group work with Black/African American males. *The Journal for Specialists in Group Work, 45*(2), 97–98. https://doi.org/10.1080/01933922.2020.1745496

Steen, S., Davis, J., & Bethea, C. (in press). Reconceptualizing the achieving success everyday group counseling model to focus on the needs of Black male middle school youth. *Journal of School-Based Counseling Policy and Evaluation.*

Steen, S., & Hines, E. M. (2020). Concluding reflections and engaged group work practice with African American children and adolescents. *The Journal for Specialists in Group Work, 45*(3), 183–184.

Steen, S., Liu, X., Shi, Q., Rose, J., & Merino, G. (2018). Promoting school adjustment for English-language learners through group work. *Professional School Counseling, 21*(1).

Steen, S., Melfie, J., Carro, A., & Shi, Q. (2022). A systematic literature review exploring achievement outcomes and therapeutic factors for group counseling interventions in schools. *Professional School Counseling, 26*(1a). https://doi.org/10.1177/2156759X221086739

Steen, S., Shi, Q., & Melfie, J. (2021). A systematic literature review of school-counselor-led group counseling interventions targeting academic achievement: Implications for research and practice. *Journal of School-Based Counseling Policy and Evaluation*, *3*(1), 6–18.

Terry Sr, C. L. (2011). Mathematical counterstory and African American male students: Urban mathematics education from a critical race theory perspective. *Journal of Urban Mathematics Education*, *4*(1), 23–49.

Thomas, D. E., Bradshaw, C. P., Bottiani, J. H., McDaniel, H. L., & Debnam, K. J. (2021). Coping power in the city: Promoting coping in African American male students. *Professional School Counseling*, *25*(1_part_4). https://doi.org/10.1177/2156759X211040002

Tinson, C. M., & McBride, C. R. (2013). Hip hop, critical pedagogy, and radical education in a time of crisis. *Radical Teacher*, *97*, 1–9.

Varelas, M., Martin, D. B., & Kane, J. M. (2012). Content learning and identity construction: A framework to strengthen African American students' mathematics and science learning in urban elementary schools. *Human Development*, *55*(5–6), 319–339.

Wang, X., Hegde, S., Son, C., Keller, B., Smith, A., & Sasangohar, F. (2020). Investigating mental health of US college students during the COVID-19 pandemic: Cross-sectional survey study. *Journal of Medical Internet Research*, *22*(9), e22817.

Washington, A. R. (2018). Integrating hip-hop culture and rap music into social justice counseling with Black males. *Journal of Counseling and Development*, *96*(1), 97–105.

Washington, A. R. (2021). Using a critical hip-hop school counseling framework to promote Black consciousness among Black boys. *Professional School Counseling*, *25*(1_part_4). https://doi.org/10.1177/2156759X211040039

Webb, L., & Brigman, G. A. (2007). Student success skills: A structured group intervention for school counselors. *The Journal for Specialists in Group Work*, *32*(2), 190–201.

Whiston, S. C., & Quinby, R. F. (2009). Review of school counseling outcome research. *Psychology in the Schools*, *46*(3), 267–272.

Whiston, S. C., Sexton, T. L., & Lasoff, D. L. (1998). Career-intervention outcome: A replication and extension of Oliver and Spokane (1988). *Journal of Counseling Psychology*, *45*(2), 150.

Whiston, S. C., Tai, W. L., Rahardja, D., & Eder, K. (2011). School counseling outcome: A meta-analytic examination of interventions. *Journal of Counseling and Development*, *89*(1), 37–55.

Zyromski, B., Dimmitt, C., Mariani, M., & Griffith, C. (2018). *Evidence-based school counseling: Models for integrated practice and school counselor education* (Vol. 22, pp. 1–12). Professional School Counseling. https://doi.org/10.1177/2156759X188018

CREATING MIRRORS OF REFLECTION AND DOORWAYS OF OPPORTUNITY: ENGAGING AND SUPPORTING ELEMENTARY BLACK MALES IN LANGUAGE ARTS

Christopher L. Small

ABSTRACT

This chapter will provide an analysis of current educational conditions of Black males within our K-12 school system and the ongoing instructional implications for school leaders working to address literacy leadership and practice. It will provide insight and motivation for school leaders as they navigate political, social, and policy systems that surround the current educational climate and instructional expectations. Readers will engage in a reflective, collaborative, and constructive learning process related to how successful school leaders enhance teaching and learning on their school campuses for Black males and what behaviors are critical to supporting teachers and students through the process. Specifically at the elementary level where foundational decoding, fluency, and comprehension skills are developed and cultivated for early learners we must be intentional with all aspects of the learning process and our instructional pedagogy. This chapter will work to expand the body of knowledge surrounding Black males as we commit to deconstructing existing and reconstructing inclusive, equitable, and just learning environments. Implications for research, policy and practice, including recommendations to support ongoing formal and informal professional learning opportunities for educators to openly discuss their

Black Males in Secondary and Postsecondary Education
Advances in Race and Ethnicity in Education, Volume 9, 87–105
Copyright © 2024 Christopher L. Small
Published under exclusive licence by Emerald Publishing Limited
ISSN: 2051-2317/doi:10.1108/S2051-231720230000009005

understanding of Black males, challenges they face, and strategies that they have found to be successful will be disclosed.

Keywords: Black male; critical literacy; professional learning; literacy leadership; cultural proficiency; culturally responsive teaching

THE BLACK MALE AND LITERACY
The Skin We Breathe

Most of my male students have gravitated to me because I treat them all just like they are my own sons. I check report cards, I give advice about handling situations that they get frustrated about, I pay for lunches, and I even tell them I love them. Janet Ready, ELA Teacher (Small, 2012)

The history of Black educational experiences in the United States is complex and entails a host of struggles that have played critical roles in shaping not only the Black culture but also contribute to many of the challenges that our educational systems face even today. More specifically, the experiences of Black males in our K-12 educational system have and continue to highlight the critical academic, social, and environmental issues that result in long-term disparities that become cyclical bondages of restriction far removed from an American dream. These disparities include but are not limited to heightened levels of disciplinary action, over-representation in special education programs, underrepresentation in advanced placement or gifted programs, below grade level reading performance, and elevated stereotypical affirmation of masculinity through athletics.

According to the National Center for Education Statistics (2020), in the school year 2017–2018 the national adjusted cohort graduation rate (ACGR) for public high school students was 85% compared to that of Black students at 79% (US Department of Education). Furthermore, one third (32%) of Black students lived in poverty in 2018, compared to only 10% of White students and only 27% of Black students lived in a household with a parent that had obtained a bachelor's degree or higher in comparison to White students at 53% (U.S. Department of Education, 2020). Parallel to these figures in connection with literacy, NCES (2020) reported that based upon the 2019 National Assessment of Educational Progress for reading (NAEP), Black students at grade 4 scored 204 points in comparison to White students at 230 points (26-point difference) and Black students at grade 8 scored 244 points in comparison to Whites at 272 points (28-point difference). Moreover, the reading scores for fourth grade males was 7 points lower than that of females (217 points compared to 224 points) and 11 points lower for eighth grade males when compared to females (258 points compared to 269 points) (U.S. Department of Education, 2020). More strikingly glaring are the results from the 2022 grade four NEAP Reading Assessment that indicate the average scale score for Black males was 194 points in comparison with white males at 224 points (30-point difference) (U.S. Department of Education, 2022). These academic disparities create the tapestry of unfortunate cyclical life circumstances that we often see unfold as economic hardships due to the higher rates of unemployment. Moreover, social complexities that are rooted in fragmented educational systems that were legally developed and cultivated to be exclusionary and homogeneously Eurocentric also become central to the disconnection of Black males in our schools.

In this context, one must ask why graduation rates and literacy performance, particularly for Black males, are so devastatingly low. What frameworks of our educational system have seemingly failed to result in the successful completion of Black males in secondary education? What central tenets of positionality, curriculum, instruction, and school leadership can be used to reframe the matriculation of Black males through the educational process? While some policymakers, researchers, and school leaders may gravitate toward the development of increased pressure of standardized assessments as the culprit for these devastating levels of Black male performance, one must consider the cause of low student performance even prior to this mass onset of high stakes testing at the primary and secondary level. The fact remains that many "students are not reading and writing at levels that enable them to compete in a rapidly changing information age" (Irvin et al., 2007, p. 3). Black males, in particular, who are unable to reach grade level literacy benchmarks in elementary school become situated early on down a pathway of future school challenges of success. The possession of the basic literacy skills needed for the successful completion of middle and high school is by far the highest predictor for graduation outcomes. If students cannot read, comprehend, and respond to assignments in required core courses or successfully understand what is being asked during standardized tests at the middle and high school level, they are doomed to academic standstills that eventually result in dropping out, thus, resulting in the cycle of predisposition to poverty, higher incarceration rates, and physical and mental health issues. Failure of public schools in America to foster the completion of Black male students, who graduate at much lower rates than their White and Asian peers, must be considered one of the most urgent and alarming problems in the educational arena.

Another underlying reality that we must also address is the idea that our educational systems often operate from the assumption and perspective that all students begin school with the same academic skill-set necessary to be successful (Darling-Hammond et al., 2020; Hale, 2001; Small, 2012). This misconception is problematic for Black males who may begin school without early literacy readiness skills or with cultural capital deficits related to Eurocentric frameworks. Early school failure breeds the feeling of disconnectedness for Black males in their learning environment, uncertainty about their cognitive ability, and causes them to feel maladjusted (Mincey, 1994). As the Black male matriculates through school, his early feelings of inadequacy or inability to read and write on grade level plagues his future educational experiences. For Black males to develop a desire to continue their investments and interaction with educational institutions they must be motivated to engage in the educational process. The instructor's ability to use instructional practices and content that can build upon their current range of background knowledge and social capital is pivotal in this matriculation and engagement process. Ideally, there is an academic cycle that should perpetuate itself as Black males pass through the phases of secondary education – positive motivational experiences of student engagement with one's peers and teachers that enhances opportunities for students to develop positive outlooks and connections with academic success. Over time, these cycles of engagement and motivation continue to perpetuate an identity with education that can be spoiled for students who cannot relate to traditional Eurocentric instructional material.

Many teachers grapple with providing students of today, specifically Black males, with what they need the most – relational voice in their academic process. With the onset of the COVID-19 pandemic and the increasing presence of social justice and racial crises situations across the country, students bring with them even more racialized and economic trauma that has yet to be unpacked. Moreover, political turmoil and legislative policy that capitalizes on inflamed verbiage and labeling terminology only exasperates the tensions that students bring with them to our educational campuses. Having someone that cares about your personal well-being as much as they care about your academic success is an untapped resource that must be leveraged as we navigate next steps in addressing the achievement and opportunity gaps that exist today. For Black males, these relationships and constructs like Critical Literacy are rooted in the very skin that they breathe each day as they walk onto our campuses (Robinson, 2019). Furthermore, the dismantling of deficit thinking and countering discussions of dehumanization with those of asset-based and strength-based approaches serve as tools to displace negative imagery and uproot historical misconceptions and stereotypes plaguing Black male learners.

Scholars have examined the alarming literacy rates of young Black males, standards-based instructional practices within schools, and frameworks for literacy instruction. However, few have examined the cross-sections of these constructs and their relation to the positionality of Black males within our classrooms and the importance of their voice that must be a part of the process. Moreover, this chapter will explore key strategies for educators to consider when working to mediate the factors impacting Black male students, specifically in terms of literacy and the role of teachers and school leaders within the process. Four dimensions of this process including: (1) use of culturally relevant pedagogy and universal design frameworks that build upon prior knowledge (Lee, 1995; Tatum, 2008), (2) engaging Black males in authentic and critical literacy discussions that seek to analyze and critique their realities within the context of their own environments as a core component of their curriculum (Comber, 2001; Lee, 1995; Tatum, 2008), and (3) utilizing academic and personal goal setting data structures as a starting point when addressing the needs of elementary Black males to establish authentic learning relationships (Rutledge et al., 2020).

INVISIBLE BUT PRESENT – CRITICAL LITERACY

Their biggest obstacle is who they are and where they come from. And it's very sad for me because the kids don't stand a chance. What they need is not a priority. Where they come from is what determines what they are going to get. And if they don't have advocates, they are not going to get a whole lot anywhere. Monica Ready, ELA Teacher (Small, 2012)

When approaching the learning process for Black males and the development of foundational literacy skills, we must be careful not to enter the educational arrangement with deficit thinking or the perception that Black males are to be pitied due to the color of their skin, dialects or languages spoken, or their socioeconomic status. Instead, through intentional critical literacy-based approaches we should begin to provide opportunities for our classrooms and schools to situate themselves as mirrors of reflections and doorways of opportunity for these students. As Ms. Ready points out, the unpacking of who and what makes a Black male student who he is not always a part of the learning experience, nor is it seen as something of value. Being in the educational process and being a part of the educational process are two very different things.

Due to current educational frameworks that have been historically Eurocentric, Black males often struggle to identify how they are best included in language arts classrooms. From lack of representation in texts used to provide instruction to the lack or representation and voice in determining social and academic goals, to the perception of Black males only being viewed from one dimensional lens. These frameworks within our current systems of education create and advance the status quo in defining not only what should be learned, but also how it will be learned and from whose perspective. Moreover, this paints a picture for Black males within our classrooms as being present and accounted for, but invisible and not included in the process.

Ladson-Billings (2009) explains that "students come to school with knowledge and that that knowledge must be explored and utilized in order for students to become achievers" (p. 56). Our young elementary Black males possess a wealth of knowledge and skill that has yet to take root and be systematically appreciated as an asset in our schools of today. If we are going to see the trajectory of change in achievement outcomes based upon current systems of measurement, then we must also begin to utilize the strengths that students of color bring with them from their cultures and social contexts as a vehicle to reach the expected end. This can also be situated in relation to the idea of critical literacy. Critical literacy theories "encompass social, political and historical contexts and allow students to examine the influence of institutions on their everyday lives" (Wood & Jocius, 2013, p. 663). Ladson-Billings (2009) explained that teachers "help students make connections between their local, national, racial, cultural, and global identities...they encourage a community of learners; they encourage their students to learn collaboratively...they view the content of the curriculum critically...they help students develop knowledge by building bridges and scaffolding for learning" (p. 25).

Cultivating the idea of mirrors of reflections allows for young scholars to engage in self-assessment and reflection as a process of truly unpacking who they are and what resources and talents Black males bring to the table. This process of looking in the mirror also allows for educators and school leaders to nurture learning environments for Black males that seek to address and improve academic and personal achievement. This occurs through an on-going process of critically challenging the long held traditional approaches to language arts courses centered on Eurocentric frameworks and stereotypical views for people of color. Whereby, Black males then begin to metacognitively construct doorways of opportunity and perceptions of their place and personal value. In working with young Black males, a part of the instructional planning process must include the voice of representation within the classroom. In the contexts of literacy, this is important not only within the context as a character or protagonist within the text, but Black boys must also be represented within the lists of curated authors and illustrators that make up our Language Arts curriculum.

Curriculum Adoption Frames Instructional Practices

Instructional materials and classroom libraries help to set the stage for diversity and inclusion within our classroom settings (Ajoke, 2017). School leaders and teachers have a responsibility to ensure that the literary texts being utilized to teach state standards and skills include not only fictional and non-fictional texts, but that they encompass a diverse set of perspectives that includes various cultures and linguistic backgrounds. This process of procurement of diverse and culturally relevant instructional texts and classroom libraries that provides students with opportunities for exploration and the building of doorways of opportunities is not something that can be done haphazardly or on the fly. Instructional planning for any subject takes time and preparation. For Black male success, this becomes even more important in the process as we look for ways to rewrite the narrative of their space within our classrooms and engage them in critical literacy discussions. In fact, there are a number of notable award-winning publications that were written and/or illustrated by African-Americans and are also situated from the perspective of a Black male protagonist (see Table 5.1).

Sonia Nieto (2004) articulates that a student "who emerges into our culturally diverse society speaking only one language and with a mono-cultural perspective on the world can legitimately be considered educationally ill-prepared" (p. xv). Each year schools and organizations across the nation often coordinate celebrations, create door decorations, read and listen to clips of the *I Have a Dream* speech, publish social media blasts, and pay tribute to what we recognize as Black History Month. In this context, students engage in related curricular activities and educators, arguably, make efforts to incorporate literature and texts that highlight diverse backgrounds. However, these displays of Blackness, justice, inclusion, and civil rights are often tucked away at the conclusion of the month of February until the following year and never revisited again. Thus, insinuating that students of color are temporal, seasonal, and confined to the 20 school days

Table 5.1. Notable Texts That Feature Black Males.

Grade Level	Genre	Title	Author(s)	Year
4–8	NonFiction	Anthony Burns: The Defeat and Triumph of a Fugitive Slave	Hamilton, Virginia	1993
4–8	Fiction	As Brave as You	Reynolds, Jason	2016
4–8	NonFiction	Bad News for Outlaws: The remarkable Life of Bass Reeves, Deputy U.S. Marshal	Nelson, Vaunda	2020
4–8	Fiction	Before and Ever After	Woodson, Jacqueline	2020
4–8	NonFiction	Black Diamond: The Story of the Negro Baseball Leagues	McKissack, Pat	2003
4–8	Fiction	The Crossover	Alexander, Kwame	2017
4–8	NonFiction	Twelve Rounds of Glory: The story of Muhammad Ali	Smith Jr., Charles	2007
K-3	NonFiction	Before John was a Jazz Giant: A Song of John Coltrane	Weatherford, Carole	2008
K-3	Fiction	Bird	Elliott, Zetta	2008
K-3	Fiction	Henry's Freedom Box	Levine, Ellen	2008
K-3	Fiction	My People	Langston Hughes	2009
K-3	Fiction	The Bat Boy & His Violin	Curtis Gavin	2002
K-3	Fiction	Undefeated	Alexander, Kwame	2019

Note: While not exhaustive, this table is designed to highlight publications to support diverse text selections for educators.

of the year each February. As Nieto (2004) also alludes, these types of seasonal displays of integrated culture result in students who are disconnected from the various cultures and voices that make up our society because they are not embedded or explored throughout the year. On the contrary, instructional materials and classrooms should invest year around in the use of fiction and non-fiction text that showcase multidimensional authors and illustrators of diverse cultural and linguistic backgrounds.

CULTURAL PROFICIENCY AND CULTURALLY RESPONSIVE TEACHING AS A MODEL FOR SCHOOLS AND DISTRICTS

Cultural proficiency involves "a mindset, a worldview, a way a person or an organization makes assumptions for effectively describing, responding to, and planning for issues that arise in diverse environments" (Lindsey et al., 2019, p. 5). As our schools have become increasingly more centralized in the crossfire of politics, policy, and stakeholder interests, educators and school leaders have had to increasingly become more agile and intentional in our plans to address issues of social justice, crisis management, and diversity within our campuses. For some schools and districts, the idea of cultural proficiency is difficult and also can be an uncomfortable shift in paradigm of thought. More specifically, it serves as a transitional point of shifting our viewing of cultural differences or diversity in perspective *from* the lens of deficit-based constructs *to* one of collaborative interactions that are rooted in the mutually respected value of cultural differences as being an asset to the collective educational experiences of all students (Lindsey et al., 2019). For Black males in particular, this paradigm shift is critical to their maturation and development within our schools.

"Culturally responsive teaching can be defined as using the cultural knowledge, prior experiences, frames of reference, and performance styles of ethnically diverse students to make learning encounters more relevant to and effective for them. It teaches to and through the strengths of the student" (Gay, 2018, p. 36). Additionally, Tatum (2008) articulates in his arguments about the significant role that instructional text selection plays in Black male development that we must go "beyond a solely cognitive focus – such as skill or strategy development, to include a social, cultural, political, spiritual, or economic focus" (p. 164). This resonates with the idea that for Black males to become and to see themselves as the critical scholars that we know they can be, we must move beyond simply allowing them to be mere consumers of texts as the spoken final truth to the role to critical users of texts to guide complex thinking, questioning, and development of new narratives. Specifically, as it relates to the role and space for Black males in the scheme of the greater society. This process also works to unpack negative and socially accepted stereotypes that are often destructive for Black males as they journey through the educational system. As teachers and school leaders look to build these doorways of opportunity and explore the mirrors of insight into Black males, we should intentionally consider not just the title of the literary texts used for instruction, but also the characterizations, themes, point of view, and relationship to illustrative infographics within the texts that also help to build critical literacy skills for students. In our intentionality in the design and development of classroom lessons and literacy experiences for Black males, we can begin to foster an inclusive learning community with rich interpersonal connections for fostering student success with literacy.

CLASSROOM CLIMATE AND ENRICHMENT THROUGH GOAL SETTING

> I dress this way because at home and on the streets this is what gets me my respect. I know y'all be wanting us to pull our pants up and stuff, but that ain't cool in my hood. I know sagging ain't going to get me no good job so I am trying to do better. Some of the teachers here be trippin' about our clothes and stuff, but I think we should be able to wear what we want. Kirkland Ready, ELA Student (Small, 2012)

The idea of taking on an asset-based mindset for Black males requires an intentional focus to be placed upon their strengths and potential for success. It requires educators to step back from what they may hold to be true based upon their previous experiences and learning and intentionally focus on the seen and unseen as well as the heard and unheard voices of Black males as they perceive their navigation in their school, home, and community settings. The lived experiences of Kirkland Ready is one that is all too common in our schools where we place so much emphasis on things like clothing or mannerisms that we lose sight of the bigger picture and the terrain that Black males are asked to face each day. In many cases, our schools are situated with the unwritten rule and intention of "fixing" our students to perform and succeed in one unified and standardized way. When Black males don't fit into these molds for learning, we begin to then see the gradual disengagement and declines in literacy performance. Our shifts to things like common core and mandated testing standardization for measuring achievement and promotion have further pushed us along this pipeline of removing the student from the center of what we do each day as educators. This is not to say that matrices of gauging student progress and learning should not be used in the educational field, however, there must be a balance and an effort to also meet students where they are, develop individual goals and objectives and celebrate their progress toward literacy improvement.

Safe Spaces for Student Success

Novak (2016) explains that "instead of wasting time trying to transform them from individuals into standardized learners, we need to teach them as they are and allow them to be the most successful people they can be" (p. 14). This starts with unpacking the *why* and engaging Black males in understanding the *why* behind what they are learning and *why* it's important to their future success. In creating this space to understand the *why* "the teacher builds engagement by giving students choices, minimizing threats and distractions, encouraging them to set their own goals, promoting expectations that optimize motivation, [facilitating] personal coping skills, and developing self-assessment" (Novak, 2016, p. 36). Each of these intentional items are important in establishing and maintaining a school climate of collective achievement and systems of support. If we want greater student achievement and increased student engagement for Black males, we need to change the student experience on our campuses. When we change the learning narrative and change our teaching, we expand the doorway of opportunity beyond the current status quo.

A key pillar in this process of establishing our *why* along with an academic and social culture for Black male achievement is that of collaborative relationship through goal setting. Additionally, this process of creating space for Black males and cultivating their learning through collaborative and supporting relationships during the early educational learning experiences is critical to their success and trajectory (Wood & Jocius, 2013). Unfortunately, "Black male disengagement with schooling develops in the early grades and continues to intensify as they progress through school" (Davis, 2003, p. 521; Hucks, 2011). Part of this disengagement can be attributed to some of the common standardized structures for evaluations conducted as part of early childhood and beginning literacy process that often include student behavior and social interactions as a major predictor for kindergarten readiness. For Black males, our schools are in fact a critical piece of the puzzle "as they make meaning of who they are, what they are supposed to do, and how others perceive them" (Davis, 2003, p. 520; Hucks, 2011). In as much, creating spaces early on in the educational arena for young Black males to feel included and understand their *why* at a developmentally appropriate level is the key. If students don't learn the way that we teach, then we must teach the way that they learn. In the context of literacy, the powerful nucleus of this mindset is that when we shift our thinking and approach so will our students.

"Culture is not formed by motivational speeches or statements of values. It is formed by repeated practice – using every minute of every day to build good habits" (Bambrick-Santoyo, 2018, p. 222). Along with building inclusive and engaging educational cultures for Black males, we should also consider the narrative that educators have the power to create and foster. Cultivating achievement mindsets by creating the right conditions and relationships for everyone to reach greatness is achievable. Hattie (2012) noted in his study on effect sizes for program influences that impacted student achievement that some of the most highly influential items included that of teacher–student relationships (0.72) and student self-reported grades/student expectations (1.44). Moreover, Delpit (2006) outlines in her lessons for teachers that "children of color, particularly African-American, seem especially [responsive] to their relationship between themselves and their teacher. I have concluded that it appears that they learn not only from a teacher but also for a teacher. If they don't feel connected to a teacher on an emotional level, then they will not learn, they will not put out the effort" (p. 227). Specifically for Black males, forming these individual relationships for success and cultivating a consistent mutual practice of building collaborative instructional success becomes critical. Coupled with strategies for establishing high expectations and celebrating success along the way, we begin to re-imagine the possibilities for Black males to also be a formidable force within our classrooms and on our campuses.

Literacy Goals That Give Value Within and Beyond the Classroom

Connecting back to the *why* for students, student goals should, "produce something of value – something that is personally or culturally relevant" and "have specificity for a big impact" (Jensen, 2019, p. 45). These two components are important when considering the landscape and societal contexts of home, school, and community that Black males face. In many cases, not only are Black males working to fit into and meet the expectations of our educational systems that require standardized performance measures and behaviors, but they are also working through the frameworks of Black masculinity and their place in the context of their surroundings. Specifically, for areas of literacy instruction, understanding why these authors or these genres of content or these perspectives are being used help to make connections for personal growth and development. Understanding that literacy is not just about content knowledge, but more importantly it's about developing lifelong skills and competencies for navigating the world outside of the classroom and cultivating the resilience and coping skills needed when faced with complex challenges. If we want Black males to be motivated to go somewhere they have never been, we must encourage, model, and set them up to do things they may have never done. By working with students to set high and lofty individual literacy goals and expectations for themselves, we challenge them to be great beyond measure and situate them with the confidence in knowing that we are also there to help them along the way and never give up. Finally, working to establish intermediate check-point goals and supportive strategies to navigate toward the end goal with specific data evidence on progress being made is important to the process.

Similar to adults, setting high lofty goals can initially be very exciting but over time it can be challenging to maintain that same energy and motivation especially if you are faced with challenges. In the contexts of literacy, improvements in areas of literacy skills like decoding, fluency, and comprehension don't just happen without specific efforts. Unfortunately, the idea of just trying harder to improve reading or frustration and fatigue often further perpetuates the trajectory of Black males becoming disengaged with classroom instruction and thus not experiencing achievement. Thus, setting intermediate check-point goals that reaffirm Black males, illustrate progress toward high expectations, and offer opportunities for relational affirmation are important parts of the process. Moreover, developing a collaborative classroom culture that is formed by repeated practices of allowing students to also encourage and support one another, especially during difficult times, helps to cultivate a literacy-rich learning environment where Black males find their true place and resolve to their *why*.

This sense of safety and community of belonging does not manifest on its own or develop without specific efforts by teachers and school leaders to build capacity by modeling and walking the walk. As a community of learners, both adults and students have strengths and areas in need of growth. Mobilizing our reflective mirrors for all parties allows for Black male students to experience and see the growth of not only themselves but also that of their peers and teachers as we engage in this process as a whole. Teachers and school leaders who are willing and able to share and be transparent about their personal struggles and journey with language arts and content area reading allows for students to peer through the doorway of the learning process. Over time students begin to also develop resilience and solace in knowing that struggle and delays in progress is not a sentence to failure and unintelligent exile. Hence, we must continue to cultivate the growth-mindset and social-emotional learning so that temporary shortfalls don't transform into long-term desolation of student success.

As we expect the best of Black males and create classroom climates enthralled with euphoric opportunities for them to feel safe, valued, heard, and connected, we empower them to reach beyond what they may have ever imagined for themselves as a Black male reader. High student achievement and literacy calls for these types of shared values that give way to relentless intellectual thinking and exploration of the many lived truths and experiences of the world around us.

PROFESSIONAL LEARNING FOR BLACK MALE LITERACY

Several years ago, the founder of Westside Preparatory School based in Chicago, IL, created the following metaphorical image of how she described educational excellence in schools. In her book Ordinary Children, Extraordinary Teachers, Collins (1992) outlines that as a conduit for "Excellence":

> I bear the flame that enlightens the world. I fire the imagination. I give might to dreams and wings to the aspirations of men.
>
> I create all that is good, stalwart, and long-lasting. I build for the future by making my every effort superior today...
>
> I am the parent of progress, the creator of creativity, the designer of opportunity, and the molder of human destiny...
>
> I wear the wisdom and contributions of all ages. I dispel yesterday's myths and find today's facts. I am ageless and timeless...
>
> I banish mediocrity and discourage being average...
>
> I stir ambition and forge ideals and create keys that open the door to worlds never dreamed.
>
> I am the source of creation, the outlet of inspiration, the dream of aspiration. (pp. 218–219)

As educators and school leaders, we have the opportunity to operate in the image of educational excellence and to cultivate new doorways of opportunities for Black males. If there is ever a time to invest in the professional learning of adults the time is now. Teachers not only need support in learning best practices and research surrounding Black males and literacy, but also need support in collaborating through professional networks and courageous conversations about supporting Black males inside and outside of classroom walls. Tangential to teacher professional development, they also need to experience educational leaders that also engage in ongoing learning as a role model. Researchers of the School Redesign Network noted that "intensive professional development, especially when it includes application of knowledge to teachers' planning and instruction, has a greater chance of influencing teaching practices, and in turn, leader to gains in student learning" (Darling-Hammond et al., 2009, p. 9). Additionally, effective professional development for adult learners should be "relevant and applicable while honing their knowledge and experiences [and] should always be accompanied by opportunities to set goals, self-assess, and self-direct [learning]" (Fisher et al., 2021, p. 34).

If we are going to achieve the excellence we desire for students within our classrooms, we must include the journey of looking inwardly to identify ways in which we as adults can reshape our current practices to intercede in unlocking the potential for our Black male students. Personalizing the professional learning process to meet the unique needs of our educators and school leadership pool in a way to not only ensure that adult learners are able to address their everyday challenges of literacy instruction, but also helps to maximize the experience and expertise that they also bring to the table. Schmoker (1999) outlines that "schools improve when purpose and effort unite [and] one key is leadership that recognizes its most vital function: to keep everyone's eye on the prize of improved student learning" (p. 111). This concept of continuous school improvement must also take into consideration the improving of student learning for all subgroups and allocating specific attention to Black males so that they are not left to chance.

Transforming Stagnant Professional Development Be strategic with whole-group professional learning that is founded on sit and get principles. Adult learners bring with them knowledge and expertise that should be utilized to shape the professional learning process and engage in the content being covered. Whole faculty professional learning can be helpful for setting the foundation and sharing needed introductory knowledge of specific content but not for all things learning. Training for literacy is an ongoing process and cannot be done in isolated pockets of disconnect.

Encourage Teachers and Administrators to Set Personal and Professional Learning Goals and Tasks. If you want to see continual literacy growth and development within Black males, it starts with the adults. Make time to identify aspects of your professional pedagogy that can be improved and make a conscious effort to seek out learning opportunities specifically around literacy development. Build upon areas of strength and build your professional network of colleagues to share ideas and best practices. Don't be afraid to ask students what worked well with the lesson and what can be improved. Inventory your students and use the qualitative data to drive literacy instruction.

Encourage and Build Capacity Through Teacher Efficacy and Professional Learning Communities. Specialized learning communities with targeted goals become powerful instructional tools and resources for improving student literacy and learning campus wide. Utilize cycles of inquiry, lesson study best practices, and learning walks to identify effective planning and instructional approaches within these learning communities. Intentionally charging this collaborative process to connect to school vision and meet the needs of target groups like Black males creates a clear agenda for moving from intention to practical application.

Create Opportunities to Share Learning and check the Pulse with Supportive Structures. Professional learning should not be done in isolation or as an added duty but should be embedded into our larger continuous school improvement process. Adults are goal-oriented and should feel respected for their work and contributions. Periodic temperature checks with accountability partners, opportunities to present new findings and resources, and the flexibility to update learning goals help in keeping the process fluid.

Professional learning post COVID-19 pandemic are vital to ensuring that Black males don't further slip into learning and opportunity gaps. Systems and expectations for professional learning must also be coupled with targeted collaborative efforts to address Black male literacy and success. Presented in Table 5.2 is a selection of potential professional learning topics centered around improving literacy instruction for Black males.

The advocacy and work toward equitable opportunities for Black males within our educational pipelines has been an ongoing fight for decades, yet countless numbers of young Black males continue to represent statistically significant and disproportionate numbers in our calculations for high school

Table 5.2. Professional Learning Topics.

Professional Learning Topics to Support Black Male Literacy Improvement.
1. Prioritize language development learning opportunities in the primary grades. African American males must be immersed in rich language experiences and have many experiences with grade-level vocabulary.
2. Avoid narrow approaches to literacy development. Embed professional learning on the intersections of reading, writing, and intellectual development as a collective process.
3. Improve teacher and school leader quality by focusing on the multiple phases and signs of literacy development. Efforts should be made to audit reading programs and practices to meet the diverse learning styles and diversity content.
4. Examine curriculum orientations and clearly define the purposes of literacy instruction with the recognition that a focus on test scores alone can become problematic as African American males move beyond the primary grades.
5. Become knowledgeable about current practice and research on reading and writing achievement for African American males.
6. Recognize that increasing the volume of experiences students have interacting with texts significantly correlates with their overall reading success.

Source: Adopted from Tatum (2012 as cited in Lewis et al., 2012, pp. 95–96).

dropouts and students reading below grade level. Moreover, the key instructional practices and pedagogy contained within this chapter lend themselves to the idea that good teaching is good teaching for all students. However, the argument can be made that there are specific and significant impacts when implemented and applied for young Black males within our classrooms and schools. The use of culturally relevant pedagogy and universal design frameworks, authentic and critical literacy discussions, utilization of academic and personal goal setting data structures and ongoing formal and informal professional learning opportunities are all significant components of understanding literacy challenges with Black males and how we can begin to address these issues strategically and intentionally.

Points of Reflection:

- What strategies do you currently use to build a sense of collective efficacy and community within your classroom or school? How might you intentionally and critically reflect on the effectiveness of current strategies to ensure Black males are included and have a voice in the journey toward their success?
- Reflect on your school and district practices for instructional material selections for literacy. What is the process for devoting specific attention to curating material that is reflective of multiple backgrounds and perspectives of lived experiences? What other themes or topics could be explored from fiction and nonfiction texts to draw connections with students? How might students' lived experiences be integrated into the school or district literacy plan?
- Engage in an intentional listening tour to collect feedback on what students' perceptions are about existing text and language arts classes. How might you

better support students in thinking about fiction and nonfiction texts more critically?
– What strategies do you currently use to establish learning environments that go beyond a single narrative in perspective and perception of social, cultural, political, and economic frameworks? How might you work to consistently thread critical literacy and multiple perspectives into your work and pedagogy to understand implications on student success and development?
– Reflect on your school and district practices vertical and horizontal curriculum alignment. What is the process for ensuring that the continuum of learning through a diverse set of texts and perspectives is comprehensive and spread throughout your system of learning and not isolated to a few select moments in time or specific classrooms or subject areas? How might your instructional staff or leadership team work to align schoolwide systems and initiatives to ensure reflective processes are in place for addressing the diversification of year around curriculum platforms?
– Engage in an intentional listening tour to collect feedback on what students' perceptions are of their role and place in the educational setting. What roles or stereotypes do Black males report they feel assigned to? What areas of your school do Black males feel they are excluded from?

Recommendations for Doorways of Opportunity for Black Male Literacy and Achievement

Unfortunately, there is no "one size fits all" solution or an all-inclusive app that will magically bridge the gaps and correct the challenges that Black males face regarding literacy. Furthermore, many of the recommendations and practices are not only good for Black males but are in fact good for all students and educators. Identifying fiction and nonfiction texts that reflect the diverse cultures, lived experiences and languages of origin, and the use of them consistently throughout the school year with various disciplines has shown to be effective for creating equitable learning opportunities for Black males. Secondly, approaching critical literacy and critical conversations with an open mind and allowing Black males to express their thoughts and ideas from their lived experiences and perspective helps to create to collaborative culture needed in early literacy and educational programs. Additionally, involving Black males in the literacy process through collaborative goal setting efforts in developing lifelong skills and competencies for navigating the world outside of the classroom is significant to cultivating the needed when faced with complex challenges.

Moreover, creating a safe space for students to share successes and challenges as it relates to literacy and content that builds a community of learners of mutual accountability and collaboration. Finally, we must reframe and re-invest in professional learning as a continuous improvement process and not a one stop shop that lays to collect dust on a forgotten bookshelf. School leaders must model professional learning and make it a priority for adults on our campuses and ensure it is practical and relative to current challenges faced in classrooms. If we want to cultivate successful Black male students who thrive in literacy rich environments, then we must create the climate and synergy to ensure it manifests and becomes the expectation and not the exception. Investments in these efforts will result in needed changes of literacy programming, our instructional methods for strategic teaching and needed adjustments to literacy interventions to close achievement gaps, specifically for school improvement plans and literacy decision trees that account for progress monitoring strategies within our school. Teachers and school leaders can then begin to collect and utilize measurable results of Black males as evidence of student progress to continue to build horizontally capacity across departments and vertically across grade levels.

Research

The voices of Black males in education have also become lost in the shuffle of educational research, policy, and practice. As a system, we base decisions and intentional frameworks on numerical outcomes and oftentimes forget about the voices, perspectives, and lived experiences that make up our data findings. As we have discussed throughout this chapter, there is a living pulse of untapped resources that reside in the perspectives and experiences that Black males bring to the table. Continuing to conduct rigorous research that includes and amplifies the voices or Black males is critical. For example, gathering the perspectives from Black males regarding their perceptions of factors that impede or enhance their literacy success is worthy of exploration. In this context, it would be useful to gather insights from not only Black males that may be reading below grade level, but also Black males that have seen success in literacy.

In addition, engaging in research and dissemination activities to identify and highlight strategies utilized by Black males to navigate their academic journey, combat social and cultural norms and stigma, and define their space as a Black male both inside and outside the school walls are also areas for further inquiry. Furthermore, triangulating this type of data from such studies with those that explore teacher and school leader experiences become critical. Particularly in drawing conclusions and bringing about application for practice for teachers and school leaders when dealing with the Black male population for literacy.

Recommendations for Policy

It is through the policy arena that we give educational practices and our instructional philosophy life and strength. Policies are intended to guide decision-making within our schools, but they also captivate the spirits by which we frame the truths and epistemologies that guide the day-to-day educational practices on our campuses. The idea that he who holds the pen wields the power and also writes our legacy is very much applicable to the nuances that we have seen from year after year related to Black males. Policymakers and legislative advisors and assistants must continue to be cognizant of the portrayals we capture related to Black males and policies that disproportionately disenfranchise students of color within our educational system. Whose story we tell and from whose perspective is a question that in many cases isn't up for debate.

Polices that guide textbook adoption, curriculum exclusion, and funding structures for schools and subgroups most in need are areas that must be given specific attention and intentional rigorous research. We have an opportunity to step back and critically review what we currently rely on as the status quo of normality for curriculum adoptions within our schools and provide a space to courageously research and discuss ways to do things not just differently but doing them better and for the success of all students. Continuing to look at data outcome measures for national, state, and local student code of conduct reporting and zero tolerance policies that are not also adjoined to restorative justice initiatives and measures to ensure access to ongoing high equality literacy experiences is critical. Moreover, a rigorous review of policies related to assignment grading and tracking that penalizes rate of learning with failure as opposed to mastery of a skill or standard over time would also be useful in gathering insight. District leaders must also be involved in a thorough review of local educational policies that disproportionately impact Black males. Investments in funding early childhood programming with strong foundational emphases on phonological awareness, decoding, and vocabulary development are needed for Black males. We have work to do, and we can help to change the navigational direction of Black males to not just exist in our society, but live life to its fullest and thrive.

CONCLUSION

When approaching the learning process for Black males and the development of foundational literacy skills, we must be careful not to enter the educational arrangement with deficit thinking or the perception that Black males are to be pitied and given passes for social promotion in our schools. Instead, through intentional critical literacy-based approaches that encompass culturally relevant instructional practices for literacy improvement with intentional frameworks for collaborative goal setting and monitoring we can begin to provide opportunities for our classrooms and schools to situate themselves as mirrors of reflections and doorways of opportunity. Moreover, professional learning structures facilitated by school leaders for literacy instruction post the COVID-19 pandemic are vital to ensuring that Black males don't further slip into learning and opportunity gaps. Systems and expectations for professional learning must also be coupled with targeted collaborative efforts to address Black male literacy and success. Black males have been misunderstood, misrepresented, and type-casted with countless stereotypes that discount the array of social-emotional trauma that plague their lives (Wright, 2021). Ultimately, we must start at the root with a critical review of our foundational literacy approaches if we are to unmask breakdowns in our current systems and rebuild intentional systems to address Black male success and literacy. With investments in continuous rigorous research and practical application of findings specific to Black male literacy, we will shift the trajectory of our current school outcomes. The results of the additional research that situates Black male voices as a part of the framework will also be critical in this journey to eradicate issues of low literacy performance and pipelines to high school dropouts. We can change the story line for Black males in our schools, and it is up to us to make it a priority if we are going to create and walk through the doorways of opportunity.

AUTHOR NOTE

This chapter is based upon the dissertation completed by Small (2012). There is no known conflict of interest to disclose. Florida State University.

This chapter received no specific grant or funding assistance from any funding agency, commercial, or not-for-profit sector.

REFERENCES

Ajoke, A. (2017). The importance of instructional materials in teaching of English as a second language. *International Journal of Humanities and Social Science Invention, 6*(9), 36–44. https://www.ijhssi.org/papers/v6(9)/Version-3/F0609033644.pdf

Bambrick-Santoyo, P. (2018). *Leverage leadership 2.0: A practical guide to building exceptional schools.* Jossey-Bass.

Collins, M. (1992). *Ordinary children, extraordinary teachers.* Hampton Roads.

Comber, B. (2001). Negotiating critical literacies. *School Talk, 6*(3), 1–2. https://doi.org/10.4324/9781410600288

Darling-Hammond, L., Flook, L., Cook-Harvey, C., Barron, B., & Osher, D. (2020). Implications for educational practice of the science of learning and development. *Applied Developmental Science, 24*(2), 97–140. https://psycnet.apa.org/doi/10.1080/10888691.2018.1537791

Darling-Hammond, L., Wei, R., Andree, A., Richardson, N., & Ophanos, S. (2009). *Professional learning in the learning profession: A status report on teacher development in the United States and abroad.* National Staff Development Council. https://edpolicy.stanford.edu/sites/default/files/publications/professional-learning-learning-profession-status-report-teacher-development-us-and-abroad.pdf

Davis, J. (2003, September). Early schooling and academic achievement of African American males. *Urban Education, 38*(5), 515–537. https://doi.org/10.1177/0042085903256220

Delpit, L. (2006). Lessons from teachers. *Journal of Teacher Education, 57*(3), 220–231. https://doi.org/10.1177/0022487105285966

Fisher, D., Frey, N., Smith, D., & Hattie, J. (2021). *The distance learning playbook for school leaders: Leading for engagement & impact in any setting.* Corwin.

Gay, G. (2018). *Culturally responsive teaching: Theory, research, and practice.* Teachers College Press.

Hale, J. (2001). *Learning while Black: Creating educational excellence for African – American children.* John Hopkins University Press.

Hattie, J. (2012). *Visible learning for teachers: Maximizing impact on learning.* Routledge.

Hucks, D. (2011). New visions of collective achievement: The cross-generational schooling experiences of African-American males. *The Journal of Negro Education, 80*(3), 339–357. https://www.jstor.org/stable/41341138

Irvin, J., Meltzer, J., & Dukes, M. (2007). *Taking action on adolescent literacy: An implementation guide for school leaders.* Association for Supervision and Curriculum Development.

Jensen, E. (2019). *Poor students, rich teaching: Seven high-impact mindsets for students from poverty.* Solutions Tree Press.

Ladson-Billings, G. (2009). *The dreamkeepers: Successful teachers of African-American children.* Jossey-Bass.

Lee, C. (1995). Signifying as a scaffold for literacy interpretation. *Journal of Black Psychology, 21*(4), 357–381. https://doi.org/10.1177/00957984950214005

Lewis, S., Casserly, M., Simon, C., Uzzell, R., & Palacios, M. (2012). *A call for change: Providing solutions for black male achievement.* Houghton Mifflin Harcourt.

Lindsey, R., Nuri-Robins, K., Terrell, R., & Lindsey, D. (2019). *Cultural proficiency: A manual for school leaders* (4th ed.). Corwin.

Mincey, R. (1994). *Nurturing young black males. Challenges to agencies, programs, and social policy.* University Institute Press.

Nieto, S. (2004). *Affirming diversity: The sociopolitical context of multicultural education* (4th ed.). Pearson.

Novak, K. (2016). *UDL now: A teacher's guide to applying universal design for learning in today's classrooms.* CAST.

Robinson, S. A. (2019, July). Critical literacy and its impact on African American boys' reading identity. *Gifted Child Today, 42*(3), 150–156. https://doi.org/10.1177/1076217519842200

Rutledge, S., Cannata, M., Brown, S., & Traeger, D. (2020). *Steps to schoolwide success: Systemic practices for connecting social-emotional and academic learning.* Harvard Education Press.

Schmoker, M. (1999). *Results: The key to continuous school improvement* (2nd ed.). ASCD.

Small, C. (2012). *Student engagement and achievement of middle school black males in single-gender and co-educational reading classes.* Doctoral dissertation. Florida State University. https://diginole. lib.fsu.edu/islandora/object/fsu:183118/datastream/PDF/download/citation.pdf

Tatum, A. (2008). Toward a more anatomically complete model of literacy instruction: A focus on African American male adolescents and texts. *Harvard Educational Review, 78*(1), 155–180. https://doi.org/10.17763/haer.78.1.6852t5065w30h449

U.S. Department of Education. (2020). *The condition of education 2020.* National Center for Education Statistics at IES. https://nces.ed.gov/pubs2020/2020144.pdf

U.S. Department of Education. (2022). *Average scale scores for grade 4 reading, by gender, race/ ethnicity.* [Data Set]. https://www.nationsreportcard.gov/ndecore/xplore/NDE. Accessed on December 2022.

Wood, S., & Jocius, R. (2013). Combating 'I hate this stupid book!': Black males and critical literacy. *The Reading Teacher, 66*(8), 661–669. https://doi.org/10.1002/trtr.1177

Wright, B. (2021). Five wise men: African American males using urban critical literacy to negotiate and navigate home and school in an urban setting. *Urban Education, 56*(3), 451–483. https://doi.org/ 10.1177/0042085917690203

CHAPTER 6

PROMOTING POSITIVE ACADEMIC AND SOCIAL-EMOTIONAL DEVELOPMENT FOR BLACK BOYS: FOCUS ON STRENGTHS-BASED PROTECTIVE FACTORS

Marcel Jacobs and Scott L. Graves Jr.

ABSTRACT

Black boys report experiencing more school-based racial discrimination than any other group (Butler-Barnes et al., 2019). Additionally, Black boys are viewed as older and less innocent than their peers beginning as early as 10 years old (Goff et al., 2014). Black boys are also suspended and expelled at much higher rates than other students (Graves & Wang, 2022). As such, there needs to be an investment in asset-based research designed to understand the factors that can help Black boys cope with these perceptions. Consequently, this chapter will discuss strengths based protective factors that will aid in the promotion of positive outcomes in Black boys.

Keywords: Black boys; asset; based; coping skills; protective factors; strengths based; positive outcomes

The education of Black boys has been plagued by opportunity gaps since the advent of Brown vs Board of Education (Tatum, 2021), resulting in an inadequate experience in the educational system. More specifically, Black boys have the lowest rates of reading proficiency nationally. According to the National Assessment of Educational Progress (NAEP), 57% of Black boys read at the below basic level in fourth grade, compared to 26% of white and 49% of Latino

Black Males in Secondary and Postsecondary Education
Advances in Race and Ethnicity in Education, Volume 9, 107–121
Copyright © 2024 Marcel Jacobs and Scott L. Graves Jr.
Published under exclusive licence by Emerald Publishing Limited
ISSN: 2051-2317/doi:10.1108/S2051-231720230000009006

boys (Nation Assessment for Educational Progress, 2022). From a practical perspective, this number demonstrates that over 50% of Black boys in the United States cannot read. Table A1, in Appendix A, presents the results of the NAEP Trial Urban District Assessment (TUDA). The TUDA is designed to focus on academic achievement in urban school districts. This shows that in many cities such as Detroit and Milwaukee, more than 80% of Black boys in fourth grade are unable to read.

The preschool-to-prison pipeline refers to exclusionary disciplinary practices occurring alongside low levels of academic achievement (Mallett, 2016). It has been shown that exclusionary practices like out-of-school suspension and expulsion more than double the chance of students being arrested (Cuellar & Markowitz, 2015). One reason for this being that students suspended before 12 years of age are more likely to associate with deviant peers (Novak, 2019). These associations can lead to a host of negative behaviors including substance use, lower school connectedness, and teacher reported problem behavior (Price et al., 2019; Rudasill et al., 2014; Wang & Dishion, 2012). Suspensions have a host of other negative outcomes including a decreased likelihood of completing high school or college (Mittleman, 2018). One particular explanation for this is that more suspensions translate to less time spent in school. The implications this has for Black boys is concerning given the unequal distribution of disciplinary action taken against them. U.S. Department of Education, Office for Civil Rights (2017) data presents that Black students (13%) are more likely to receive an out-of-school suspension than any other group. This statistic is even higher when examining Black boys alone; 17.6% of Black male students received one or more out-of-school suspensions, which was double that of the next highest group (Native American males 9.1%; U.S. Department of Education, Office for Civil Rights, 2017). Rates of disproportionality begin as early as preschool. Black boys make up a total of 19% of boys enrolled in preschool; however, they account for 45% of the suspensions to preschool boys (Graves & Wang, 2022). As these students spend less time in school, there is less time spent learning and less opportunities for true engagement with classroom material. In fact, Black students lose five times as many days of time spent learning than white students because of out-of-school suspensions. Heafner and Fitchett (2015) mention how instructional time is crucial for Black students, given the existing opportunity gap that continues to persist. The COVID-19 pandemic has made the opportunity for instructional time more difficult for Black boys. As many schools used a distance learning format, many Black families lacked the resources (computers, internet, etc.) for their children to appropriately engage in school material (Bailey et al., 2021).

Many reasons explain the disproportionate rates of exclusionary discipline, and as more research is done in this area, more data have begun to show that many of the factors are subjective. It's important to note that Black boys in the United States have long been stereotyped and seen as a danger or threat (Smiley & Fakunle, 2016). Black boys are perceived to be physically bigger, and more violent and aggressive for simply having a more Black sounding name. As Black boys are often perceived from this perception of aggressive and violent, they are often seen as older and treated as such by authority figures (Hines et al., 2021). Additionally, Black boys with more stereotypical features (dark skin, wide nose, etc.) tend to be associated with the criminal Black man stereotype more so than Black boys without them (Kleider-Offutt et al., 2017). For example, a teacher having knowledge of a student in poverty or unwarranted responses to minor infractions have been shown to be more responsible for suspensions than behaviors themselves (Jacobsen et al., 2019; Petras et al., 2011; Skiba et al., 2002, 2014). Further supporting this is the fact that differences in discipline take place even though the same or very similar behaviors are engaged by non-Black students, and this occurs all throughout Black students' schooling (Okonofua & Eberhardt, 2015; United States Department of Education, Office of Civil Rights, 2016). Home–school dissonance that occurs between students and staff is another reason for such disproportionality. Home–school dissonance happens when a student has demands and values in the home that differ from those in the school (Arunkumar et al., 1999). As a result, Black students' home values are likely to become devalued by those within the school (Gay, 2000), leading to what is known as cultural conflict. Humor for example, is one area in which cultural conflict may result in a Black boy being unnecessarily suspended. Milner (2012) mentions that often, humor is used to de-escalate tension or avoid confrontation in many Black households. However, white teachers may see this use of humor as rude, which could then lead to disciplinary action being taken against the student. This type of conflict is highly likely for Black boys given the racial makeup of schools. In the 2018–2019 school year, Black students made up 15% of the public-school population, while 79% of the teacher workforce was white (Schaeffer, 2021). These numbers again demonstrate that the chances of students' values being devalued are high, which gives a partial explanation for the discipline disparities. Such disparities in discipline have become so prevalent; the US Department of Education has formally addressed it through a Dear Colleague Letter on the Nondiscriminatory Administration of School Discipline (Lhamon, 2014). The letter states that schools are obligated to avoid and redress the racial discrimination that occurs in the handling of student discipline.

With the high rates of disproportionality of exclusionary discipline rates for often negative perceptions of Black boys, one would expect interventions and supports to be implemented that looks at this population in a more positive light. Strengths-based interventions are one type of support that has been shown to help Black boys in different ways. Strengths-based interventions can be described as those that assess and enhance the strengths of students and seek to create positive outcomes such as increased self-efficacy and resilience (Craig & Furman, 2018). This is opposed to interventions that instead focus on dysfunction and the risk of students. Richard et al. sought to reduce the negative impact chronic stress has on Black boys and girls by enhancing resilience through a strengths-based intervention (2016). The intervention used, the Civic Engagement Curriculum, included multiple activities such as learning about the meaning of community, reading passages from prominent Black leaders, having conversations with antiviolence community leaders, and peer circle activities. They found the intervention to increase self-efficacy and self-confidence in leadership, as well as life satisfaction for the sample. Many professionals who interact and work with Black boys on a regular basis (school psychologists, counselors, clinical psychologists) endorse the use of strengths-based practices such as these (Nichols & Graves, 2018). However, less than 50% of each respective profession indicates actively using strengths-based assessment and intervention practice (Nichols & Graves, 2018). While this may be the case, there are several documented practices that have been demonstrated to improve the trajectory of Black boys. It is important that the strategies used when working with Black boys are strength-based in nature in order to promote positive growth as was done by Richards et al. (2016). In this chapter we will examine research and data on the academic and behavioral outcomes of Black boys. Afterward, protective factors will be discussed in order to provide guidance toward a strengths-based approach to working with Black boys. Finally, recommendations for research, practice, and policy are given.

PROTECTIVE FACTORS

As Black boys grow and develop, a variety of obstacles and factors may prevent them from realizing their full potential. Many of these factors play themselves out within the home and community environment, while many others appear within the schools they attend. These, on top of the surprising statistics described earlier in this chapter, it is imperative to identify factors that will help support these students. These factors, also known as protective factors, could help to deter many negative outcomes for Black boys, both academic and social emotional. Within this section of this chapter, we will be discussing a total of three protective factors that have the ability to assist in the positive development of Black boys.

RACIAL IDENTITY

One protective factor which has a strong research base is the concept of racial identity. Racial identity may be defined as one's personal attitude about the significance and meaning of what it means to belong to a particular racial group, or what it means to be Black in the current discussion. One particular theory within this idea, the multidimensional model of racial identity (MMRI) holds that there are multiple dimensions to one's racial identity (Sellers et al., 1998). The four dimensions of the MMRI are: racial salience (how relevant race is to one's self-concept at a specific moment), racial centrality (how important race is in the definition of one's identity), the regard one holds for their race (positive or negative feelings toward one's racial group), and their racial ideology (personal beliefs and ideas about how members of one's race should act). The utilization of these dimensions helps to demonstrate that two people may similarly identify as Black but may have completely different ideas about what it means to be Black given they differ within any of the dimensions. Researchers have long explored the way in which Black youth develop their own racial identity, as well as the impact of racial identity on many life outcomes.

Racial discrimination is not something uncommon for Black children and adults to encounter. Many instances of discrimination occur as a result of untrue stereotypes held about racial groups. It has been found that students as young as 10 years old become aware of the stereotypes society may hold about their race (McKown & Weinstein, 2003). Seaton and Douglass (2014) sought to examine the frequency of discriminatory acts Black students encountered within their schools over a 2-week period. They found that 97% of their sample of 75 students experienced discrimination every day for the study period. Similarly high rates of discrimination have been noted in other research as well (Seaton et al., 2008). These discriminatory practices are often carried out by teachers as noted in interviews with Black adolescents (Hope et al., 2015). Such discrimination has a negative impact on the social and academic well-being of these students. As students in the Hope et al. (2015) study mention, many teachers implement classroom behavior management practices that problematize Black students. This can lead to unjust and overutilization of disciplinary action against Black students. This often can lead to more time spent away from instruction, which contributes to low achievement scores for Black boys. Additionally, racial discrimination has been positively associated with depressive symptoms for Black youth (Seaton & Douglass, 2014). Racial identity, however, can moderate the distress linked with racial discrimination (Sellers & Shelton, 2003). Specifically, the nationalism racial ideology and low public regard were shown to moderate the relationship. This nationalist ideology is in stark contrast with discrimination as those with such an ideology appreciate Black culture and are often resistant to the marginalization of their race. For public regard, because students believed other groups negatively view Black students, students may have been prepared to cope with the discriminatory distress. These findings further demonstrate the importance of the four MMRI elements and how they work to impact behavior. One study done by Butler-Barnes and colleagues (2013) supported the positive impact of racial identity. In their study, Black adolescents responded to questionnaires regarding their private regard (racial pride), academic persistence, discrimination, and self-efficacy beliefs. They found that students with average levels of private regard experienced greater academic persistence and self-efficacy than those with low levels; additionally, students with high levels of private regard saw greater levels of persistence and self-efficacy than those with average levels. Similar findings were shown by Leath et al. (2019); however, race centrality was the dimension of focus. Here, high levels of racial centrality and belongingness with other Black people in the school or community was a significant predictor of academic efficacy for Black boys. We agree with the authors of the study in that though work should be done to lessen negative external factors such as discrimination and bias, finings such as these point to the personal strengths Black boys have that can promote their well-being.

STUDENT–TEACHER RELATIONSHIPS

Given that Black boys spend a considerably large amount of their time in school, it is imperative to identify protective factors within this environment. One of the most salient factors within schools that impacts students is the relationship they hold with their teachers. The first interaction most Black boys have within schools is of course with their teachers, and student–teacher relationships will continue throughout their academic career. These relationships are particularly important for Black boys given that teachers often have negative perceptions of their race (Graves & Howes, 2011; McGrady & Reynolds, 2013). These negative perceptions can then result in conflictual relationships between Black boys and their teachers (Goldberg & Iruka, 2022). This issue is very much prevalent within education given the difference in demographics between students and teachers. As a result only 7% of the teacher workforce is Black and 15% of students within the United States are Black (National Center for Education Statistics, 2022); therefore, Black boys may not frequently encounter Black teachers. Such negative ideas about Black boys are less likely to occur when Black students have Black teachers. For instance, Graves and Howes (2011) showed within their study that the negative perceptions of Black boys were no different than other racial groups when Black students were matched with Black teachers. However, racial match between teacher and student is not required for quality relationships to take place. When teachers take time to acknowledge and understand the unique identity of Black boys, they are more likely to have a positive view of their teacher (Leverett et al., 2022). The importance of these quality relationships begin as early as Pre-K for Black boys. Evidence has shown that when the quality of these relationships increases, teachers also reported increases in the language abilities in Pre-K for Black boys (Goldberg & Iruka, 2022). Development of language abilities is especially important for Black boys as their reading scores have been consistently low for many decades (Nation Assessment for Educational Progress, 2019). Student–teacher relationships are also critical during the transition from middle to high school, which many researchers describe as the most difficult transition for students given high rates of failure and dropout (Longobardi et al., 2016). Not only do student–teacher relationships aide in the academic success of students, but also their mental health outcomes. For example, teachers and parents reported lower rates of conduct and peer problems, hyperactivity, and greater prosocial skills when student–teacher relationships were high quality (Miller-Lewis et al., 2014). Taken further, the negative impact of trauma lessens when students have a caring adult in their lives (Nicholson et al., 2018). Given that Black students are at a high risk of experiencing traumatic experiences (Morsy & Rothstein, 2019), helping these students overcome the negative consequences of trauma is important. For example, increased drug use is a behavior associated with higher exposure to trauma (Carliner et al., 2016); however, teachers have the ability to reduce or even nullify this increase when they form strong bonds with their students (Forster et al., 2017).

EXTRACURRICULAR ACTIVITIES

Extracurricular activities refer to activities that may be offered by a school or other organization but aren't directly connected to academic learning. This can include sports, music and the arts, religious organizations, and many more. Black students in general have historically participated in these activities at a moderate rate; nationally, about 16.5% Black 12th grade students participated in academic clubs, 45.4% in sports, 24% in music, and 17.5% in vocational clubs in 2004 (National Center for Education Statistics, 2016). Participation in extracurricular activities stands to hold many benefits for Black boys for a variety of reasons. It is firstly important to consider the social and economic circumstances many Black boys live with on a daily basis. In 2019, the poverty rate for Black people was 18.8% compared to the national rate of 10.5% (Creamer, 2020). Other research has also found Blacks to be impacted by concentrated poverty at disproportionate rates (Federal Interagency Forum on Child and Family Statistics [FIFCSF], 2013). Poverty has many unfortunate side effects, one of which includes community and familial violence. Exposure to violence can often lead students to joining gangs, where they may engage in antisocial behaviors, often after school (Garo et al., 2018). Given that exposure to this violence and its impacts are more likely to occur in Black communities, extracurricular activities are particularly important for Black boys. As many of these activities occur after school, they would provide boys with opportunities to engage in not only fun activities related to their personal interests, but ones actively promoting their positive development. For instance, students engaging in extracurricular activities had an increased sense of belonging as well as school engagement (NFHS, 2015), both of which are protective factors for students. Ensuring Black boys are engaged is important as it is both associated with a higher Grade Point Average (GPA) when levels are high, and an increased chance of dropping out when rates are low (Griffin et al., 2020). School belongingness is also particularly important for Black boys. Murphy and Zirkel (2015) found that when Black middle school students felt a sense of belonging in school, they set high expectations for themselves and had a high sense of academic self-efficacy. This is important because Oberle et al. (2019) found that middle school students who pick up an extracurricular activity are likely to have better mental health outcomes as well. This means that students who initially feel disconnected from their school may begin to feel a greater sense of belonging if joining a school club the next year. These activities also help Black youth develop a variety of prosocial values such as understanding the importance of a college education or having a good paying job (Tolan et al., 2013). However, students involved in extracurricular activities also receive many academic benefits. Often, if not always, schools will require students to hold a minimum GPA in order to participate in school extracurriculars (Fox et al., 2010). This in itself can be a motivating factor for many Black boys. These students know that in order to continue participating in their activity, they must consistently work hard to maintain good grades. In this instance, the activity would be an extrinsic factor; however, given students would need to be engaged to maintain good grades, they may very well become intrinsically motivated to do well in school (Shaffer, 2019). Marchetti et al. (2016) also found positive correlates between academics and extracurricular activity involvement. In their study of high school juniors from low-socioeconomic status (SES) backgrounds, they found students who met ACT reading and math benchmark scores were more likely to participate in extracurricular activities. Such findings are key for Black boys because they often come from low-SES backgrounds and the impact standardized tests have in perpetuating the opportunity gap is considerable (White et al., 2016).

One way in which extracurricular activities benefit Black boys is through the social connection students gain. Many extracurricular activities are team-based, meaning that students must learn to work well with others in order to find success (Lawhorn, 2008). This provides Black boys an opportunity to develop social skills that can translate well into other contexts. These activities also allow students to form positive relationships with supportive adults (Fredricks, 2011). This is especially important for Black boys, who as mentioned before are likely to reside in impoverished neighborhoods. Impoverished neighborhoods are often times under-resourced fiscally, as well as socially (Lacour & Tissington, 2011). Horvat and colleagues' study (2003) demonstrate that working and lower class families often lack the social capital that middle class families are afforded. As mentioned before, community violence is not uncommon in such neighborhoods. Community violence is a risk factor for a variety of undesirable social and emotional outcomes such as anxiety, depression, and posttraumatic stress disorder (Kennedy & Ceballo, 2014) demonstrating the social impact of poverty. Therefore, providing boys with positive models who they can connect with is essential. The different social skills and values Black boys develop during their extracurriculars can carry over into the classroom, hence the academic benefits. Hard work ethic, collaboration, and perseverance are all valued traits within the classroom that boys can also learn to value in their activities (Broh, 2002).

RECOMMENDATIONS

Research

From a research standpoint there are specific gaps that must be addressed before Black boys reach their optimal potential. A student's reading identity is validated by being represented in texts which reflect their social and cultural background; unfortunately, Black boys are not represented in the text that they read at school, which can hinder this reading identity (Robinson, 2020; Wood & Jocius, 2013). When asked about their preferences for reading passages written specifically to reflect their racial and cultural backgrounds, Black students indicated that self-identity (i.e., the tendency to identify with the story) was the primary reason they liked the passages (Cartledge, 2016). Results such as these point to the engaging power of representation for Black boys. Another aspect of school-related inequalities for Black boys reading disparities is teacher–child relationships. Black boys are the group most likely to have teacher–child relationships characterized by high conflict and low warmth; and this topology is predictive of lower academic achievement (Spilt et al., 2012). Given that Black male teachers represent less than 2% of the workforce, solutions as to how teachers of other races can better serve Black children is warranted.

Practice

From a practical standpoint, psychological and educational research have shown that implementing culturally focused programming is more impactful for Black youths academic and social development. More specifically, Graves and colleagues (2017) implemented a culturally modified version of the Strong Start social-emotional learning program (Whitcomb & Damico, 2016) with 31 Black boys. The purpose of their study was to examine the effectiveness of the culturally adapted learning program on the development of both social-emotional knowledge and assets of Black male students. Outcomes of the intervention showed positive effects for self-regulation and self-confidence; it was also shown that the students' social-emotional knowledge also increased. Relatedly Graves and Aston (2018) implemented the Brothers of Ujima intervention in a school setting, being the first to do so. The purpose of this strength-based culturally relevant intervention is to strengthen positive self-esteem, ethnic identity, and prosocial behaviors while reducing negative behaviors among Black adolescent boys. Fourteen Black boys ages 10–14 from an urban school participated in the intervention, no control group was included in the study. Results indicated that the intervention improves individuals' Afrocentric values. As a result of these documented effects, practitioners should concentrate on using culturally focused and culturally modified interventions for Black boys in schools. These types of interventions have proven to be more effective than interventions that are delivered without modifications (Hall et al., 2016).

Policy

Black boys face numerous hurdles when attempting to develop a reading identity, and their reading performance cannot be explained by one specific factor (Harris & Graves, 2010; Robinson, 2019). Historically, teachers have had lower expectations for Black boys in comparison to Black girls (Gershenson et al., 2018). In their examination of the effect of student–teacher demographic match on teacher expectations, Gershenson et al. (2018) found that white teachers consistently had lower expectations for Black students, but this effect was significantly larger for Black boys than any other group. These lowered expectations have resulted in lower reading achievement (Rowley et al., 2014). It has been documented that the instructional practices of teachers who have high expectations translate to higher levels of academic achievement (Rubie-Davies et al., 2020).

As previously mentioned, Black students make up a total of 14% of the public-school population in the United States. However, only 2% of the teacher workforce are Black males (Griesbach, 2021), meaning that many Black boys do not see teachers who look like them within school buildings, and they are likely to have low expectations placed on them. Moving forward, we believe that continuous efforts should be made in the recruitment of Black teachers as their presence has been shown to be beneficial for Black boys. Gershenson and colleagues (2018) found a 39% decrease in dropout rates for Black boys exposed to Black teachers during elementary school. College aspirations were also found to be increased due to this exposure. Schools such as Clemson University, Alabama A&M University, and North Carolina Central University (NCCU) have implemented initiatives to increase the number of Black male teachers. Clemson's Call Me MISTER (acronym for Mentors Instructing Students Toward Effective Role Models) program provides Black undergraduate men with tuition assistance, in addition to academic, social and job-searching support throughout the program (Clemson University, 2022). The Marathon Teaching Institute of NCCU and Males for Alabama Education (M.AL.E.) Scholarship Program Alabama A&M University provides similar support in addition to mentorship opportunities from Black male teachers (Alabama A&M University, 2020; NC Central University, 2022). We believe that more universities should emulate initiatives like these in order to further increase the recruitment and retention of Black male teachers. The ultimate outcome of such programs would be better academic, as well as social-emotional outcomes for Black boys of the future.

CONCLUSION

Ensuring the most optimal outcomes of Black boys is an endeavor that all individuals should care about. The statistics and research presented in this chapter highlight several areas of need such as improved reading achievement and decreases in perceived behavioral incidents in schools. Utilizing a strength-based approach and developing constructs such as racial identity, improved student–teacher relationships, and increasing involvement in extracurricular activities have the potential to create progress toward realizing these goals.

REFERENCES

Alabama A&M University. (2020, October 30). *M.A.L.E. scholarship announced.* https://www.aamu.edu/about/inside-aamu/news/black-male-teachers-wanted.html

Arunkumar, R., Midgley, C., & Urdan, T. (1999). Perceiving high or low home-school dissonance: Longitudinal effects on adolescent emotional and academic well-being. *Journal of Research on Adolescence, 9*(4), 441–466. https://doi.org/10.1207/s15327795jra0904_4

Bailey, D. H., Duncan, G. J., Murnane, R. J., & Au Yeung, N. (2021). Achievement gaps in the wake of COVID-19. *Educational Researcher, 50*(5), 266–275. https://doi.org/10.3102/0013189X211011237

Broh, B. A. (2002). Linking extracurricular programming to academic achievement: Who benefits and why? *Sociology of Education, 75*(1), 69–95. https://doi.org/10.2307/3090254

Butler-Barnes, S. T., Chavous, T. M., Hurd, N., & Varner, F. (2013). African American adolescents' academic persistence: A strengths-based approach. *Journal of Youth and Adolescence, 42*(9), 1443–1458. https://doi.org/10.1007/s10964-013-9962-0

Butler-Barnes, S. T., Richardson, B. L., Chavous, T. M., & Zhu, J. (2019). The importance of racial socialization: School-based racial discrimination and racial identity among African American adolescent boys and girls. *Journal of Research on Adolescence, 29*(2), 432–448. https://doi.org/10.1111/jora.12383

Carliner, H., Keyes, K. M., McLaughlin, K. A., Meyers, J. L., Dunn, E. C., & Martins, S. S. (2016). Childhood trauma and illicit drug use in adolescence: A population-based national comorbidity survey replication–adolescent supplement study. *Journal of the American Academy of Child & Adolescent Psychiatry, 55*(8), 701–708. https://doi.org/10.1016/j.jaac.2016.05.010

Cartledge, M. J. (2016). *Testimony in the spirit: Rescripting ordinary Pentecostal theology.* Routledge.

Clemson University. (2022). *Call me MISTER.* https://www.clemson.edu/education/programs/programs/call-me-mister.html

Craig, S. L., & Furman, E. (2018). Do marginalized youth experience strengths in strengths-based interventions? Unpacking program acceptability through two interventions for sexual and gender minority youth. *Journal of Social Service Research, 44*(2), 168–179. https://doi.org/10.1080/01488376.2018.1436631

Creamer, J. (2020). *Inequalities persist despite decline in poverty for all major race and Hispanic origin groups.* US Census Bureau.

Cuellar, A., & Markowitz, S. (2015). School suspension and the school to prison pipeline. *International Review of Law and Economics, 43*, 98–106. https://doi.org/10.1016/j.irle.2015.06.001

Federal Interagency Forum on Child and Family Statistics (FIFCSF). (2013). *America's children: Key national indicators of well-being, 2013.* U.S. Government Printing Office.

Forster, M., Gower, A. L., Borowsky, I. W., & McMorris, B. J. (2017). Associations between adverse childhood experiences, student-teacher relationships, and non-medical use of prescription medications among adolescents. *Addictive Behaviors, 68*, 30–34. https://doi.org/10.1016/j.addbeh.2017.01.004

Fox, C. K., Barr-Anderson, D., Neumark-Sztainer, D., & Wall, M. (2010). Physical activity and sports team participation: Associations with academic outcomes in middle school and high school students. *Journal of School Health, 80*(1), 31–37. https://doi.org/10.1111/j.1746-1561.2009.00454.x

Fredricks, J. A. (2011). Engagement in school and out-of-school contexts: A multidimensional view of engagement. *Theory into Practice, 50*(4), 327–335. https://doi.org/10.1080/00405841.2011.607401

Garo, L., Allen-Handy, A., & Lewis, C. W. (2018). Race, poverty, and violence exposure: A critical spatial analysis of African American trauma vulnerability and educational outcomes in Charlotte, North Carolina. *The Journal of Negro Education, 87*(3), 246–269. https://muse.jhu.edu/article/802652

Gay, G. (2000). *Culturally responsive teaching.* Teachers College Press.

Gershenson, S., Hart, C. M., Hyman, J., Lindsay, C., & Papageorge, N. W. (2018). *The long-run impacts of same-race teachers.* National Bureau of Economic Research. https://www.nber.org/papers/w25254

Goff, P. A., Jackson, M. C., Di Leone, B. A. L., Culotta, C. M., & DiTomasso, N. A. (2014). The essence of innocence: Consequences of dehumanizing Black children. *Journal of Personality and Social Psychology, 106*(4), 526–545. https://doi.org/10.1037/a0035663

Goldberg, M. J., & Iruka, I. U. (2022). The role of teacher – Child relationship quality in Black and Latino boys' positive development. *Early Childhood Education Journal.* https://doi.org/10.1007/s10643-021-01300-3

Graves, S. L., Jr., & Aston, C. (2018). A mixed-methods study of a social emotional curriculum for Black male success: A school-based pilot study of the Brothers of Ujima. *Psychology in the Schools, 55*(1), 76–84. https://doi.org/10.1002/pits.22088

Graves, S., & Howes, C. (2011). Ethnic differences in social-emotional development in preschool: The impact of teacher child relationships and classroom quality. *School Psychology Quarterly, 26*(3), 202–214. https://doi/10.1037/a0024117

Graves, S. L., Jr., Herndon-Sobalvarro, A., Nichols, K., Aston, C., Ryan, A., Blefari, A., Schutte, K., Schachner, A., Vicoria, L., & Prier, D. (2017). Examining the effectiveness of a culturally adapted social-emotional intervention for African American males in an urban setting. *School Psychology Quarterly, 32*(1), 62. https://doi.org/10.1037/spq0000145

Graves, S., & Wang, Y. (2022). It's not that they are big, it's just that they are Black: The impact of body mass index, school belonging, and self esteem on Black boys' school suspension. *School Psychology Review*. https://doi.org/10.1080/2372966X.2022.2072693

Griesbach, R. (2021, December 1). Local Alabama program shows promise in putting more Black male teachers in classrooms. https://www.al.com/news/2021/11/local-alabama-program-shows-promise-in-putting-more-black-male-teachers-in-classrooms.html

Griffin, C. B., Stitt, R. L., & Henderson, D. X. (2020). Investigating school racial climate and private racial regard as risk and protector factors for Black high school students' school engagement. *Journal of Black Psychology*, *46*(6–7), 514–549. https://doi.org/10.1177/0095798420946895

Hall, G. C. N., Ibaraki, A. Y., Huang, E. R., Marti, C. N., & Stice, E. (2016). A meta-analysis of cultural adaptations of psychological interventions. *Behavior Therapy*, *47*(6), 993–1014. https://doi.org/10.1016/j.beth.2016.09.005

Harris, T. S., & Graves, S. L., Jr. (2010). The influence of cultural capital transmission on reading achievement in African American fifth grade boys. *Journal of Negro Education*, *79*(4), 447–457. https://www.muse.jhu.edu/article/806962

Heafner, T. L., & Fitchett, P. G. (2015). An opportunity to learn US history: What NAEP data suggest regarding the opportunity gap. *High School Journal*, *98*(3), 226–249. https://doi.org/10.1353/hsj.2015.0006

Hines, E. M., Fletcher, E. C., Jr., Ford, D. Y., & Moore, J. L., III. (2021). Preserving innocence: Ending perceived adultification and toxic masculinity toward Black boys. *Journal of Family Strengths*, *21*(1), 1. https://par.nsf.gov/servlets/purl/10353524

Hope, E. C., Skoog, A. B., & Jagers, R. J. (2015). "It'll never be the White kids, it'll always be us" Black high school students' evolving critical analysis of racial discrimination and inequity in schools. *Journal of Adolescent Research*, *30*(1), 83–112. https://doi.org/10.1177/0743558414550688

Horvat, E. M., Weininger, E. B., & Lareau, A. (2003). From social ties to social capital: Class differences in the relations between schools and parent networks. *American Educational Research Journal*, *40*(2), 319–351. https://doi.org/10.3102/00028312040002319

Jacobsen, W. C., Pace, G. T., & Ramirez, N. G. (2019). Punishment and inequality at an early age: Exclusionary discipline in elementary school. *Social Forces*, *97*(3), 973–998. https://doi.org/10.1093/sf/soy072

Kennedy, T. M., & Ceballo, R. (2014). Who, what, when, and where? Toward a dimensional conceptualization of community violence exposure. *Review of General Psychology*, *18*(2), 69–81. https://doi.org/10.1037/gpr0000005

Kleider-Offutt, H. M., Knuycky, L. R., Clevinger, A. M., & Capodanno, M. M. (2017). Wrongful convictions and proto-typical black features: Can a face-type facilitate misidentifications? *Legal and Criminological Psychology*, *22*(2), 350–358. https://doi.org/10.1111/lcrp.12105

Lacour, M., & Tissington, L. D. (2011). The effects of poverty on academic achievement. *Educational Research and Reviews*, *6*(7), 522–527. https://doi.org/10.5897/ERR.9000349

Lawhorn, B. (2008). Extracurricular activities. *Occupational Outlook Quarterly*, *9*, 16–21.

Leath, S., Mathews, C., Harrison, A., & Chavous, T. (2019). Racial identity, racial discrimination, and classroom engagement outcomes among Black girls and boys in predominantly Black and predominantly White school districts. *American Educational Research Journal*, *56*(4), 1318–1352.

Leverett, P., D'Costa, S., & Baxa, M. (2022). The impact of student-teacher relationships on Black middle school boys. *School Mental Health*, *14*, 254–265. https://doi.org/10.1007/s12310-022-09504-7

Lhamon, C. (2014). Dear colleague letter: Resource comparability. https://www2.ed.gov/about/offices/list/ocr/letters/colleague-resourcecomp-201410.pdf

Longobardi, C., Prino, L. E., Marengo, D., & Settanni, M. (2016). Student-teacher relationships as a protective factor for school adjustment during the transition from middle to high school. *Frontiers in Psychology*, *7*. https://doi.org/10.3389/fpsyg.2016.01988

Mallett, C. (2016). The school-to-prison pipeline: A critical review of the punitive paradigm shift. *Child and Adolescent Social Work Journal*, *33*(1), 15–24. https://doi.org/10.1007/s10560-015-0397-1

Marchetti, R., Wilson, R. H., & Dunham, M. (2016). Academic achievement and extracurricular school activities of at-risk high school students. *Educational Research Quarterly*, *39*(4), 3–20.

McGrady, P. B., & Reynolds, J. R. (2013). Racial mismatch in the classroom: Beyond black-white differences. *Sociology of Education*, *86*(1), 3–17. https://doi.org/10.1177/0038040712444857

McKown, C., & Weinstein, R. S. (2003). The development and consequences of stereotype consciousness in middle childhood. *Child Development*, *74*(2), 498–515. https://doi.org/10.1111/1467-8624.7402012

Miller-Lewis, L. R., Sawyer, A. C., Searle, A. K., Mittinty, M. N., Sawyer, M. G., & Lynch, J. W. (2014). Student-teacher relationship trajectories and mental health problems in young children. *BMC Psychology*, *2*(1), 1–18. https://doi.org/10.1186/s40359-014-0027-2

Milner IV, H. R. (2012). Beyond a test score: Explaining opportunity gaps in educational practice. *Journal of Black Studies*, *43*(6), 693–718. https://doi.org/10.1177/0021934712442539

Mittleman, J. (2018). A downward spiral? Childhood suspension and the path to juvenile arrest. *Sociology of Education*, *91*(3), 183–204. https://doi.org/10.1177/0038040718784603

Morsy, L., & Rothstein, R. (2019). Toxic stress and children's outcomes: African American children growing up poor are at greater risk of disrupted physiological functioning and depressed academic achievement. *Economic Policy Institute*, 1–32. https://www.epi.org/publication/toxic-stress-and-childrens-outcomes-african-american-children-growing-up-poor-are-at-greater-risk-of-disrupted-physiological-functioning-and-depressed-academic-achievement/

Murphy, M. C., & Zirkel, S. (2015). Race and belonging in school: How anticipated and experienced belonging affect choice, persistence, and performance. *Teachers College Record*, *117*(12), 1–40. https://doi.org/10.1177%2F016146811511701204

Nation Assessment for Educational Progress. (2019). *The nation's report card.* https://www.nationsreportcard.gov/ndecore/xplore/NDE

National Assessment of Educational Progress. (2022). *Data tools NAEP data explorer.* https://www.nationsreportcard.gov/ndecore/landing

National Center for Education Statistics. (2016). Percentage of high school seniors who participate in various school-sponsored extracurricular activities, by selected student characteristics: 1992 and 2004 [Table 227.30]. *The Digest of Education Statistics, 2014.*

National Center for Education Statistics. (2022). *Characteristics of public school teachers.* Condition of education. U.S. Department of Education, Institute of Education Sciences. https://nces.ed.gov/programs/coe/indicator/clr

NC Central University. (2022). *Marathon teaching institute.* https://www.nccu.edu/soe/marathon-teaching-institute

Nichols, K., & Graves, S. L., Jr. (2018). Training in strength-based intervention and assessment methodologies in APA-accredited psychology programs. *Psychology in the Schools*, *55*(1), 93–100. https://doi.org/10.1002/pits.22090

Nicholson, J., Perez, L., & Kurtz, J. (2018). *Trauma-informed practices for early childhood educators: Relationship-based approaches that support healing and build resilience in young children.* Routledge. https://doi.org/10.4324/9781315141756

Novak, A. (2019). The school-to-prison pipeline: An examination of the association between suspension and justice system involvement. *Criminal Justice and Behavior*, *46*(8), 1165–1180. https://doi.org/10.1177/0093854819846917

Oberle, E., Ji, X. R., Guhn, M., Schonert-Reichl, K. A., & Gadermann, A. M. (2019). Benefits of extracurricular participation in early adolescence: Associations with peer belonging and mental health. *Journal of Youth and Adolescence*, *48*(11), 2255–2270. https://doi.org/10.1007/s10964-019-01110-2

Okonofua, J. A., & Eberhardt, J. L. (2015). Two strikes: Race and the disciplining of young students. *Psychological Science*, *26*(5), 617–624. https://doi.org/10.1177/0956797615570365

Petras, H., Masyn, K. E., Buckley, J. A., Ialongo, N. S., & Kellam, S. (2011). Who is most at risk for school removal? A multilevel discrete-time survival analysis of individual- and context-level influences. *Journal of Educational Psychology*, *103*(1), 223–237. https://doi.org/10.1037/a0021545

Price, J., Drabick, D. A., & Ridenour, T. A. (2019). Association with deviant peers across adolescence: Subtypes, developmental patterns, and long-term outcomes. *Journal of Clinical Child and Adolescent Psychology, 48*(2), 238–249. https://doi.org/10.1080/15374416.2017.1405351

Richards, M., Romero, E., Deane, K., Carey, D., Zakaryan, A., Quimby, D., Gross, I., Thomas, A., Velsor-Friedrich, B., Burns, M., & Patel, N. (2016). Civic engagement curriculum: A strengths-based intervention serving African American youth in a context of toxic stress. *Journal of Child & Adolescent Trauma, 9*(1), 81–93. https://doi.org/10.1007/s40653-015-0062-z

Robinson, M. (2019). Two-spirit identity in a time of gender fluidity. *Journal of Homosexuality.* https://doi.org/10.1080/00918369.2019.1613853

Robinson, S. A. (2020). Culturally responsive representation in graphic novels matter for African American boys with reading disabilities. *Journal of African American Males in Education (JAAME), 11*(1), 23–36.

Rowley, S. J., Ross, L., Lozada, F. T., Williams, A., Gale, A., & Kurtz-Costes, B. (2014). Framing Black boys: Parent, teacher, and student narratives of the academic lives of Black boys. *Advances in Child Development and Behavior, 47,* 301–332. https://doi.org/10.1016/bs.acdb.2014.05.003

Rubie-Davies, C., Meissel, K., Alansari, M., Watson, P., Flint, A., & McDonald, L. (2020). Achievement and beliefs outcomes of students with high and low expectation teachers. *Social Psychology of Education, 23,* 1173–1201. https://doi.org/10.1007/s11218-020-09574-y

Rudasill, K. M., Niehaus, K., Crockett, L. J., & Rakes, C. R. (2014). Changes in school connectedness and deviant peer affiliation among sixth-grade students from high-poverty neighborhoods. *The Journal of Early Adolescence, 34*(7), 896–922. https://doi.org/10.1177/0272431613511330

Schaeffer, K. (2021, December 14). *America's public school teachers are far less racially and ethnically diverse than their students.* Pew Research Center. https://www.pewresearch.org/fact-tank/2021/12/10/americas-public-school-teachers-are-far-less-racially-and-ethnically-diverse-than-their-students/

Seaton, E. K., Caldwell, C. H., Sellers, R. M., & Jackson, J. S. (2008). The prevalence of perceived discrimination among African American and Caribbean Black youth. *Developmental Psychology, 44*(5), 1288–1297. https://doi.org/10.1037/a0012747

Seaton, E. K., & Douglass, S. (2014). School diversity and racial discrimination among African-American adolescents. *Cultural Diversity and Ethnic Minority Psychology, 20*(2), 156–165. https://doi.org/10.1037/a0035322

Sellers, R. M., & Shelton, J. N. (2003). The role of racial identity in perceived racial discrimination. *Journal of Personality and Social Psychology, 84*(5), 1079–1092. https://doi.org/10.1037/0022-3514.84.5.1079

Sellers, R. M., Smith, M. A., Shelton, J. N., Rowley, S. A., & Chavous, T. M. (1998). Multidimensional model of racial identity: A reconceptualization of African American racial identity. *Personality and Social Psychology Review, 2*(1), 18–39. https://doi.org/10.1207/s15327957pspr0201_2

Shaffer, M. L. (2019). Impacting student motivation: Reasons for not eliminating extracurricular activities. *Journal of Physical Education, Recreation and Dance, 90*(7), 8–14. https://doi.org/10.1080/07303084.2019.1637308

Skiba, R. J., Arredondo, M. I., & Williams, N. T. (2014). More than a metaphor: The contribution of exclusionary discipline to a school-to-prison pipeline. *Equity & Excellence in Education, 47*(4), 546–564. https://doi.org/10.1080/10665684.2014.958965

Skiba, R. J., Michael, R. S., Nardo, A. C., & Peterson, R. L. (2002). The color of discipline: Sources of racial and gender disproportionality in school punishment. *The Urban Review, 34*(4), 317–342. https://doi.org/10.1023/A:1021320817372

Smiley, C., & Fakunle, D. (2016). From "brute" to "thug": The demonization and criminalization of unarmed Black male victims in America. *Journal of Human Behavior in the Social Environment, 26*(3–4), 350–366. https://doi.org/10.1080/10911359.2015.1129256

Spilt, J. L., Hughes, J. N., Wu, J. Y., & Kwok, O. M. (2012). Dynamics of teacher–student relationships: Stability and change across elementary school and the influence on children's academic success. *Child Development, 83*(4), 1180–1195. https://doi.org/10.1111/j.1467-8624.2012.01761.x

Tatum, A. W. (2021). *Teaching black boys in the elementary grades: Advanced disciplinary reading and writing to secure their futures*. Teachers College Press.

The National Federation of State High School. (2015). *The case for high school activities*. https://www.nfhs.org/articles/the-case-for-high-school-activities/

Tolan, P., Lovegrove, P., & Clark, E. (2013). Stress mitigation to promote development of prosocial values and school engagement of inner-city urban African American and Latino youth. *American Journal of Orthopsychiatry, 83*(2–3), 289. https://doi.org/10.1111/ajop.12038

U.S. Department of Education, Office of Civil Rights. (2016, October). 2013–2014 civil rights data collection. A first look. https://www2.ed.gov/

U.S. Department of Education, Office for Civil Rights. (2017). Civil rights data collection, "2013–14 Discipline Estimations by Discipline Type" and "2013–14 Estimations for Enrollment". See Digest of Education Statistics 2017, table 233.28.

Wang, M. T., & Dishion, T. J. (2012). The trajectories of adolescents' perceptions of school climate, deviant peer affiliation, and behavioral problems during the middle school years. *Journal of Research on Adolescence, 22*(1), 40–53. https://doi.org/10.1111/j.1532-7795.2011.00763.x

Whitcomb, S. A., & Damico, D. M. P. (2016). *Merrell's strong start – Grades K-2: A social and emotional learning curriculum* (2nd ed.). Paul H. Brookes Publishing Co.

White, G. W., Stepney, C. T., Hatchimonji, D. R., Moceri, D. C., Linsky, A. V., Reyes-Portillo, J. A., & Elias, M. J. (2016). The increasing impact of socioeconomics and race on standardized academic test scores across elementary, middle, and high school. *American Journal of Orthopsychiatry, 86*(1), 10–23. https://doi.org/10.1037/ort0000122

Wood, S., & Jocius, R. (2013). Combating "I hate this stupid book!": Black males and critical literacy. *The Reading Teacher, 66*(8), 661–669. https://doi.org/10.1002/trtr.1177

APPENDIX A

Table 6.A1. Reading Achievement of fourth Grade Boys.

Jurisdiction	Percent of Students Below Basic		
	Black Boys	White Boys	Latino Boys
National average	57	26	49
Atlanta	61	5	–
Baltimore city	73	–	59
Charlotte	47	12	42
Chicago	64	20	53
Cleveland	71	43	74
Dallas	70	–	57
Detroit	81	–	65
District of Columbia	64	9	49
Houston	71	–	57
Louisville	65	25	54
Memphis	59	–	52
Miami	47	–	29
Milwaukee	81	34	73
New York city	59	30	56
Philadelphia	74	–	80

CHAPTER 7

AN ANTIRACIST APPROACH TO COUNSELING GIFTED BLACK BOYS WITH DISABILITIES

Renae D. Mayes, E. Mackenzie (Ken) Shell
and Stephanie Smith-Durkin

ABSTRACT

While the literature on twice exceptionality is growing, it often focuses on twice exceptionality generally, overlooking within group differences that may create unique experiences for students. As such, there is a need to explicitly detail these differences to push the knowledge base forward. This chapter focuses on the unique needs and experiences of twice exceptional (2E) Black boys as they navigate K-12 schools. Further, this chapter details the ways in which school counselors may respond to their needs through comprehensive, antiracist school counseling practices. Finally, implications for policy and research are discussed.

Keywords: Black boys; gifted education; special education; antiracism; twice exceptional; school counselors

INTRODUCTION

Black boys in K-12 schools have a myriad of experiences that often shape their opportunities both in and outside of schools (Hines et al., 2022). For example, Black boys often have limited access to rigorous courses and gifted education while also being disproportionately represented in special education and the most exclusive educational settings (Hines et al., 2020; Shell, 2020). What is often not understood are the experiences and unique needs of Black boys who are at the intersection of gifted and special education. These gifted students with

Black Males in Secondary and Postsecondary Education
Advances in Race and Ethnicity in Education, Volume 9, 123–140
Copyright © 2024 Renae D. Mayes, E. Mackenzie (Ken) Shell and Stephanie Smith-Durkin
Published under exclusive licence by Emerald Publishing Limited
ISSN: 2051-2317/doi:10.1108/S2051-231720230000009007

disabilities, also known as twice exceptional (2E) students, are often misunderstood by their peers and educators as they work to navigate K-12 schools (Foley-Nicpon & Assouline, 2015). Part of this confusion relates to the somewhat competing characteristics related to both giftedness and disability status which 2E students are trying to make meaning of while educators and their peers are often trying to do the same. While greater strides have been made in the education of 2E students, what often is overlooked are the ways in which other identities (i.e., race, gender identity, etc.) can further complicate K-12 experiences. As such, this chapter will focus on this intersection to detail the experiences and unique needs of 2E Black boys along with implications for professional school counselors.

LITERATURE REVIEW
Experiences of 2E Black Boys in K-12 Schools

The K-12 schooling experiences for 2E Black boys is filled with numerous potholes which they must navigate. First, it must be noted that Black boys are likely to be overlooked for gifted education (Mayes & Moore, 2016a). In particular, educator bias in the gifted referral process can play a critical role in essentially blocking Black boys from gifted education (Owens, Ford, Lisbon, Jones, & Owens, 2016). For example, educator bias may view Black boys through a stereotypical, negative lens which views behaviors as aggressive, lazy, and uninterested in learning whereas behaviors may really be excitement and enthusiasm about the learning process (Mayes et al., 2016; Owens, Ford, Lisbon, & Owens, 2016). Additionally, educators may lack an understanding of the ways in which disability and giftedness exist on different spectrums. So when viewing a Black boy with a disability, educators may view behaviors through a restrictive lens that only views Black boys negatively because of their culture and disability (Mayes & Moore, 2016a; Owens, Ford, Lisbon, & Owens, 2016). When behaviors are viewed through a negative lens, teachers are less likely to see Black boys for their gifted potential, thus less likely to refer them to be tested. As such, Black boys are likely to be seen for their disability status and placed in the most restrictive educational settings, leaving virtually no opportunity for general education courses let alone gifted education (Mayes & Moore, 2016a, 2016b). Should Black boys with disabilities be referred for gifted education, they are likely subjected to standardized testing measures which have been shown to be poor assessments for understanding the brilliance of Black youth (Mayes & Moore, 2016a).

However, should Black boys be seen and correctly identified as being gifted and having a disability, their inclusion and experience in gifted education can still be challenging. First, as gifted education is not regulated in the same way special education is through federal legislation (IDEA), there is no guarantee that 2E Black boys will have access to gifted education (Mayes, 2016). In fact, it is quite possible that schools may opt for additional supports (i.e., pull out services) to be put into students' schedules which may not leave space for a student to participate in gifted or accelerated courses (Mayes, 2016). Thus, they may "count" as being gifted for that particular school/district, they have virtually no opportunity to grow and hone those skills as a part of their K-12 schooling process. Even with such documentation of giftedness despite lack of gifted education services, that information may not be shared with special and general educators who might find ways to leverage such as a part of their particular courses (Mayes, 2016).

To be clear, experiences in gifted education for 2E Black boys can present its own unique challenges as access does not ensure being welcomed into affirming spaces. Often 2E students, especially Black boys, are one of a few students who share similar identities (i.e., cultural identity, disability status, etc.; Mayes & Moore, 2016a, 2016b). As bias and discrimination are often a part of the identification process, these same issues show up in the gifted education classroom (Owens, Ford, Lisbon, & Owens, 2016). Bias and discrimination can further complicate 2E Black boys opportunity to form meaningful relationships with their peers and educations. Educators, in particular, may have limited understanding of 2E Black boys as cultural beings and may lack understanding of the intersections of race, disability, and giftedness. As such, educators may view 2E Black boys as not belonging in gifted education and may refuse to provide appropriate accommodations as outlined in the individualized education plan (IEP; Mayes, 2016; Mayes et al., 2014). As 2E Black boys experience hostility from educators and peers in gifted education, they may disengage from learning opportunities which may severely limit or even lead to undermatching with postsecondary opportunities (Mayes et al., 2014).

Beyond academic experiences, 2E Black boys are likely to experience challenges in developing healthy, positive identities. In particular, while socioemotional learning is vital for holistic development, often schools implement curriculum that are steeped in white supremacy that dehumanizes students (Drake & Oglesby, 2020; Mayes et al., 2022). As such, socioemotional learning leads to the continued dehumanization and policing of Black boys through the use of greater punitive and disciplinary measures when compared to peers (Girvan et al., 2017; Hines et al., 2022). These K-12 environmental challenges certainly contribute to the messages that 2E Black boys must contend with as they work to understand their own uniqueness. As they grapple with external messages, they are also working to make meaning of the intersection of their own identities (i.e., culture, gender identity, disability status, giftedness, etc.). If 2E Black boys are unable to disentangle these negative external messages from their own internal understandings, they are likely to develop poor self-esteem and underachieve which may push them to disengage with schooling (Mayes et al., 2018). Further, much of US schooling is still reflective of colonial roots which functions to protect whiteness (Drake & Oglesby, 2020). With these roots still intact, when disparities occur, it's often attributed to the individual and personal failings of 2E Black boys rather than for the systemic issues which created said disparities (Girvan et al., 2017; Hines et al., 2022).

The Role of School Counselors

As 2E Black boys move through their academic careers, school counselors can assist in ensuring they are recognized for their strengths and not diminished to their disabilities. Professional school counselors work in K-12 schools as educational leaders and mental health professionals, leading the charge of systemic educational change and student advocacy (American School Counseling Association [ASCA], 2017). School counselors must work diligently to create inclusive, culturally sustaining school environments that empower all students to achieve to their highest potential, including those identified as gifted and those with disabilities (Foley-Nicpon & Assouline, 2015; Smith-Durkin, 2022).

In their position statement regarding gifted and talented programs, ASCA encourages school counselors to consider the individual needs of gifted and talented students as well as monitor the appropriateness of gifted programs (ASCA, 2019b). Specifically, for identified gifted students from historically marginalized backgrounds, ASCA pushes school counselors to address underrepresentation in specialized programs and teacher bias in testing and selection. Although they are not responsible for gifted assessments, school counselors should collaborate with 2E Black boys, their families, school staff, and community members to foster student well-being as well as academic and postsecondary success (ASCA, 2019b; Mayes et al., 2014). Through the implementation of comprehensive school counseling programs (CSCPs), such as the ASCA National Model, school counselors can align school goals and activities to serve the needs of all students, including 2E Black boys (ASCA, 2019a, 2019b). CSCPs ensure school counselors are intentional in their interventions to serve all students, regardless of ability, race, and gender identity. Interventions and activities should be designed to meet the unique needs of all students and strive to close achievement and opportunity gaps (Smith-Durkin, 2022).

ASCA National Model
The ASCA National Model is one of the better known school counseling frameworks that provide counselors with guidance and resources to assist with the implementation of impactful initiatives supporting the academic, career, and social/emotional well-being of all students (ASCA, 2019a). The model is divided into four components: (a) define, (b) manage, (c) assess, and (d) deliver. Each component contains resources to support program development as well as outline culturally sustaining school counseling (Grothaus et al., 2020).

In the ASCA National Model, the *define* component refers to school counselor and student standards that detail the expectations for those in the school counseling profession (ASCA, 2019a). These standards assist new and current school counselors to "develop, implement, and assess school counseling programs to improve student outcomes" (ASCA, 2019a, p. xiii). In supporting 2E Black boys, school counselors *assess* school gifted programs and student access to advanced coursework (Smith-Durkin, 2022). School counselors also assess for any student exposure to micro-aggressions and bias that prevent 2E Black boys from reaching their full academic potential (ASCA, 2019b).

School counselors *manage* their counseling programs by implementing impactful and effective activities to benefit all students (ASCA, 2019a; Smith-Durkin, 2022). School counseling program mission and vision statements should be inclusive, align with school goals, and focus on equitable educational outcomes for students. By utilizing school data, including advanced course and gifted program enrollment of students from historically marginalized backgrounds, school counselors ensure school outcome goals are equitable. An analysis of collected data assists school counselors in the creation of school action plans that address opportunity, achievement, information, and attainment gaps for 2E Black boys (Smith-Durkin, 2022).

Lastly, school counselors *deliver* developmentally and culturally appropriate activities and services that positively affect student achievement outcomes (Smith-Durkin, 2022). When working specifically with 2E Black boys, school counselors can implement small group counseling sessions so students have a safe space to share their experiences and increase their self-awareness (ASCA, 2019a). School counselors should also provide professional development opportunities for school staff, addressing bias and discrimination in student referrals for specialized programs (ASCA, 2019b).

School counselors play an important role in the creation of educationally and culturally inclusive school environments (Smith-Durkin, 2022). The ASCA emphasizes school counselors promoting student equitable access to rigorous coursework as well as the intentional development of interventions that tackle the overrepresentation of students from historically marginalized backgrounds in special education programs (Smith-Durkin, 2022). To eliminate barriers, it is essential that school counselors implement antiracist practices and move school staff from focusing on student deficits to celebrating student strengths (Holcomb-McCoy, 2022; Smith-Durkin, 2022).

THE NEED FOR ANTIRACISM IN SCHOOL COUNSELING

For decades, educational institutions have perpetuated bias and inequity and as a result, caused irreparable harm to Black and brown students (Ladson-Billings & Tate, 1995; Smith-Durkin, 2022). To assure their comprehensive school counseling programs are culturally confirming, it is imperative that school counselors work to eliminate biases and inequities existing in their school (Grothaus et al., 2020). The commitment to antiracist school counseling dismantles racist practices and policies and honors the humanness of historically marginalized students, families, and communities (Holcomb-McCoy, 2022; Love, 2019). School counseling antiracist work involves more than recognizing oppressive systems; it is the active removal of oppressive systems and policies that unfairly target Black and Brown children (Holcomb-McCoy, 2022). Along those same lines, Mayes and Byrd (2022) describe antiracist school counseling as the:

Ongoing process of (a) believing that racism is ever-present and plagues all systems of society, (b) unlearning colonial ways of being, (c) learning about the roots of racism and how all oppression is intersectional, (d) consistently addressing one's own racist behaviors or internalized oppression, (e) challenging ways of thinking and doing that may feel normal, (f) using critical theories to develop and sharpen a lens to identify oppression, and (g) actively engaging in rooting out oppressive beliefs and policies wherever you find them, even within yourself. (p. 21)

School counselors must be antiracist leaders in their schools – identifying and addressing racist and discriminatory practices. 2E Black boys are also twice stigmatized for their racial identity and disabilities as they face both racism and ableism in schools. This stigmatization isolates and excludes 2E Black boys from the free and appropriate education in which all children are entitled to as they are likely to be surveilled and pushed out of school with little regard to their needs and system failures. Antiracist school counselors address this stigmatization directly with school staff, purposely dismantling old systems and creating new policies that celebrate diversity and serve every student (Betters-Bubon et al., 2022; Smith-Durkin, 2022). School staff, including teachers and school counselors, are mostly white women holding white middle class expectations for their students (Betters-Bubon et al., 2022; Haugen et al., 2021). To prevent such staff bias from permeating into classrooms and school environments, counselors serve as a mouthpiece for historically marginalized students and advocate for change (ASCA, 2021).

Antiracist school counselor advocates promote equity, healing, and liberation of Black youth from white supremacist systems (Edirmanasinghe et al., 2022; Holcomb-McCoy, 2022; Love, 2019; Mayes & Byrd, 2022). Self-awareness is necessary to invoke change; therefore, school counselors must also acknowledge their own biases in course recommendations and selections (Betters-Bubon et al., 2022; Simmons, 2019; Smith-Durkin, 2022). They must engage in active learning and studying of educational and institutional racism as well as participate in conversations regarding race, racism, injustice, and inequities (ASCA, 2021). School counselors hold a privilege that their students do not, thus, they have a responsibility to use their privilege to create equitable outcomes for all students.

ANTIRACISM AND MULTITIERED SYSTEMS OF SUPPORT (MTSS) – IMPLICATIONS FOR SCHOOL COUNSELOR PRACTICE

Black boys face systemic racism and structural barriers in traditional US school settings which mitigate healthy development of their racial, gender, and academic identities, including risks of over-identification for special education services and under-identification for gifted education services, lowered access to rigorous courses, increased placement in more restrictive academic settings, higher suspension/expulsion rates, and lower college-going and completion rates (Mayes & Moore, 2016a; Shell, 2020). For Black boys who have been identified for both a gifted designation and a learning disability, 2E students, the structural barriers persist and include an overemphasis on the disability(ies) and an underemphasis on giftedness by teachers, micro and macroaggressions in gifted programming, and the challenges of being one of a few marginalized students in gifted classes (Mayes & Moore, 2016a). The structural barriers and systemic racism that cause harm to 2E Black boys and other marginalized students require school counselors to investigate and implement policies and interventions that remove barriers and disrupt systems by implementing antiracist school counseling praxis (Mayes & Byrd, 2022). In schools that use MTSS, school counselors can integrate antiracist practices into their comprehensive school counseling program and MTSS frameworks (Betters-Bubon et al., 2022; Mayes & Byrd, 2022). The tiered model of prevention/intervention of MTSS aligns well with the ASCA's tiered model of comprehensive school counseling programs (Ziomek-Daigle et al., 2016).

Multitiered Systems of Support (MTSS)

MTSS frameworks incorporate "academic (i.e., Response to Intervention [RtI]) and behavioral support systems (i.e., Positive Behavior Interventions and Supports [PBIS])" (Betters-Bubon et al., 2022, p. 2) and social-emotional and mental health supports (Edyburn et al., 2022) for all students within a school. Research in public health and prevention and a socio-ecological behavior model undergird MTSS frameworks (Fallon et al., 2021). School counselors operating in an MTSS framework can differentiate their comprehensive counseling program by offering universal services to all students and targeted interventions to students who need more academic, behavioral, or social-emotional supports (Edirmanasinghe et al., 2022). MTSS implementation may vary in individual schools or districts, but most models involve a three- or four-tiered framework (Shell et al., 2019). Typical models use the three-tiered framework with developmentally appropriate prevention and intervention strategies embedded in each tier to improve student outcomes (Hines et al., 2022; Sugai et al., 2019). Broadly, Tier 1 of the models consists of school-wide research-based primary or universal prevention with concurrent progress monitoring to strengthen academic, behavioral, and social-emotional development. Tier 2 of the model involves the provision of intensive instruction and support for students who need more supports after receiving the assessments and interventions administered in Tier 1. This support may consist of small group instruction or tutorial support. Finally, if supports provided in Tier 2 fail to provide additional protective factors for identified students, they move to Tier 3 where they receive more specialized/individualized interventions with increased frequency and monitoring (Hines et al., 2022; Shell et al., 2019).

School Counselors and MTSS

School counselors play a critical role in the development of systemic practices to meet the academic, behavioral, social/emotional, and career needs for all students. Their comprehensive school counseling programs should support educational equity and promote equitable access to high-quality educational practices. Hines et al. (2017) noted that

...school counselors acknowledge the broad, systemic societal inequities that are present within and outside of school and assume responsibility in taking action to eliminate said inequities.

This means that school counselors for social justice focus on historically underserved and marginalized groups. (p. 9)

When school counselors focus on the needs of minoritized students within their comprehensive school counseling programs, they create a context where their efforts can benefit outcomes for all students (Shell et al., 2019). School counselors serve as essential leaders within MTSS and have the training to make unique contributions to the MTSS process because of their skills in advocacy, leadership, collaboration, consultation, and the effective use of data to inform decisions (Belser et al., 2016). School counselors play an essential role in decreasing the opportunity gaps in access to academic, behavioral, and mental health support for 2E Black boys (Mayes et al., 2014). More specifically, school counselors can use an MTSS framework to structure their intentional interventions to support student success through a data-driven, evidence-based model that encourages targeted interventions in a tiered approach for 2E Black boys (Hines et al., 2022).

Catch-22 of MTSS

Multiple studies have shown the benefits of MTSS implementation for student outcomes, including decreased suspension and expulsion rates, increased school attendance rates, and decreased special education referrals (Betters-Bubon et al., 2022). In spite of those promising outcomes, MTSS implementation has not closed opportunity gaps for minoritized students, especially Black boys. Despite the improved data associated with MTSS implementation, Black students still bear the brunt of exclusionary discipline practices in US schools (Heidelburg et al., 2022). The persistent opportunity gaps between minoritized students and their white peers and longstanding issue of disproportionality in gifted education and special education imply that race- or culturally-neutral MTSS implementation is not effective (Shell et al., 2019). Traditional MTSS frameworks cannot sufficiently mitigate the harms of institutional and systemic racism embedded in the American education system (Heidelburg et al., 2022). Harm mitigation requires an equity-focused, culturally responsive, antiracist MTSS framework that supports students' growth and dismantles school policies and barriers that exacerbate inequities (Hines et al., 2022; Mayes & Byrd, 2022).

Critical Race Theory (CRT)

Ladson-Billings and Tate introduced CRT in education as a framework to critique race and racist systems within the field of education (Ladson-Billings & Tate, 1995). This theory empowers counselors to analyze racialized disparate outcomes by centering those disparate outcomes within a larger discussion of racism in schooling (Howard & Navarro, 2016). CRT offers tools to interrogate current practices within an MTSS framework by providing an apt framework to analyze structural biases and appearances of fairness and neutrality. There are six key tenets within CRT: (a) permanence and intersectionality of race and racism, (b) a critique of liberalism and positivist thought, (c) counter storytelling, (d) whiteness as property, (e) intersectionality, and (f) interest convergence. Permanence and intersectionality of race and racism refer to ways that racism shows up in individual and institutional acts and the social construction of race and racial difference. Twice exceptional Black boys likely experience racism from interactions with educators and from the policies, histories, and structures of public schools within the United States (Ladson-Billings, 2021). Critique of liberalism refers to the notion that color-evasive or race-neutral policies are necessary now because the United States is a postracial society and no longer needs to redress the harms of racism (Ladson-Billings & Tate, 1995). Counter storytelling may perhaps seem the more important tenet for 2E Black boys. Counter storytelling allows for the centering of the narratives of Black youth as they discuss their lives, resistance to dominant narratives that devalue their existence, and speak their truths about experiences with racist systems meant to deter their growth (Ladson-Billings & Tate, 1995). Whiteness as property highlights the ways that policies and structures often, ultimately, benefit white people (Ladson-Billings & Tate, 1995). In schools, curriculum and expectations center whiteness and exclude minoritized students and their experiences. Moreover, whiteness as property speaks to the disproportionality of Black students in gifted programs and exclusionary discipline rates for Black students (Girvan et al., 2017). Intersectionality refers to the multiple, intersecting axes of oppression experienced by individuals with multiple minoritized identities (Ladson-Billings & Tate, 1995). For example, Black boys with disabilities experience exclusionary practices at school because of racism and ableism (Annamma et al., 2016). The last tenet, interest convergence, details the ways that racial progress or progress toward equity in schools only happens because the progress benefits whiteness as well (Ladson-Billings & Tate, 1995). For example, scholars note how the *Brown v Board of Education* ruling preserved the appearance of fairness and caring in whiteness while allowing for resegregation of public schools through other means, including special education (Ladson-Billings & Tate, 1995; Shell, 2020). When applied to MTSS, CRT premises assert that the continued inequities produced by the processes of MTSS are not happenstance.

Applying CRT as a foundational framework can help school counselors understand race and the impact of racism in schools and the systemic barriers and policies that twice-exceptional Black boys face. CRT provides a framework for school counselors to address issues of discrimination within the MTSS framework. Additionally, the use of CRT allows school counselors to conceptualize a culturally responsive, antiracist MTSS framework for addressing their own biases while creating systemic prevention and intervention supports.

Antiracist Multitiered Systems of Support

To create an antiracist MTSS framework, school counselors who are participating and co-creating those systems must engage in their own critical self-reflection and personal learning (Betters-Bubon et al., 2022; Hines et al., 2022). School personnel who lack a critical understanding of their biases and the impacts of culture on learning may construe their pedagogy and interventions as race-neutral or culturally neutral. Supposedly race-neutral or culturally neutral practices reify the normality of white supremacy while leaving biased or racist practices unchallenged and unmitigated in classrooms and schools (Howard & Navarro, 2016). Counselors in an antiracist MTSS framework need to have an awareness of their own dispositions, beliefs, intersectional identities, and cultural backgrounds and their power dynamics when interacting with students and communities (Khalifa et al., 2016; Ratts & Greenleaf, 2017). This critical self-awareness must be an iterative process that allows the school counselor to interrogate their own practices and mitigate potential oppressive practices (Khalifa et al., 2016; Ratts & Greenleaf, 2017). The process of developing a critical consciousness is especially important for school counselors as they contend with their beliefs about 2E Black boys and how school and community policies evince power, privilege, and oppression (Mayes & Byrd, 2022). Moreover, the development of a critical consciousness allows counselors to grasp the ways white supremacist ideals underpin every policy and law in the school and community (Mayes & Byrd, 2022). This critical consciousness permits school counselors to interrogate the ways prior school counseling prevention and intervention activities have actively harmed Black students, especially 2E Black boys (Hines et al., 2022; Mayes & Byrd, 2022). For example, critical consciousness and self-reflections allow school counselors to understand how they have contributed to disproportionality in both gifted and special education which limited educational access and success for Black students (Shell, 2020). Critical consciousness helps school counselors move beyond awareness to actions to disrupt white supremacist systems that reproduce sociohistorical inequities (Mayes & Byrd, 2022). Critical consciousness permits school counselors to honor the full humanity of 2E Black boys, their families, and their communities (Ladson-Billings, 2021).

Tier 1 – Universal

The Tier 1 level should ideally serve all students within the school (Sugai et al., 2019). School counselors can work in an MTSS team to review the school's curricula, policies, and procedures to determine how the policies reify white supremacist ideals of compliance, surveillance of minoritized students, or silencing the voices of students and their communities of care (Mayes & Byrd, 2022). As antiracist personnel, school counselors use both their critical consciousness and cultural responsiveness to examine their biases about Black boys and twice-exceptional Black boys. Then, they must work to dismantle curricula that exclude equitable access to the core curriculum for all students (Hines et al., 2022).

Assessment and Use of Data

As data-driven practitioners, school counselors collect and analyze data to assess inequities in student achievement for minoritized students, to determine equity in academic attainment and access to services, to evaluate school climate and culture, and to determine the school's professional development needs (Betters-Bubon et al., 2022; Hines et al., 2017; Shell, 2021). Further, school counselors use data to develop and implement their comprehensive school counseling programs and to create and monitor systems of accountability for redressing inequities, improving access to opportunities, and increasing equitable student academic, career, and social/emotional growth (Hines et al., 2017; Shell, 2021). The review of data should answer the following questions: Who was referred to special education? Which students were referred for gifted education or more rigorous courses? Which students are being referred to the office for discipline issues? What are my biases as we review data? What are the counter stories that may help explain the data? Which students are benefitting from the MTSS framework? Which students are disadvantaged by the MTSS framework? Using both qualitative and quantitative school data to answer these questions may frame prevention and intervention efforts for 2E Black boys. For example, if data shows that Black boys are disproportionately referred to the office for disciplinary issues, the team can investigate from whom the referrals originate (i.e., teachers and/or grade levels), types of interventions implemented, and what types of trainings or consultations might be required to disrupt the referral patterns and improve cultural responsiveness.

Collecting Counter Stories
Scholarship suggests that public schools and educators within them often blame minoritized students for their persistent challenges in education (Green, 2017; Khalifa et al., 2016). This blame shows up as deficit-oriented opinions and beliefs about minoritized students, their families, and communities and serves as a barrier to an equity-based educational environment (Khalifa et al., 2016). The prevailing narrative about individual and cultural deficits masks knowledge about systemic racism, concentrated poverty, and other inequitable community conditions (Green, 2017) and their effects on students and their families (Bryan et al., 2022). Twice exceptional Black boys suffer from the effects of deficit-oriented opinions and beliefs about their racial and disability identities (Mayes & Moore, 2016a). School counselor preparation and training provide tools to gather counter stories of 2E Black boys and their communities. Those counter stories allow school counselors to infuse strengths-based, culturally responsive, antiracist practices into counseling, consultation, and staff development interventions (Bryan et al., 2022; Mayes & Byrd, 2022; Schulz et al., 2014). Additionally, school counselors can evaluate and facilitate discussions regarding the contribution of school processes, adult actions and adult interactions to disparate school outcomes for 2E Black boys (Carter et al., 2017).

Consultation
School counselor access to data allows for disaggregation and examination to unearth inequitable patterns of referral for discipline or special education. This

data helps counselors target teachers for consultation, training, and difficult conversations about equity issues (Carter et al., 2017; Khalifa et al., 2016). Consultation is an essential skill for school counselors to use collaboratively with other stakeholders to create culturally responsive school settings (Hines et al., 2022; Schulz et al., 2014) and to discuss students' academic, behavioral, and/or socioemotional needs or outcomes (Shell, 2021). The collaborative nature of consultation permits school counselors and educational partners to find solutions to increase equity, access to educational opportunities, and create additional supports for students within the schools and their communities (Betters-Bubon et al., 2022; Hines et al., 2017). School counseling consultation with teachers and administrators reinforces improvements in pedagogy and access to educational opportunities in a culturally responsive school environment (Schulz et al., 2014).

Professional Development
The development of workshops/trainings for teachers, administrators, and staff members serves as an essential area of culturally responsive advocacy for school counselors (Schulz et al., 2014; Shell, 2021). These trainings promote a culturally responsive school environment by helping participants understand their multi-cultural identities, power and privilege within the school, and the school's socio-political dynamics to further the evaluation of the school's practices and mission (Schulz et al., 2014). Furthermore, the professional development helps to create anti-discriminatory practices by incorporating students' cultural and linguistic experiences into classroom guidance lessons (Hines et al., 2017; Mayes & Byrd, 2022) and promoting teachers' use of strengths-based approaches with minoritized students (Hines et al., 2017; Mayes & Byrd, 2022). The strengths-based training involves assisting school staff members to identify the cultural practices and assets in the students, their families, and communities and to infuse those assets into curricular activities to engage students and improve educational outcomes (Bryan et al., 2022; Schulz et al., 2014). The strengths-based approach provides a counter story to color-evasiveness/race-neutrality, deficit-laden beliefs about minoritized students and their communities, and behaviors that oppress 2E Black boys (Schulz et al., 2014; Shell, 2021).

Community Partnerships
Scholars encourage school counselors to develop and cultivate collaborations with community stakeholders and agencies to build antiracist practices within MTSS (Bryan et al., 2022). The collaborations often improve the schools' abilities to promote culturally responsive, antiracist school contexts, and culturally affirming school environments (Bryan et al., 2022; Hines et al., 2017). The partnerships prove invaluable in addressing inequities that 2E Black boys face with the caveat that schools alone cannot redress all inequities (Galloway & Ishimaru, 2017). Acting as facilitators with teachers, administrators, staff, students and their families, and community stakeholders allows school counselors to build supports and cultivate strengths to remove systemic barriers to school

success (Bryan et al., 2022; Hines et al., 2017). Community partnerships also provide opportunities for school counselors to learn about, address, and advocate for community-based issues that impact 2E Black boys and the ways that schooling has caused harm to those students as well (Bryan et al., 2022; Khalifa et al., 2016). The mutually beneficial, reciprocal nature of the partnership may mitigate challenges in the neighborhoods in which Black students live which, in turn, would improve educational outcomes for Black students (Green, 2017). School–community partnerships also engender mutual trust and welcoming environments between the schools and the communities in which they are embedded (Bryan et al., 2022).

Tier 2 – Targeted/Small Group Work

School counselors can incorporate antiracist practices in Tier 2 using a more targeted approach such as small groups. School counselors implement culturally responsive, antiracist counseling with small groups that emphasizes student empowerment while simultaneously focusing on strengths-based approaches that accentuate and incorporate students' cultural practices, worldviews, counter stories, talents, and gifts (Betters-Bubon et al., 2022; Hines et al., 2022; Mayes & Byrd, 2022; Shell, 2021). For example, small groups can assist 2E Black boys to address common challenges throughout the academic year and provide a supportive space (Edirmanasinghe et al., 2022; Hines et al., 2020). Small group approaches can help 2E Black boys work on positive identity development, understand their strengths and challenges as 2E students, and help students understand and navigate special education and gifted education processes (Mayes & Moore, 2016a).

To address systemic issues within the school, school counselors might offer small groups as workshops for administrators, faculty, and staff emphasizing topics such as strengths and challenges of 2E Black boys or community resources that serve as additional support for students and parents (Mayes & Moore, 2016a) to promote cultural responsiveness and antiracist praxis.

Tier 3 – Individualized

A subset of 2E Black boys may require additional supports where they receive interventions with increased frequency and duration. Tier 3 supports increase the intensity and duration of interventions (Sugai et al., 2019). School counselors can support 2E Black boys through individual counseling or specialized consultation on behalf of the students (Hines et al., 2022; Sugai et al., 2019). Critical consciousness is important as school counselors interrogate their biases about 2E Black boys and examine referral patterns and interventions to ascertain systemic biases that would lead to Tier 3 interventions (Hines et al., 2022). More importantly, tertiary interventions should continue to emphasize student empowerment, focus on strengths-based approaches for 2E Black boys, and interrogate the systemic oppression faced by 2E Black boys (Hines et al., 2022).

IMPLICATIONS FOR POLICY

In addition to practice, it is important to discuss implications for policy as policy often guides practices in K-12 schooling. Said differently, K-12 schools create and implement policies that not only indicate values and beliefs, but also what resources are embedded into school structures. As such, developing policies that center antiracism is paramount to the humanity and success of Black children, especially 2E Black boys (Hines et al., 2022). This includes dismantling zero-tolerance disciplinary policies and socioemotional policies and practices that perpetuate white supremacy (Drake & Oglesby, 2020; Hines et al., 2022). Further, dismantling restrictive gifted identification models that rely on culturally biased teacher referrals and tests in favor of holistic identification policies is needed. Instead, K-12 schools should create and implement culturally responsive policies that center restorative justice, Black joy, and student and family voice while sustaining homeplace (Mayes & Byrd, 2022; Mayes et al., 2022). These policies may include a gifted identification process that utilizes a multidisciplinary team including family and community members to assess student strengths in addition to the use of student portfolios to indicate creativity. This holistic identification process can be a part of a more comprehensive process to address gifted education from identification to enrollment and participation through the Gifted Program Advocacy Model (G-PAM; Grantham, 2003; Grantham et al., 2005).

Additionally, policy should reflect a commitment to culturally responsive training and practice for school counselors, educators, and administrators. Hines et al. (2022) recommend a policy at the district level that requires ongoing training in antiracist MTSS models to reflect the work needed across all tiers to ensure culturally responsive practice. This training should include a general framework and also sessions tailored to school counselors, educators, and administrators' unique roles in tier 1, 2, and 3 in order to address racism and ableism that may be embedded in each subsequent tier.

IMPLICATIONS FOR RESEARCH

More research is needed to not only capture 2E Black boys' experience holistically, but also to build strengths-based models that capture successes in K-12 schools. As such, much of the current empirical literature is based on small sample sizes that, while valuable, lack generalizability. This is perhaps a consequence of challenges within the identification process that contribute to the seemingly small "identified" 2E Black youth population. More research should take quantitative approaches that may engage in comparative studies across districts to understand factors that support or hinder academic, socioemotional, and career development for 2E Black boys. It would also be important to engage in inquiries that aim to understand within group differences among 2E Black boys. In particular, these studies may investigate differences related to disability (learning disability, autism, behavioral disorders) in addition to community context (i.e., socioeconomic status, enrollment in minority majority and predominately white schools, etc.). Future studies may also investigate the unique role and understandings of staff, such as school counselors and school psychologists in supporting the success of 2E Black boys. Results from these students can support the development of K-12 models aimed at 2E Black boys thriving regardless of school and community setting.

CONCLUSION

While Black boys may have a challenging road to navigate in K-12 schools, school counselors can offer support and guidance to meet their unique needs. Further, as school counselors engage in comprehensive antiracist practices, they can protect Black boys while challenging and building structures to support their success systemically. These antiracist practices allow for sustainable approaches that not only benefit 2E Black boys but all students who deserve to be seen for their brilliance, joy, and humanity.

AUTHOR NOTE

We recognize and acknowledge the labor upon which our country, state, and institution are built. We remember that our country was built on the labor of enslaved people who were kidnapped and brought to the United States from the African continent and recognize the continued contribution of their survivors. We also acknowledge all immigrant and indigenous labor, including voluntary, involuntary, trafficked, forced, and undocumented peoples who contributed to the building of the country and continue to serve within our labor force. We recognize that our country is continuously defined, supported, and built upon by oppressed communities and peoples. We acknowledge labor inequities and the shared responsibility for combatting oppressive systems in our daily work.

REFERENCES

American School Counselor Association. (2017). *The school counselor and school counseling programs.* https://schoolcounselor.org/Standards-Positions/Position-Statements/ASCAPosition-Statements/The-School-Counselor-and-School-Counseling-Program

American School Counselor Association. (2019a). *The ASCA national model: A framework for school counseling programs* (4th ed.). Author.

American School Counselor Association. (2019b). *The school counselor and gifted and talented programs.* https://schoolcounselor.org/Standards-Positions/Position-Statements/ASCA-Position-Statements/The-School-Counselor-and-Gifted-and-Talented-Stude

American School Counselor Association. (2021). *The school counselor and anti-racist practices.* https://www.schoolcounselor.org/Standards-Positions/Position-Statements/ASCA-Position-Statements/The-School-Counselor-and-Anti-Racist-Practices

Annamma, S. A., Jackson, D. D., & Morrison, D. (2016). Conceptualizing color-evasiveness: Using dis/ability critical race theory to expand a color-blind racial ideology in education and society. *Race, Ethnicity and Education, 20*(2), 147–162. https://doi.org/10.1080/13613324.2016.1248837

Belser, C., Shillingford, M., & Joe, J. (2016). The ASCA model and a multi-tiered system of supports: A framework to support students of color with problem behavior. *The Professional Counselor*, *6*(3), 251–262. https://doi.org/10.15241/cb.6.3.251

Betters-Bubon, J., Pianta, R., Sweeney, D., & Goodman-Scott, E. (2022). Antiracism starts with us: School counselor critical reflection within an MTSS framework. *Professional School Counseling*, *26*(1a), 34–56.

Bryan, J., Henry, L. M., Daniels, A. D., Edwin, M., & Griffin, D. M. (2022). Infusing an antiracist framework into school-family-community partnership. In C. Holcomb-McCoy (Ed.), *Antiracist counseling in schools and communities* (pp. 129–149). American Counseling Association.

Carter, P., Skiba, R., Arredondo, M., & Pollack, M. (2017). You can't fix what you don't look at: Acknowledging race in addressing racial discipline disparities. *Urban Education*, *52*(2), 207–235. https://doi.org/10.1177/0042085916660350

Drake, R., & Oglesby, A. (2020). Humanity is not a thing: Disrupting white supremacy in K-12 social emotional learning. *Journal of Critical Thought and Praxis*, *10*. https://doi.org/10.31274/jctp.11549

Edirmanasinghe, N., Goodman-Scott, E., Smith-Durkin, S., & Tarver, S. Z. (2022). Supporting all students: Multi-tiered systems of support from an antiracist and critical race theory lens. *Professional School Counseling*, *26*(1), 1–12. https://doi.org/10.1177/2156759X221109154

Edyburn, K. L., Bertone, A., Raines, T. C., Hinton, T., Twyford, J., & Dowdy, E. (2022). Integrating intersectionality, social determinants of health, and healing: A new training framework for school-based mental health. *School Psychology Review*, 1–23. https://doi:10.1080/2372966x.2021.2024767

Fallon, L. M., Veiga, M., & Sugai, G. (2021). Strengthening MTSS for behavior (MTSS-B) to promote racial equity. *School Psychology Review*, 1–16. https://doi.org/10.1080/2372966x.2021.1972333

Foley-Nicpon, M., & Assouline, S. G. (2015). Counseling considerations for the twice-exceptional client. *Journal of Counseling and Development*, *93*, 202–210. https://doi.org/10.1002/j.1556-6676.2015.00196x

Galloway, M. K., & Ishimaru, A. M. (2017). Equitable leadership on the ground: Converging on high-leverage practices. *Education Policy Analysis Archives*, *25*, 2. https://doi.org/10.14507/epaa.25.2205

Girvan, E. J., Gion, C., McIntosh, K., & Smolkowski, K. (2017). The relative contribution of subjective office referrals to racial disproportionality in school discipline. *School Psychology Quarterly*, *32*(3), 392.

Grantham, T. C. (2003). Increasing Black student enrollment in gifted programs: An exploration of the Pulaski County Special School District's advocacy efforts. *Gifted Child Quarterly*, *47*, 46–65.

Grantham, T. C., Frasier, M. M., Roberts, A. C., & Bridges, E. M. (2005). Parent advocacy for culturally diverse gifted students. *Theory into Practice*, *44*(2), 138–147.

Green, T. L. (2017). Enriching educational leadership through community equity literacy: A conceptual foundation. *Leadership and Policy in Schools*, *17*(4), 487–515. https://doi.org/10.1080/15700763.2017.1326148

Grothaus, T., Johnson, K. F., & Edirmanasinghe, N. (2020). *Culturally sustaining school counseling: Implementing diverse, equitable, inclusive programs*. American School Counseling Association.

Haugen, J. S., Bledsoe, K. G., Burgess, M., & Rutledge, M. L. (2021). Framework of anti-racist school counseling competencies: A delphi study. *Journal for Counseling Development*, 1–14. https://doi.org/10.1002/jcad.12422

Heidelburg, K., Phelps, C., & Collins, T. A. (2022). Reconceptualizing school safety for Black students. *School Psychology International*. https://doi.org/10.1177/01430343221074708

Hines, E. M., Hines, M. R., Moore, J. L., III, Steen, S., Singleton, P., II, Cintron, D., Traverso, K., Golden, M. N., Wathen, B., & Henderson, J. A. (2020). Preparing African American males for college: A group counseling approach. *Journal for Specialists in Group Work*, *45*(2), 129–145. https://doi.org/10.1080/01933922.2020.1740846

Hines, E. M., Mayes, R. D., Harris, P. C., & Vega, D. (2022). Using a culturally responsive MTSS approach to prepare Black males for postsecondary opportunities. *School Psychology Review*, 1–15.

Hines, E. M., Moore, J. L., Mayes, R. D., Harris, P. C., Vega, D., Robinson, D. V., Gray, C. N., & Jackson, C. E. (2017). Making student achievement a priority: The role of school counselors in turnaround schools. *Urban Education*, *55*(2), 216–237. https://doi.org/10.1177/0042085 916685761

Holcomb-McCoy, C. (2022). *Antiracist counseling in schools and communities*. American Counseling Association.

Howard, T. C., & Navarro, O. (2016). Critical race theory 20 years later: Where do we go from here? *Urban Education*, *51*(3), 253–273. https://doi.org/10.1177/0042085915622541

Khalifa, M. A., Gooden, M. A., & Davis, J. E. (2016). Culturally responsive school leadership. *Review of Educational Research*, *86*(4), 1272–1311. https://doi.org/10.3102/0034654316630383

Ladson-Billings, G. (2021). I'm here for the hard re-set: Post pandemic pedagogy to preserve our culture. *Equity & Excellence in Education*, *54*(1), 68–78. https://doi.org/10.1080/10665684.2020. 1863883

Ladson-Billings, G., & Tate, W. (1995). Toward a critical race theory of education. *Teachers College Record*, *97*(1).

Love, B. (2019). *We want to do more than survive: Abolitionist teaching and the pursuit of educational freedom*. Beacon Press.

Mayes, R. D. (2016). Educators' perceptions of twice exceptional African American males. *Journal of African American Males in Education*, *7*(1), 20–34.

Mayes, R. D., & Byrd, J. A. (2022). An antiracist framework for evidence-informed school counseling practice. *Professional School Counseling*, *26*(1a), 18–33.

Mayes, R. D., Harris, P. C., & Hines, E. M. (2016). Meeting the academic and socio-emotional needs of twice exceptional African American students through group counseling. In J. L. Davis & J. L. Moore, III (Eds.), *Gifted children of color around the world* (pp. 53–69). Information Age Publishing.

Mayes, R. D., Hines, E. M., & Harris, P. C. (2014). Working with twice-exceptional African American students: Information for school counselors. *Interdisciplinary Journal of Teaching and Learning*, *4*(2), 125–139.

Mayes, R. D., Hines, E. M., & Moore, J. L., III. (2018). When the rubber meets the road: Educating and supporting twice exceptional African American students. In S. B. Kaufman (Ed.), *Twice exceptional: Supporting and educating bright and creative students with learning difficulties* (pp. 290–298). Oxford University Press.

Mayes, R. D., & Moore, J. L., III. (2016a). The intersection of race, disability, and giftedness: Understanding the education needs of twice-exceptional, African American students. *Gifted Child Today*, *39*(2), 98–104.

Mayes, R. D., & Moore, J. L., III. (2016b). Adversity and pitfalls of twice exceptional urban learners. *Journal of Advanced Academics*, *27*(3), 167–189.

Mayes, R. D., Pianta, R., Oglesby, A., & Zyromski, B. (2022). Principles of antiracist social emotional justice learning. *Theory into Practice*, *61*(2), 178–187. https://doi.org/10.1080/00405841.2022. 2036063

Owens, C. M., Ford, D. Y., Lisbon, A. J., Jones, S. G., & Owens, M. T. (2016). Too bad to be gifted: Gifts denied for Black males with emotional and behavioral needs. *The Wisconsin English Journal*, *58*(2), 121–139.

Owens, C. M., Ford, D. Y., Lisbon, A. J., & Owens, M. T. (2016). Shifting paradigms to better serve twice-exceptional African-American learners. *Behavioral Disorders*, *41*(4), 196–208.

Ratts, M. J., & Greenleaf, A. T. (2017). Multicultural and social justice counseling competencies: A leadership framework for professional school counselors. *Professional School Counseling*, *21*(1b), 1–9. https://doi.org/10.1177/2156759X18773582

Schulz, L. L., Hurt, K., & Lindo, N. (2014). My name is not Michael: Strategies for promoting cultural responsiveness in schools. *Journal of School Counseling*, *12*(2). http://jsc.montana.edu/articles/v12n2.pdf

Shell, E. M. (2020). Exploring school counselors' preparation to address disproportionality of African American students in special education. *Teaching and Supervision in Counseling*, *2*(1). https://doi.org/10.7290/tsc020108

Shell, E. M. (2021). School counselors as leaders for social justice and equity. *Taboo: The Journal of Culture and Education, 20*(2), 58–71. https://digitalscholarship.unlv.edu/taboo/vol20/iss2/4

Shell, E. M., Johnson, L. V., & Getch, Y. Q. (2019). Good intentions, poor outcomes: Centering culture and language diversity within response to intervention. *Journal of School Counseling.* http://jsc.montana.edu/articles/v17n24.pdf

Simmons, D. (2019). How to be an antiracist educator. *ASCD.* https://www.ascd.org/el/articles/how-to-be-an-antiracist-educator

Smith-Durkin, S. D. (2022). *A phenomenological investigation of school counselor antiracist social justice practices.* Unpublished doctoral dissertation. Old Dominion University.

Sugai, G., La Salle, T. P., Everett, S., & Feinberg, A. B. (2019). Multi-tiered systems of support: The what, why, and how for school counselors. In E. Goodman-Scott, J. Betters-Bubon, & P. Donohue (Eds.), *The school counselor's guide to multi-tiered systems of support* (pp. 1–28). Routledge.

Ziomek-Daigle, J., Goodman-Scott, E., Cavin, J., & Donohue, P. (2016). Integrating a multi-tiered system of supports with comprehensive school counseling programs. *The Professional Counselor, 6*(3), 220–232. https://doi.org/10.15241/jzd.6.3.220

CHAPTER 8

CREATING POSITIVE ACADEMIC OUTCOMES FOR BLACK MALES: A SCHOOL COUNSELOR'S ROLE AS ADVOCATE AND CHANGE AGENT IN ELEMENTARY, MIDDLE, AND HIGH SCHOOL

Bobbi-Jo Wathen, Patrick D. Cunningham,
Paul Singleton II, Dejanell C. Mittman,
Sophia L. Ángeles, Jessica Fort, Rickya S. F. Freeman
and Erik M. Hines

ABSTRACT

School counselors are committed to serving students' social-emotional, post-secondary, and academic needs while they navigate primary and secondary school (American School Counselor Association, 2019). Much has been said about the ways in which school counselors can impact postsecondary outcomes and social emotional health. It is important that we also address the ways school counselors can impact positive academic outcomes as it is intertwined in postsecondary options and success. For Black males, academic success has traditionally been met with systemic barriers (i.e., school-to-prison pipeline, lower graduation rates, lower incomes, higher unemployment rates, and lower college going rates (National Center for Edcuation Statisitics, 2019a, 2019b, 2020a, 2020b) and low expectations. School counselors are charged to be

Black Males in Secondary and Postsecondary Education
Advances in Race and Ethnicity in Education, Volume 9, 141–161
Copyright © 2024 Bobbi-Jo Wathen, Patrick D. Cunningham, Paul Singleton II, Dejanell C. Mittman,
Sophia L. Ángeles, Jessica Fort, Rickya S. F. Freeman and Erik M. Hines
Published under exclusive licence by Emerald Publishing Limited
ISSN: 2051-2317/doi:10.1108/S2051-231720230000009008

leaders and change agents for social justice and equity in our schools by the American School Counselor Association (ASCA, 2019) and can impact systemic change. This chapter will explore ways in which school counselors can impact positive academic outcomes for Black males. School counselors as change agents and advocates are positioned to make a real impact for Black male academic success. The authors will also provide some recommendations and best practices for elementary, middle, and high school counselors as they work with students, teachers, and families from an anti-deficit model as outlined by Harper (2012).

Keywords: Black males; school counselors; academic success; change agents; social justice; anti-deficit

INTRODUCTION

Society has developed a stereotypical perception of Black males as being "...hostile, volatile, academically inferior, and emotionally disturbed" (Holcomb-McCoy, 2007, p. 255), viewed through deficit lens which permeates the perception of educators and the systemic framework of educational policies and practices (Rhoden, 2017). These perceptions have impacted access to rigorous coursework, school discipline, perceptions of college readiness, and perceptions of emotional regulation (cite). Furthermore, in 1999, Steele wrote about the ways in which stereotype threat has created extreme performance anxiety that has sabotaged the success of Black males in education settings.

These are not just perceptions; the NAEP 2019 test reported that 82% of Black students are below proficiency in reading and 89% in mathematics in the fourth grade. By eighth grade, those numbers increase to 85% and 86%, respectively, and by 12th grade, students scoring below proficiency in math for Black students rise to 92% (National Center for Education Statistics, 2019a). Black male students are also going to and completing college at lower rates than their peers, becoming incarcerated at higher rates, and these differences in achievement are worrisome to families, school districts, and teachers alike.

While school counselors are not classroom teachers and do not teach academic content, they are charged with supporting academic growth and advocating for fair and equitable access to academic opportunities within schools. School counselors focus their work in three domains in their work within schools: academic, social/emotional, and career (ASCA, 2020). School counselors have a unique view of schools and systems as their work requires a consultation model to serve all stakeholders in schools (Dinkmeyer & Carlson, 2006). Because of this viewpoint on student success, school counselors work through a holistic approach that includes things like executive functioning and social/emotional well-being while keeping postsecondary goals in mind. In this chapter, we will outline some concrete strategies for school counselor, researchers, and policymakers in elementary, middle, and high schools as they support positive academic outcomes for Black males.

LITERATURE REVIEW
Mental Health

Although the focus of this chapter is on the academic outcomes of Black males in elementary, middle, and high school, it is impossible to separate academic outcomes from their ecological and social/emotional roots. According to Maslow's (1943) Hierarchy of Needs, individuals are motivated to fulfill basic needs, including food, safety, love, and self-esteem, before addressing more complex needs such as self-actualization. Similarly, students' learning and achievement in school are impacted by social determinants of health, including food insecurity, socioeconomic status, incarceration rates, and neighborhood quality and safety, as well as mental health and well-being (Burleson & Thoron, 2014; Xanthos et al., 2010). Ultimately, as a group, Black males are disproportionately impacted by social/systemic factors as well as mental health challenges, adversely impacting overall rates of academic success (Cokley et al., 2014; Walker, 2021; Xanthos et al., 2010).

One important indicator of the mental health of Black males is the suicide rate, which has been increasing by 73% for Black youth (Congressional Black Caucus, 2019). Additionally, the suicide rate is significantly higher for Black males as compared to Black females (Centers for Disease Control and Prevention, 2021). While there are many underlying factors that likely contribute to this troubling trend, it is important to consider factors such as trauma exposure, lack of mental health support, and criminalization of behavior (Cokley et al., 2014; Holcomb-McCoy, 2022; Walker, 2021; Walker & Goings, 2017). First, it is important to acknowledge that Black students tend to encounter traumatic experiences at a higher rate than their white peers due to disparate policies in schools and the community (Walker, 2021). These traumatic experiences may include racial trauma, exclusionary discipline practices in schools, community trauma, and individual exposure to traumatic experiences (Walker, 2021; Walker & Goings, 2017), which are associated with increases in mental health challenges including anxiety, depression, and externalizing behaviors (Cokley et al., 2014; Walker & Goings, 2017). Unfortunately, a lack of access to mental health services tends to accompany these mental health challenges faced by Black males, as demonstrated by inequities regarding rates of mental health diagnosis, access to treatment, and treatment prognosis (Holcomb-McCoy, 2022). In schools, when Black males display externalizing behaviors associated with the trauma they've experienced, their behavior tends to be criminalized, leading to exclusionary discipline practices or experiences with school resource officers (Cokley et al., 2014). Additionally, research demonstrates that even when they do receive mental health support, Black and brown people in America tend to receive lower quality care than their white peers (Agency for Healthcare Research and Quality, 2017).

Family Engagement

Another factor that has been shown to relate to student academic outcomes is school–family–community (SFC) partnerships. More specifically, research has suggested that partnerships between schools and families built on trust and two-way communication lead to more successful academic outcomes for students (Bryk & Schneider, 2002; Henderson & Mapp, 2002; Hill & Tyson, 2009; Jeynes, 2015). Unfortunately, family engagement practices in schools tend to follow an inequitable and outdated model of involvement that prioritizes showing up to events or meetings at school or volunteering in the classroom (Ishimaru, 2019). These institutional scripts about parent involvement contribute to the further marginalization of families who cannot or choose not to participate in education in this way, leading to attitudes of judgment and blame (Ishimaru, 2019). Educators who ascribe to the outdated model of parent involvement see families as the primary reason for educational disparities, believing that families who do not ascribe to their views of engagement either do not care or do not value their child's education. These beliefs disproportionately impact Black families, as they are more likely to work multiple jobs or work hours that make it difficult for them to attend school functions (Turney & Kao, 2009). Additionally, some families may choose not to engage directly with the school due to past negative experiences with school from their childhood or as a parent (Bergman & Mapp, 2021). And when educators ascribe to outdated beliefs regarding family engagement, it can further exacerbate racial inequities in schools (Ishimaru, 2019).

Families' lack of involvement in the traditional sense does not mean that they do not care about their child or their academic success, and it also does not mean that they are not engaging in their child's education at home. In fact, home-based engagement practices are the most effective form of family engagement (DeSpain et al., 2018; Epstein et al., 2018). To promote more equitable outcomes for Black males in education, a shift in educational practices around family engagement is needed, emphasizing the value of families and home-based engagement strategies. School counselors play a vital role in advancing this work in schools (Bryan, 2005; Bryan & Henry, 2008, 2012; Bryan & Holcomb-McCoy, 2007).

Academic Access

Unfortunately, Black male students are consistently at a disadvantage in the educational system. It is well-documented that schools have failed to adequately serve Black males (Howard, 2010). From the onset of their educational trajectories, young Black males are already at a disadvantage as they enter kindergarten approximately nine months behind in reading and math. Less developed reading and math skills at kindergarten entry are significant predictors of later school success (Friedman-Krauss et al., 2016). Moreover, Black students often attend under resourced schools with a larger number of inexperienced teachers (Darling-Hammond, 2001). As students, they are more likely to be retained (National Center for Education Statistics, 2019b).

More worrisome is the fact that young Black males are susceptible to disciplinary actions at higher rates than their non-Black peers (Riddle & Sinclair, 2019). For example, during the 2018–2019 academic year, Black preschool students "accounted for 18.2% of total preschool enrollment but received 43.3% of one or more out of school suspensions" (U.S. Department Of Education, Office For Civil Rights, 2021, p. 7). Relatedly, Black youth tend to be over diagnosed with oppositional defiant disorder and conduct disorder (Fadus et al., 2020) though they are least likely to receive a diagnosis of ADHD (Coker et al., 2016). It is these exclusionary practices that keep young Black male students out of the classroom in the most formative academic learning years.

The trend continues through high school where Black males have higher dropout rates, lower participation in college level coursework, and are identified through special education services more (Hines et al., 2020; Natinal Center for Education Satisitics, 2020a). The trends and perceptions of Black males as they enter public education continue to hold them hostage and only increase in severity as they progress through k-12 systems.

College and Career Readiness

The trends that began at the start of schooling continue to plague Black males as they enter college and/or the workforce. Black males had the highest unemployment rate in the Q2 2021 jobs report at 7.1% (US Bureau of Labor Statistics, 2021). While jobs increased across the board in 2022, Black males did not see the same gains. In Q1 of 2022 to white males saw a 6.5% increase, while Black males only saw a 3% increase in full time employment (US Bureau of Labor Statistics, 2022).

Black males continue to have the lowest college enrollment rates of the male population (Natinal Center for Education Statistics, 2020a). Black males are enrolling in college at 34% which is only 3% lower than white males. However, completion rates for Black males are only 16%, while white males are completing college at 32% (Schott, 2015). Much has been written about how to support Black males as they explore and enroll in college. Research points to leveraging mentorships, school–family connections, culturally sustaining practices, and services that school counselors provide to held Black males as they explore and transition to college (Bryan et al., 2012; Hines et al., 2020; Holcomb-McCoy, 2022).

RECOMMENDATIONS

Elementary School Counselors

Elementary school represents the foundation for academic and social development for children. It is during these formidable years that students learn to read, write, problem-solve, and interact with peers and adults outside of their family. Through a positive and supportive elementary experience, children are empowered to matriculate through school with the skills, mindsets, and behaviors necessary to succeed.

Recommendations for Research
Academically, Black males' low performance reflects the "cumulative effect of systemic challenges evident in many minoritized communities" (Wint et al., 2022, p. 196). More precisely, these disparities are largely due to the opportunity gap. According to Griffin et al. (2021), the opportunity gap "focus[es] on the unequal and inequitable distribution of educational resources and opportunities that result in radically different levels of academic success for children based on their race" (pp. 1–2). When students are provided with educational resources and opportunities, academic achievement can be improved (Kim, 2006). In agreement with scholars like Moore et al. (2021) who argue that the "aforementioned education trends among young men and boys of color is nauseating and necessitates a sense of urgency for practical education solutions and policies" (p. 1). Much of the current research demonstrates these points in high school students; there is not sufficient research that points specifically to elementary school students, especially when it comes to early identification of gifted Black male students.

Recommendations for Practicing School Counselors
We highlight specific ways in which elementary school counselors, who are trained to be agents of change and educational leaders, can leverage resources to affirm the resiliency of Black males and their families to ensure their educational advancement. In what follows, we detail practices elementary school counselors can engage with the stakeholders in their community, including other teachers, students, and families. These practices help change the narrative and produce positive academic outcomes for Black males.

Elementary school is a main entry point into a school system for families. Often the way in which a family is welcomed into a system can have a large impact on the way in which that family engages with that school system, and therefore impacting their child's experience in school. School counselors contribute to family involvement and advocating for the academic needs of their students. One thoroughly researched way to affect change for Black males is through SFC partnerships (Bryan & Henry, 2012). These partnerships can provide support, programs, and opportunities that Black males need to succeed academically (Griffin et al., 2021). School counselors can serve as the catalyst in forming these partnerships which will in turn create opportunities for family members to be involved with their child's education and promote strategies that will address academic challenges and systemic racial bias (Bryan & Henry, 2012). As school counselors seek to implement SFC partnerships, it is important for them to consider models that highlight the following equity-focused principles: democratic collaboration, empowerment, social justice, and strengths (Griffin et al., 2021). These foci ensure equitable opportunities and resources all while building partnerships with families and communities.

Recommendations for Policy

To ensure that more Black males have access to school counselors in elementary school, educational policymakers and politicians must work together to enact policies that prioritize the hiring of elementary school counselors. Currently, only 23 states in addition to the District of Columbia ensure that K to eighth graders have access to school counseling (American School Counselor Association, 2022). Access to school counselors must also be met with protections that ensure that school counselors have manageable caseloads of students so that they may deliver "programs [that] are comprehensive in scope, preventive in design and developmental in nature" (American School Counselor Association, 2019, par. 1). The evidence is clear that when students have access to not only school counselors but can interact with them frequently via individual counseling sessions, small groups, and guidance lessons, students gain greater opportunities to succeed academically (Steen & Kaffenberger, 2007).

Middle School Counselors

Recommendations for Research

The impact of the school counselor has led researchers to look beyond the classroom and counseling office to see how school counselors can account for and create positive outcomes for African American males. Researchers contend that understanding the experiences and success strategies of Black male students is critical in that it can counter prevailing narratives of academic deficits which have dominated education literature (Howard et al., 2016; Warren et al., 2016). Further, it is important to note that the available research on the experiences of Black males who excel and have positive academic outcomes due to their interaction with a school counselor has been conducted primarily at the high school level (Hackett et al., 2018) or college level (Brooms, 2021), but limited when focusing on Black males in middle school (Nelson, 2016). We recommend that researchers explore this specifically with middle school Black males.

There are various factors like school–family involvement, community, and educational perspective, and relationships that strongly influence Black male achievement (Nelson, 2016; Wint et al., 2021). Consequently, understanding the lives and experiences of Black males is critical in addressing negative school experiences and developing positive practices that facilitate academic excellence (Hackett et al., 2018). Promoting and teaching excellence is central in middle school when social and educational demands begin to increase due to developmental changes and the transition from elementary school to middle school (Mintro, 2014).

Recommendations for Practicing School Counselors

Middle school is a vulnerable time for young males. Not only are they learning more independence, but they are also navigating a confusing time as many begin to experience the symptoms of puberty. Trust is essential at this point of development. Several researchers have examined the impact of relationships and trust in Black males finding that trust (in oneself, in others, and in the institution) can influence Black males' academic achievements while also serving as a form of motivation for Black males to continue to strive for and achieve their vision of a successful postsecondary outcome (Brooms, 2017; Carey, 2018; Huerta et al., 2013; Rhoden, 2017). This idea was furthered by Holland (2015) who found trust to be a critical factor in creating successful student–counselor relationships that could facilitate access to vital college information and improve help-seeking behaviors.

We recommend that counselors emphasize a commitment to cultivating trust and understanding between the counselor and student. Consider how the various structures and systems shape the schooling experience of Black males from their perspective (Howard et al., 2016). Empathy and understanding leads to stronger trust between the counselor and student. According to Bryk and Schneider (2002), trust is characterized by four main aspects: respect, personal regard, competence in core responsibilities, and personal integrity.

Due to the various academic and achievement gaps that Black males face and the need to create more positive outcomes, building relational trust should be considered important for counselors to foster with Black males, so they can be empowered to attain their educational goals. According to Bryk and Schneider (2002), relational trust is the social exchanges of schooling organized around a distinct set of role relationships. For school counselors, relational trust focuses on the amount and extent that they are willing to commit to in order to create a positive schooling environment that will lead to positive outcomes for Black males (Bryk & Schneider, 2002; Rhoden, 2017) also viewed this relationship of trust as an essential component of a student's educational experience because it plays a significant role in how they build relationships and also how those relationships can be leveraged. Trust is important when considering to support the needs of Black males (Howard et al., 2016; Rhoden, 2017).

High School Counselors

Recommendations for Research

Black males are historically placed at a disadvantage long before they step into high school and have been historically identified as at risk and marginalized within the education system (Rhoden, 2017). For some Black males, resistance to negative perceptions is exhibited through refusal of positioning practices and dominant ideologies that contribute to such disparities and instead correlate the acquisition of education to access to power (Allen, 2017). For others, these stereotypes are internalized, and resistance comes in the form of disengagement, exhibiting behaviors that minimize academic success (Allen, 2017). By high school, we see the impact of these factors in alarming numbers for Black males in comparison to their white peers. Research shows that they are disproportionately placed in special education (Gardner et al., 2014) and overrepresented in exclusionary discipline (Bottiani et al., 2017) which both contribute to higher dropout rates and impedes postsecondary success. When the research continues to expose such trends in data, it illuminates the need to further examine how to produce positive academic outcomes for Black male students at the high school level.

According to the American School Counselor Association (2019), school counselors are culturally responsive, and data-driven practitioners are uniquely positioned in schools to help address the academic, social/emotional, college, and career needs of students. The training of school counselors equips them with the skills needed to create interventions that address barriers of marginalized communities (Cook Sandifer & Gibson, 2020). At the high school level, it becomes imperative for school counselors to engage in proactive leadership and advocacy when working with Black males (Carey & Dimmitt, 2012). To ensure students are being supported holistically, considering their cultural and ethnic backgrounds, school counselors must advocate for equitable practices and policies that work to improve educational experiences (American School Counseling Association, 2021a). It continues to be important that research explores the ways in which school counselors can be change agents, as ASCA recommends, for the benefit of Black males' academic outcomes. This is especially important in the changing landscape of education and the challenges students are coming to school with postpandemic.

Recommendations for Practicing School Counselors
It is common for Black males to be taught by educators who view them through a deficit lens and project low expectations of success (Goings & Shi, 2018). Black males are more likely to be placed in lower-level courses and less likely to be identified as gifted and talented in comparison to their white peers (Bailey & Paisley, 2004). The lack of recommendations for Black males into rigorous courses deemed essential for academic postsecondary preparation can be attributed to the implicit biases of educators (Johnson, 2020). To address this concern, it is imperative for school counselors to develop and maintain a strong belief that all students, no matter their race, have the ability to achieve high levels of success (Uwah et al., 2008). In addition, it is equally important to use data to guide students into rigorous courses that align with their postsecondary goals (Paolini, 2019). Some schools even implement "challenge by choice" policies that allow students to enroll in rigorous coursework without a required recommendation by a teacher. School counselors should have conversations with families and students about these opportunities and discuss student strengths as they are enrolling in coursework.

Recommendations for Policy
Late high school students are at higher risk of entering the justice system as both juveniles and adults. There are specific combinations of charges and age that can land a 16-year-old in prison with adults' long lasting involvement in the justice system. To address disproportionate discipline, policies must be revised to decrease the overrepresentation of Black males. Zero tolerance policies first emerged in the 1980s, heavily used by the federal government to address

drug-related crimes (Kyere et al., 2020). It was then adopted in schools and gave life to exclusionary discipline measures that inflicted more so upon Black males leading to dropout and incarceration (Greer sr & Webb, 2020). Widely adopted discipline measures fueled the school-to-prison pipeline that largely affects Black male students (Gonsoulin et al., 2012). Kyere et al. (2020) posits that instead of embedding zero-tolerance policies in disciplinary measures, schools should aim to create responsiveness that reflects racial and cultural sensitivity. Inserting more restorative justices practices talked about earlier will ensure that students are in the classroom more and engaged with the community positively.

RECOMMENDATIONS FOR K-12

The recommendations above highlight research, practice, and policy for specific grade levels; however, we found that there are many recommendations that are applicable across K-12 education that are important to discuss.

Recommendations for Practicing School Counselors

Informing Culturally Responsive Practices Among School Staff
Black male students are denied equal and equitable access to learning opportunities because of systematic racial bias (Griffin et al., 2021). There is also evidence of systematically biased teacher expectations: studies have shown that non-Black teachers have lower educational expectations for Black students than Black teachers (Bryan et al., 2012). As school counselors, it is critical to collaborate with teachers and school staff on behalf of African American students to confront and combat implicit biases and negative expectations of Black males. School counselors can help school stakeholders adopt culturally responsive thinking through the reading and discussion of certain anti-racist texts (Griffin et al., 2021) and encouraging teachers to use culturally responsible materials, like cultural modeling, that engage African Americans in the learning process (Bryan et al., 2012).

Utilizing Multitiered Systems of Support (MTSS) in Conjunction With the Comprehensive Counseling Program
School counselors can have a lasting impact on behavior development and student academic success through MTSS (Ziomek-Daigle et al., 2016). MTSS provides an evidenced-based framework for both instruction and intervention that improve learning outcomes for students. Through participation in MTSS teams, school counselors can work to problem-solve and make informed decisions about the academic output of African American males. School counselors should strive to know the systems of support and ensure that implementation of intervention is done with fidelity before a decision is made about important things like course placement, diagnoses, and special education. Through MTSS, school counselors should advocate for equitable education and work to remove systemic barriers (ASCA, 2021b).

Perception and Peer Capital

Black males must be viewed as whole people, in need of social, emotional, physiological, academic, and intellectual support. This support cannot be based on guilt or out of pity for their circumstances. Nor should it strip them of the agency, cultural practices, language, and resourcefulness that these young men bring to school with them. One way to do this is by cultivating empathy and connectedness as a professional disposition of our counselors and teachers regardless of bias or differences (Whitford & Emerson, 2019). Due to school counselors being change agents and based on their training in culturally responsive counseling, school counselors can offer details for thinking about how to help teachers to see the world from students' social and cultural points of view (O'Connor, 2018).

Stakeholders within a school aspiring to support Black males should refrain from internalizing and passing on negative stories or depictions of young men of color based on their past mistakes (Warren, 2014). Educators must look beyond a young man's behavior characteristic of "disengagement" or "resistance" and rather look to understand how such feelings developed over time (Warren, 2014). The impact of factors such as teacher bias, learning environments, discipline practices, home environments, and disparities in a family's economic resources can prove to be an ongoing barrier for Black males (Howard et al., 2016). Thus, it is important for school counselors to not only display a genuine desire to understand the root causes of the various factors that may inhibit a student but also be proactive, rather than reactive when fostering relationships with their students.

It can be equally beneficial to create and invest in clubs, groups, and organizations that create a sense of community in middle school settings, as well as in out-of-school contexts (Grant et al., 2021). Schools and school counselors must carve out a defined space where young men of color can self-affirm, provide one another multiple forms of support, and receive mentorship and access to men of color who provide multiple images of success. If these spaces cannot be created, Black males will likely create these spaces and avenues of support on their own (Howard et al., 2016). Schools need to permit and encourage the organic development of such spaces and brotherhood among Black males, especially in schools where they are underrepresented (Howard et al., 2016).

Special Education Practices

Black males are overrepresented in special education primarily due to subjective and unreliable practices in the identification process (Adkison-Bradley et al., 2006). To address this, there must be emphasis placed on revising the referral process. School counselors need to be more involved in the referral and placement process by evaluating the external and internal factors that inhibit student achievement and using data to properly inform and guide proposed recommendations (Adkison-Bradley et al., 2006). They can do so by disaggregating the data by race, gender, and socioeconomic status and develop intervention strategies to provide students the academic support needed (Ford & Russo, 2016). It is important for educators to differentiate their instruction to meet the needs of students to ensure they have equitable access to education (Gardner et al., 2014). Additionally, educators must develop the skills necessary to understand culturally influenced behaviors, such as speech and language differences, and disassociate them from being a learning disability to instead seeing an opportunity for increased regular education support (Gardner et al., 2014). A critical component of this process is parent collaboration. It is common for parents to be uninformed of the intricate details of the planning and placement team and may lack an understanding of how their student is being assessed and identified. School counselors can intervene by delivering information to families through online platforms and informational to support them in advocating for their child (Ford & Russo, 2016).

Addressing Discipline Disparities
Black males are more likely to have higher rates of exclusionary discipline such as suspensions, expulsions, and office referrals (Bottiani et al., 2017). The more they are excluded from the classroom, the higher the risk of dropping out of high school becomes (Allen, 2017). Due to self-concept and identity issues, Black males typically will dissociate from school and exhibit disengaged behaviors that tend to be misinterpreted by school staff leading to exclusionary discipline and retention (Tatum, 2006). It is imperative to develop interventions that aim to address student behaviors and teach self-regulating skills. Social emotional learning should be incorporated into the skills taught to Black males to help them learn positive coping strategies to improve emotional regulation and increase positive behaviors (Smith et al., 2017). Restorative justice practices (RJP) can be used to implement social emotional learning. RJP is a tiered approach that addresses student behavior through the lens of repairing harm and teaching essential skills to decrease misbehavior and increase emotional and physical awareness (Smith et al., 2017). School counselors can engage in conversations with students that seek to resolve the harm done to the school environment and aim to teach an understanding of self-awareness and accountability opposed to punitive punishment (Smith et al., 2017). They can then discuss ways for the student to repair the harm done to the school environment and allow them to continue to be a part of the greater school community. An RJP tool includes facilitated individual conversations or circles which involve members of the community of whom the undesired behaviors impacted (Smith et al., 2017) The social/emotional development skills of school counselors make them highly qualified and ideal candidates for coordinating restorative practice initiatives and training for students and staff (Smith et al., 2017). These learning opportunities can help students learn to regulate emotions and, therefore, keep them engaged in learning in the classroom.

Mental Health

According to the Council for Accreditation of Counseling and Related Educational Programs (2016), school counseling programs are required to provide training that addresses the characteristics and warning signs of trauma and crisis which reflect courses taught in mental health programs. School counselors should be able to shift their attention toward the mental health needs of students as an early intervention effort to help improve overall student well-being and academic success (ASCA, 2019). Black teens commonly have limited access to mental health support and are less likely to seek it (Banks, 2021) The negative stigmas around mental health concerns have deterred Black males away from seeking support (Lindsey et al., 2010). Counseling groups led by school counselors to support Black male mental health need to foster a safe space for them to learn social and emotional coping skills (Furey, 2015). We offer this focus as an academic intervention because we understand that when students are struggling with mental health, they are not able to access parts of their brain that allow for skills needed to academic success like memory recall, processing new learning, and critical thinking skills.

Recommendations for Policy

School Counselor Duties

Ensuring real change requires policy and legislation practices that meet the needs of Black males and works to close the opportunity gap. Educational leaders must be wary of the policies that constrain school counselors' abilities to address "systemic inequities and opportunity gaps" which lead to the educational disenfranchisement of young Black males (Griffin et al., 2021, p. 11). It is imperative that educational leaders at the district-level or site-level do not impose noncounseling duties (e.g., attendance and registration) (Dollarhide et al., 2007) upon school counselors. Burdening school counselors with noncounseling duties prevents them from engaging in "interventions associated with positive student outcomes," including counseling, consultation, curriculum, and coordination (Scarborough & Culbreth, 2008, p. 455). Equally important is ensuring that school districts clearly define the role of school counselors, and that this role is understood by school principals. Finally, it would behoove administrators to become familiar with the American School Counselor Association (ASCA) National Model and, subsequently, school counselors' appropriate roles, given that this is positively correlated with implementation of a school counseling program (Fye et al., 2017).

Professional Development

While school counselors are the advocates and change agents, they do not work in silos. School districts should also offer professional development specifically geared toward African American male achievement. An example of a school district that prioritized equity and diversity for Black males was the *Guilford County African American Male Initiative*. The school district conducted several professional development sessions and was able to demonstrate how building meaningful student–teacher relationships led to fewer office referrals, more equitable approaches to discipline, and increased culturally responsive literacy instruction (Brinkley et al., 2018). Lastly, a concerted anti-racist effort by all stakeholders should inform all staff training to ensure the academic achievement of Black males.

Leveraging Capital (Community, Peers, and Self)
There are numerous examples of interventions aimed specifically at bridging the gap that Black males face in regard to academic achievement. In fact, these programs in their various incarnations (e.g., mentoring programs and community wrap-around services) have been positioned as innovative strategies for confronting the academic issues that have plagued African American male students (Washington, 2010). Establishing school–community partnerships that are ingrained in the school's policy is crucial. SFC partnerships are "collaborative initiatives and relationships among school personnel, family members, and community members and representatives of community-based organizations such as universities, businesses, religious organizations, libraries, and health and social service agencies" (Bryan & Henry, 2012).

These types of partnerships can create a space for Black males and community members to support one another and develop trust across disparate demographics and diverse social and community groups (Davidson & Case, 2018). While the school/institutions are important, there are community-based spaces that can help Black male achievement. Policies, practices, and partnerships that acknowledge, incentivize, and even replicate effective pedagogies and leadership in community-based spaces (e.g., community centers and barbershops) should be encouraged (Green, 2017).

The research on SFC partnerships indicates that they have positive academic, social, and behavioral outcomes for many children (Henry, 2014). In recent years, it has been found that when schools, families, and communities partner together to assist children, academic achievement outcomes, such as achievement scores, discipline referrals, and attendance, all improve with academic achievement increasing across all sociodemographics (Henderson & Mapp, 2002). By creating policy that leverages SFC partnerships, students will be provided valuable resources that will address issues of concern such as the disproportionate referrals and suspensions or low achievement of Black male students. Further, these partnerships create opportunities and spaces for stakeholders to become more engaged in their student's education (Bryan & Henry, 2012; Garrow & Kaggwa, 2012). We recommend that policymakers use this research and further research to make informed policy, especially in a postpandemic school environment.

Reshaping the Special Education Referral Process
There is a need for reshaping the identification process for special education to reflect the initiatives set out in the Individuals with Disabilities Education Act

(IDEA) which considers cultural differences which minimize discriminatory practices in regards to socioeconomic status and personal bias (Gardner et al., 2014). For example, the Board of Assessment and Testing states that IQ tests used in the identification process do not reflect the cultural or social experience of Black males and, therefore, need revision (Adkison-Bradley et al., 2006). IDEA includes clear guidelines to help monitor racial disparity. For example, schools must examine disaggregated data, review disciplinary measures, and use assessments that are evidence-based and consider cultural and linguistic differences (Gardner et al., 2014). Moving away from racially biased assessments like the IQ test as a primary tool for identification is recommended. Referrals should be monitored to examine any recurring trends (Ford & Russo, 2016), which will help illuminate factors contributing to disproportionately.

Cultural Sustainability Training
Stakeholders in education must provide and mandate adequate and effective training for school counselors and staff members to strengthen their cultural sustainability skills. Mandated training in these areas will allow educators to gain a deeper understanding of the multilayered factors that contribute to student identity and aid in minimizing judgment (Howard et al., 2016). School leaders should collaborate with outside partners, such as local universities and consultants, to incorporate seminars and training around cultural competency to recognize and address unintended bias (Holcomb-McCoy, 2022). Every Student Succeeds Act is designed to hold schools accountable in creating systems that address the inequities in education that students of color face and look to improve postsecondary outcomes (Cook-Harvey et al., 2016) Policies that embed cultural sustainability within their curriculum will increase student engagement (Butler, 2003). When coursework has cultural relevance and provokes a sense of connection to the content, it is likely that students will be invested and engaged in curriculum.

LIMITATIONS

School counselors play a vital role in the academic development of Black males in schools. Recent research on the impact of the COVID-19 pandemic on learning outcomes for students shows that educational disparities are becoming more extreme, especially for Black males (Banks, 2021; Bansak & Starr, 2021). While all children and adolescents have been impacted by the pandemic in some way, whether through school closures and disrupted learning or more serious issues like food and shelter insecurity, the pandemic's impact has had a disproportionate impact on those children who were already vulnerable (Dorn et al., 2020; Van Lancker & Parolin, 2020). Impacting the most basic level of need, increased job loss led to increases in food and home insecurity (Van Lancker & Parolin, 2020). Additionally, teens have reported increased feelings of depression, stress, and anxiety, while their perceptions of the availability of adults to talk to when feeling stressed have decreased (YouthTruth, 2021).

As was emphasized earlier, academic achievement is greatly impact by physical security and mental health (Burleson & Thoron, 2014; Maslow, 1943; Xanthos et al., 2010). Research has demonstrated that the pandemic has generated significant disruptions in learning for students, resulting in large groups of students starting the 2021–2022 school year half of a grade-level behind their contemporaries in reading and math (Bansak & Starr, 2021). When compounded by issues regarding safety and security as well as the mental health concerns mentioned previously, there is a concern that these disruptions could have long-lasting impacts on historically minoritized groups including Black males (Van Lacker & Parolin, 2020). This is especially true because Black students were more likely to have their education moved to remote learning (Oster et al., 2021) and less likely to have access to stable internet during this period of online learning (Dorn et al., 2020).

It is the responsibility of school counselors to act as advocates on behalf of Black males, who have been impacted by growing academic disparities that have been created systemic injustice and exaggerated by the pandemic (Holcomb-McCoy, 2022). To do this, school counselors should operate with an anti-racist lens, utilizing data and their comprehensive school counseling program to identify opportunities to elevate academic opportunities and outcomes for Black males. As we discussed in this chapter, school counselors have a wide range of advocacy tools at all levels of K-12 education that can and should be enacted while the nation responds to the aftermath of the pandemic.

CONCLUSION

In this chapter, we have talked in depth about the ways in which the education system has failed Black male students. There are repeated and compounded issues that plague Black males at every level of their journey through education. School counselors, policymakers, and researchers have a responsibility to act, so that Black males can harness all of their potential free from the shackles of oppression that feed the system.

REFERENCES

Adkison-Bradley, C., Johnson, P. D., Rawls, G., & Plunkett, D. (2006). Overrepresentation of African American males in special education programs: Implications and advocacy strategies for school counselors. *Journal of School Counseling, 4*(16), n16.

Agency for Healthcare Research and Quality. (2017). *National healthcare quality and disparities report.* https://www.ahrq.gov/research/findings/nhqrdr/nhqrdr17/index.html

Allen, Q. (2017). "They write me off and don't give me a chance to learn anything": Positioning, discipline, and Black masculinities in school. *Anthropology & Education Quarterly, 48*(3), 269–283.

American School Counseling Association. (2021a). *The school counselor and anti-racist-practices.*

American School Counseling Association. (2021b). *The school counselor and multitiered system of supports*. https://www.schoolcounselor.org/Standards-Positions/Position-Statements/ASCA-Position-Statements/The-School-Counselor-and-Multitiered-System-of-Sup

American School Counselor Association. (2019). *National model: A framework for school counseling programs* (4th ed.). American School Counselor Association.

American School Counselor Association. (2022). *State school counseling mandates & legislation*. https://www.schoolcounselor.org/About-School-Counseling/State-Requirements-Programs/State-School-Counseling-Mandates-Legislation

Bailey, D. F., & Paisley, P. O. (2004). Developing and nurturing excellence in African American male adolescents. *Journal of Counseling and Development, 82*(1), 10–17.

Banks, A. (2021). Black adolescent experiences with COVID-19 and mental health services utilization. *Journal of Racial and Ethnic Health Disparities*, 1–9.

Bansak, C., & Starr, M. (2021). Covid-19 shocks to education supply: How 200,000 U.S. households dealt with the sudden shift to distance learning. *Review of Economics of the Household, 19*(1), 63–90. https://doi.org/10.1007/s11150-020-09540-9

Bergman, E. B., & Mapp, K. L. M. (2021). *Embracing a new normal: Toward a more liberatory approach to family engagement*. Carnegie Corporation of New York. https://doi.org/10.15868/socialsector.38504

Bottiani, J. H., Bradshaw, C. P., & Mendelson, T. (2017). A multilevel examination of racial disparities in high school discipline: Black and white adolescents' perceived equity, school belonging, and adjustment problems. *Journal of Educational Psychology, 109*(4), 532.

Brinkley, B., Hines, E., Jones, A., McMillian, E. G., Sturdivant, B., & Walker, M. (2018). Fixing systems, not kids: Changing the narrative of Black males in Guilford county schools. *Voices in Urban Education, 48*, 19–25. https://files.eric.ed.gov/fulltext/EJ1174511.pdf

Brooms, D. R. (2017). Black otherfathering in the educational experiences of Black males in a single-sex urban high school. *Teachers College Record, 119*(12), 1–46. https://doi-org.ezproxy.lib.uconn.edu/10.1177/016146811711901102

Brooms, D. R. (2021). "He wanted everybody to succeed": Black males, relational trust, and school counseling. *Professional School Counseling, 25*(1_part_4), 2156759. https://doi.org/10.1177/2156759X211040035

Bryan, J. (2005). Fostering educational resilience and achievement in urban schools through school-family-community partnerships. *Professional School Counseling*, 219–227.

Bryan, J., Day-Vines, N. L., Griffin, D., & Moore-Thomas, C. (2012). The disproportionality dilemma: Patterns of teacher referrals to school counselors for disruptive behavior. *Journal of Counseling and Development, 90*(2), 177–190. https://doi.org/10.1111/j.1556-6676.2012.00023.x

Bryan, J., & Henry, L. (2008). Strengths-based partnerships: A school-family-community partnership approach to empowering students. *Professional School Counseling, 12*(2), 2156759. https://doi.org/10.1177/2156759X0801200202

Bryan, J., & Henry, L. (2012). A model for building school family community partnerships: Principles and process. *Journal of Counseling and Development, 90*(4), 408–420. https://doi.org/10.1002/j.1556-6676.2012.00052.x

Bryan, J., & Holcomb-McCoy, C. (2007). An examination of school counselor involvement in school-family-community partnerships. *Professional School Counseling, 10*(5), 2156759. https://doi.org/10.1177/2156759X0701000501

Bryk, A. S., & Schneider, B. (2002). *Trust in schools: A cored resource for improvement*. Russell Sage Foundation.

Burleson, S. E., & Thoron, A. C. (2014). *Maslow's hierarchy of needs and its relation to learning and achievement*. University of Florida IFAS Extension. http://edis.ifas.ufl.edu

Butler, S. K. (2003). Helping urban African American high school students to excel academically: The roles of school counselors. *High School Journal, 87*(1), 51–57.

Carey, J., & Dimmitt, C. (2012). School counseling and student outcomes: Summary of six statewide studies. *Professional School Counseling, 16*(2), 146–153.

Centers for Disease Control and Prevention. (2021). *1991–2019 High school youth risk behavior survey data [Data file]*. http://nccd.cdc.gov/youthonline

Coker, T. R., Elliott, M. N., Toomey, S. L., Schwebel, D. C., Cuccaro, P., Tortolero Emery, S., Davies, S. L., Visser, S. N., & Schuster, M. A. (2016). Racial and ethnic disparities in ADHD diagnosis and treatment. *Pediatrics, 138*(3), e20160407. https://doi.org/10.1542/peds.2016-0407

Cokley, K., Cody, B., Smith, L., Beasley, S., Miller, I. S. K., Hurst, A., Awosogba, O., Stone, S., & Jackson, S. (2014). Bridge over troubled waters: Meeting the mental health needs of black students. *Phi Delta Kappan, 96*(4), 40–45. https://doi.org/10.1177/0031721714561445

Congressional Black Caucus. (2019). *Ring the alarm: The crisis of Black youth suicide in America.* National Black Justice Coalition.

Cook Sandifer, M. I., & Gibson, E. M. (2020). School counselors as social justice change agents: Addressing retention of African American males. *Journal of School Counseling, 18*(21), n21.

Cook-Harvey, C. M., Darling-Hammond, L., Lam, L., Mercer, C., & Roc, M. (2016). *Equity and ESSA: Leveraging educational opportunity through the every student succeeds act.* Learning Policy Institute.

Darling-Hammond, L. (2001). Inequality in teaching and schooling: How opportunity is rationed to students of color in America. In *The right thing to do, the smart thing to do: Enhancing diversity in the health professions – Summary of the symposium on diversity in health professions in Honor of Herbert W. Nickens, M.D.* (pp. 208–233). The National Academies Press. https://doi.org/10. 17226/10186

Davidson, K., & Case, M. (2018). Building trust, elevating voices, and sharing power in family partnership. *Phi Delta Kappan, 99*(6), 49–53.

DeSpain, S. N., Conderman, G., & Gerzel-Short, L. (2018). Fostering family engagement in middle and secondary schools. *The Clearing House, 91*(6), 236–242. https://doi.org/10.1080/00098655. 2018.1524743

Dinkmeyer, D. C, Jr., & Carlson, J. (2006). *Consultation: Creating school-based interventions* (3rd ed.). Routledge.

Dollarhide, C. T., Smith, A. T., & Lemberger, M. E. (2007). Critical incidents in the development of supportive principals: Facilitating school counselor-principal relationships. *Professional School Counseling, 10*(4), 2156759. https://doi.org/10.1177/2156759X0701000409

Dorn, E., Hancock, B., Sarakatsannis, J., & Viruleg, E. (2020). *COVID-19 and learning loss—Disparities grow and students need help.* McKinsey & Company.

Epstein, J. L., Sanders, M. G., Sheldon, S. B., Simon, B. S., Salinas, K. C., Jansorn, N. R., Van Voorhis, F. L., Martin, C. S., Thomas, B. G., Greenfeld, M. D., Hutchins, D. J., & Williams, K. J. (2018). *School, family, and community partnerships: Your handbook for action.* Corwin Press.

Fadus, M. C., Ginsburg, K. R., Sobowale, K., Halliday-Boykins, C. A., Bryant, B. E., Gray, K. M., & Squeglia, L. M. (2020). Unconscious bias and the diagnosis of disruptive behavior disorders and ADHD in African American and Hispanic Youth. *Academic Psychiatry, 44,* 95–102. https://doi.org/10.1007/s40596-019-01127-6

Ford, D. Y., & Russo, C. J. (2016). Historical and legal overview of special education over-representation: Access and equity denied. *Multiple Voices for Ethnically Diverse Exceptional Learners, 16*(1), 50–57.

Friedman-Krauss, A., Barnett, W. S., & Nores, M. (2016). *How much can high-quality universal pre-K reduce achievement gaps?* Center for American Progress and National Institute on Early Education Research. https://www.americanprogress.org/issues/early-childhood/reports/2016/04/05/132750/how-much-can-high-quality-universal-pre-k-reduce-achievement-gaps/

Furey, A. W. (2015). *Adolescent mental health: Exploring the school counselor experience.* Northeastern University.

Fye, H. J., Miller, L. G., & Rainey, J. S. (2017). Predicting school counselors' supports and challenges when implementing the asca national model. *Professional School Counseling, 21*(1). https://doi. org/10.1177/2156759X18777671

Gardner, R., III, Rizzi, G. L., & Council, M., III. (2014). Improving educational outcomes for minority males in our schools. *Interdisciplinary Journal of Teaching and Learning, 4*(2), 81–94.

Garrow, G. L., & Kaggwa, E. B. (2012). Providing solutions for Black male achievement: Partnerships and mentoring. In M. Casserly, S. Lewis, C. Simon, R. Uzzell, & M. Palacios (Eds.), *A call for change: Providing solutions for Black male achievement* (pp. 193–220). Council of the Great City Schools. http://files.eric.ed.gov/fulltext/ED539625.pdf

Goings, R., & Shi, Q. (2018). Black male degree attainment: Do expectations and aspirations in high school make a difference? *Spectrum: A Journal on Black Men, 6*(2), 1–20.

Gonsoulin, S., Zablocki, M., & Leone, P. E. (2012). Safe schools, staff development, and the school-to-prison pipeline. *Teacher Education and Special Education, 35*(4), 309–319.

Grant, K. L., Springer, S. I., Tuttle, M., & Reno, M. (2021). Small-group counseling intervention to support career exploration of rural middle school students. *The Journal for Specialists in Group Work, 46*(1), 108–127.

Green, T. L. (2017). From positivism to critical theory: School-community relations toward community equity literacy. *International Journal of Qualitative Studies in Education, 30*(4), 370–387.

Greer Sr, D., & Webb, T. E., Jr (2020). School counselors and African American students: Counseling within the psychology of the Black experience. *Urban Education Research & Policy Annuals, 7*(1).

Griffin, D., Williams, J. M., & Bryan, J. (2021). School – Family – Community partnerships for educational success and equity for Black male students. *Professional School Counseling, 25*(1c), 1–14. https://doi.org/10.1177/2156759X211040036

Hackett, E. M., Ponterotto, J. G., Zusho, A., & Jackson, M. A. (2018). Rising out of the gap: Early adolescent Black males and academic success. *Qualitative Report, 23*(10).

Harper, S. R. (2012). *Black male student success in high education: A report from the national Black male achievement study.* University of Pennsylvania, Center for the study of Race and Equity in Education. https://web-app.usc.edu/web/rossier/publications/231/Harper%20(2012)%20Black%20Male%20Success.pdf

Henderson, A. T., & Mapp, K. L. (2002). *A new wave of evidence: The impact of school, family, and community connections on student achievement. Annual synthesis, 2002.* National Center for Family & Community Connections with Schools, Southwest Educational Development Laboratory.

Henry, L. M. (2014). *Just Love: A collaborative evaluation of a faith-based school-family-community partnership through the voices of the children.* Doctoral Dissertation. http://scholarcommons.usf.edu/cgi/viewcontent.cgi?article=6433&context=etd

Hill, N. E., & Tyson, D. F. (2009). Parental involvement in middle school: A meta-analytic assessment of the strategies that promote achievement. *Developmental Psychology, 45*(3), 740–763. https://doi.org/10.1037/a0015362

Hines, E. M., Harris, P. C., Mayes, R. D., & Moore, J. L., III. (2020). I think of college as setting a good foundation for my future: Black males navigating the college decision making process. *Journal for Multicultural Education, 14*(2), 129–147. https://doi.org/10.1108/JME-09-2019-0064

Holcomb-McCoy, C. (2007). Transitioning to high school: Issues and challenges for African American students. *Professional School Counseling, 10*(3). https://doi.org/10.1177/2156759X0701000306

Holcomb-McCoy, C. C. (2022). *School counseling to close opportunity gaps: A social justice framework for success* (2nd ed.). Corwin Press, Inc.

Holland, M. M. (2015). Trusting each other: Student-counselor relationships in diverse high schools. *Sociology of Education, 88*(3), 244–262.

Howard, T. C. (2010). *Why race and culture matter in schools: Closing the achievement gap in America's classrooms.* Teachers College Press.

Howard, T. C., Douglas, T. R. M., & Warren, C. A. (2016). "What works": Recommendations on improving academic experiences and outcomes for Black males. *Teachers College Record, 118*(6), 1–10.

Huerta, J., Watt, K. M., & Reyes, P. (2013). An examination of AVID graduates' college preparation and postsecondary progress: Community college versus 4-year university students. *Journal of Hispanic Higher Education, 12*(1), 86–101.

Ishimaru, A. M. (2019). *Just schools: Building equitable collaborations with families and communities.* Teachers College Press.

Jeynes, W. H. (2015). A meta-analysis: The relationship between father involvement and student academic achievement. *Urban Education, 50*(4), 387–423. https://doi.org/10.1177/0042085914525789

Johnson, L. E., Jr. (2020). *Perception, beliefs, or implicit bias: Investigating the relationship between teacher recommendation and African American males selection in gifted and advanced placement courses.* Doctoral dissertation. Youngstown State University.

Kim, J. S. (2006). Effects of a voluntary summer reading intervention on reading achievement: Results from a randomized field trial. *Educational Evaluation and Policy Analysis, 28*(4), 335–355. https://doi.org/10.3102/01623737028004335

Kyere, E., Joseph, A., & Wei, K. (2020). Alternative to zero-tolerance policies and out-of-school suspensions: A multitiered centered perspective. *Journal of Ethnic & Cultural Diversity in Social Work, 29*(5), 421–436.

Lindsey, M. A., Joe, S., & Nebbitt, V. (2010). Family matters: The role of mental health stigma and social support on depressive symptoms and subsequent help seeking among African American boys. *Journal of Black Psychology, 36*(4), 458–482. https://doi.org/10.1177/0095798409355796

Maslow, A. H. (1943). A theory of human motivation. *Psychological Review, 50*(4), 370–396. https://doi.org/10.1037/h0054346

Moore, J. L., Hines, E. M., & Harris, P. C. (2021). Introduction to the special issue: Males of color and school counseling. *Professional School Counseling, 25*(1), 1–7. https://doi.org/10.1177/2156759X211040045

National Center for Education Statistics. (2019a). *Nation's report card.* National Assessment of Educational Progress. https://www.nationsreportcard.gov/ndecore/xplore/NDE

National Center for Education Statistics. (2019b). *Indicator 15: Retention, suspension, and expulsion.* https://nces.ed.gov/programs/raceindicators/indicator_rda.asp

National Center for Educational Statistics. (2020a, May). *College enrollment rates.* https://nces.ed.gov/programs/coe/indicator_cpb.asp

National Center for Educational Statistics. (2020b, May). *Status dropout rates.* https://nces.ed.gov/programs/coe/indicator_coj.asp

Nelson, J. D. (2016). Relational teaching with Black boys: Strategies for learning at a single-sex middle school for boys of color in New York city. *Teachers College Record, 118*(6), 25–47.

O'Connor, P. (2018). How school counselors make a world of difference. *Phi Delta Kappan, 99*(7), 35–39.

Oster, E., Jack, R., Halloran, C., Schoof, J., McLeod, D., Yang, H., Roche, J., & Roche, D. (2021). Disparities in learning mode access among K-12 students during the COVID-19 pandemic, by race/ethnicity, geography, and grade level—United States, September 2020–April 2021. *Morbidity and Mortality Weekly Report, 70*(26), 953–958. https://doi.org/10.15585/mmwr.mm7026e2

Paolini, A. C. (2019). School counselors promoting college and career readiness for high school students. *Journal of School Counseling, 17*(2), n2.

Rhoden, S. (2017). "Trust me, you are going to college": How trust influences academic achievement in Black males. *The Journal of Negro Education, 86*(1), 52–64.

Riddle, T., & Sinclair, S. (2019). Racial disparities in school-based disciplinary actions are associated with county-level rates of racial bias. *Psychological and Cognitive Sciences, 116*(17), 8255–8260. https://doi.org/10.1073/pnas.1808307116

Scarborough, J. L., & Culbreth, J. R. (2008). Examining discrepancies between actual and preferred practice of school counselors. *Journal of Counseling and Development, 86*(4), 446–459. https://doi.org/10.1002/j.1556-6678.2008.tb00533.x

Schott. (2015). *Black Lives Matter: The Schott 50 state report on public education and black males.* http://blackboysreport.org/

Smith, L. C., Garnett, B. R., Herbert, A., Grudev, N., Vogel, J., Keefner, W., & Baker, T. (2017). The hand of professional school counseling meets the glove of restorative practices: A call to the profession. *Professional School Counseling, 21*(1). https://doi.org/10.1177/2156759X18761899

Steen, S., & Kaffenberger, C. J. (2007). Integrating academic interventions into small group counseling in elementary school. *Professional School Counseling, 10*(5), 2156759. https://doi.org/10.1177/2156759X0701000510

Tatum, A. W. (2006). Engaging African American males in reading. *Educational Leadership, 63*(5), 44–49.

Turney, K., & Kao, G. (2009). Barriers to school involvement: Are immigrant parents disadvantaged? *The Journal of Educational Research*, *102*(4), 257–271. https://doi.org/10.3200/JOER.102.4.257-271

U.S. Bureau of Labor Statistics. (2021, November 20). *Unemployment Rate – 20 Yrs. & over, Black or African American Men*. Federal Reserve Bank of St. Louis. https://fred.stlouisfed.org/series/LNS14000031

U.S. Bureau of Labor Statistics. (2022, March 30). *Unemployment Rate – 20 Yrs. & over*. Federal Reserve Bank of St. Louis. https://fred.stlouisfed.org/series/LNS14000024

U.S. Department Of Education, Office For Civil Rights. (2021). *An overview of exclusionary discipline practices in public schools for the 2017–18 school year*. https://www2.ed.gov/about/offices/list/ocr/docs/crdc-exclusionary-school-discipline.pdf

Uwah, C. J., McMahon, H. G., & Furlow, C. F. (2008). School belonging, educational aspirations, and academic self-efficacy among African American male high school students: Implications for school counselors. *Professional School Counseling*, *11*(5). https://doi.org/10.1177/2156759X0801100503

Van Lancker, W., & Parolin, Z. (2020). COVID-19, school closures, and child poverty: A social crisis in the making. *The Lancet Public Health*, *5*(5), e243–e244.

Walker, D. K. (2021). Parenting and social determinants of health. *Archives of Psychiatric Nursing*, *35*(1), 134–136. https://doi.org/10.1016/j.apnu.2020.10.016

Walker, L. J., & Goings, R. B. (2017). A dream deferred: How trauma impacts the academic achievement of African American youth. In *Linking health and education for African American students' success* (pp. 3–12). Routledge.

Warren, C. A. (2014). Perspective divergence and the mis-education of Black boys... like me. *Journal of African American Males in Education*, *5*(2).

Warren, C., Douglas, T., & Howard, T. (2016). In their own words: Erasing deficits and explaining what works to improve K-12 and post-secondary Black male school achievement. *Teachers College Record*, *118*(6). https://doi.org/10.1177/016146811611800607

Washington, A. R. (2010). Professional school counselors and African American males: Using school/community collaboration to enhance academic performance. *Journal of African American Males in Education (JAAME)*, *1*(1), 26–39.

Whitford, D. K., & Emerson, A. M. (2019). Empathy intervention to reduce implicit bias in pre-service teachers. *Psychological Reports*, *122*(2), 670–688.

Wint, K. M., Opara, I., Gordon, R., & Brooms, D. R. (2021). Countering educational disparities among Black boys and Black adolescent boys from pre-k to high school: A life course-intersectional perspective. *The Urban Review*, 1–24.

Wint, K. M., Opara, I., Gordon, R., & Brooms, D. R. (2022). Countering educational disparities among Black boys and Black adolescent boys from pre-k to high school: A life course-intersectional perspective. *The Urban Review*, *54*, 183–206. https://doi.org/10.1007/s11256-021-00616-z

Xanthos, C., Treadwell, H. M., & Holden, K. B. (2010). Social determinants of health among African–American men. *Journal of Men's Health*, *7*(1), 11–19. https://doi.org/10.1016/j.jomh.2009.12.002

YouthTruth. (2021). *Learning from student voice: Emotional & mental health*. https://youthtruthsurvey.org/wp-content/uploads/2019/12/YouthTruth-Learning-from-Student-Voice-Emotional-and-Mental-Health.pdf

Ziomek-Daigle, J., Goodman-Scott, E., Cavin, J., & Donohue, P. (2016). Integrating a multi-tiered system of supports with comprehensive school counseling program. *The Professional Counselor*, *6*(3), 220–232. http://tpcjournal.nbcc.org/integrating-a-multi-tiered-system-of-supports-with-comprehensive-school-counseling-programs/

CHAPTER 9

COUNSELING BLACK MALE STUDENT-ATHLETES IN K-16

Paul C. Harris, Janice Byrd, Hyunhee Kim, Miray D. Seward, Araya Baker, Alagammai Meyyappan, Deepika Nantha Kumar and Tia Nickens

ABSTRACT

The authors focus on using Critical Race Theory (CRT) as a lens through which to analyze the holistic welfare development of Black male student-athletes, namely their identity development and overall college and career readiness. The authors contend that if structured and delivered well with the appropriate supports, athletics can be more of a mobilizing mechanism for Black males versus an exploitive one. Specifically, athletic identity does not have to be exclusive, but rather one aspect of the student-athletes' multidimensional sense of self. To this end, the authors outline specific research, practice, and policy recommendations that address the unique challenges of Black male student-athletes in K-16.

Keywords: Black males; student athletes; critical race theory; identity development; college readiness; career readiness

INTRODUCTION

Adolescents experience competing priorities in their development related to self-identification, self-efficacy, interpersonal relationships, and future planning. Playing a sport adds an unexpectedly complex layer to these stage-related tasks,

Black Males in Secondary and Postsecondary Education
Advances in Race and Ethnicity in Education, Volume 9, 163–177
Copyright © 2024 Paul C. Harris, Janice Byrd, Hyunhee Kim, Miray D. Seward, Araya Baker, Alagammai Meyyappan, Deepika Nantha Kumar and Tia Nickens
Published under exclusive licence by Emerald Publishing Limited
ISSN: 2051-2317/doi:10.1108/S2051-231720230000009009

especially for Black males (Harris et al., 2020). For example, in high school, Black male student athletes experience less educational benefit than their white counterparts, particularly as their status moves from junior varsity to varsity (Harris, 2014). Researchers emphasize that Black student-athletes are socialized to over rely on sport as their primary means to achieving success and upward mobility (Beamon, 2008). Therefore, their academic and career success is hampered in ways their white counterparts do not experience. For example, Harper et al. (2013) found that despite Black males making up only 2.8% of college undergraduates, they still represented 58.4% of the football and basketball teams for the 76 schools within the top six conferences in the National Collegiate Athletic Association (NCAA). At the same time, only 50.2% of Black male athletes graduated with a degree as compared to all student athletes (66.9%).

Given the reality that their over-identification with the athlete role could put them at risk, it is important to have a better understanding of societal influences that shape Black male student-athletes' identities. The emancipatory nature of Critical Race Theory (CRT) provides an appropriate lens through which to view and serve the needs of Black male student-athletes. The authors focus on using CRT as a lens through which to analyze the holistic welfare development of Black male student-athletes, namely their identity development and overall college and career readiness. The authors contend that if structured and delivered well with the appropriate supports, athletics can be more of a mobilizing mechanism for Black males versus an exploitive one. Specifically, athletic identity does not have to be exclusive, but rather one aspect of the student-athletes' multidimensional sense of self. To this end, the authors outline specific research, practice, and policy recommendations that address the unique challenges of Black male student-athletes in K-16.

CRT

CRT focuses on moving toward justice for people of color (Delgado & Stefancic, 2001; Ladson-Billings, 2013; McCoy & Rodricks, 2015). While CRT originally emerged from legal scholarship, its application has extended beyond the legal field and has been used in the analysis of the Black male student-athlete experience (Cooper & Hawkins, 2015; Singer, 2005). One tenet of CRT that is particularly relevant to counseling Black male student-athletes is that racism is, and always has been, a pervasive and entrenched reality. Further, CRT elevates the importance of voice-centeredness and storytelling, in contradiction to the positivist tradition. This includes elevating the voices of Black male student-athletes in an effort to both facilitate their empowerment and to allow the centrality of their voices to inform and guide the necessary interventions aimed at serving their unique needs, as well as the holistic welfare of all Black males who may follow in their path given similar socialization experiences.

Black Male Identity Development

CRT as a framework allows for close scrutiny of the myriad forms of racism that many of these student-athletes face throughout their lived experience, whether in the form of structural barriers or personal affronts. The framework is also conducive to examining the social forces giving rise to the overrepresentation of Black males in revenue sports. Thus, CRT leaves space for the ostensible benefits of athletic participation to be held in tension with coexisting risks and inequities.

The reality that Black boys are collectively stereotyped as antiintellectual and antischool, susceptible to criminality should be discussed in understanding Black male student-athletes' overidentification with their athlete role. In other words, we should enhance our critical awareness of Black male students' experiences of being marginalized with their academics, while getting recognized with their athletic talents at school. As Davis (2005) states, Black boys become both fetishized and loathed at school. Black boys are forced to navigate this seemingly dichotomous positionality in their schools and become susceptible to severe academic disengagement by middle and high school. In fact, statistics indicated that less than half of Black boys enrolled in high school during 2014 graduated on time with their peers, compared to a 30 to 40% higher rate for their white male counterparts (Spielberg, 2014).

Teachers' implicit biases could be one of the reasons for their progressive disaffiliation and disengagement in school over time (Rashid, 2009). For instance, Gilliam et al. (2016) found that preschool teachers misperceived Black boys as more disruptive than students from other backgrounds who exhibited the same age-appropriate types of misbehavior. This deep-seated distrust from educational institutions, at such an early age, has direct implications for Black male student-athletes in college, not the least of which includes lower self-efficacy and a systemically foreclosed academic identity.

Literature has also pointed to the fact that Americans generally overestimate the age of Black boys between ages 10 and 17, by about 4.5 years (Goff et al., 2014). This same study also revealed that the typical American misperceives Black boys as less innocent and less deserving of protection. As stated above, this commonplace adultification of Black boys can cause teachers to frame Black boys' misbehavior in a way that is stripped of childish naivete and perceived as less innocent than their peers (Ferguson, 2000; Goff et al., 2014). In addition to the stereotyping of Black criminality in schools, the dominant culture's conflation of dangerousness with Black masculinity renders Black boys disproportionately profiled and targeted by police officers. From 2010 to 2014, for instance, police killed Black boys over age 10 at almost three times the rate of white boys and men (Buehler, 2017). The psychological impact of this disproportionality cannot be underestimated, as a recent study determined that exposure to police brutality and murders correlated positively with emotional distress among Black adults, in general (Bor et al., 2018). Such erasure of Black boys' childhood innocence can engender a dual sense of hypervisibility and invisibility that speaks to an inability to imagine Black boys as sentient beings outside of situations in which they are policed or framed as aggressors. Interestingly, sports, particularly revenue-generating, high contact sports like football, provide a space within which aggression is not only tolerated, but praised and encouraged. However, such praise only extends as far as the entertainment value of their athletic performance can go, potentially rendering them just as invisible, disempowered, and marginalized in the sporting arena as they are in others.

The erasure of Black boys' childhood innocence can engender a vulnerable sense of hypervisibility, while also underscoring a parallel invisibility that withholds the humanizing of Black boys and men as sentient beings. Franklin (2014) conceptualized the "invisibility syndrome paradigm" to describe Black boys' and men's intrapsychic struggle to forge a healthy personal identity in the face of gendered racial stress, at every turn. Here, invisibility connotes feeling that one's "abilities, personality, and worth are not valued or even recognized because of prejudice or racism" (Franklin, 2014). Franklin's framing of invisibility extends previous definitions of prejudice and racism, as "ways in which people devalue, disadvantage, demean, and in general, unfairly regard others." From this groundwork, Franklin outlined seven dynamic elements of invisibility syndrome relevant to Black boys' identity development and mental health:

> 1) feeling a lack of recognition or appropriate acknowledgement; 2) feeling a lack of satisfaction or gratification from any racially stressful encounter; 3) self-doubt about one's legitimacy; 4) a lack of validation; 5) perceived disrespect; 6) perceived challenges to dignity; 7) a sense that one's identity is being uprooted or shaken. (p. 15–16)

Emotional invisibility can result from the convergence of invisibility syndrome and the rampant adultification of Black boys and young men. Once Black boys are no longer perceived to be child-like – which is much sooner than usual – they are effectively abandoned social-emotionally.

The dearth of Black male role models (Bryant & Zimmerman, 2003) only compounds this societal afterthought/oversight. For instance, numerous scholars have theorized about the significant role of professional membership in laying the groundwork for the positive identity development of Black adolescent boys (Quigley & Mitchell, 2018). Black boys, however, are also sentient beings with holistic needs, and therefore require the same investment of nurturance, tenderness, and thoughtfulness as any other child. Several artistic and spiritual mentorship programs designed for Black boys have emerged over the past decade (Chatman, 2019; Jackson et al., 2014; Watson et al., 2015), but demand for these specific types of holistic mentorship programs still outpaces their availability. This widespread neglect of Black boys' intrapsychic world can lead to adults under-engaging Black boys and young men in ongoing emotional (Dunbar et al., 2017), gender (Hill, 2002; Howard et al., 2013), and racial (Stevenson et al., 2002) socialization. Not only that, but society's emotional negligence of Black boys has the potential to derail and destabilize an already complex identity development process. Sports can make this process even more complex when early recruiting pushes young Black males into navigating tasks and decisions that are developmentally incongruent with their age and typical maturity level.

Despite these challenges, an innovative conceptualization of the gendered racial identity development of Black male students still holds the potential to be socially transformative. With greater collaborative and interdisciplinary consideration about how to forge sufficient protective factors for this demographic, educational practitioners and scholars alike, in tandem with families, mentors, and counselors, can raise the consciousness of institutions and communities, and exchange insights about the collective benefit of unconventional investments in Black boys' and young men's social-emotional well-being and stability. One of many spaces within which to target such efforts includes the college preparatory process for Black male student-athletes. Emphasizing eligibility to play, for example, without similar attention to readiness for college and career can simply reproduce the aforementioned identity challenges, only now disguised by the prestige of being a college athlete.

College and Career Readiness Versus NCAA Eligibility for Black Male Student-Athletes

There are various factors considered in determining the initial eligibility of prospective student-athletes to play at Division I or II schools. Some factors include traditional admission measures such as ACT/SAT test scores, high school coursework and GPA on courses that the NCAA approves. Lately, the NCAA has attracted criticism for not paying adequate attention to the academic experience of student-athletes and their preparation for future careers (August, 2020; Dent et al., 2014; Ganim, 2014). In particular, Black males – who comprise less than 3% of the undergraduate student body population, but constitute over 50% of the players in NCAA's highest revenue sports, basketball and football (Harper et al., 2013; Harris, 2014) – are significantly disadvantaged. Despite the NCAA claiming that all its student-athletes, Black football players included, have a rewarding academic experience (Gallup, 2020), demographic data suggests this is not the case. Compared to nonathlete Black male students and student-athletes from other racial groups, research shows that Black male student-athletes in Division 1 institutions are less likely to graduate (Harris, 1995; Vereen et al., 2015). Given the disparities in college graduation rates among Black male student-athletes, it is important to examine the gap between NCAA,s Initial-Eligibility standards and the readiness of Black male student athletes for postsecondary education and career. We utilize David Conley's Four Keys model to draw this distinction.

David Conley (2012) defines college and career ready as "qualify for and succeed in entry-level, credit-bearing college courses leading to a baccalaureate or certificate, or career pathway-oriented training programs without the need for remedial or developmental coursework" (Conley, 2012). To operationalize this definition, Conley (2012) identifies four components as essential for students to be successful in their postsecondary pursuits (a) key cognitive strategies (e.g., formulating a hypothesis, identifying sources, problem solving) (b) key content knowledge (e.g., foundational content, technical knowledge) (c) key learning skills and techniques (e.g., ownership of learning and specific learning techniques), and (d) transition knowledge (e.g., skills and knowledge needed to successfully navigate postsecondary environments). Through taking into account the different types of knowledge and skills that students need to successfully transition into their postsecondary pathways, Conley emphasizes on the complex and contextual nature of college and career readiness.

According to Conley, both cognitive strategies and content knowledge are key components of the academic aspect of college and career readiness (Conley, 2007, 2012). In discussing content knowledge, Conley draws our attention to the importance of challenging curriculum content. While research shows that a rigorous high school curriculum has a positive effect on college success (Morgan et al., 2018), the opportunity for Black male student-athletes to access a rigorous curriculum is limited. Research shows that the likelihood of college enrollment, persistence and success improves with the number of Advanced Placement (AP) and Dual Enrollment (DE) courses that students, particularly from minority groups, take while in high school (Curry et al., 2021; The College Board, 2016); and yet, according to a 2020 report by The Education Trust, Black students from low income households remain underrepresented in AP courses (Curry et al., 2021; Morgan et al., 2020). Furthermore, in college, academic advisors are more likely to recommend "easy to pass" majors to student athletes (Beamon, 2008) to ensure academic eligibility, and this can lead Black male student athletes to feel more academically disengaged.

In discussing learning skills and strategies, Conley notes that taking ownership of learning is a most important factor for postsecondary transition (Conley, 2012). Self-efficacy, which is a component of ownership of learning, improves as individuals master experiences and begin to perceive themselves as successful (Bandura, 1977; Conley & French, 2014). For many Black male athletes, however, the opportunities to experience success in academics are very limited. Despite the NCAA's mandate that student-athletes devote no more than 20 hours a week toward athletic activities; the participation of student athletes in athletic related activities frequently exceeds this weekly limit (Benford, 2007; Huml et al., 2019) and eventually has an adverse effect on their academic engagement. For Black males, whose rates of postsecondary readiness are already lower than their white peers, overidentification with their athletic identity comes at the expense of their academic identity development (Harper et al., 2013; Harris, 2014). Additionally, studies show that Black male student-athletes are confronted with negative stereotypes about their academic abilities from professors and peers (Comeaux & Harrison, 2007; Cooper, 2016; Harrison & Lawrence, 2004), and internalizing these stereotypes can further impact their beliefs in their own academic capabilities.

Another key factor in Conley's Four Keys model on college and career readiness is transition knowledge, which includes awareness of financial aid processes, postsecondary program options, college culture, career pathways, and self-advocacy skills (Conley, 2012). However, as previously mentioned, Black males demonstrate lower levels of college and career readiness, and among Black male athletes, this lack of preparation and/or socialization can be noted in their choice of program major or degree, their regrets over college major choice, and their uncertainty around life after college (Curry et al., 2021). Furthermore, despite Black males being a sliver of the US population (6%), both professional football and basketball have high percentages of Black athletes, at 66% and 82%

respectively (Morris & Adeyemo, 2012). In contrast, Black males are significantly underrepresented in fields such as law (2%) or medicine (3%) (Morris & Adeyemo, 2012), facts which suggest that Black males have fewer visible career role models outside of athletics.

In summary, the NCAA's Initial-Eligibility standards focus on a limited set of measures to determine a student athletes' eligibility. While Conley (Conley 2007, 2010) argues that high school graduation requirements are not determining factors of postsecondary success because high school courses are not aligned with college level curriculum, NCAA's Initial-Eligibility requirements continue to place a heavy emphasis on these scores. In doing so, the NCAA fails to account for the broader knowledge and skills that student athletes require to succeed in postsecondary pathways, thereby creating a gap between eligibility and readiness. This gap is particularly pronounced for Black male athletes, who are already leaving high school with lower capital to navigate their postsecondary pathways, and are faced with even more complex challenges as they go forth in their academic and career advancement. It is critical, then, that targeted interventions are implemented to mitigate these dynamics in such a way that helps promote a multidimensional sense of self for Black male student-athletes. Harris et al. (2020) detail a group counseling intervention, MP3, that effectively accomplishes this end.

Men Passionately Pursuing Purpose (MP3)

Given the harmful effects of over-identification with the athlete role, practitioners should consider supporting Black male student-athletes in their development of their multidimensional sense of self beyond their athletic identity (Conley, 2010). As many Black male student-athletes perceive that their counselors do not understand their unique situations and needs (Harris et al., 2021), practitioners should privilege the voice of Black male student-athletes to inform interventions with them. For example, K-12 school counselors should utilize group counseling to curate a space for the voices of Black male student-athletes to be leveraged, amplified, and empowered in the company of their peers. Group counseling could help them "recognize shared feelings or thoughts, develop a desire to help others, believe in their growth, feel a sense of belonging and trust, experience a release of feelings associated with experiences, engage in introspection, assume responsibility for life decisions, and ultimately see themselves as more than just an athlete" (Harris et al., 2020, p. 146). For example, Harris et al. (2020) provided a group counseling intervention named *Men Passionately Pursuing Purpose (MP3)* and found that the intervention helped participants with a positive sense of self and connections with others/brotherhood, both critical for college and career readiness and overall wellness. Having a safe space to explore their identities and lived experiences helped them recognize who they wanted to be beyond sports. Feeling connected to other Black male student athletes in a group also helped them experience universality and learn from each other to cope with their challenges and pursue their goals in and out of sports. There are eight sessions in the MP3 group experience, and session topics and activities include: (1) Establishing rapport with each other and facilitator through structured activity; (2) Discovering strengths through genogram development and sharing; (3) Reflection upon identities through responding the prompt "Who am I without the ball?" (4) Writing a statement of purpose and outlining strategic plan to passionately pursue purpose during high school years; (5) Engaging mental contrasting skills through reflecting upon what is in and outside of one's locus of control and their respective impacts; (6) Building capacity for making healthy decisions within one's locus of control; (7) Analyzing the importance and utility of accountability, and drafting specific plans to incorporate accountability into daily living; and (8) Reflection upon progress gained through group experience.

Recommendations

Research

Despite the challenges and disadvantages that Black male student-athletes experience, counseling literature has paid scant attention on how to address and serve the needs of Black male student-athletes. Harries et al. (2021) in their qualitative study with Black male student-athletes, reported that participants had pretty limited perceptions of their school counselors (e.g., "She just couldn't understand where I was coming from a lot of the time." "It's almost like she wasn't listening in a sense. Or, she was listening but wasn't understanding"). Avent Harris and Wong (2018) also indicated that Black male college students' tendency of not actively seeking help for mental health services. In line with evidence-based counseling practice, more empirical studies are required to support counselors to be equipped with better knowledge and skills in serving the needs of Black male student-athletes. A lack of their understanding might put Black male student-athletes at risk and contribute to the harmful exploitation of them through sport.

Future research should continue to reveal any discrepancies or opportunity gaps between Black male student-athletes and their counterparts, which could help counselors advocate and address their needs. Researchers could consider using CRT as a framework to examine the effects of racism on Black male student-athletes' experiences and explore intersectionality of Black male student-athletes (e.g., Blackness, maleness, and student-athlete). Particularly, researchers are encouraged to pay attention to Black male student athletes' overidentification with their role in sport (Harris et al., 2021). Future studies could benefit from exploring external and internal factors that contribute to Black male student-athletes' experiences (e.g., academic success, college and career readiness, and mental health), which could shed lights on how to support Black male student-athletes to develop their holistic identity that leads to academic and career success.

Practice

K-16 counselors can utilize a myriad of interventions to effectively serve the unique needs of Black male student-athletes. From individual counseling techniques, to group counseling strategies, to community partnerships, counselors can directly and indirectly build on the strengths of Black student-athletes in a way that facilitates their healthy identity development and overall wellness. Specifically, with targeted intervention, Black male athletes can thrive in their academic, emotional, and career development.

In addition to providing direct service to Black male student athletes, practitioners, particularly school counselors should work with educators and other stakeholders to facilitate their critical consciousness. Literature confirms that Black male student athletes with a positive support system, strong academic identity, and solid racial pride can thrive in both athletics and academics, despite the challenges they encounter (Cooper & Cooper, 2015). Still, in reality, even gifted Black male student-athletes also encounter negative stereotypes of being Black males, such as *dumb jock*, which often makes them difficult to explore their academic and career identities outside sports (Dexter et al., 2021). Educators should be encouraged to examine their implicit biases and support Black male student-athletes to develop their multidimensional sense of self. Moreover, such consultation on the part of school counselors should extend to community partners as well.

School counselors and higher counselors, alike, are often expected to take on a variety of responsibilities, often making it more difficult to provide the mental health services they are trained to deliver. Moreover, the needs of some students extend beyond that of what can be provided in the school building. In a qualitative study by Harris and colleagues (2021), one participant reported that his school counselor only checked in with him to make sure he was up to date on coursework. Another participant in the same study reported that he was not sure if his school counselor understood the challenges he faced. Given the current increasing demand for mental health services in school districts, Black male student-athletes are often left with minimal support from school counselors while having to navigate different identities, such as being a Black man in a colonial system rooted in oppression, being a student, being an athlete, etc. Innovative community partnerships spearheaded by school counselors can help ensure that Black male student-athletes have access to mental health services in and out of school. For example, partnering with local universities would give Black male student-athletes access to mental health counselors and allow for future mental health counselors to receive training in school settings. Such a partnership would enable student mental health care on multiple tiers: from their teachers, school counselors, and the embedded mental health counselors. Furthermore, this eases the pressure that is placed on school counselors.

A key challenge to this process is upholding the ethical principle of non-maleficence whereby counselors should avoid "actions that cause harm" (ACA, 2014) and ensuring that the mental health counselors that serve Black male student-athletes have the appropriate background and training to work with historically marginalized groups. This training should include ensuring the counselor has an understanding of cultural humility by teaching them to constantly self-evaluate and engage in learning. Moreover, encouraging counselors to use frameworks and theories that take into account the role of systemic factors, such as CRT, Relational-Cultural Theory, Black Feminist Thought, Liberation Psychology, etc., can be crucial when working with Black male student-athletes.

Policy

We make seven recommendations that have the potential to ensure Black male student-athletes are developing healthy identities and improving their overall wellness, specifically in their college and career readiness. Firstly, we recommend that the NCAA's Initial-Eligibility requirements be expanded to include a wider range of skills, knowledge, and behaviors that are deemed critical for postsecondary success. Doing so can help ensure that academic identity will not be left behind in favor of an exclusive athletic identity. Secondly, targeted supports for Black male student-athletes should be implemented to help improve their academic success, graduation rates, and life readiness. Thirdly, as part of any academic and career development supports, career assessments should be administered to every Black male student-athletes as part of a holistic assessment of what a congruent program major might be for them to study while in college. Our fourth recommendation is for more training to be provided to faculty on how to interact positively with Black male student-athletes, specifically, faculty can be educated on how to facilitate the empowerment of Black male student-athletes such that they are seen and validated for more than their athletic success, and that sports participation is not seen as a liability for their academic progress. Faculty can also more intentionally create opportunities for Black male student-athletes to develop their leadership outside of the classroom and sport. Our fifth recommendation is for specific mentoring programs to be implemented that focus on promoting a multidimensional sense of self. MP3 could definitely be adapted for use at the college level to accomplish this. Our sixth recommendation would be for universities and athletic departments alike improve support and awareness of mental health issues among Black male student-athletes. And lastly, our seventh recommendation is to reframe student-athletes' time commitment to allow them to integrate better into the campus culture.

BIBLIOGRAPHY

August, R. A. (2020). Understanding career readiness in college student-athletes and identifying associated personal qualities. *Journal of Career Development*, *47*(2), 177–192. https://doi.org/10.1177/0894845318793936

Avent Harris, J. R., & Wong, C. D. (2018). African American college students, the Black church, and counseling. *Journal of College Counseling*, *21*(1), 15–28.

Aymer, S. R. (2016). "I can't breathe": A case study—Helping Black men cope with race-related trauma stemming from police killing and brutality. *Journal of Human Behavior in the Social Environment*, *26*(3–4), 367–376. https://doi.org/10.1080/10911359.2015.1132828

Bandura, A. (1977). Self-efficacy: Toward a unifying theory of behavioral change. *Psychological Review*, *84*, 191–215.

Beamon, K. K. (2008). "Used goods": Former African American college student athletes' perception of exploitation by Division I universities. *The Journal of Negro Education*, *77*(4), 352–364.

Benford, R. D. (2007). The college sports reform movement: Reframing the "edutainment" industry. *The Sociological Quarterly*, *48*, 1–28.

Bond, M. J., & Herman, A. A. (2016). Lagging life expectancy for black men: A public health imperative. *American Journal of Public Health*, *106*(7), 1167–1169. https://doi.org/10.2105/AJPH.2016.303251

Bor, J., Venkataramani, A. S., Williams, D. R., & Tsai, A. C. (2018). Police killings and their spillover effects on the mental health of black Americans: A population-based, quasi-experimental study. *The Lancet*, *392*(10144), 302–310. https://doi.org/10.1016/S0140-6736(18)31130-9

Brook, J. S., Whiteman, M., & Finch, S. (1993). Role of mutual attachment in drug use: A longitudinal study. *Journal of the American Academy of Child & Adolescent Psychiatry*, *32*(5), 982–989. https://doi.org/10.1097/00004583-199309000-00015

Bryant, A. L., & Zimmerman, M. A. (2003). Role models and psychosocial outcomes among African American adolescents. *Journal of Adolescent Research*, *18*(1), 36–67. https://doi.org/10.1177/0743558402238276

Buehler, J. W. (2017). Racial/ethnic disparities in the use of lethal force by US police, 2010–2014. *American Journal of Public Health*, *107*(2), 295–297. https://doi.org/10.2105/AJPH.2016.303575

Burton, L. (2007). Childhood adultification in economically disadvantaged families: A conceptual model. *Family Relations*, *56*(4), 329–345. https://doi.org/10.1111/j.1741-3729.2007.00463.x

Chatman, M. C. (2019). Advancing Black youth justice and healing through contemplative practices and African spiritual wisdom. *The Journal of Contemplative Inquiry*, *6*(1).

Clark, R., Anderson, N. B., Clark, V. R., & Williams, D. R. (1999). Racism as a stressor for African Americans: A biopsychosocial model. *American Psychologist*, *54*(10), 805–816. https://doi.org/10.1037/0003-066X.54.10.805

Coates, T. (2015). *Between the world and me*. Spiegel & Grau.

Cohen, G. L. (2017). Self-affirmation facilitates minority middle schoolers' progress along college trajectories. *Proceedings of the National Academy of Sciences*, *114*(29), 7594–7599. https://doi.org/10.1073/pnas.1617923114

Comeaux, E., & Harrison, C. K. (2007). Faculty and male student-athletes: Racial differences in the environmental predictors of academic achievement. *Race, Ethnicity and Education*, *10*(2), 199–214. https://doi.org/10.1080/13613320701330726

Conley, D. T. (2007). *Redefining college readiness* (Vol. 3). Educational Policy Improvement Center.

Conley, D. T. (2010). *College and career ready: Helping all students succeed beyond high school*. Jossey-Bass.

Conley, D. T. (2012). *A complete definition of college and career readiness*. Educational Policy Improvement Center.

Conley, D. T., & French, E. M. (2014). Student ownership of learning as a key component of college readiness. *American Behavioral Scientist*, *58*(8), 1018–1034. https://doi.org/10.1177/0002764213515232

Cook, E. (2013). A rigorous curriculum really matters. *Principal Leadership*, *13*(8), 36–40.

Cooper, J. N. (2016). 'Focus on the bigger picture': An anti-deficit achievement examination of Black male scholar athletes in science and engineering at a historically white university (HWU). *Whiteness and Education*, *1*(2), 109–124. https://doi.org/10.1080/23793406.2016.1272627

Cooper, J. N., & Cooper, J. E. (2015). "I'm running so you can be happy and I can keep my scholarship": A comparative study of Black male college athletes' experiences with role conflict. *Journal of Intercollegiate Sport*, *8*(2), 131–152. https://doi.org/10.1123/jis.2014-0120

Cooper, J. N., & Hall, J. (2014). Understanding Black male student athletes' experiences at a historically black college/university. *Journal of Mixed Methods Research*, *10*(1), 46–63. https://doi.org/10.1177/1558689814558451

Cooper, J., & Hawkins, B. (2015). Athletic migration experiences of black athletes. In B. Hawkins, J. Cooper, A. Carter-Francique, & J. K. Cavil (Eds.), *The athletic experience at historically black colleges and universities: Past, present, and persistence* (pp. 107). Rowman & Littlefield.

Crain, W. C. (1992). *Theories of development* (3rd ed.). Prentice Hall.

Cross, W. E., Jr., Parham, T. A., & Helms, J. E. (1991). The stages of Black identity development: Nigrescence models. In R. L. Jones (Ed.), *Black psychology* (pp. 319–338). Cobb & Henry Publishers.

Curry, J. R., Soares, F. A., Maclin, J. E., & Csaszar, I. (2021). Black male collegiate athletes' perceptions of their career and academic preparation: A mixed methods study. *Journal of College Access, 6*(3), 111–140.

Davis, J. E. (2005). Black boys at school: Negotiating masculinities and race. In *Educating our black children* (pp. 183–196). Routledge.

Delgado, R., & Stefancic, J. (2001). *Critical race theory: An introduction.* NYU Press.

Dent, M., Sanserino, M., & Werner, S. (2014). *Do colleges drop the ball with student-athletes?* http://www.post-gazette.com/sports/college/2014/06/01/Do-colleges-drop-the-ball-with-student-athletes/stories/201406010120

Dexter, M. R., Collins, K. H., & Grantham, T. C. (2021). Extending the scholar baller model to support and cultivate the development of academically gifted Black male student-athletes. *Gifted Child Today, 44*(4), 203–215. https://doi.org/10.1123/jis.2014-0120

Douglass, F. (1857). *My bondage, my freedom.* Orton & Co.

Dunbar, A. S., Leerkes, E. M., Coard, S. I., Supple, A. J., & Calkins, S. (2017). An integrative conceptual model of parental racial/ethnic and emotion socialization and links to children's social-emotional development among African American families. *Child Development Perspectives, 11*(1), 16–22. https://doi.org/10.1111/cdep.12218

Erikson, E. H. (1968). *Identity: Youth & crisis.* Norton.

Ferguson, A. (2000). *Bad boys* (pp. 29–30). University of Michigan Press.

Fonagy, P., Steele, M., Steele, H., Leigh, T., Kennedy, R., Mattoon, G., & Target, M. (1995). Attachment, the reflective self, and borderline states: The predictive specificity of the Adult Attachment Interview and pathological emotional development. In S. Goldberg, R. Muir, & J. Kerr (Eds.), *Attachment theory: Social, developmental, and clinical perspectives* (pp. 233–278). Analytic Press, Inc.

Franklin, A. J. (2014). The invisibility syndrome. In *The use of personal narratives in the helping professions* (pp. 121–130). Routledge.

Gallup. (2020). *A study of NCAA student-athletes: Undergraduate experiences and post-college outcomes.* https://www.gallup.com/education/312941/ncaa-student-athlete-outcomes-2020.aspx

Ganim, S. (2014). CNN analysis: Some college athletes play like adults, read like 5th graders. http://www.cnn.com/2014/01/07/us/ncaa-athletes-reading-scores/index.html

Geller, A., Fagan, J., Tyler, T., & Link, B. G. (2014). Aggressive policing and the mental health of young urban men. *American Journal of Public Health, 104*(12), 2321–2327. https://doi.org/10.2105/AJPH.2014.302046

Gilliam, W. S., Maupin, A. N., Reyes, C. R., Accavitti, M., & Shic, F. (2016). Do early educators' implicit biases regarding sex and race relate to behavior expectations and recommendations of preschool expulsions and suspensions. *Yale University Child Study Center, 9*(28), 1–16.

Gilligan, C. (1993). *In a different voice: Psychological theory and women's development.* Harvard University Press.

Goff, P. A., Eberhardt, J. L., Williams, M. J., & Jackson, M. C. (2008). Not yet human: Implicit knowledge, historical dehumanization, and contemporary consequences. *Journal of Personality and Social Psychology, 94*(2), 292. https://doi.org/10.1037/0022-3514.94.2.292

Goff, P. A., Jackson, M. C., Di Leone, B. A. L., Culotta, C. M., & DiTomasso, N. A. (2014). The essence of innocence: Consequences of dehumanizing Black children. *Journal of Personality and Social Psychology, 106*(4), 526–545. https://doi.org/10.1037/a0035663

Goyer, J. P., Garcia, J., Purdie-Vaughns, V., Binning, K. R., Cook, J. E., Reeves, S. L., Gregory, A., Skiba, R. J., & Noguera, P. A. (2010). The achievement gap and the discipline gap: Two sides of the same coin? *Educational Researcher, 39*(1), 59–68. https://doi.org/10.3102/0013189X09357621

Hamre, B. K., & Pianta, R. C. (2001). Early teacher – Child relationships and the trajectory of children's school outcomes through eighth grade. *Child Development, 72*(2), 625–638. https://doi.org/10.1111/1467-8624.00301

Harper, S. R., Williams, C. D., Jr, & Blackman, H. W. (2013). *Black male student-athletes and racial inequities in NCAA Division I college sports.* University of Pennsylvania, Center for the Study of Race & Equity in Education.

Harrell, S. P. (2000). A multidimensional conceptualization of racism-related stress: Implications for the well-being of people of color. *American Journal of Orthopsychiatry, 70*(1), 42–57. https://doi.org/10.1037/h0087722

Harris, S. M. (1995). Psychosocial development and Black male masculinity: Implications for counseling economically disadvantaged African American male adolescents. *Journal of Counseling and Development, 73*(3), 279–287. https://doi.org/10.1002/j.1556-6676.1995.tb01749.x

Harris, P. C. (2014). The sports participation effect on educational attainment of black males. *Education and Urban Society, 46*(5), 507–521. https://doi.org/10.1177/0013124512446219

Harris, P. C., Mayes, R. D., Freeman, C., Eberly, B., Tatby, N., & Wiener, S. (2020). Men passionately pursuing purpose (MP3): A group counseling intervention for Black male student athletes. *The Journal for Specialists in Group Work, 45*(2), 146–164. https://doi.org/10.1080/01933922.2019.1679931

Harrison, C. K., & Lawrence, S. M. (2004). College students' perceptions, myths, and stereotypes about African American athleticism: A qualitative investigation. *Sport, Education and Society, 9*(1), 33–52. https://doi.org/10.1080/1357332042000175809

Harris, P. C., Seward, M. D., Mayes, R. D., Elopre, L., & Wengert, E. (2021). "We got to do better": Interactions between school counselors and Black male student-athletes. *Professional School Counseling, 25*(1 part_4), 1–9.

Hill, S. A. (2002). Teaching and doing gender in African American families. *Sex Roles, 47*(11), 493–506. https://doi.org/10.1023/A:1022026303937

Hoberman, J. M. (1997). *Darwin's athletes: How sport has damaged Black America and preserved the myth of race.* Houghton Mifflin Harcourt.

Howard, L. C., Rose, J. C., & Barbarin, O. A. (2013). Raising African American boys: An exploration of gender and racial socialization practices. *American Journal of Orthopsychiatry, 83*(2–3), 218–230. https://doi.org/10.1111/ajop.12031

Huml, M. R., Bergman, M. J., Newell, E. M., & Hancock, M. G. (2019). From the playing field to the classroom: The academic challenges or NCAA Division I athletes. *Journal for the Study of Sports and Athletes in Education, 13*(2), 97–115. https://doi.org/10.1080/19357397.2

Jackson, I., Sealey-Ruiz, Y., & Watson, W. (2014). Reciprocal love: Mentoring Black and Latino males through an ethos of care. *Urban Education, 49*(4). https://doi.org/10.1177/00420859135193

Klopfenstein, K. (2004). The advanced placement expansion of the 1990s: How did traditionally underserved students fare? *Education Policy Analysis Archives, 12*(68). https://doi.org/10.14507/epaa.v12n68.2004

Ladson-Billings, G. (2013). Critical race theory – What it is not. In *Handbook of critical race theory in education* (pp. 54–67). Routledge.

Landrine, H. (1992). Clinical implications of cultural differences: The referential versus the indexical self. *Clinical Psychology Review, 12*(4), 401–415. https://doi.org/10.1016/0272-7358(92)90124-Q

Lee, J., Grigg, W., & Donahue, P. (2007). *The Nation's Report Card [TM]: Reading 2007. National Assessment of Educational Progress at Grades 4 and 8. NCES 2007-496.* National Center for Education Statistics.

Levant, R. F., & Pollack, W. S. (Eds.). (1995). *A new psychology of men.* Basic Books/Hachette Book Group.

Majors, R., & Billson, J. M. (1993). *Cool pose: The dilemma of Black manhood in America.* Simon and Schuster.

Marcia, J. E. (1980). Identity in adolescence. In J. Adelson (Ed.), *Handbook of adolescent psychology.* Wiley.

McCoy, D. L., & Rodricks, D. J. (2015). *Critical race theory in higher education: 20 years of theoretical and research innovations: ASHE higher education report* (Vol. 41(3)). John Wiley & Sons.

Morgan, I., Socol, A. R., & Patrick, K. (2020, January 9). *Inequities in advanced coursework.* The Education Trust.

Morgan, T., Zakem, D., & Cooper, W. (2018). From high school access to postsecondary success: An exploratory study of the impact of high-rigor coursework. *Education Sciences, 8*(4), 191. https://doi.org/10.3390/educsci8040191

Morris, J. E., & Adeyemo, A. O. (2012). Touchdowns and honor societies. *Phi Delta Kappan, 93*(5), 28–32. http://web.b.ebscohost.com/ehost/pdfviewer/pdfviewer?vid=19&sid=1670729-4517-4d84-959c-bff6cc83f901%40sessionmgr198&hid=110

Moynihan, D. P. (1965). *The Negro family: The case for national action* (No. 3). US Government Printing Office.

Muss, R. E. (1996). *Theories of adolescence* (6th ed.). McGraw-Hill.

O'Neil, J. M. (1981). Patterns of gender role conflict and strain: Sexism and fear of femininity in men's lives. *Personnel & Guidance Journal, 60*(4), 203–210. https://doi.org/10.1002/j.2164-4918.1981.tb00282.x

Ogbu, J. U. (1987). Variability in minority school performance: A problem in search of an explanation. *Anthropology & Education Quarterly, 18*(4), 312–334. https://doi.org/10.1525/aeq.1987.18.4.04x0022v

O'Neil, J. M. (2008). Summarizing 25 years of research on men's gender role conflict using the Gender Role Conflict Scale: New research paradigms and clinical implications. *The Counseling Psychologist, 36*(3), 358–445. https://doi.org/10.1177/0011000008317057

Phinney, J. S. (1996). When we talk about American ethnic groups, what do we mean? *American Psychologist, 51*(9), 918–927. https://doi.org/10.1037/0003-066X.51.9.918

Pleck, J. H. (1984). *The myth of masculinity*. MIT Press.

Quigley, M. W., & Mitchell, A. B. (2018). "What works": Applying critical race praxis to the design of educational and mentoring interventions for African American males. *Journal of African American Males in Education, 9*(2).

Rashid, H. M. (2009). From brilliant baby to child placed at risk: The perilous path of African American boys in early childhood education. *The Journal of Negro Education, 78*(3), 347–358. https://doi.org/10.1177/01614681211051995

Schott Foundation for Public Education. (2015). *Black lives matter: The Schott 50 state report on public education and Black males*. http://blackboysreport.org/

Sewell, T. (1997). *Black masculinities and schooling. How Black boys survive modern schooling*. Trentham Books Ltd.

Sheftall, A. H., Vakil, F., Ruch, D. A., Boyd, R. C., Lindsey, M. A., & Bridge, J. A. (2022). Black youth suicide: Investigation of current trends and precipitating circumstances. *Journal of the American Academy of Child & Adolescent Psychiatry, 61*(5), 662–675. https://doi.org/10.1016/j.jaac.2021.08.021

Singer, J. N. (2005). Understanding racism through the eyes of African American male student-athletes. *Race, Ethnicity and Education, 8*(4), 365–386. https://doi.org/10.1080/13613320500323963

Spielberg, W. (2014). Trying not to learn—How Black boys respond to the education system. *The Psychology of Black Boys and Adolescents, 2 volumes*, 163.

Steinberg, L., & Scott, E. S. (2003). Less guilty by reason of adolescence: Developmental immaturity, diminished responsibility, and the juvenile death penalty. *American Psychologist, 58*(12), 1009–1018. https://doi.org/10.1037/0003-066X.58.12.1009

Stevenson, H. C., Jr, Cameron, R., Herrero-Taylor, T., & Davis, G. Y. (2002). Development of the teenager experience of racial socialization scale: Correlates of race-related socialization frequency from the perspective of Black youth. *Journal of Black Psychology, 28*(2), 84–106. https://doi.org/10.1177/0095798402028002002

Stock, M. L., Gibbons, F. X., Beekman, J. B., Williams, K. D., Richman, L. S., & Gerrard, M. (2018). Racial (vs. self) affirmation as a protective mechanism against the effects of racial exclusion on negative affect and substance use vulnerability among black young adults. *Journal of Behavioral Medicine, 41*(2), 195–207. https://doi.org/10.1007/s10865-017-9882-7

The College Board. (2016). *Performance and success: 2015 program results*. The College Board. https://www.collegeboard.org/program-results/2015/performance

The Education Trust. (2020, January 9). *Black and Latino students shut out of advanced coursework opportunities*. https://edtrust.org/press-release/black-and-latino-students-shut-out-of-advanced-coursework-opportunities/

Utsey, S. O., Payne, Y. A., Jackson, E., & Jones, A. M. (2002). Racism quality of life indicators, and life satisfaction among elderly African Americans. *Cultural Diversity and Ethnic Minority Psychology, 8*(3), 224–233. https://doi.org/10.1037/1099-9809.8.3.224

Vereen, L., Hill, N. R., & Lopez, M. (2015). African American athletes and higher education. In J. R. Curry & M. A. Shillingford (Eds.), *African American students' career and college readiness: The journey unraveled* (pp. 309–340). Lexington Books.

Watkins, L. O. (2004). Epidemiology and burden of cardiovascular disease. *Clinical Cardiology*, *27*(S3), 2–6. https://doi.org/10.1177/2047487318825350

Watson, J., Washington, G., & Stepteau-Watson, D. (2015). Umoja: A culturally specific approach to mentoring young African American males. *Child and Adolescent Social Work Journal*, *32*(1), 81–90. https://doi.org/10.1007/s10560-014-0367-z

Wong, Y. J., & Rochlen, A. B. (2005). Demystifying men's emotional behavior: New directions and implications for counseling and research. *Psychology of Men and Masculinity*, *6*(1), 62–72. https://doi.org/10.1037/1524-9220.6.1.62

PART II

POSTSECONDARY SETTINGS

CHAPTER 10

THE LIVED EXPERIENCES OF COLLEGIATE BLACK MEN

Derrick R. Brooms, Marcus L. Smith
and Darion N. Blalock

ABSTRACT

This chapter takes a panoramic view to explore the lives of collegiate Black men. We begin with brief reflections from our own experiences to position ourselves to and alongside Black men's lives and college years. After setting the stage through our own reflections, we explore the literature on Black men's lives during their college years and pay particular attention to their social statuses, campus engagement, and health and well-being. Two critical components in many Black men's collegiate experiences are how they are projected in wider US society through deficit-based perspectives and repositioned away from educational success. We interrogate these realities and advance a discussion on ways to improve the conditions, environment, and understanding of their college journeys and possibilities. We conclude with recommendations for research, practice, and policy.

Keywords: Black men; higher education; representations; athletics; health and well-being

This chapter takes a panoramic view to explore the lives of collegiate Black men. We begin with brief reflections from our own college-related experiences to position ourselves as part of the larger collective of Black men's lives and their college years. After setting the stage through our own reflections, we explore Black men's lives during their college years and pay particular attention to representations of Black boys and men in the media, Black men's athletic endeavors and athletic identity, and survey some challenges they experience and their health

Black Males in Secondary and Postsecondary Education

Advances in Race and Ethnicity in Education, Volume 9, 181–200

Copyright © 2024 Derrick R. Brooms, Marcus L. Smith and Darion N. Blalock

Published under exclusive licence by Emerald Publishing Limited

ISSN: 2051-2317/doi:10.1108/S2051-2317202300000009010

and well-being. Two critical components in many Black men's lives during their collegiate experiences are how they are projected in wider US society through deficit-based perspectives and how they are repositioned away from educational success. We interrogate these realities and advance a discussion on ways to improve the conditions, environment, and understanding of their college journeys and possibilities. We conclude with recommendations for research, practice, and policy.

RESEARCHERS' POSITIONALITIES: BEING BLACK AND MALE IN HIGHER EDUCATION

We are three Black men engaged with and connected to Black collegiate men from several vantage points. Thus, as we discuss further below, our focus on Black college men's lived experiences and positive outcomes are both subjective and personal and serve as the foundation of much of our individual efforts, professional endeavors, and work/community-based engagements. We approach this work through our own experiences, which makes it imperative that we begin by discussing and sharing our own positionalities.

I (first author) currently serve as a faculty member, researcher, and youth worker; I have a research agenda focused on the lives, education, and future of Black boys and men. My current and ongoing work also is anchored in a philosophy of Black education and is informed by my experiences as a secondary school teacher, administrator, and athletic coach as well as my mentoring, community-based work, and advocacy with Black families and Black youth related to educational equity and racial justice. I am a first-generation college graduate who attended a private, elite, predominantly white higher education institution. During my college years, I struggled to navigate the institution primarily because of my family's working-class background, lack of academic preparedness and college knowledge, culture shock (given the hyper-segregation that I experienced in my home city), and the ways that I was denigrated and presumed incompetent and unworthy by white counterparts and faculty. All of these, both individually and collectively, created racial battles that I had to navigate, and contributed to my nonbelonging. Additionally, I had several family-based challenges that made my college years even more difficult. My educational and lived experiences as well as my community and professional experiences inform the lens through which I engage in my pedagogy, service, research, and praxis.

I (second author) currently hold the positionality of a Black male PhD student and researcher. My research agenda is currently focused on the well-being, development, and mentoring that Black male college athletes receive from their Black and white sport coaches. This research is being led and developed through my continuing education in sociology, more broadly my work explores the intersection of Black masculinity, education, and sports. By providing a view of Black boys and men that moves beyond the monolithic physicality that many Black men are reduced to, my scholarship works toward broadening the range of educational and occupational outcomes of Black men. Like many other Black athletes, my high school and college years were spent as a student-athlete training in male-dominated spaces, developing a skill set and identity that I would struggle to shed as I transitioned into adulthood. Additionally, I spent eight years of my early adulthood tirelessly chasing the dream of being a Division I college basketball coach, with the purpose of serving as a mentor and support for the young Black men that I coached. My educational and lived experiences position me uniquely to understand the hyper-focused ways that Black boys are disproportionately socialized and cultivated to be athletes at the expense of a more holistic development. The perspectives I've gained from both my academic and athletic experiences inform the ways I engage in my teaching, service, and research.

I (third author) currently work as a higher education professional in the realm of undergraduate student recruitment focusing on both prospective transfer and first-year students at a large, public, elite, predominantly white institution. Primarily, my role is to engage in efforts to increase the pipeline of community college transfers, especially those from in-state institutions. Prior to this position, I supported students as an academic advisor at a community college where my philosophy was to partner with students in creating academic plans that reflected their personal and professional goals. In both roles, my central aim has been to provide holistic support and ensure students are aware of and able to access the vast resources and opportunities available within higher education. I am particularly sensitive to the needs of traditionally underrepresented and underserved populations like those of racially minoritized, first-generation college status, and working-class backgrounds. This sensitivity stems from my identity as a first-generation college graduate who attended a private, elite, predominantly white institution. Many of my challenges I encountered stemmed directly from my lack of knowledge for navigating college, despite attending a high school with a college centric curriculum. My early years in college also were challenging due to the culture shock and racial microaggressions I experienced as a Black man from a working class family, which caused me to disengage from campus life and focus primarily on academics. My experiences have led me to seek out roles focused on student support and access and have directly influenced the ways I engage students.

Collectively, we understand how our positionalities inform how we read and make sense of Black men's lives and college experiences. In this work, we appreciate Black men's experiential knowledge, and we intentionally center Blackness as we survey the literature on Black men's collegiate experiences (Clark & Brooms, 2021).

EXPLORING BLACK MEN'S COLLEGIATE EXPERIENCES

Black boys' and men's educational pathways, including their matriculation into and through college, continue to be an important arena of investigation particularly related to their lives, experiences, and outcomes. Part of the realities that

Black men face in higher education is threefold. First, all too often Black men are discussed through a singular axis focus that homogenizes their lives and experiences. That is, a set of experiences for a specific group of Black men become the driving force for stories told about them within the higher education landscape. Second, Black college men have a full range of experiences across higher education institutional types, which helps display how institutional context matters to their collegiate years. Third, Black men themselves as well as their experiences go well beyond only focusing on their academic selves or academic experiences. As we take up in this chapter, there is a great need for a broader perspective of viewing and understanding Black men's college years, so that we can better appreciate multiple factors that contribute to their experiences and outcomes.

One of the prevailing constraints that Black college men must endure and navigate is their presumed disinterest in education (Brooms, 2021; Hines et al., 2021; Howard, 2014). This narrative takes many forms and continues to dominate the lenses through which many people (mis)perceive Black college men, from denigrating those who participate in collegiate athletics (particularly football and basketball) to lowered expectations for those who focus their studies in specific majors (e.g., science, technology, engineering, and mathematics) to wide-ranging deficit-based views held about them that continue to underestimate and under-appreciate their intellect and academic abilities. As opposed to the popularized narrative that they don't care about school, research demonstrates and continues to affirm Black boys' and men's educational aspirations and desires (Brooms, 2021; Hines et al., 2020; Wright et al., 2020). Some of this research affirms how they acknowledge college as "setting a good foundation for my future" (Hines et al., 2020) while other research also shows that their higher education pursuits are connected to their desires to achieve some of their personal and educational goals (Brooms, 2017, 2021; Brooms & Davis, 2017; Cuyjet, 2006; Frierson et al., 2009; Warde, 2008). Even further, existing research demonstrates that some Black men actually increase their academic efforts in order to prove others wrong, to overcome invisibilities, or even to achieve against the odds (Brooms, 2017; Hrabowski et al., 1998; Moore et al., 2003).

In contrast and conflict with their desires are a range of hindrances that continue to constrain and delimit their experiences. A good deal of research also reveals numerous challenges and obstacles that Black men face in college, which ultimately have resulted in lowered expectations, less support, and diminished views of this student population (Cuyjet, 2006; Palmer et al., 2014; Wood & Palmer, 2015). Some of the challenges that Black college men face include gendered and racial microaggressions and a hostile campus climate (Brooms, 2017; Smith et al., 2016), negative messaging about their ability to do well academically (Goings, 2018), and racism (Jenkins, 2006; Robertson & Chaney, 2015; Smith et al., 2007). Each of these factors, individually and collectively, impede Black men's potential, academic performances, and social engagements during their college years. Additionally, these tensions undermine their sense of belonging and mattering on many college campuses (e.g., see Harper & Wood, 2015; Hilton et al., 2012; Strayhorn, 2018).

In order to make sense of the lived experiences of Black college men, we explore three specific domains: (1) representations in the media, (2) athletic endeavors, and (3) on-campus experiences. We provide a survey of literature and briefly discuss pertinent issues in each of these domains. In addition, we also offer a brief discussion of Black college men's health and well-being and end with recommendations.

Black Boys and Men in the Media

Mass media within the United States continues to play a prominent role in influencing and shaping its citizens' attitudes, beliefs, and understandings of race and racism as well as their perceptions of particular racial groups (hooks, 2004). While mass media never has been quite objective, there seems to be an increasingly concerted effort across media outlets to denigrate, vilify, and silence Black people, with an emphasis on Black boys and men (e.g., see Dow, 2016; Drake, 2016; hooks, 2004). As higher education institutions discuss the importance of diversity, equity, and inclusion in relation to Black men collegians, it is imperative that they also acknowledge the discourse and perceptions of these men as ignoring it can demonstrate a lack of care for their lives and relegate them to marginal mattering – or even doom (Brooms, 2021; Carey, 2019; Young, 2018). In this chapter, as we explore the lived experiences of collegiate Black men, we call attention to the messages, representations, and projections about Black boys and men precisely because, in this country, to be Black always already means that one's being and humanity are constantly under attack. Even further, these mediated messages both precede and follow Black boys and men into and across social institutions, including the higher educational landscape. Indeed, that Black boys and men continue to be repositioned away from personal and educational success within US society has, is, and always will be a problem that threatens their lives and life outcomes, especially given the prevalence of anti-Blackness.

In the recent past, both broadcast media and social media have served as the lens through which violence perpetrated against Black men and boys, including murder and infringements by law enforcement agents and vigilantes, have been recorded and circulated repeatedly. Not only have Black boys and men been the victims of horrific murders, many also have experienced a social death in the form of character assassination and vilification during the coverage of their stories as well as from opinions shared online (e.g., see Brown & Johnson, 2014; Curry, 2014). Primarily informed by a gendered anti-Blackness lens, which is rooted in racialized-gendered denigrations and is a social construction of Black men as always already problem, threat, and awaiting criminal (e.g., see Anderson, 2008; Brooms, 2021; Young, 2018), the social death(s) of Black boys and men provide fertile ground for mischaracterizations and misperceptions of them and fuels their miseducation. Multiple experiences provide examples of Black boys' and men's social death that also can be weaponized against them and reverberate across the broader scope of their lives.

In 2012, unarmed 17-year-old Trayvon Benjamin Martin was stalked and murdered by 28-year-old neighborhood watchman, George Zimmerman, who followed the teen after being instructed not to by local police. During the court trial and after, it seemed that Trayvon was being tried for his own murder given the hyper-focus on his clothing attire and presentation of self. Zimmerman was found not guilty and one may argue that publicly the verdict had been decided already by many given the ways in which Trayvon was portrayed (see Brown & Johnson, 2014; Madison, 2015). Importantly, the practice of presumed Black male guilt is generational and part of American heritage, from the Scottsboro Boys and Central Park 5 to numerous individuals that can be identified historically and contemporarily, such as Tamir Rice, Kalief Browder, and Stephon Clark, to name but a few. These realities reveal the historical and ongoing condemnation and criminalization of Black boys and men (e.g., see Brooms & Perry, 2016; Jenkins, 2006; Oliver, 2003; Rios, 2015). And, within the higher education landscape, researchers have identified how some Black men on various college campuses already "fit the description" of presumed guilt or even as unwanted and undesirable "guests" simply because of their racialized and gendered identities (Brooms, 2017; Smith et al., 2007).

In empirical studies that examine Black men's collegiate experiences, researchers provide ample evidence that societal tensions influence the ways in which they are perceived. For instance, researchers continue to show that Black boys and men are accosted by lowered expectations and negative stereotypes while also reporting having their intellect, aptitude, and acumen rejected and dismissed (e.g., see Abrica et al., 2020; Jett, 2022; Moore et al., 2003). Brown (2012) investigated the perceived influence of societal dissonance, self-efficacy, and institutional support on the academic success of a selected group of Black collegiate men at a predominantly white institution (PWI). The researcher found that diminished views of Black men were prevalent among the participants in the study with one student contending, "I think it plays a major part on how we interact with other students and then, how it affects us in class" (p. 94). Without question, societal stereotyping of Black boys and men lends to a whole host of challenges that Black men experience within higher education, not least of which is stereotype threat (Robertson & Chaney, 2015; Steele & Aronson, 1995), racial microaggressions (Harden, 2019; Robinson-Perez, 2021), invisibilities (Abrica et al., 2020; Allen, 2020; Brooms, 2021), and racial battle fatigue (Smith et al., 2011, 2016). Any of these on their own increases the burdens that Black men experience and must navigate in their college years regardless of institutional type and, even further, could compound themselves into negative or troubling coping behaviors and outcomes.

A good deal of some Black men's college efforts includes challenging and resisting racial stereotypes, including those from wider society that follow them in and across social institutions as well as those generated within higher education that continuously denigrates their character and being. Their efforts to resist these stereotypes are not simply just about themselves individually but are much broader and are aimed at Black boys and men as a collective (e.g., see Brooms & Davis, 2017; Brown, 2012). Thus, numerous Black college men recount stories and experiences of having been placed "at-risk" along their educational journeys, much of which is predicated on delimiting views and misperceptions of them and their abilities. Additionally, these experiences may even contribute to how they construct and perform their Black masculine identities on campus (Allen, 2020; Ford, 2011; Harris et al., 2011).

Black Men, Athletics, and Athletic Identities

This section focuses on Black men's athletic participation and identities relative to their college years and also beyond given our view that their college experiences provide pathways to their futures. In particular, we discuss some of the larger social and institutional factors that lead to Black men being disproportionately socialized into college athletes. We start by highlighting some of the debilitating factors of US culture, educational system, and athletic sports complex that hinder the academic potential of Black boys and men. While these factors paint a somewhat or even sometimes grim reality for Black boys, we also provide a narrative of hope by illuminating the need for Black parents and caregivers to support the development of a critical consciousness in our Black boys and young men. We see this consciousness as necessary as it will empower Black men to leverage their athletic prowess for positive academic and career outcomes as they navigate collegiate athletics.

Research shows that many Black college athletes arrive at predominantly white college campuses where there is a higher percentage of Black men as members of the high-profiled basketball and football teams than there is Black men represented as a percentage of the general student population (Hawkins, 2010). This racial juxtaposition demonstrates the value that US colleges ascribe to Black male athletic ability over their academic ability and what can be construed as their potential societal contributions. Some of the push factors that comprise a system of racial disadvantage that leads to Black boys and men being overrepresented in sports include but are not limited to: unequally funded K-12 public schools, where an overrepresentation of white teachers provide colorblind and whitewashed lesson plans to Black students (Abdul Rahman, 2022; Howard, 2014), and a racially biased college standardized testing system limits students' potentials (Knoester & Au, 2015; Meier & Knoester, 2017). Pull factors include a US culture that communicates through the media and Black communities that Black boys are better suited to excel at physical endeavors such as sports than intellectual endeavors (Hoberman, 1997; Kumah-Abiwu, 2020). Additionally, sports is a fun activity that has been characterized as a less racist meritocratic space that values the physical abilities of Black men (Brooks & Althouse, 2000).

Starting with the K-12 educational system helps to expose the process that is designed to disadvantage and diminish the academic potential of the Black boys that it is supposed to serve (Lewis et al., 2010). The US education system provides Black youth in general with an economically inferior, culturally deficient, and heavily policed educational experience when compared to that which white students receive (Bryan, 2017; Howard, 2014; Jenkins, 2006). These disadvantages work to diminish Black boys' academic acumen and interests, lowers their status in educational spaces, and thus pushes them to focus on more physically intensive sporting activities (particularly basketball and football), with the intended purpose of them accessing greater social mobility opportunities. The previously described deficient K-12 experience is then coupled with a racially biased system of standardized testing, which is a better predictor of economic-rich zip codes than it is cognitive ability and potential for societal impacts (e.g., see Knoester & Au, 2015; Thompson & Allen, 2012). Universities use this flawed system of standardized testing to "raise the profile" of their institutions, particularly related to selectivity, which at the same time serves as an enrollment barrier that hinders further education of nonathlete Black men across the country.

The educational system is coupled with a US culture that historically has excluded Black people from every cognitive elite position in the society (Hoberman, 1997) and a media that provides too many depictions of Black athletic heroes while suppressing Black intellectual role models (Edwards, 1969; Harrison et al., 2017). These factors combine to limit and marginalize the number of nonathlete Black men on college campuses and thus reproduce Black men's place as a physically gifted lower class in colleges and larger society. The system of college athletics further works to incentivize Black men's sports participation by offering high profile college scholarships and relaxing institutional standards of grade point averages and standardized test requirements in trade for the athletic labor of Black men (Beamon, 2010; Shropshire, 1997). As young Black boys grow up, they see themselves in the high-profiled Black athletes that the media showcases on television and magazine covers. These powerful media representations foster ideas, attitudes, and belief systems in these young boys about what type of identity and lifestyle they should choose for themselves (Beamon, 2010).

In addition, we also see these pathways included in pop culture as well. For instance, in Baby Keem's 2021 hit song "Range Brothers," featuring rap star Kendrick Lamar, Lamar taps into the athletic identity and lifestyle that many Black boys and men are considering or may subscribe to. Athletic identities are fostered through family, neighborhood, and media encouragement of early and consistent sports participation. This hyper focus on sports participation often leads to lower levels of academic achievement, higher expectations for professional sports careers as a means to upward social mobility, and lower levels of career maturity (Beamon, 2010; Harrison et al., 2011; Howard, 2014). These athletic identities are endorsed in and developed by a disproportionate number of young Black boys and as these boys age toward manhood, they begin basing their identity and self-worth on athletic participation and success, so much so that many college athletes' identities become foreclosed. Connecting back to Lamar, and research scholars (e.g., Harrison et al., 2011), the usual trappings of the masculine athletic lifestyle of material wears (cars, clothes, and jewelry), sexual conquest (attractive women), and sports glory (notoriety and roar of the crowd) can be harmful and empty. Lamar urges Black athletes to raise their level of consciousness and resist these intellectually and emotionally vacant temptations.

Sports participation, which often is seen as a positive masculine rite of passage and safe haven from the pathologies of crime, prison, and substance abuse that impact Black men, does not come without constraints, tensions, and challenges (Hawkins, 2010). Black boys who learn valuable skills of teamwork, discipline, and dedication through their sports participation can experience a decrease in academic and occupational potential due to over-investment in sports participation. As a result, while sports can have positive effects on Black boys and men, it is up to the individual and their family and support group to navigate and extract the social, educational, and occupational value out of their sports participation. A mindfulness of the previously stated anti-Black US educational system, culture, and media depictions that work against Black boys is important to reduce the over-centering of athletics in their lives in favor of a more holistic development. A healthy and balanced navigation of the illusion-filled sports pathway will help to expose Black boys and men to more robust social, academic, and professional pathways.

As Lamar concludes in "Range Brothers," he places an emphasis on the confusion, depression, and sense of loss that many Black men may face as their athletic careers come to an end and they are then forced to transition into an uncertain and unfamiliar labor market. The years that Black men have spent focused on cultivating an athletic identity, which often requires placing a priority on athletic participation over academic or intellectual interests, can be seen as problematic. The idea of athletic identity foreclosure has been used to describe the difficulty that many athletes face in transitioning away from sports and into the labor market. For instance, Beamon (2012) found that Black men college athletes excessively base their identity and self-worth on athletic participation and success and thus have lower rates of academic achievement and experience difficulties transitioning away from sports and into the labor market. Identity foreclosure has been found to occur when individuals make premature commitments to occupational or ideological roles that are socially and parentally acceptable in order to avoid identity crises (Brewer & Petitpas, 2017). These definitions and findings bolster support for the importance of providing holistic development for Black boys that exposes them to a variety of people, institutions, and experiences that can enhance their educational and life trajectories. A more holistic approach to development helps to develop and strengthen the nonathletic identities of Black men (Cooper, 2016).

A few explicit examples are warranted. Lenny Cooke was a talented high school basketball athlete who was once regarded as a top-tier recruit. Although Cooke was talented, his athletic mindset led to "misjudgment, arrogance, and attitude" (Squadron, 2019) as well as a failed NBA dream. After an early life that was impacted by poverty, a learning disability, and a culture that values the Black body over the Black mind, Cooke followed some bad advice, forgoing his college eligibility to enter the 2002 NBA draft. Cooke was not drafted and opted to play multiple short stints with professional basketball teams overseas. In 2004, Cooke was in a serious car accident where he suffered multiple broken bones and was forced to use a wheelchair for over two years. The combination of a shattered hoop dream and a broken body caused him to live in the past and struggle transitioning to life after basketball. Now, Cooke serves as a mentor who is committed to developing a critical consciousness within young aspiring athletes, he says "My blessing is to share my story... Prevent them from going through what I went through" (Squadron, 2019). The loss of purpose that Cooke experienced is shared by many Black men college athletes, particularly those at Division I schools whose competitive playing careers may end prematurely or before they desire. One high profile college example is former South Carolina star running back Marcus Lattimore, who experienced depression following injuries that abruptly ended his college career and likely derailed his NFL career. Lattimore was quoted as saying, "When you cut those lights off after you've played football, you need to know who you are outside of that. There's a lot more to life...than football" (USCA, 2018).

As these examples and research reveal, Black college athletes can experience a loss of purpose and identity and are often metaphorically lost without the sport that they have spent most of their lives developing an identity around. While acknowledging that in most cases there is no true replacement for the adrenaline rushing void left by sports participation, Cooke's and Lattimore's experiences highlight the importance of broadening Black college men's interests and skill set in a more holistic manner to help them envision and maintain a sense of purpose across multiple possibilities in their lives that include and go beyond athletics. Given the multiple transitions that they will experience – such as completing or transitioning out of college and completing or ending collegiate athletic participation – preparing Black men for various pathways in their postcollege years is crucial for their health and well-being as well as their life outcomes.

Given the nature of the athletic performance incentive structure, the academic support that collegiate Black men student-athletes receive often focuses on short-term goals of eligibility, less rigorous degree progress, and fails to properly prepare them for the labor market. This short-term mindset geared toward the appearance of academic success, quite regularly fails to develop Black men collegians holistically, creating less satisfied and engaged student-athletes (Beamon, 2012). The academics being housed under the athletics model have been known to result in educational neglect and academic exploitation due in part to academic clustering, pressure to select less-demanding majors, and academic fraud (Cooper et al., 2017). An example of a historic academic scandal was found at the University of North Carolina (UNC) in 2011.

From 1993 to 2011, UNC's African American Studies Department offered courses that were open to any student on campus, but mainly benefited student-athletes, allowing them to maintain athletic eligibility. The allegations included UNC's student-athletes being disproportionately enrolled in classes that provided high grades, little to no attendance, and required one test. Because the National Collegiate Athletic Association (NCAA) could not prove that these classes were created to benefit exclusively athletes by the record provided by UNC, the NCAA did not have the legislative power to classify the behavior as fraudulent (Tracy, 2017). This lack of incriminating evidence, combined with the lack of NCAA jurisdiction set the stage for few systemic changes to be made to address academic corruption (Ganesan, 2021). The scandal at UNC as well as others at Auburn and Michigan are high-profiled examples of the exploitative system that puts the tools for academic oversight in the hands of the same institutions that profit from athletic labor. Given the complexities of this exploitative system and the tremendous pressure to perform on Black athletes, systemic changes need to be made to prevent the foreclosure of Black men's identities. Until change comes, Black men must attempt to resist these systems of oppression themselves with the goal of getting the education that will provide them and their family with opportunities to prepare them for their future lives, roles, and responsibilities.

Being Black, Being Male on Campus – and On-Campus Experiences

In addition to the ways that they are projected in the media and their athletic endeavors, how Black men navigate their broader on-campus experiences matters a great deal to their college years. As noted briefly above, research on Black men's college experiences reveal the challenges, opportunities, and successes that Black men endure and navigate on campus. As discussed within a range of studies, researchers identify challenges that Black men experience across all institutional types, across two-year and four-year institutions as well as Historically Black Colleges and Universities (HBCUs), predominantly white institutions (PWIs), and Hispanic-Serving Institutions (HSIs). Studies reveal that Black men struggle related to accessing higher education, their preparedness for the academic rigors of college, navigating campus climate (e.g., conservatism and racism), and negotiating social domains, such as peer relationships and engagement on campus (see Brooms, 2017, 2021; Cuyjet, 2006; Hilton et al., 2012; Palmer et al., 2014; Palmer & Wood, 2012; Wood & Palmer, 2015).

Much of Black men's experiences, particularly in some of the more recent studies, is marked by anti-Blackness, discrimination, and stereotypes (Abrica et al., 2020; Brooms, 2017; Robertson & Chaney, 2015; Smith et al., 2016). Primarily, researchers continue to find that collegiate Black men are accosted by various forms of anti-Black racism within campus domains (e.g., academic, social, and cultural) that are connected to the broader societal misperceptions, denigrations, and dismissals of their lives. These studies detail how Black-maleness, the combined impact of Black men's racialized and gendered identities renders them as simultaneously invisible and hypervisible and expose them to a variety of forms of gendered racism (see Brooms, 2017; Mutua, 2006). In line with Brooms (2017), considering Black men's collegiate experiences within Blackmaleness "helps better appreciate the concomitant pushes and pulls that Black males experience within wider society in general and how various components of being Black and men are enacted on them during their college years," which helps make clear how Black men are problematized and are always already the subject and object of surveillance and scrutiny (p. 19).

Although they face a range of structural challenges, studies show peer relationships, social engagement on campus, and connections with faculty are important contributors to Black men's college experiences (Flowers, 2003; Goings, 2017). While they may face various forms of microaggressions, stereotypes, and racism (e.g., see Robertson & Chaney, 2015; Smith et al., 2016), Black men's campus connections and engagement can serve as a buffer and help propel their academic performances and sense of belonging while also contributing to their health and well-being as well (Brooms & Davis, 2017; McGowan & Pérez, 2020; Strayhorn, 2017, 2018).

Faculty Interactions and Relationships. Research confirms the importance of Black men collegians' interactions and relationships with faculty and how these can be fruitful to their matriculation (Brooms, 2020; Flowers, 2003; Goings, 2017; Wood & Ireland, 2014). For instance, in their study of 59 Black college men who attended three different HWIs, Brooms and Davis (2017) found that relationships with faculty were an essential component of their on-campus networks. Even more specifically, they described relationships with Black faculty members as being critical to their development as they received additional support and academic assistance; the faculty members also provided them with a sense of comfort and support. Further, these relationships with faculty can contribute to Black college men's campus "village," which provides them with "a system of support that honors students' holistic selves" (Brooms, 2020, p. 933; also see Burt et al., 2019; Palmer & Gasman, 2008). Also, positive relationships with faculty can help facilitate Black men's transition to college, persistence, and retention in higher education (Brooms & Davis, 2017; Burt et al., 2019; Moore & Toliver, 2010). In addition, studies demonstrate that faculty also can limit Black men's college success efforts; here, faculty may disregard or question Black men's intellectual abilities, hold low expectations for their academic skills and interests, and perpetrate racial microaggressions or hold stereotypical views of them (Brooms, 2017; Harden, 2019; Harper et al., 2018; Smith et al., 2016).

Engagement on Campus. Another critical component of Black men's college experiences includes their engagement in campus organizations, activities, and programming, such as race- or culture-based organizations, fraternities, and men of color programs. Previous research pointed out the need for nuancing the approaches to studying Black men's college experiences given some of their unique lived experiences and needs (e.g., Howard-Hamilton, 1997; Simms et al., 1993; Taylor & Howard-Hamilton, 1995). For instance, Simms et al. (1993) noted that academic and social support services are critical factors that influence the academic success of Black college men. They also asserted that extracurricular activities contribute to students' adjustment to college. Howard-Hamilton (1997) specified that because of numerous societal dilemmas that many Black men face, they may internalize personal burdens and emotional scars "from fighting institutional racism and seeing their African American brothers fall victim to the system" (p. 17). Research on Black men's experiences in fraternities reveals how this engagement can provide opportunities for students to develop meaningful relationships with peers, enhance their skills, and provide leadership opportunities (Harper & Harris, 2006; McGuire et al., 2020).

More recently, researchers have focused on Black men's experiences in Black Male Initiative programs – or other men of color programs (Brooms, 2017, 2018; Druery & Brooms, 2019). Collectively, these studies reveal a number of ways that Black men are able to engage in meaningful interactions on campus with their Black male peers, feel supported and encouraged through involvement, and benefit from personal and professional development opportunities. As an example, in studying Black male students' experiences in a retention program,

Simmons (2013) found that a combination of personal and institutional factors contributed to students' persistence. Among the findings, the researcher noted that students held high aspirations and goals, developed positive relationships with peers and faculty, and viewed their participation in student organizations as important to their academic experience and personal growth. Similarly, in a qualitative study of 23 Black male college students in a BMI program, Brooms and colleagues (2015) found that students benefited from meaningful interactions and connections with Black male students and university personnel, felt empowered through self-discovery and personal development, and were aided by positive role models and professional development opportunities. In specific reference to the men's self-empowerment and possibilities for positive contributions, one participant noted, "I learned that I have the potential to make a change simply by completing my goals and achieving success" (p. 114).

Other studies that focus on Black men's experiences in student-centered programs, such as summer bridge programs (McGowan & Pérez, 2020), living learning communities (Cintron et al., 2020), scholars and other support programs (Maton et al., 2011; Simmons, 2013), and even subject-based collectives, such as mathematics communities (Jett, 2021), can be impactful as well. For instance, McGowan and Pérez (2020) found for the Black men collegians in their study, all of whom participated in a summer bridge program, older peers used peer pedagogies to help students navigate campus. The program contributed to the men's peer networks, offered students academic and social support, and helped create bridges to students' cultural wealth. Collectively, these studies, and others, reveal the positive contributions and multiple opportunities that engaging in out-of-classroom endeavors offer to collegiate Black men.

IMPLICATIONS

The goal of this chapter was to discuss the lived experiences of collegiate Black men. In particular, we explored how they are framed and portrayed in wider US society to help create a context for some of their on-campus experiences. Additionally, we also talked about their endeavors across athletics, relationships with faculty, and engagement on campus. Through examining multiple domains within this chapter, we identified some of the constraints that Black men experience as well as some of the opportunities and supports. Through this panoramic view, we identify several implications for education research, practice, and policy.

Research

As researchers explore Black men's college experiences, investigations that also consider how they are portrayed and positioned in wider society, particularly the media, they should continue to interrogate how media (mis)representations contribute to dominant narratives about Black boys and men in educational contexts (e.g., see Brooms, 2021; hooks, 2004; Kumah-Abiwu, 2020). Future research should investigate how collegiate Black men perceive media representations, especially given the continued increase in anti-Black violence perpetrated against Black peoples, and how these might matter to their sense of self and educational endeavors. Also, future research should explore how Black men who participate in college athletics are being prepared for college life beyond athletics (e.g., see Beamon, 2010; Cooper, 2016; Edwards, 1969; Harrison et al., 2011). This research could explore their academic engagement and continue to develop recommendations for collegiate athletic programs for meeting the needs of Black men collegians. Additionally, the performance driven nature of sports puts constraints on Black men's time, energy, and curriculum choices all for the intended purpose of athletic competition. Future research should continue to analyze the taken for granted nature of sports in educational spaces and more critically assess the role of sports in under-developing and supporting Black men's sense of self and their holistic identities.

Practice

As our discussion makes clear, it is important that educators and stakeholders pay close attention to how dominant narratives impact and can influence campus culture and climate. Future practice in student and academic services in higher education must include increasing awareness and action plans to respond to the varying needs of college Black men. Future practitioners should develop more holistic and culturally competent mentoring strategies that contribute to collegiate Black men's holistic development across multiple identities – academically, athletically, socially, and culturally. Finally, in attempting to meet some of their needs, programs and activities need to be developed that place the lives of Black men collegians at the center of focus. Not only can such efforts support their transition to college and enhance their sense of belonging, but they also can contribute to their retention, satisfaction, development, performance, and graduation (e.g., see Brooms, 2018; Cintron et al., 2020; Druery & Brooms, 2019; McGowan & Pérez, 2020; Strayhorn, 2018). Importantly, Black men also should be part of the processes of developing and refining these practices, including identifying needs and aspirations as well as potential parameters, supports, and partnerships. Engaging Black men in creating and refining these practices also ensures that their perspectives can serve as a form of both assessment and accountability for the various goals that are adopted and the intended outcomes.

Policy

Greater efforts are needed to include collegiate Black men as part of the conversations and discussions about campus life and how colleges and universities consider improving their policies and practices. Black men collegians should be strategic partners of each venture in which there are considerations for how to improve their educational experiences and outcomes. Additionally, policies should be created that ensure that there is a greater emphasis on supporting Black men's holistic development, regardless of their entrée points to the institution: such as first-time students, first-generation status, transfer status, academic self and nonathletic endeavors, as well as racial, cultural, and gender identities. Within the athletic domain, as an example, one way this could be accomplished is by tracking these activities within athletic departments and developing assessments that report out progress and (lack) of accomplishments – such as the current graduation report card for Division I athletics. Additionally, efforts to meet the needs of Black men collegians should be tied to institutional priorities and strategic plans so that such efforts can be sustained and woven into the culture of the institution.

CONCLUSION

Nearly three decades ago, Davis (1994) asserted that collegiate Black men experience education in problematic ways and, as a result, "have common needs for support and integration" in college which implies that institutions should "provide services that can meet these needs more effectively" (p. 630). As discussed throughout this chapter, there are several areas that impact the lives of Black men collegians that need greater attention, some of which are reflected in the college society nexus that often shapes how they are perceived, positioned, and treated. Given these realities, much more efforts are needed to ensure that Black men are provided with holistic support that can position them better to thrive academically, socially, and personally in higher education contexts.

REFERENCES

Abdul Rahman, M. (2022). *Cognitive dissonance and the reproduction of the Black achievement gaps in the US.* Cambridge Scholars Publishing.

Abrica, E. J., Garcia-Louis, C., & Gallaway, C. D. J. (2020). Antiblackness in the Hispanic-serving community college (HSCC) context: Black male collegiate experiences through the lens of settler colonial logics. *Race, Ethnicity and Education, 23*(1), 55–73. https://doi.org/10.1080/13613324.2019.1631781

Allen, Q. (2020). (In)visible men on campus: Campus racial climate and subversive Black masculinities at a predominantly White liberal arts university. *Gender and Education, 32*(7), 843–861. https://doi.org/10.1080/09540253.2018.1533924

Anderson, E. (Ed.). (2008). *Against the wall: Poor, young, Black, and male.* University of Pennsylvania Press.

Beamon, K. (2010). Are sports overemphasized in the socialization process of African American males? A qualitative analysis of former collegiate athletes' perception of sport socialization. *Journal of Black Studies, 41*(2), 281–300. https://doi.org/10.1177/0021934709340873

Beamon, K. (2012). "I'm a baller": Athletic identity foreclosure among African-American former student-athletes. *Journal of African American Studies, 16*(2), 195–208. https://doi.org/10.1007/s12111-012-9211-8

Brewer, B. W., & Petitpas, A. J. (2017). Athletic identity foreclosure. *Current Opinion in Psychology, 16,* 118–122. https://doi.org/10.1016/j.copsyc.2017.05.004

Brooks, D. D., & Althouse, R. C. (2000). *Racism in college athletics: The African American athlete's experience.* Fitness Information Technology.

Brooms, D. R. (2017). *Being Black, being male on campus: Understanding and confronting Black male collegiate experiences.* State University of New York Press.

Brooms, D. R. (2018). Exploring Black male initiative programs: Potential and possibilities for supporting Black male success in college. *The Journal of Negro Education, 87*(1), 59–72. https://doi.org/10.7709/jnegroeducation.87.1.0059

Brooms, D. R. (2020). "Helping us think about ourselves": Black men's sense of belonging through connections and relationships with faculty in college. *International Journal of Qualitative Studies in Education, 33*(9), 921–938. https://doi.org/10.1080/09518398.2019.1687956

Brooms, D. R. (2021). *Stakes is high: Trials, lessons, and triumphs in young Black men's educational journeys.* State University of New York Press.

Brooms, D. R., & Davis, A. R. (2017). Staying focused on the goal: Peer bonding and faculty mentors supporting Black males' persistence in college. *Journal of Black Studies, 48*(3), 305–326. https://doi.org/10.1177/0021934717692520

Brooms, D. R., Goodman, J., & Clark, J. (2015). "We need more of this": Engaging Black men on college campuses. *College Student Affairs Journal, 33*(1), 105–123. https://muse.jhu.edu/article/601457

Brooms, D. R., & Perry, A. R. (2016). "It's simply because we're Black men": Black men's experiences and responses to the killing of Black men. *The Journal of Men's Studies, 24*(2), 166–184. https://doi.org/10.1177/1060826516641105

Brown, A. L., & Johnson, M. W. (2014). Blackness enclosed: Understanding the Trayvon Martin incident through the long history of Black male imagery. In V. E. Evans-Winters & M. C. Bethune (Eds.), *(Re)teaching Trayvon: Education for radical justice and human freedom* (pp. 11–24). Sense.

Brown, R. (2012). Societal perceptions of African American males in higher education and the adverse impact it has on their academic achievement at predominantly White institutions. In T. Hicks & A. Pitre (Eds.), *Research in studies in higher education: educating multicultural college students* (pp. 87–116). University Press of America.

Bryan, N. (2017). White teachers' role in sustaining the school-to-prison pipeline: Recommendations for teacher education. *The Urban Review, 49*(2), 326–345. https://doi.org/10.1007/s11256-017-0403-3

Burt, B. A., Williams, K. L., & Palmer, G. J. M. (2019). It takes a village: The role of emic and etic adaptive strengths in the persistence of Black men in engineering graduate programs. *American Educational Research Journal, 56*(1), 39–74. https://doi.org/10.3102%2F0002831218789595

Carey, R. L. (2019). Imagining the comprehensive mattering of Black boys and young men in society and schools: Toward a new approach. *Harvard Educational Review, 89*(3), 370–396. https://doi.org/10.17763/1943-5045-89.3.370

Cintron, D. W., Hines, E. M., Singleton, P., & Golden, M. N. (2020). Improving the retention and GPAs of Black males at a predominantly white institution: A living and learning community approach. *Journal of African American Males in Education, 11*(1), 37–57. https://jaamejournal.scholasticahq.com/article/18098.pdf

Clark, J. S., & Brooms, D. R. (2021). Unapologetic Black inquiry: Centering Blackness in education research. In C. E. Matias (Ed.), *The handbook of critical theoretical research methods in education* (pp. 303–318). Routledge.

Cooper, J. N. (2016). Excellence beyond athletics: Best practices for enhancing Black male student athletes' educational experiences and outcomes. *Equity & Excellence in Education, 49*(3), 267–283. https://doi.org/10.1080/10665684.2016.1194097

Cooper, J., Nwadike, A., & Macaulay, C. (2017). A critical race theory analysis of big-time college sports: Implications for culturally responsive and race-conscious sport leadership. *Journal of Issues in Intercollegiate Athletics, 10*, 204–233.

Curry, T. (2014). Michael Brown and the need for a genre study of Black male death and dying. *Theory & Event, 17.*

Cuyjet, M. J. (2006). African American college men: Twenty-first-century issues and concerns. In M. J. Cuyjet (Ed.), *African American men in college* (pp. 3–23). Jossey-Bass.

Davis, J. E. (1994). College in Black and White: Campus environment and academic achievement of African American males. *The Journal of Negro Education, 63*(4), 620–633. https://doi.org/10.2307/2967299

Dow, D. M. (2016). The deadly challenges of raising African American boys: Navigating the controlling image of the "thug". *Gender & Society*, *30*(2), 161–188. https://doi.org/10.1177/0891243216629928

Drake, S. C. (2016). A meditation on the soundscapes of Black boyhood and disruptive imaginations. *Souls*, *18*(2–4), 446–458. https://doi.org/10.1080/10999949.2016.1230827

Druery, J. E., & Brooms, D. R. (2019). "It lit up the campus": Engaging Black males in a culturally enriching environment on campus. *Journal of Diversity in Higher Education*, *12*(4), 330–340. https://doi.org/10.1037/dhe0000087

Edwards, H. (1969). *The revolt of the Black athlete*. University Of Illinois Press.

Flowers, L. A. (2003). Effects of college racial composition on African American students' interactions with faculty. *College Student Affairs Journal*, *23*, 54–63.

Ford, K. A. (2011). Doing fake masculinity, being real men: Present and future constructions of self among Black college men. *Symbolic Interaction*, *34*(1), 38–62. https://doi.org/10.1525/si.2011.34.1.38

Frierson, H. T., Pearson, W., Jr., & Wyche, J. H. (2009). *Black American males in higher education: Diminishing proportions*. Emerald Publishing Limited.

Ganesan, R. (2021, August 29). Ten years since UNC's academic scandal – and we still haven't learned. *The Daily Tar Heel*. https://www.dailytarheel.com/article/2021/08/opinion-who-is-to-blame-unc-sports-scandal

Goings, R. (2017). Traditional and nontraditional high-achieving Black males' strategies for interacting with faculty at a historically Black college and university. *The Journal of Men's Studies*, *25*, 316–335. https://doi.org/10.1177/1060826517693388

Goings, R. (2018). "Making up for lost time": The transition experiences of nontraditional Black male undergraduates. *Adult Learning*, *29*(4), 158–169. https://doi.org/10.1177/1045159518783200

Harden, Y. S. (2019). *Stereotypes of a Black male misunderstood (and it's still all good): Exploring how African American/Black male students experience and perceive racial microaggressions at a community college*. [Unpublished doctoral dissertation]. Northeastern University.

Harper, S. R., & Harris, F., III. (2006). The role of Black fraternities in the African American male undergraduate experience. In M. J. Cuyjet (Ed.), *African American men in college* (pp. 129–153). Jossey-Bass.

Harper, S. R., Smith, E. J., & Davis, C. H. F. (2018). A critical race case analysis of Black undergraduate student success at an urban university. *Urban Education*, *53*(1), 3–25. https://doi.org/10.1177/0042085916668956

Harper, S. R., & Wood, J. L. (Eds.). (2015). *Advancing Black male student success from preschool through PhD*. Stylus.

Harris, F., III, Palmer, R. T., & Struve, L. E. (2011). "Cool posing" on campus: A qualitative study of masculinities and gender expression among Black men at a private research institution. *The Journal of Negro Education*, *80*(1), 47–62. https://www.jstor.org/stable/41341105

Harrison, L., Bimper, A. Y., Smith, M. P., & Logan, A. D. (2017). The mis-education of the African American student-athlete. *Kinesiology Review*, *6*(1), 60–69. https://doi.org/10.1123/kr.2016-0039

Harrison, L., Jr., Sailes, G., Rotich, W. K., & Bimper, A. Y., Jr. (2011). Living the dream or awakening from the nightmare: Race and athletic identity. *Race, Ethnicity and Education*, *14*(1), 91–103. https://doi.org/10.1080/13613324.2011.531982

Hawkins, B. (2010). *The new plantation: Black athletes, college sports, and predominantly white NCAA institutions*. Palgrave MacMillan.

Hilton, A. A., Wood, J. L., & Lewis, C. W. (Eds.). (2012). *Black males in postsecondary education: Examining their experiences in diverse institutional contexts*. Information Age.

Hines, E. M., Harris, P. C., Mayes, R. D., & Moore, J. L., III. (2020). I think of college as setting a good foundation for my future: Black males navigating the college decision making process. *Journal for Multicultural Education*, *14*(2), 129–147. https://doi.org/10.1108/JME-09-2019-0064

Hines, E. M., Mayes, R. D., Hines, M. R., Henderson, J. A., Golden, M. N., Singleton, P., Cintron, D. W., Wathen, B. J., Wright, C. G., Vega, D., & Slack, T. (2021). "You are going to school": Exploring the precollege experiences of first-year Black males in higher education. *Professional School Counselor*, *25*(1c), 1–12. https://doi.org/10.1177%2F2156759X211040044

Hoberman, J. (1997). *Darwin's athletes: How sport has damaged Black America and preserved the myth of race.* Houghton Mifflin Company.

hooks, b. (2004). *We real cool: Black men and masculinity.* Routledge.

Howard, T. C. (2014). *Black male(d): Peril and promise in the education of African American males.* Teachers College Press.

Howard-Hamilton, M. F. (1997). Theory to practice: Applying developmental theories relevant to African American men. *New Directions for Student Services, 80,* 17–30.

Hrabowski, F. A., III, Maton, K. I., & Greif, G. L. (1998). *Beating the odds: Raising academically successful African American males.* Oxford University Press.

Jenkins, T. S. (2006). Mr. Nigger: The challenges of educating Black males within American society. *Journal of Black Studies, 37*(1), 127–155. https://doi.org/10.1177/0021934704273931

Jett, C. C. (2021). "Third floor respect": A Black masculinist examination of Morehouse College's mathematics learning community. *Journal of Higher Education, 93*(2), 248–272. https://doi.org/10.1080/00221546.2021.1971486

Jett, C. C. (2022). "I have the highest GPA, but I can't be valedictorian?": Two Black males' exclusionary valedictory experiences. *Race, Ethnicity and Education, 25*(2), 290–308. https://doi.org/10.1080/13613324.2019.1599341

Knoester, M., & Au, W. (2015). Standardized testing and school segregation: Like tinder for fire? *Race, Ethnicity and Education, 20*(1), 1–14. https://doi.org/10.1080/13613324.2015.1121474

Kumah-Abiwu, F. (2020). Media gatekeeping and portrayal of Black men in America. *The Journal of Men's Studies, 28*(1), 64–81. https://doi.org/10.1177/1060826519846429

Lewis, S., Simon, C., Uzzell, R., Horwitz, A., & Casserly, M. (2010). *A call for change: The social and educational factors contributing to the outcomes of Black males in urban schools.* Council of the Great City Schools.

Madison, E. (2015). Media portrayals of the Trayvon Martin tragedy. *Cultural Studies, 15*(4), 278–282. https://doi.org/10.1177/1532708615578418

Maton, K., Hrabowski, F., & Pollard, S. (2011). African American males in the Meyerhoff Scholars Program: Outcomes and processes. In W. Tate, H. Frierson, & H. Frierson (Eds.), *Beyond stock stories and folktales: African Americans paths to STEM fields: Diversity in higher education* (Vol. 11, pp. 47–70). Emerald Publishing Limited.

McGowan, B. L., & Pérez, D. (2020). "A community built just for me": Black undergraduate men bridging gaps to community cultural wealth. *Journal of the First-Year Experience & Students in Transition, 32*(1), 43–57. https://www.acuho-i.org

McGuire, K. M., McTier, T. S., Ikegwuonu, E., Sweet, J. D., & Bryant-Scott, K. (2020). "Men doing life together": Black Christian fraternity men's embodiments of brotherhood. *Men and Masculinities, 23*(3–4), 579–599. https://doi.org/10.1177/1097184X18782735

Meier, D., & Knoester, M. (2017). *Beyond testing: Seven assessments of students and schools more effective than standardized tests.* Teachers College Press.

Moore, J. L., III, Madison-Colmore, O., & Smith, D. M. (2003). The prove-them-wrong syndrome: Voices from unheard African-American males in engineering disciplines. *The Journal of Men's Studies, 12*(1), 61–73. https://doi.org/10.3149%2Fjms.1201.61

Moore, P. J., & Toliver, S. D. (2010). Intraracial dynamics of Black professors' and Black students' communication in traditionally White colleges and universities. *Journal of Black Studies, 40*(5), 932–945. https://doi.org/10.1177/0021934708321107

Mutua, A. D. (2006). Theorizing progressive Black masculinities. In A. D. Mutua (Ed.), *Progressive Black masculinities* (pp. 3–42). Routledge.

Oliver, M. (2003). African American men as "criminal and dangerous": Implications of media portrayals of crime on the "criminalization" of African American men. *Journal of African American Studies, 7*(2), 3–18. http://www.jstor.org/stable/41819017

Palmer, R. T., & Gasman, M. (2008). "It takes a village to raise a child": The role of social capital in promoting academic success of African American men at a Black college. *Journal of College Student Development, 49*(1), 52–70. https://doi.org/10.1353/csd.2008.0002

Palmer, R. T., & Wood, J. L. (Eds.). (2012). *Black men in college: Implications for HBCUs and beyond.* Routledge.

Palmer, R. T., Wood, J. L., Dancy, T. E., & Strayhorn, T. L. (2014). *Black male collegians: Increasing access, retention, and persistence in higher education (ASHE Higher Education Report)*. John Wiley & Sons.

Rios, V. R. (2015). Policed, punished, dehumanized: The reality for young men of color living in America. In D. Johnson, P. Y. Warren, & A. Farrell (Eds.), *Deadly injustice: Trayvon Martin, race, and the criminal justice system* (pp. 59–80). New York University Press.

Robertson, R. V., & Chaney, C. (2015). The influence of stereotype threat on the responses of Black males at a predominantly white college in the south. *Journal of Pan African Studies, 7*(8), 20–42.

Robinson-Perez, A. (2021). "The heaviest thing for me is being seen as aggressive": The adverse impact of racial microaggressions on Black male undergraduates' mental health. *Race, Ethnicity and Education*, 1–21. https://doi.org/10.1080/13613324.2021.1969902

Shropshire, K. L. (1997). Colorblind propositions: Race, the SAT, & (and) the NCAA. *Stanford Law and Policy Review, 8*(1), 141–158.

Simmons, L. D. (2013). Factors of persistence for African American men in a student support organization. *The Journal of Negro Education, 82*(1), 62–74.

Simms, K., Knight, D., & Dawes, K. (1993). Institutional factors that influence the academic success of African American men. *The Journal of Men's Studies, 1*(3), 253–262. https://doi.org/10.3149/jms.0103.253

Smith, W. A., Allen, W. R., & Danley, L. L. (2007). "Assume the position...you fit the description": Psychosocial experiences and racial battle fatigue among African American male college students. *American Behavioral Scientist, 51*(4), 551–578. https://doi.org/10.1177/00027 64207307742

Smith, W. A., Hung, M., & Franklin, J. D. (2011). Racial battle fatigue and the miseducation of Black men: Racial microaggressions, societal problems, and environmental stress. *The Journal of Negro Education, 80*(1), 63–82. https://www.jstor.org/stable/41341106

Smith, W. A., Mustaffa, J. B., Jones, C. M., Curry, T. J., & Allen, W. R. (2016). "You make me wanna holler and throw up both my hands!": Campus culture, Black misandric microaggressions, and racial battle fatigue. *International Journal of Qualitative Studies in Education, 29*(9), 1189–1209. https://doi.org/10.1080/09518398.2016.1214296

Squadron, A. (2019, December 19). Lenny Cooke opens up about the final chapter of his playing career. *Slam*. https://www.slamonline.com/the-magazine/lenny-cooke-story/

Steele, C. M., & Aronson, J. (1995). Stereotype threat and the intellectual test performance of African Americans. *Journal of Personality and Social Psychology, 69*, 797–811. https://doi.org/10.1037//0022-3514.69.5.797

Strayhorn, T. L. (2017). Factors that influence the persistence and success of Black men in urban public universities. *Urban Education, 52*(9), 1106–1128. https://doi.org/10.1177/0042085915623347

Strayhorn, T. L. (2018). *College students' sense of belonging: A key to educational success* (2nd ed.). Routledge.

Taylor, C. M., & Howard-Hamilton, M. F. (1995). Student involvement and racial identity attitudes among African American males. *Journal of College Student Development, 36*(4), 330–336.

Thompson, G. L., & Allen, T. G. (2012). Four effects of the high-stakes testing movement on African American K-12 students. *The Journal of Negro Education, 81*(3), 218–227. https://www.jstor.org/stable/10.7709/jnegroeducation.81.3.0218

Tracy, M. (2017, October 13). N.C.A.A.: North Carolina will not be punished for academic scandal. *The New York Times*. https://www.nytimes.com/2017/10/13/sports/unc-north-carolina-ncaa.html

University of South Carolina Athletics. (2018, January 23). Lattimore aims to make a difference in new role with Gamecocks. *University of South Carolina Athletics*. https://gamecocksonline.com/news/2018/01/23/lattimore-aims-to-make-a-difference-in-new-role-with-gamecocks

Warde, B. (2008). Staying the course: Narratives of African American males who have completed a baccalaureate degree. *Journal of African American Studies, 12*(1), 59–72. https://doi.org/10.1007/s12111-007-9031-4

Wood, J. L., & Ireland, S. M. Y. (2014). Supporting Black male community college success: Deter-
minants of faculty-student engagement. *Community College Journal of Research and Practice,
38*(2), 154–165. https://doi.org/10.1080/10668926.2014.851957
Wood, J. L., & Palmer, R. T. (2015). *Black men in higher education: A guide to ensuring student success.*
Routledge.
Wright, C., Pickup, T., & Maylor, U. (2020). *Young British African and Caribbean men achieving
educational success.* Routledge.
Young, A. A. (2018). *Are Black men doomed?* Wiley.

CHAPTER 11

THE OVERLOOKED CONVERSATION: BLACK MALE SUCCESS IN COMMUNITY COLLEGES

Jasmin L. Spain and Nicholas T. Vick

ABSTRACT

The success of Black males in community colleges across the nation is at a pivotal turning point. Due to increased social unrest in America and the global challenges of the COVID-19 pandemic, there is a renewed focus on equitable outcomes for marginalized, underrepresented, and minoritized student groups. Consequently, institutions have sought to identify innovative and effective solutions to recruit, engage, retain, and graduate Black males.

In this chapter, best practices focused on the areas of advising, engagement, instruction, and programing will be discussed. The authors call for a strategic shared responsibility between Academic Affairs and Student Services to promote the educational, civic, and social success of Black males. The importance of workforce development for nondegree seeking Black male students will be explored. It is vital for community college professionals to develop cultural competency by developing a shared understanding of values and language. Other areas to be emphasized include developing consistency for psychological safe spaces, disaggregating student data, and providing access to key services and resources.

Keywords: Black males; student success; community college; equity; retention; cultural competency

Black Males in Secondary and Postsecondary Education
Advances in Race and Ethnicity in Education, Volume 9, 201–217
Copyright © 2024 Jasmin L. Spain and Nicholas T. Vick
Published under exclusive licence by Emerald Publishing Limited
ISSN: 2051-2317/doi:10.1108/S2051-231720230000009011

Picture this: A young, Black male is a first-generation college student entering his first class of the fall semester at the beginning of the academic year. He, like most of his classmates, is excited for this moment. He believes he is prepared, motivated to succeed, and knows what to expect. After all, he attended a summer orientation on campus to learn about campus resources such as advising, counseling, tutoring, and financial aid. Unfortunately, he will feel pressured throughout the fall semester due to the demands of a part-time job and other familial responsibilities. Despite this student's best efforts, he will fail three of his four classes and enter the spring semester on academic probation. Worse, his motivation to continue will falter, and he will ultimately decide that college is simply not for him. Consider for a moment the societal implications that this decision will have on his immediate and distant future.

Although the example above is fictional, this vignette is very much a representation of the hardships and outcomes that many Black males face in community colleges on a national scale. Even more damaging is that Black male students are often labeled as aggressive, lazy, rude, misguided, uninformed, nonchalant, and/or disconnected. These negative stereotypes and myths ignore the reality that Black males are oftentimes hard working and driven to be successful. They are intelligent, charismatic, creative, and resilient among many other positive characteristics. Some Black males might easily navigate the challenges of college life while others may need a stronger and more formal support system. Regardless, Black males deserve an enriching, challenging, and supportive educational environment.

The success of Black males in community college requires a shared and intentional responsibility by all facets of the institution but especially academic and student affairs. These units have the most interactions with Black males and shoulder the primary responsibility. Beyond shared responsibility, there is also a need for community college professionals to acknowledge the transition from access to success to equitable outcomes. The central mission of focusing on equity is noteworthy and can be accomplished through a nuanced understanding of challenges and opportunities facing community colleges in the present and the future.

In this chapter, best practices focused on the areas of advising, engagement, instruction, and programing will be discussed. The authors call for a strategic shared responsibility between Academic Affairs and Student Services to promote the educational, civic, and social success of Black males. The importance of workforce development for nondegree seeking Black male students will be explored. It is vital for community college professionals to develop cultural competency by developing a shared understanding of values and language. Other areas to be emphasized include developing consistency for psychological safe spaces, disaggregating student data, and providing access to key services and resources.

We will begin with one of the most critical success strategies for Black males in higher education, which is the strategic planning of the pipeline from secondary education to postsecondary education. This foundation for Black male achievement bridges the gap in relationships by creating an environment that brings the community college academic expectations and programatic structure and support to Black males in high school. These intentional measures have the intention to prepare them for ongoing success upon high school graduation into community college enrollment. This includes early rapport with community college leaders, reduced economic challenges for campus exposure (i.e., transportation for college tours), and early access to dual-enrolled courses and workforce credentials for immediate employment. To note, we provide a list of national Black male events in Appendix A (Spain & Vick, in press).

ESTABLISHING A PIPELINE

The establishment of pipeline programs is essential to the exposure of Black male students to the rigors of higher education. This arrangement is especially key with high school students. These pipeline programs include structures that provide college readiness, academic preparation such as summer bridge programs, career exploration, financial literacy, mentorship, as well as psycho-social-emotional development. These programs also make intentional efforts to expose Black males to opportunities to obtain college credit or employment experience in advance by way of career and college readiness courses and/or preapprentice experiences. These pipeline programs require collaboration from key partners and stakeholders who provide leadership at both the local school board level, as well as the community college, not to exclude potential public policy representatives, county and city officials, potential funders, and of course the students themselves. These pipeline initiatives provide support staff (ideally Black male or female representation) to build rapport, seeking to eliminate trust barriers that will hinder students from receiving this assistance that will contribute to their persistence and graduation from high school.

In a recent survey conducted by Pitt Community College's North Carolina (NC) pipeline program for Black males at their six public high schools in Pitt County, NC, the following quantitative outcomes were revealed:

(1) 95% of the students shared that they had a plan for success by the time of graduation. Of this percentage, students shared that their involvement in the program helped them to decide to enroll in the local community college to pursue a degree (43%) or complete short-term certification programs to begin gainful employment (38%). The remainder shared that their goals were to join the military or to begin working.
(2) 89% of the students shared that the program played a critical role in the awareness of their strengths and talents via various career exploration inventories.
(3) 83% shared that they were knowledgeable of the community college academic programs, continuing education opportunities, and student support services.
(4) 87% shared that the mentorship received helped enhance their levels of maturity, and cultural and personal development.

To support the quantitative feedback, qualitative feedback included statements such as:

(5) "It was more of a learning process for me. Takes me step-by-step of what I need to do. This community college is striving for you to be successful."

(6) "This experience was very informative, positive, and well put together."

(7) "I want to say that this was very helpful because I was gonna give up... it was perfect!"

Areas of improvement were explored as well. Feedback included an increase in the duration of each high school visit, more visits to the community college campus opposed to predominant engagement at the high school campus, and an increased emphasis on entrepreneurship. These data display the impact of early exposure, rapport building with support staff, and awareness of expectations can aid in college readiness and success.

IMPACT OF COVID-19 AND SOCIAL AND RACIAL JUSTICE

Although pipeline programs have proved to be a successful strategy for establishing a foundation for the continued pursuit of educational attainment, these programs were challenged with the psychological effects of the highly publicized deaths of unarmed Black Americans by law enforcement. This struggle was married to another public health crisis in the form of the unpredicted COVID-19 pandemic. Both world changing events generated a more in-depth conversation around diversity, inclusion, and more importantly, equity.

On March 14, 2021, Inside Higher Ed released an article entitled "Reopening with Equity" (Burke, 2021). The article was written to assess the educational, economic, psychological, and social impact of COVID-19 and viral displays of social and racial injustice. Higher education leaders were forced to evaluate and determine whether their delivery of instruction and support services were equitable to support successful recruitment, retention, learning, and engagement.

"I'm really optimistic that we have champions all across the state who are deeply committed to equity for students and deeply committed to institutional change. I really feel hopeful for what we'll be able to accomplish" (Arnett, 2022). These champions for change include institutional leaders who value investing financial and human capital to create and/or support programs and initiatives designed to support minority or underperforming student populations. As Dr Tamara Stevenson, Chief Diversity Officer and Vice President of Diversity, Equity and Inclusion at Westminster College in Salt Lake City, Utah, stated "higher ed cannot deny these inequities, cannot deny the racial hostility of this country and how it impacts students" (Arnett, 2022).

These inequities have presented psychological and social concerns for Black males, therefore affecting recruitment, but more notably retention and enrollment. COVID-19 and the ongoing systemic and institutional racist structures impacted the enrollment rates of colleges and universities nationwide. Community colleges were affected the most with a decline of enrollment of 10% in fall

2020 and an additional decline of 5% in fall 2021. This especially applies to the number of Black males, which saw a decline of almost 15% from spring 2020 to spring 2021. However, these champions of change have used the aforementioned inequities and current trend of low enrollment as leverage to address these concerns through intentional positions and/or programs designed for the success of Black males and minoritized males (Graham, 2022).

Due to families being affected by the pandemic having experienced extreme economic loss, including financial resources and employment, this has served as a factor in lower enrollment rates (Graham, 2022). Self-sacrifice and survival, especially for family, aid in the pressures of addressing the economic loss. This pressure mentally and emotionally takes precedence over enrolling or returning to college, despite community colleges structured affordability to potentially attend as a part-time student.

There have, however, been public school and community college leaders who have partnered with one another, using specific language and intentional efforts to support students. For example, Pennsylvania's city of Philadelphia public school system and the Community College of Philadelphia (CCP). Per the Superintendent of Philadelphia's, Dr William Hite, Jr there was the obvious need for success: a focus on reliable technology, an aggressive focus on mental, emotional, physical well-being. "We had to provide a lot of resources for young people to create the circumstances and conditions to be educated in a pandemic" (Herder, 2021). This feeder public school system created the space to extend beyond providing tangible support and intensifying the voice of belonging and matter created by CCP's Center of Male Engagement (CME) Project Director, Derrick Perkins. The director believes at the core of these challenges is communication, more listening and less talking. "Too often, we try to decide what is in the best interest of our students, and then wonder why it doesn't meet their needs... A student needs to know we care about them and what that care actually looks like in practice" (Herder, 2021).

An example of another common solution is Hillsborough Community College's (HCC) efforts that not only saw the benefit of partnering with their public school system to support bolster enrollment, but also saw the benefit of transfer agreements with two- to four-year institutions by providing a clear, and seamless transition into Florida A&M University and the University of South Florida. HCC also tapped into one of the most influential staples of the Black community, faith-based leaders promoting, supporting, and encouraging postsecondary enrollment (Herder, 2021).

PROGRAMS AND INITIATIVES

Throughout the country, whether it be historically Black colleges and universities (HBCUs), predominately white institutions (PWIs), minority serving institutions (MSIs), and community colleges, there are an abundance of student services, intentional programing, and structures of support to meet the noninstructional, holistic needs of college student development and growth. These consistent support services and leadership opportunities for personal and professional development include student activities and student government, TRiO programs, career services, accessibility services, counseling, veterans affairs, work study, and more. However, of the many services and opportunities offered or provided to college students, initiatives established to support Black males in college are inconsistent. This is a challenge to the ability of Black males to establish a sense of belonging on campus and the hope of a critical mass of Black male students to counter their declining enrollments.

Across the country, community colleges have done a great job of piecemealing support systems for Black males. For the sake of political correctness, or to obtain funding, efforts to support initiatives for male students identified as men of color, Black, Indigenous, and people of color (BIPOC), or minority male tend to receive more attention. However, higher education administrators and practitioners not only have been seeking ways to engage Black males on campus to enhance their collegiate experiences but also assist in their psychosocial development. There are community colleges and statewide systems that have been successful establishing programs and/or taking steps to provide intentional services. Four of them that we would like to highlight and share their program/initiative uniqueness include three institutions and one state system: Milwaukee Area Technical College, Wisconsin (WI), Compton College, California (CA), City College of Philadelphia (PA), and the North Carolina Community College System.

Men of Color Initiative (MOCI) – Milwaukee Area Technical College (MATC)

Located in the Midwest in the state of Wisconsin, Milwaukee Area Technical College's three campus institution, is home of the MOCI. The city of Milwaukee is described as having a diverse economy, low cost of living, cultural and educational experiences, with great proximity to Lake Michigan. In contrast, the city includes high levels of crime, uncomfortable winters, and property tax, just to name a few not so desired living conditions (Home & Money, 2022). MATC is the largest Wisconsin technical college of the system's institutions, with an enrollment of close to 30,000 students, of which more than half are women. Half of the enrollment is also students of color (Milwaukee Area Technical College, 2022). These statistics mirror the diverse makeup of the city's population, of which a little more than half of a million citizens reside (United States Census Bureau, 2022). Students who identify as Black, as well as citizens who identify as Black lead the racial minority demographic.

Of the robust student life experiences, initiatives, and programing, designed to support a very diverse student body, the MOCI has an ideal, yet not so-common successfully implemented approach to their umbrella for Black Male Achievement (Milwaukee Area Technical College, 2021). This approach includes:

(1) Academic advising/coaching,
(2) Cultural and educational programing,
(3) Career and workforce support,

(4) Peer to peer mentoring relationships.

In comparison to other initiatives at institutions focused on men of color, ownership of carrying out MATC's efforts are divided up into three staff leaders/administrators who specialize in the areas aforementioned in their model. Those positions include an Academic Advisor, Coordinator for Student Experience, and the Veteran Specialist.

What is unique about this cross-campus collaboration is that the institution provided a financial incentive, and considered these duties as "stretch assignments." These stretch assignments modified their job descriptions to expand their work portfolio by dedicating a specific percentage of their roles and responsibilities to the MOCI, of which each staff member obtained the title of Project Manager of MATC Men of Color Initiative. This additional responsibility also increased the data proven amount of service to men of color at MATC, which is complimented by the duties of their original position prior to the stretch assignment.

Center for Male Engagement (CME) – City College of Philadelphia (CCP)

Located in Philadelphia, PA, the CME at the CCP is one of the country's most notable programs in one of the largest cities in the country, ranking number six in 2020 (World Population Review, 2022). Focused on Black males, the CME provides its Black male students with intentional and targeted support to promote academic and nonacademic success while seeking to obtain their educational goals.

The CME is designed to enhance their skill sets, cultivate a sense of belonging and build resolve as they pursue a degree at CCP and continue beyond (Community College of Philadelphia, 2022). Services provided by the CME include:

(1) Staff support – Campus advocacy in the form of support coaches offered to students to assist in their navigation through barriers to obtain academic achievement, while receiving personal and professional development.
(2) Technology – Computers made readily available for students, including software and a repository of resources, located in the CME.
(3) Academic support – Staffing is provided to support the academic coursework in the subjects of math, English, and science. This assistance establishes academic success in core courses that will establish a firm ground for advanced and/or future coursework to obtain their educational goals.
(4) Summer bridge – In an effort to expose Black males to the collegiate experience at the CCP, the CME Next Level Summer Enrichment Program is designed to provide students with early exposure to campus life and begin to provide the foundational structure for academic success. Eligibility requirements include being admitted to the institution, completion of the Free Application for Federal Student Aid (FAFSA) and Pennsylvania Higher

Education Assistance Agency (PHEAA), and be a first-time student at the institution.

(5) Holistic experiences – To assist in the development of well-rounded students, additional services, and opportunities for growth include cultural enrichment, career development, student leadership development, attendance at various events in the arts, as well as exposure to various four-year institutions.

In comparison to other initiatives or programs designed to support Black male success, the CME has the benefit of providing a physical location on campus where students can receive academic support, mentoring, and participate in healthy social engagement in a safe environment. On the other hand, programs that solely rely on staffing to create this environment in one's office, or a space on campus not specifically designed for Black male engagement, CME provides a location that presents a place of psychological safety and trust, while also providing a location to offer the various academic resources and services afore-mentioned. The CME was founded in 2009, of which Derrick Perkins serves as the Director.

Minority Male Success Initiative (MMSI) – North Carolina Community College System (NCCCS)

Based on the number of community colleges, North Carolina ranks as the third largest community college system in the United States (North Carolina Community College System, 2022a, 2022b). North Carolina community colleges serve on average 3,375 students (Community College Review, 2022). Of the various methods to provide accessible opportunities for degree and/or diploma obtainment and developing cultural and global international focused workforce training to meet the needs of employers, various programs, and services are offered to support barriers students encounter. For Black and minoritized males, the state-funded MMSI was established to provide institutions with support to increase retention and completion rates on their respective campuses.

Each institution, under grant requirements and at their discretion, has the freedom to create the structure, delivery, marketing, and implementation of their MMSI program to meet their institutional needs regarding Black and minoritized males. Funds are awarded through a request for proposal (RFP) submission, with each community college outlining a plan of action to increase academic achievement outcomes based on the grant requirements. Over the course of the last decade, submissions included utilizing funds toward three focus areas:

(1) Programatic – Providing personal and professional development opportunities including on and off-campus programs, retreats, campus tours, etc.

(2) Early Alert – Advanced software and technology designed to support student success through engagement with faculty and staff, and track student outcomes.

(3) Staff – Hiring staff to provide one on one academic and success coaching, as well as mentoring.

The usage of technology to accompany success coaching and mentoring has been utilized to support the success of Black and minoritized males. Most recently, 11 North Carolina community colleges partnered with Watermark (formerly Aviso Retention). Per John "JJ" Evans, PhD, who serves as the Associate Director of Student Life at the North Carolina Community College System, "The shared goal among the NCCCS and Aviso Retention is to provide a well-balanced mix of human intervention and technology-driven capabilities to help students achieve their academic and personal goals... we firmly believe that the power to close the higher education equity gap lies in technology-enabled success coaching, predictive analytics and early intervention" (PR Newswire, 2021). The success of the collaborative strategy is in the ability to provide technological wrap around services among faculty, academic advisors, institutional advancement offices, as well as student support services. The grant commitment is three years, requiring each institution to submit a new nonguaranteed RFP to continue to receive funding. The first program, previously named Minority Male Mentoring, was established in 2003.

Compton College

Per Wil Del Pilar, Vice President of Higher Education Policy at the Education Trust, "We shouldn't be talking about opening up normal, we should be talking about opening up better. We know that a lot of four-year and two-year institutions weren't providing the best services to low-income students and students of color" (Burke, 2021). During the course of the COVID-19 pandemic, there have been negative impacts to the success of Black males enrolled in higher education, with a significant increase in dropout rates and a significant decrease in enrollment.

However, there have been discussions from thought leaders, educators, and administrators around equity about the increased support for Black males. As institutions seek to resume business as usual, of the many institutions who took steps to "open better" and address this concern was Compton College, located outside of Los Angeles in Compton, CA, with the hiring of its first Director of Black and Males of Color Success in 2021.

Supported, endorsed and financially supported by the college's President and Chief Executive Officer (CEO) Keith Curry, the Director position was created intentionally and specifically to recruit, retain, and graduate Black males at Compton College. The creation of this position was in response to losing more than 1,000 Black and minoritized males from fall 2019 to fall 2021. Serving as the Director is Antonio Banks, Ed.D., whose position goals are to provide academic coaching and support to help students as they navigate through guided pathways, provide cultural and academic programing, and identify support service within the fields of study students are pursuing (Weissman, 2022). With limited staffing (Director only), and the responsibility of offering strategic direction in improving the educational outcomes of Black and males of color, campus community partnerships are established to evaluate and assess student outcomes, key performance indicators (KPIs), student support services, early alert systems, student leadership and academic support.

RESIDENTIAL VERSUS NONRESIDENTIAL CAMPUSES AND MEETING BASIC NEEDS

At the conclusion of a student's secondary education experience are the numerous options to explore as they enter into the early stages of adulthood. These options include employment, the military, or furthering their education at a college or university. Unlike primary and secondary school education that provide instruction and extracurricular experiences for two semesters per academic calendar year, which typically operates over the course of 10 months, institutions of higher education typically operate in three semesters per academic calendar year: fall, spring/winter, and summer.

For those students who seek to pursue higher education, they have various options as to how they prefer to receive their instruction, and journey through their post-secondary experience. For the sake of equitable instruction for all institutions, course delivery varies including traditional face-to-face instruction, online, hybrid, and the hybrid flexible (HyFlex) classroom. However, for the sake of the lived and extracurricular experiences, community colleges primarily differ from four-year institutions in three major basic needs categories: housing, food, and transportation. Per Maslow's Hierarchy of Needs, food and housing rest in the physiological needs, whereas transportation is identified as a safety/security need. All three needs are very critical. When speaking of college students, motivation is the core of learning per Maslow's Hierarchy, where students must meet these needs in order to reach their fullest potential (Kuhn, 2017; McLeod, 2007). For students in community colleges, the needs of housing, food, and transportation are more critical than those attending four-year residential institutions.

Residence halls and campus housing create experiences for those students to live and learn in an environment conducive to holistic growth through intentional programing, socialization, and leadership opportunities such as residence hall assistants. On residential campuses, campus dining is provided to students to have the opportunity to continue their residential living experience by providing meals daily. While both housing and dining accommodate these students, both also provide spaces in which transportation is not a barrier for both housing and food are provided on their residential campuses. Most community colleges do not offer all three, if they offer them at all. Although all three affect community college students in general, Black males have another need to accompany food, transportation, and housing, which is employment or income. Among adult learners per race and ethnicity groups in 2018, Hispanics had the highest employment–population ratio, whereas Black men had the lowest, both of which are considered a longstanding pattern (U.S. Bureau of Labor Statistics, 2018).

With the lack of food, housing, and provided transportation at community colleges, along with the high unemployment rates of Black males, the barriers to successfully complete college are exacerbated. The challenges of meeting the needs of food, housing, and transportation require income in order to meet those needs unlike these needs being provided by four-year institutions. The financial resources to meet these basic needs take priority, not only for themselves but also for their families, much of which are identified as low-income, first-generation college students. The priority to meet these needs, depending on each student's financial state, can determine whether employment is better used to meet these needs in order to meet their personal and educational needs, or if employment is better served to meet their personal needs alone.

Unlike four-year institutions with students who compete for admittance, community colleges have been at the forefront for affordable, seamless access to gain a postsecondary education, especially for Black males (Cuyjet & Pope, 2006). However, meeting the basic needs of food, housing, transportation, and employment are proven barriers to Black male retention and completion.

RESEARCH

Make an informed decision. Disaggregate the data! Disaggregating the data, by gender and race specifically, will provide institutions with a clearer image of the challenges to Black male student success. Disaggregating data empowers institutions to identify various challenges but support institutional decisions, especially financial ones, to provide resources to address enrollment, retention, and graduation outcomes. This includes investing in hiring staff or budgets to create initiatives for Black male success. Every institutional department can conceivably disaggregate their data. For example, the office of admissions can track how many Black applicants are successfully onboarded. Financial aid can determine the percentage of Black applicants receiving financial support through scholarships or grants. Of course, each academic department can closely monitor if instructional initiatives are successful in closing any existing equity gaps that may impact Black males. An outcome of disaggregating data is the opportunity to disaggregate institutional and departmental processes as well.

Mental health and the promotion of workforce development. With decreased interest in transfer goals and an increase in identifying employment, Black males have focused on obtaining stackable and/or certifications to make them marketable for the workforce. There have been critics who argued that the shift from a community colleges origin of preparing students to transfer to four-year colleges or universities to focusing on obtaining jobs yielding limited economic and social benefits would not be beneficial long term (Cuyjet & Pope, 2006). However, a focus on workforce development enhances economic values in communities by addressing potential unemployment concerns which could potentially limit crime, and a continuance of providing highly-skilled workers for successful business and industry. And for students who are from low-income homes and are first-generation, the economic benefit can be more attractive. This also supports students who desire to pursue a degree after establishing a work history through the usage of credit from prior learning (CPL).

PRACTICE

Regular and frequent attendance at and/or participation in notable academic, social, and personal development events. The majority of Black males who attend these events not only promote holistic growth but also engagement and exposure with other Black and minoritized males from other institutions and in different geographical regions. Professional development experiences are provided locally and statewide; however, there are annual events held nationally to consider engaging Black and minoritized males.

Identify campus stakeholders to assist based on interest. Gauging interest from campus-stakeholders regarding Black male success on community college campuses have led to institutions identifying specific faculty and staff to serve this population. This includes roles such as academic advisors and financial aid counselors to name a couple. This is pivotal to ensure the same intentional effort at-potential populations such as student-athletes, veterans, etc. receive. There has also been efforts to create "stretch assignments" for specific staff based on interest, advanced degree aspirations, and employee goals such as was done at Milwaukee Area Technical College (WI). Another consideration is creating a nonworking advisory board or committee, with a roster balance of community leaders serving as clergy, business men/women, educators, legal system representatives, politicians, and mental health providers.

Advising with immediacy and patience. When advising Black males, it is vital to respond quickly to questions and concerns but also to wait patiently for any follow up questions or subsequent actions. This balance is necessary to ensure that the student feels supported yet not pressured. Admittedly, this approach will not be found within any standard advising theory, but it is recommended to ensure that Black males are able to build positive relationships based on trust and understanding.

An advisor should be astutely aware of the Black male students on his or her caseload and take appropriate steps to ensure a connection is established and maintained. Advisors should use all available tools to respond to Black males including email, phone, and text. To further personalize this process, it is critical for advisors to know how their assigned students prefer to communicate. Regular check-ins and even after-hours availability might be required to provide advising to Black males with a sense of both urgency and calmness.

Equity minded instructional practices. One of the most important interactions for a Black male during his time as a student at a community college will be with his instructors. One useful framework that various colleges endorse is called The 4 Connections. This framework emerged from work at Odessa College in efforts to improve the college's success rates. These strategies are listed below along with a brief explanation.

• Interact with students by name: Instructors are encouraged to learn the names of all students in face-to-face class and begin using their names throughout the first week. This simplistic strategy will help to create a personalized classroom in which students feel like they are more recognized and not simply a number.

Some Black males may even have nicknames that they prefer to be called, so it provides an excellent opportunity for instructors to create a welcoming environment.

- Check in regularly: For this strategy, instructors monitor student progression and attendance on an ongoing basis during the semester. It might also be important to refer students to campus resources such as tutoring, advising, and counseling as needed.
- Schedule one-on-one meetings: Students do not generally understand the purpose of office hours or take full advantage of them. For those reasons, it is helpful to schedule and require one-on-one meetings with students. These meetings can help instructors clarify questions about the course content and individualize their responses.
- Practice paradox: One of the more intriguing components in the 4 connections framework is the notion of practicing paradox. This process involves having a clearly structured course along with routine communication of class expectations. All courses, whether face-to-face, online, or hybrid, need organization and consistency to enhance student learning. The second layer of practicing paradox includes instructor flexibility. Too often, instructors allow their own policies and procedures of a course to derail the success of a student. Black males suffer inordinately when an instructor is unwilling to accept a late assignment (or otherwise be flexible) simply because of a policy written in the syllabus.

Without question, it is a priority for instructors to create a classroom environment that balances the open-door concept and rigor with the community college setting. It is equally important for instructors to be content experts and to provide enriching experiences. However, the aforementioned pedagogical approaches shift the instructor into the mindset of being a student advocate. Black males will benefit from an instructor that is truly concerned with their progress and success. These various efforts will require a great deal of energy, compassion, precision, and patience on the part of the instructor but improved and equitable outcomes will be attainable.

Other instructional techniques to increase the likelihood of success for Black males are the use of high impact teaching practices. Setting high yet realistic expectations is key to ensuring that the community college classroom has an appropriate level of challenge and intrigue. Additionally, instructors may choose to provide alternative learning opportunities through classroom assessment techniques, graphic organizers, portfolios, multimedia, and contextualized assignments.

Assignments can be, when possible, tailored to a student's area of interest, intended major, or background. If an instructor seeks to better understand a Black male student's background and the student chooses to reveal something about himself that is deeply personal, that information should never be used in a punitive way by the instructor in the future. Instead, it should merely serve as a bridge to form a powerful and positive relationship between instructor and student.

Instructors will find that there are many advantages to embracing diversity within their classroom. A diverse and more informed classroom can help to dispel any preconceived stereotypes. Developing cultural competency can potentially lead to more fascinating discoveries of language, customs, history, and landmarks. In other words, a more informed classroom leads to a more informed citizenry.

First generation college students may be unfamiliar with the pressures and demands of college life. There may be additional challenges in adjusting to being independent for the first time if the student is living away from home. These factors might affect the way students manage their time when trying to be a full-time student and maintain an active social life. Faculty need to be aware of and understanding of the barriers that all students face and that these challenges may be exacerbated for some Black males. Faculty should also consider the best way to promote academic integrity within their classes. For example, taking class time to explain not only what plagiarism is but also how to avoid it will pay dividends later during the course. Finally, students should be encouraged to make mistakes and ask questions. Mistakes are opportunities to learn, and questions of genuine curiosity lead to greater understanding of course content. Unfortunately, Black males may be less prone to engage in question asking and mistake making due to a variety of socioeconomic and cultural factors. It is the instructor's responsibility to normalize these student interactions and behaviors.

Institutions can also support their faculty by providing targeted training. Tallahassee Community College (TCC) provides an equity minded and culturally responsive teaching workshop series for faculty in which participants can earn a micro credential for successful completion. This professional development series asks participants to identify and develop personalized equity goals related to their teaching, consider the functions of an equity minded syllabus, and investigate key course-level success data. The training is grounded in TCC's CARE model emphasizing connections, academics, resources, and engagement (CARE). This model is proving successful in closing equity gaps between Black and white students.

POLICY

Intentional and strategic hiring efforts to increase Black male representation. Institutions should make intentional efforts to review policies to employ faculty that will mirror the student body in which it enrolls. Black male faculty are very influential, impactful, and resourceful to the success of Black male students. To combat institutional racism, prevent discrimination or potential affirmative action violations, these efforts should be done in collaboration with human resources, the diversity officer or administrator who is trained to view, create, or revise job descriptions with an equitable lens and using verbal and visible marketing strategies in tandem with four-year colleges and universities to attract upcoming Black male graduates who will be obtaining their degrees in education in their respective disciplines. This is very critical for Black males during their primary and secondary education experiences because it promotes a foundational sense of belonging that a Black male student may never receive until college, if they are fortunate enough to enroll in a course instructed by a Black male faculty member.

Usage of student activity fees. Various community college system state board codes identify policy guidelines to utilize student activity fees. For institutions that have been unsuccessful with identifying grant funding or arriving at a budget to employ staff or fund a program/initiative for Black males, the creation of a Black male student club can assist. With the establishment of a student club, this will allow for the usage of student activities fees in carrying out the mission, values, and goals to promote and enhance Black male success on campuses. Just as the establishment of a department or hiring of a staff or faculty member, usage of these funds by the club will provide the institution and student body culturally relevant programing, provide Black males with student leadership opportunities, personal and professional development experiences, as well as develop a greater sense of belonging by being recognized by the institutions Student Government Association. Some institutions provide stipends to encourage faculty and staff to serve as student club advisors, which offsets additional compensation for their service in these roles.

Prioritize off campus partnerships. Depending on a college's surrounding local community, there may be additional partnerships that can enhance a Black male's experience while enrolled. Such partnerships could include internship opportunities, mental health services, and even financial awareness training. At TCC, under the direction of the President and a commission formed on race and equity, the College made the strategic decision to support locally owned minority businesses such as restaurants and other organizations. When an event is held on campus that requires catering, a minority owned restaurant will be included in consideration. Another specific example is when Student Affairs hosted an etiquette dinner and asked for a local minority owned organization to present on topics such as professionalism and expected behavior at business meetings. These intentional efforts signal to current and prospective students, as well as faculty, staff, and the surrounding community, that TCC is welcoming and supportive of Black students. The same president's commission also created a new local history festival to educate students and the community about Northern Florida and Tallahassee's storied history.

Celebrate and connect. The success of Black male students should be prioritized and emphasized through social media, on campus celebrations, and throughout the internal and external campus community. When Black males successfully complete a program of study at their respective community college, they should feel empowered and confident to move to the next step, whether it entails entering the workforce or transferring to a university. The transfer process should be seamless and allow Black males the opportunity to connect with other transfer students upon enrolling.

If the graduate is entering the workforce, career services can be uniquely positioned to provide assistance in job placement, internships, resume and cover letter writing, professional dress tips, and soft skills development. These priorities of transfer and workforce development are central to the mission of community colleges. Institutions should strive to recognize, in both formal and informal ways, the accomplishments of Black males and provide adequate momentum to send students forward on the next steps of their destination.

REFERENCES

Arnett, A. (2022). Is 'race fatigue' setting in? Diverse Issues in Higher Education.

Burke, L. (2021). *Reopening with equity*. Inside Higher Ed. https://www.insidehighered.com/news/2021/03/15/experts-consider-equity-and-college-reopening

Community College Review. (2022). Largest North Carolina Community Colleges. https://www.communitycollegereview.com/college-size-stats/north-carolina

Community College of Philadelphia. (2022). *Center for Male Engagement (CME)*. https://www.ccp.edu/student-support/center-male-engagement

Compton College. (2021). *Compton College hires director of Black and males of color success*. https://www.compton.edu/campusinformation/currentnews/Documents/ComptonCollegeNewsReleases/2021/CC-Hires-Director-Black-and-Males-of-Color-Success.pdf

Cuyjet, M., & Pope, M. (2006). *Meeting the challenges to African American men at community colleges*. African American Men in College.

Graham, C. (2022). Why is Black male enrollment in decline? https://www.bestcolleges.com/blog/black-male-enrollment/

Herder, L. (2021). *Panel focuses on providing support to Black male students during the pandemic*. https://www.diverseeducation.com/demographics/african-american/article/15113580/panel-focuses-on-providing-support-to-black-male-students-during-the-pandemic

Home & Money. (2022). *Pros and cons of moving to Milwaukee, WI*. https://homeandmoney.com/blog/pros-and-cons-of-moving-to-milwaukee-wi/

Milwaukee Area Technical College. (2021). *Men of Color Initiative (MOCI)*. https://matc.campuslabs.com/engage/organization/moci

Milwaukee Area Technical College. (2022). *Who we are*. https://www.matc.edu/who-we-are/index.html

North Carolina Community College System. (2022a). *Get the facts*. https://www.nccommunitycolleges.edu/get-facts

North Carolina Community College System. (2022b). *Minority male success initiative*. https://www.nccommunitycolleges.edu/student-services/student-life-and-engagement/minority-male-success-initiative

PR Newswire. (2021). *Aviso retention releases initial results of study aimed at closing the higher education equity gap for minority males*. https://www.prnewswire.com/news-releases/aviso-retention-releases-initial-results-of-study-aimed-at-closing-the-higher-education-equity-gap-for-minority-males-301272574.html

Spain, J. L., & Vick, N. T. (in press). The overlooked conversation: Black male success in community colleges. In E. M. Hines & E. C. Fletcher (Eds.), *Black males in secondary and postsecondary education: Teaching, mentoring, advising, and counseling*. Emerald Publishing Limited.

United States Census Bureau. (2022). *Quick facts: Milwaukee City, Wisconsin*. https://www.census.gov/quickfacts/milwaukeecitywisconsin

U.S. Bureau of Labor Statistics. (2018). *Labor force characteristics by race and ethnicity*. https://www.bls.gov/opub/reports/race-and-ethnicity/2018/home.htm

Weissman, S. (2022). *A decades-long 'national crisis,' and a new position*. Inside Higher Ed. https://www.insidehighered.com/news/2022/01/19/colleges-hire-staff-focused-black-men#.YpFWCbj0hsc.link

World Population Review. (2022). *The 200 largest cities in the United States by population 2022*. https://worldpopulationreview.com/us-cities

APPENDIX A

NATIONAL BLACK MALE EVENTS

Table 11.A1. Exemplary National Events.

Event	Location	Host
Black, Brown, and College Bound	Tampa, FL	Hillsborough Community College
African American Male Summit	Elk Grove, CA	African American Male Education Network & Development (A²MEND)
SAAB National Conference	TBD annually	Student African American Brotherhood (SAAB)
Uplifting Black Men Conference	Blacksburg, VA	Virginia Polytechnic Institute and State University
National M.A.I.N. Summit	Greenville, NC	The M.A.I.N. Initiative LLC & U Good, Bro?! Inc.

CHAPTER 12

PROMOTING BLACK AFFIRMATION IN ADVISING AND COACHING FOR FIRST-GENERATION BLACK MALE COLLEGE STUDENTS' SUCCESS

DeOnte Brown, Rose-May Frazier, David H. Kenton and Derrick Pollock

ABSTRACT

This chapter explores the concept of identity-conscious advising and coaching to support the development of First-Generation Black Male College Students during their undergraduate experience. Advising and coaching represent foundational practices colleges and universities use to support student success. Much like other aspects of education, institutions implement advising and coaching practices without consideration for how the identity of the student or the professional delivering the service influences student outcomes. First-Generation Black Male College Students' interactions within the college context are often framed by their visible, racial, and gender identities as opposed to their first-generation experience. First-Generation Black Male College Students experience microaggressions, discrimination, deficit perspectives, or negative stereotypes. By exploring an identity-conscious approach to relevant advising theories and coaching approaches, the chapter highlights the importance of building trusting, affirming relationships that lean into the lived experiences of First-Generation Black Male College Students without subjecting them to false, harmful stereotypes. This approach requires self-awareness on the part of educators and an understanding of the racialized dynamics that are inherent in the experience. Without addressing anti-Blackness, the impact of advising and coaching on First-Generation Black

Black Males in Secondary and Postsecondary Education
Advances in Race and Ethnicity in Education, Volume 9, 219–233
Copyright © 2024 DeOnte Brown, Rose-May Frazier, David H. Kenton and Derrick Pollock
Published under exclusive licence by Emerald Publishing Limited
ISSN: 2051-2317/doi:10.1108/S2051-231720230000009012

Male College Students is likely to have diminished or limited effects for this vital student population.

Keywords: First-generation; advising; coaching; identity; culturally relevant; Black males

INTRODUCTION

Within the Black community, 57% of Black, continuing-generation college students complete a college degree compared to 29% of Black, first-generation college students (Pew Research Center, 2021). For context, continuing-generation college students are defined as having a parent that completed a bachelor's degree, and first-generation college students have a primary parent that did not complete a college degree. It is plausible that within the Black community, the graduation rate for first-generation Black college males is lower, given that graduation rates for Black males are historically lower than their peers at 40%. Completing a college degree significantly influences economic and career outcomes for Black students. However, the path to completion includes challenges based solely on the identities they were born into – being Black, male, and first generation. Of course, everyone has identities that they are born into and shape their experience; however, the socialization processes in America often leave Black males combating deficit and harmful narratives (Harper, 2012; Kim & Hargrove, 2013; Strayhorn, 2010, 2015).

Every person experiences a socialization process that allows them to understand group membership, social norms, or expectations. Like any process within human development, socialization has its faults (Cole, 2021). The socialization process often occurs from the perspective of the dominant cultures (i.e., white people, college-educated men, etc.). Undoubtedly, a process that favors one group over others can and has produced prejudices or stereotypes about other groups. Socialization occurs daily within but is not limited to media, classrooms, homes, sports, and entertainment. In education, the effects of racialized socialization are evident in disproportionate discipline, lower enrollment in honors or college, and an over-emphasis on athletic abilities (Comeaux & Grummert, 2020; Thomas & Stevenson, 2009). Gender-based socialization often highlights strength, leadership, or directness as positive qualities for men, while those qualities can have a negative connotation for women. Socialization has also led many to believe that first-generation college students should consider themselves "lucky" to be in college, lack knowledge, or have limited exposure to opportunities.

Although it appears simple to identify the effects of socialization based on a single identity, no person is only a single identity (Cole, 2021; Crenshaw, 1989). As such, intersectionality allows us to understand better the context in which a Black, first-generation college man experiences their education. Intersectionality, coined by Kimberlé Crenshaw in 1989, focused on the fact that discrimination experienced by Black women was not a matter of race or gender discrimination but the combination or intersection of both identities. Crenshaw's work highlights that the intersection of race, gender, class, and sexual orientation within a system of inequality creates varying effects within the context of discrimination because of interconnected identities. For example, when a Black, first-generation college male is subjected to the common microaggression, "What sport do you play?" the association of being Black and a man often intersect to lead another person to ask that question. Although Crenshaw's work aids in understanding the Black female experience, it has become vitally relevant when considering that having a marginalized identity weakens the power or influence that one might have with a dominant identity. An example of this idea is Black college men possessing a dominant gender identity but a marginalized racial identity.

Anti-Blackness Perspective Within Education

For Black, first-generation college men, their race and gender are likely the two identities that will inform which socialization experiences their peers, faculty, and others in the educational environment will draw upon to guide their interactions. While the first-generation identity is essential to the student's experience, that identity is hidden and only known to others if the student shares it. However, once the first-generation identity is known, it can further alter interactions. For example, a Black college man's failure to recognize that full-time course enrollment is based on number of credit hours and not number of courses on the schedule may be construed as disengagement or lack of interest based on the narrative that Black males are less interested in education. However, if that same Black college man shares that he is first-generation college student and genuinely was unaware that courses were not all equal to the same credit-hour total, a peer, faculty, and staff member may be more likely to take additional time to explain other processes to this student to support their success. The knowledge of this hidden identity leads to a different level of compassion for the student and to some extent neutralizes the assumptions generated by race.

Given the history of America and its higher education system creating barriers to education for Black people, anti-Blackness is a driving factor in the experiences of Black, first-generation college males. While discussion of racism has existed and continues to exist in American society, further naming anti-Black racism or anti-Blackness allows for recognition that (a) dehumanization of Blackness exists, (b) intentional marginalization of Black people occurs, and (c) anti-Black policies and ideologies are allowed to exist (Council for the Democratizing Education). Within education, anti-Blackness has led to Black students questioning if they belong on campus (Brady et al., 2020; Strayhorn, 2012), have access to college engagement opportunities (Harper, 2012), or see themselves in their majors or careers of their choice (Brown, 2021). Similarly, the Black faculty and staff supporting Black students (formally or informally) must navigate anti-Blackness in their careers concerning policies or acceptable practices (Croom & Patton, 2012; Richardson, 2021).

BLACK, FIRST-GENERATION COLLEGE MEN IN HIGHER EDUCATION

The experience of Black, first-generation college men in higher education can consist of the visible identity of Black college men, and the hidden identity, of first-generation college students.

Black College Men. Black college men often exist as a population of concern or targets for intervention on campuses, given their historically low retention and graduation rates (Brooms, 2018; Hall, 2017; Harper, 2009). Several factors contribute to the status of Black college men as an at-risk group. Black college men, especially those in attendance at predominately white institutions, are likely to experience increased psychological stress due to their race and gender (Bridges, 2011; Harper, 2009). In recent years with more media attention highlighting the murders of Black boys and men – Trayvon Martin, Tamir Rice, Ahmaud Arbery, George Floyd, and so many others – Black boys and men constantly live in a state of fear. For Black college men, the college campus is not a haven but rather an extension or microcosm of society, which has socialized others into viewing them as uneducated or a threat. The undue stress of being a Black man on a college campus contributes to adverse effects on academic performance, social engagement, and sense of belonging (Bridges, 2011; Strayhorn, 2010), which influence graduation and retention.

Often, rather than being met with a supportive and engaging campus environment, Black college men encounter microaggressions, higher levels of isolation, and fewer opportunities for meaningful engagement with faculty (Jackson et al., 2013; Pendakur & Harper, 2016). Student–faculty relationships and, by extension, student–staff relationships like that of an academic advisor or coach positively impact the college experience. However, when Black college men feel that they have been negatively labeled (i.e., lazy, incompetent, just an athlete, etc.), they are less likely to seek out those meaningful relationships. Additionally, like other students with marginalized identities, Black college men can be more successful when faculty or staff engage in culturally relevant or affirming practices (Brown, 2021; Rhoden, 2017).

First-Generation College Students. Only 20% of first-generation college students complete a bachelor's degree within six years, compared to 49% of continuing-generation students (RTI, 2019). The first-generation college population is also more likely to enroll in college part-time, have dependents, and is less likely to be male, which aligns with lower college enrollment among Black males (RTI, 2019). Like Black college men, first-generation students face challenges to retention and graduation because of academic or social factors. In particular, first-generation college students have reported concerns about their academic preparedness or confidence and ability to be involved or know what their goals are regarding their education (Petty, 2014). For first-generation college students, navigating college can be an isolating experience considering that their family is less likely to understand many of the processes or elements of the experience. Similarly, faculty and staff that were continuing-generation college graduates also have a different perspective on college than the first-generation students they support.

Compounding Challenges from Identities. Considering the intersection of the visible and hidden identities, there is a greater likelihood that Black, first-generation college men are less likely to utilize resources that could combat their lack of college-going knowledge, given the perceptions that exist based on their race and gender among faculty (Carey, 2019; Gilliard, 2020; Jehangir, 2010). Black, first-generation college men may also find themselves desiring assistance but not knowing what resources are available to them because many college campuses operate from the position that students know what resources are available to them. Additionally, as both the visible and hidden identities must face feelings that they do not belong on campus, the burden of not living up to that assumption can be overwhelming for Black, first-generation college students. However, with appropriate support, these and other challenges for Black, first-generation college students can be mitigated.

PURPOSE OF ACADEMIC ADVISING AND COACHING IN HIGHER EDUCATION

Academic advising and coaching represent essential services within higher education that can influence college completion while also addressing some challenges that Black, first-generation college men may experience (Frazier, 2019). The staff that provide these services are supporting students in their transition to college, connecting to campus resources for academic, career, and personal success, or being a supportive staff member. Academic advising is a service on college campuses. The foundation of this work exists because of the expectations that early faculty members not only taught courses but often were assigned groups of students to mentor to ensure graduation. According to O'Banion (1972), "the purpose of academic advising is to help the student choose a program of study which will serve him in the development of his total potential" (p. 62). Faculty advising still exists; however, many campuses employ staff members to serve in these professional roles. As college students and the college experience have evolved, so has the purpose of advising. El-Sheikh et al. (2019) asserted the importance of academic advising to the educational process. They identified the five steps thereof: (a) exploration of life goals, (b) exploration of vocational goals, (c) selection of program, (d) selection of courses, and (e) scheduling courses.

In further support of the evolution of student needs and to lean into the exploration of life goals, professionals are employed to deliver coaching services that have garnered national recognition related to retention and graduation improvement (Bettinger & Baker, 2014; Mitchell & Gansemer-Topf, 2016; van Nieuwerburgh, 2012). Coaching remains an emerging intervention in higher education, but according to van Nieuwerburgh (2012), it is:

A one-to-one conversation focused on enhancing learning and development through increasing self-awareness and a sense of personal responsibility, where the coach facilitates self-directed

learning of the student being coached through questioning, active listening, and appropriate
challenge in a supportive and encouraging climate (p. 17).

Within the college context, coaching provides a service for students that often
allows them to identify the barriers to their success that must be addressed
(McClellan & Moser, 2011; Richman et al., 2014; Robinson & Gahagan, 2010).
The relationship that students form with an advisor or coach is representative of a
meaningful faculty–student or staff–student relationship that is often the catalyst
for belonging, engagement, and student success.

The Foundation of Advising and Coaching in Higher Education

Much of the work concerning advising and coaching follows guidance by
NACADA: The Global Community for Academic Advising. NACADA offers a
fundamental concept of advising to operationalize the implementation, core
values for advising and coaching professionals, and competencies that allow
advising and coaching to be impactful. The concept of academic advising focuses
on the "what" – curriculum of academic advising, "how" – pedagogy of academic
advising, and "why" – student learning outcomes of academic advising. Academic advising derives from theoretical perspectives in education, social sciences,
and the humanities. As such, professionals delivering academic advising and
coaching must engage in training for service delivery, documentation of service
delivery, and assessment of their service. Advising and coaching are learning
experiences that influence student growth and development. While advising was
once transactional by simply providing the list of courses, this is no longer the
primary intent. The seven core values that NACADA encourages professionals to
embrace in their daily interactions are in place to promote student growth and
development. NACADA (2017) established core values as outlined in their
association's guiding documents include (1) caring, (2) commitment, (3)
empowerment, (4) inclusivity, (5) integrity, (6) professionalism, and (7) respect.
The core values address relationship management between the student and
advisor that must center high-quality support for all students with emphasis on
diverse populations via affirmation, ethical behaviors, and high quality of service.

Core competencies represent the third element of the advising and coaching
foundation. These core competencies should guide the development of any
training program related to advising and coaching. According to the NACADA
professional development committee (2017), the purpose of the model is to
identify the broad range of understanding, knowledge, and skills that support
academic advising, guide professional development, and promote the contributions of advising to student development, progress, and success. Professional
advisors, faculty advisors, administrators, advising supervisors and mentors, and
trainers can use the model to gain the understanding and expertise to be influential allies for students. Conceptual, informational, and relational are the three
elements of the framework for the academic advising core competencies. The core
competencies represent the content knowledge (conceptual and informational),
the theories and facts of advising, combined with abilities (relational). Through
conceptual competency, an understanding of how to engage as an academic

advising and coaching professional is developed. Informational emphasizes the importance of advising and coaching professionals understanding the facts, resources, and histories of their respective campus to effectively engage in advising and coaching. Relational focuses on how or the leveraging of the relationship between the advisor/coach and student to ensure that the student can receive the information and support that is shared.

Current Approaches to Advising and Coaching

Several current approaches are worth highlighting within the context of advising and coaching. The approaches have success related to retention and graduation broadly.

Developmental advising. Various academic advising models exist to address the specific, diverse needs of heterogeneous students and improve overall retention. Developmental advising was offered as an approach that examines student development from a holistic perspective and includes the college experience, not just academics (Raushi, 1993; Sanders & Killian, 2017; Winston et al., 1982). He and Huston (2016) asserted that developmental advising "focuses on students' holistic development in both cognitive and non-cognitive aspects" (p. 216). The developmental advising approach is a strategy that academic advisors apply when meeting with students to discuss the skills and strengths required to complete program of study courses, graduate, and pursue graduate school or enter the workforce. An academic advisor practicing developmental advising demonstrates a caring attitude, initiating conversations beyond policy and responding to student cues. The advisor incorporates a holistic approach to items that influence students' success in getting involved on campus, financial stability, personal wellness, and commitment to graduation and beyond. Developmental advising has a long history as an effective approach to academic advising.

Intrusive advising. Intrusive advising is a structured intervention strategy to engage the student multiple times throughout the semester and is a response to developmental advising (Donaldson et al., 2016; Garing, 1993; Noel et al., 1985). Intrusive advising is a practical strategy to improve student retention. Tollinchi (2015) stated that intrusive academic advising addresses the four stages of college attrition development, and each stage – (a) early detection, (b) action-oriented responses, (c) campus-wide participation, and (d) professional staffing – is an extension of retention theory. An example of intrusive advising is a first-year course or seminar. Academic advisors often teach first-year seminars via a course design that aims to improve first-year retention. The advisor can provide students with institutional information before students need the resources and allow students to experience the transition from high school to college within the curriculum structure. In addition, intrusive advising allows the scheduling of one-on-one meetings to discuss goal setting, encourage involvement, and discuss any obstacles or challenges that students may be experiencing. Academic advisors have the opportunity to foster a collaborative partnership by encouraging follow-up meetings that promote relationship building and increase the sense of being a part of the campus community as soon as possible. Intrusive advising can support students in connecting with the institution, applying time management strategies, and encouraging persistence and graduation.

Nurtured advising. Williams et al. (2008) offered nurtured advising as a method that allows the advisor to exert care and act in a maternal or paternal role with a similar influence to help shape the student's life. According to Williams et al. (2008):

> This type of student-advisor relationship simulates that of a concerned family member. This relationship can improve the student matriculation processes and provides students with a sense of security. The relationship also provides a sense of connectedness where students feel that they belong to the school and that the school belongs to them. (p. 15)

Professionals consider nurtured advising a successful strategy among historically Black colleges and universities, whose student populations are predominately Black, first-generation college students.

Personal Coaching. With varying models and strategies of advising, many college and university leaders began to identify the benefits of the whole student, intrusive and nurturing aspects of advising that merge mentorship, academic preparation, and personal facilitation of success. Such pursuits of a more holistic approach are precursors to success coaching. Personal coaching in college assists students in becoming more self-aware and reflective while learning how to apply their self-management skills to be effective students. In the coaching session, students will learn how to apply institutional policies and procedures to achieve academic and personal goals (Farrell, 2007). Personal coaching in college can also be effective with vulnerable student populations such as first-generation, commuting, working adults, and returning military student populations. Similar to commuter students, online learners, or part-time students, personal coaching is popular with first-generation students who are unaware of campus life (Lefdahl-Davis et al., 2018; Melendez, 2007). Personal coaching is vital to university administrations because student service increases first-year retention metrics for student success and institutional excellence and increases revenue through student tuition.

Identity-Conscious Advising and Coaching

Advising and coaching have very well-established approaches to supporting retention and graduation. However, as institutions continue to seek ways to address systemic inequities and promote educational equity, a focus and understanding of student identity is paramount. NACADA purports that inclusivity is a core value for advising and coaching professionals to embrace daily. Identity-conscious advising does not replace any of the models of advising or coaching that were previously shared. Instead, identity-conscious advising implores the advising community to add and understand "who" – students experiencing academic advising to its core concept. Amplification of inclusivity occurs by addressing the "who."

The idea of identity-conscious advising and coaching draws upon the cultural responsiveness component of Museus (2014), Culturally Engaging Campus

Environments (CECE) Model. The CECE model focuses on the role of campus environments in influencing the experiences and outcomes of college students with diverse backgrounds. Museus (2014) found that indicators within an institution's culture such as cultural relevance (cultural familiarity, culturally relevant knowledge, meaningful cross-cultural engagement, and cultural validation) and cultural responsiveness (collective cultural orientation, humanized educational environments, proactive philosophies, and holistic support) impact student outcomes (learning, development, satisfaction, persistence, and degree completion). The impact within the relationship is influenced by students' sense of belonging, academic disposition, and academic performance.

The CECE model directly addresses several challenges experienced by Black, first-generation college men, including but not limited to feelings of isolation, lack of belonging, retention, and graduation. Specifically, the cultural responsiveness component of the CECE model focuses on the support systems, which could include advising and coaching and how the systems consider and respond to the experiences and needs of diverse students. Within cultural responsiveness, four specific indicators defined by Museus (2014) that must be addressed are:

- Collectivist Cultural Orientations – Campuses cultures that emphasize a collectivist, rather than individualistic, cultural orientation that is characterized by teamwork and pursuit of mutual success.
- Humanized Educational Environments – Availability of opportunities for students to develop meaningful relationships with faculty and staff members who care about and are committed to their success.
- Proactive Philosophies – Philosophies that lead faculty, administrators, and staff to proactively bring important information, opportunities, and support services to students, rather than waiting for students to seek them out or hunt them down on their own.
- Holistic Support – Students' access to at least one faculty or staff member that they are confident will provide the information they need, offer the help they seek, or connect them with the information or support that they require regardless of the problem or issue that they face.

Collectively, each indicator encourages identity-conscious advising and coaching to support the success of Black, first-generation college men.

- As previously highlighted, coaching is based on the idea that the student and coach are both committed to the student's success, and that the advising relationship is vital to student retention and graduation. However, Black, first-generation college men may not always feel that their coach or advisor is invested in their collective success unless consistent and intentional actions are taken to understand the student. The collectivist approach is relevant to the focus on identity-conscious advising. An example of a collectivist approach would be a coach or advisor working together to identify the barriers to success influenced by the student's identity and the action items they will take to ensure the student's success.

- Advisors and coaches can create humanized environments by providing opportunities for students to experience the range of emotions that come with being a college student, especially when race or gender becomes a factor. It could be easy for an advisor or coach to dismiss a student's experience with racism or discrimination as a general student experience, but that would run counter to the CECE model and the focus on identity-conscious advising and coaching. Similarly, advisors can create these environments by considering what their physical or virtual office space conveys to students.

- Proactive philosophies would implore advisors and coaches to respectfully show up for students at their cultural events or offer to be a resource to conduct student workshops. In addition, a proactive philosophy requires advisors and coaches to learn about the students they support to minimize harming students through microaggressions or bias incidents.

- Holistic support allows advisors and coaches to be a comprehensive resource and supporter for students. One way this can occur is by sending students messages during moments of national crisis or, at minimum, acknowledging cultural heritage months. Holistic support also means connecting Black, first-generation college men with each other as a system of support. Also, this includes connecting students with other faculty and staff that can be a resource.

For academic advisors and coaches to engage in cultural responsiveness and support of Black, first-generation college men, the core competencies must become grounded identity consciousness. For this to occur, training and development for advisors must include: 1) recognition of inequity in societal context, 2) self-awareness of own identities, 3) understanding of student identities, and 4) practice in delivering culturally appropriate support (see Table 12.1).

Recognition of inequity in context. An individual providing advising or coaching services must first acknowledge that inequities exist for specific identities in education. For Black, first-generation college men, this recognition requires an acknowledgment that anti-Blackness exists in education, and that our systemic practices create barriers for this population in achieving college success outcomes. Within this tenet, the advisor or coach must be able to identify how their respective campus perpetuates inequity for this population. Individuals are

Table 12.1. Connection Between Core Competencies and Identity-Conscious Training.

Core Competency	Identity-Conscious Elements
Conceptual	Recognition of inequity in societal context
Informational	Awareness of own identities
	Understanding of Student Identities
Relational	Delivering culturally relevant support

Note: Table developed by authors in 2023.

encouraged to review (a) campus climate surveys, (b) equity, diversity, and inclusion strategic plans, or (c) host listening sessions with students.

Awareness of own identities. Identity-conscious advising or coaching demands that the person delivering the service gain a deeper understanding of their various social identities. A stronger sense of self allows staff to approach their work with a level of authenticity that allows students to gravitate toward them. By having a deeper understanding of themselves, advisors and coaches will understand their own culture, their experiences with implicit bias, and how their lived experiences influence how they show up in their work. To engage in this tenet, advisors or coaches can complete identity or cultural-based assessments, read books about their salient identities, or attend a host or equity, diversity, or inclusion workshops incorporating self-reflection.

Understanding of student identities. While learning about oneself, advisors or coaches must also learn about the students they will support. As previously mentioned, Black, first-generation college men are often victims of negative stereotypes, which can dissuade their willingness to engage with faculty or staff. Advisors or coaches benefit from learning about their students' individualized experiences to be better informed of that student's narrative instead of focusing on broad generalizations. Broad generalizations prevent advisors and coaches from understanding the inequities within the environment and the more focused relationship-building that could occur with students. Advisors or coaches can learn more about students by creating opportunities for students to share how their identities have influenced their educational journey or asking questions that allow the student to share what feels included feels like for them or about any experiences that have positively or negatively impacted them. Advisors or coaches can also learn if there are any significant cultural norms or expectations that may impact the staff–student relationship.

Practice in delivering culturally relevant support. Providing culturally responsive support results from understanding inequity, one's own identities, and the identities of students being supported. The congruence of those three areas allows advisors and coaches to tailor their support of students based on their identities. This congruence also catalyzes continued learning to be able to adjust to the needs of the students.

RECOMMENDATIONS

Research

There is much to be learned about identity-conscious advising through empirical research. Among the most anticipated areas of inquiry would be an examination of advisor or coach intercultural competence coupled with the satisfaction of the advising or coaching experiences of students with underrepresented identities. Intercultural competence would allow for an understanding of how advisors and coaches approach the difference between their own identity and that of the students they can support. Furthermore, as first-generation students are less likely to use campus support resources, research that can lead to a greater understanding of factors that influence the engagement of Black, first-generation college men could allow advisors or coaches to tailor their support strategies around "what works." Exploring the types of culturally responsive strategies that advisors or coaches use to affect student success would also add value to research related to identity-conscious advising.

Practice

The academic advising and coaching profession can potentially enhance its impact on retention and graduation by investing more in inclusivity development. As individuals are trained, more intentionality in the topics that are covered for equity, diversity, and inclusion is essential. As advisors or coaches are expected to remain up-to-date on academic policies or expectations, having a similar expectation of remaining aware of the equity, diversity, and inclusion efforts are of equal importance. Advisors and coaches should ensure they incorporate meetings or opportunities focused on relationship-building with students. These meetings allow students with marginalized identities, such as Black, first-generation college men, to get more from experience than a transactional relationship related to courses or skill development.

Policy

Many colleges and universities have specific policies and guidelines related to academic advising or coaching. It is recommended that these policies be reviewed and updated as needed to incorporate requirements related to identity-conscious advising. For example, suppose an advising policy has a statement of purpose. In that case, language like "advising or coaching serves to meet the needs of students based on their social identities and lived experiences" communicate to faculty, staff, and students that an expectation of identity consciousness exists. Also, within policies, establishing specific goals or outcomes of advising and coaching related to identity consciousness represents essential additions. Policies should also outline minimum training expectations related to identity-conscious advising.

CONCLUSION

Enhancing advising and coaching practices to become conscious identity benefits Black, first-generation college men and other underrepresented students. The socialization process that has occurred in America for decades with respect to Black men has existed to limit their trajectory. The shifting of one's perspective requires an investment of time and commitment to learning. The ask for advisors and coaches to become more identity conscious in their work is not difficult; however, Black, first-generation college men need to be seen and understood. Since the summer of 2020, which saw many Americans begin to address racism and anti-Blackness, socially conscious messaging has become a prevalent part of corporate marketing. For example, Proctor and Gamble produced a commercial,

"These Hands," which challenged the notion that a young Black boy with "good hands" for catching a football should focus on sports which tends to become the primary narrative for athletically gifted Black boys. The commercial provides examples of other non-athletic-focused careers that can be achieved with good hands. Just as this reframing occurred in the commercial, advisors and coaches will be able to reframe their thinking through their investment in learning. However, they will also be able to affirm and validate Black, first-generation college men that they belong in college and have individuals that care about their success.

REFERENCES

Bettinger, E. P., & Baker, R. B. (2014). The effects of student coaching: An evaluation of a randomized experiment in student advising. *Educational Evaluation and Policy Analysis, 36*(1), 3–19.

Brady, S. T., Cohen, G. L., Jarvis, S. N., & Walton, G. M. (2020). A brief social belonging intervention in college improves adult outcomes for Black Americans. *Science Advances, 6*(18), eaay3689. https://doi.org/10.1126/sciadv.aay3689

Bridges, E. M. (2011). Racial identity development and psychological coping strategies of undergraduate and graduate African American males. *Journal and African American Males in Education, 2*(2), 151–167.

Brooms, D. R. (2018). Exploring Black male initiative programs: Potential and possibilities for supporting Black male success in college. *The Journal of Negro Education, 87*(1), 59–72.

Brown, D. (2021). *Educating Black collegians: Examining the influence of blackness on educational outcomes related to life and career perspectives.* All Dissertations. 2895. https://tigerprints. clemson.edu/all_dissertations/2895

Carey, R. L. (2019). Am I smart enough? Will I make friends? And can I even afford it? Exploring the college-going dilemmas of Black and Latino adolescent boys. *American Journal of Education, 125*(3), 381–415.

Cole, N. L. (2021, February 16). Understanding Socialization in Sociology. https://www.thoughtco. com/socialization-in-sociology-4104466

Comeaux, E., & Grummert, S. E. (2020). Antiblackness in college athletics: Facilitating high impact campus engagement and successful career transitions among Black athletes. *Journal of Issues in Intercollegiate Athletics*, 56–72. Special issue.

Crenshaw, K. (1989). Demarginalizing the intersection of race and sex: A Black feminist critique of antidiscrimination doctrine, feminist theory and antiracist politics. *University of Chicago Legal Forum, 1989*(8). https://chicagounbound.uchicago.edu/uclf/vol1989/iss1/8

Croom, N., & Patton, L. (2012). The miner's canary: A critical race perspective on the representation of Black women full professors. *Negro Educational Review, 62/63*(1–4), 13–39.

Donaldson, P., McKinney, L., Lee, M., & Pino, D. (2016). First-year community college students' perceptions of and attitudes toward intrusive academic advising. *NACADA Journal, 36*(1), 30–42.

El-Sheikh, O., Mohammed, B., Emad, H., & Zoromba, M. (2019). Developing corrective actions to improve academic advising process. *American Journal of Nursing, 7*(3), 286–292.

Farrell, E. F. (2007). *Some colleges provide success coaches for students.* http://www.chronicle.com/ article/Some-Colleges-Provide-Success/10133/

Frazier, R. (2019). *Postsecondary success coaching: A predictive analysis of Pell-eligible, first time in college students' transition, first-year retention, and academic success.* Dissertation. 27663401.

Garing, M. T. (1993). Intrusive academic advising. *New Directions for Community Colleges, 82*(1), 97–104.

Gilliard, L. (2020). *Rooting for everybody Black: Exploring the need for mentorship for Black first-generation students at predominantly white institutions* (p. 144). West Chester University Master's Theses.

Hall, R. R. (2017). Factors contributing to the persistence of African American and Hispanic undergraduate males enrolled at a regional predominantly White institution. *Administrative Issues Journal: Connecting Education, Practice, and Research, 7*(1), 51–65.

Harper, S. R. (2009). Negros no more: A critical race counternarrative on Black male student achievement at predominantly White colleges and universities. *International Journal of Qualitative Studies in Education, 22*(6), 697–712.

Harper, S. R. (2012). *Black male student success in higher education: A report from the national Black male college achievement study.* University of Pennsylvania, Center for the Study of Race and Equity in Education.

He, Y., & Hutson, B. (2016). Appreciative assessment in academic advising. *The Review of Higher Education, 39*(2), 213–240.

Jackson, J. R., Jackson, C. E., Liles, R. G., & Exner, N. (2013). The educated Black men and higher education. *Ideas and Research You Can Use: Vistas Online, 89,* 1–12.

Jehangir, R. (2010). *Higher education and first-generation students: Cultivating community, voice, and place for the new majority.* Springer.

Kim, E., & Hargrove, D. T. (2013). Deficient or resilient: A critical review of Black male academic success and persistence in higher education. *The Journal of Negro Education, 82*(1), 300–311.

Lefdahl-Davis, E. M., Huffman, L., Stancil, J., & Alayan, A. J. (2018). The impact of life coaching on undergraduate students: A multiyear analysis of coaching outcomes. *International Journal of Evidence Based Coaching and Mentoring, 16*(2), 6983.

McClellan, J., & Moser, C. (2011). A practical approach to advising as coaching. NACADA Clearinghouse of Academic Advising Resources website. http://www.nacada.ksu.edu/Resources/Clearinghouse/View-Articles/Advising-as-coaching.aspx

Melendez, R. (2007). Coaching students to achieve their goals: Can it boost retention? *The Hispanic Outlook in Higher Education, 17,* 21–60.

Mitchell, J. J., & Gansemer-Topf, A. M. (2016). Academic coaching and self-regulation: Promoting the success of students with disabilities. *Journal of Postsecondary Education and Disability, 29*(3), 249–256.

Museus, S. D. (2014). The Culturally Engaging Campus Environments (CECE) Model: A new theory of college success among racially diverse student populations. In M. B. Paulsen (Ed.), *Higher education: Handbook of theory and research* (pp. 189–227). Springer.

NACADA: The Global Community for Academic Advising. (2017). *NACADA core values of academic advising.*

van Nieuwerburgh, C. (2012). *Coaching in education: Getting better results for students, educators, and parents.* Routledge.

Noel, L., Levitz, R. S., & Saluri, D. (1985). *Increasing student retention: Effective programs and practices for reducing the dropout rate.* Jossey-Bass.

O'Banion, T. (1972). An academic advising model. *Junior College Journal, 42*(62–64), 66–69.

Pendakur, V., & Harper, S. R. (2016). *Closing the opportunity gap: Identity conscious strategies for retention and student success.* Stylus Publishing, LLC.

Petty, T. (2014). Motivating first-generation students to academic success and college completion. *College Student Journal, 48*(2), 257–264.

Pew Research Center. (2021). *First-Generation College Graduates Lag Behind Peers on Key Economic Outcomes.*

Raushi, T. M. (1993). Developmental academic advising. In M. C. King (Ed.), *Academic advising: Organizing and delivering services for student success* (Vol. 82, pp. 5–19). New Directions for Community Colleges.

Rhoden, S. (2017). "Trust me, you are going to college": How trust influences academic achievement in Black males. *The Journal of Negro Education, 86*(1), 52–64. https://doi.org/10.7709/jnegroeducation.86.1.0052

Richardson, A. (2021). *The impact of interlocking systems of oppression on the leadership and decision-making experiences of Black women in executive-level leadership positions at predominantly white public research institutions in the United States.* All Dissertations. 2948. https://tigerprints.clemson.edu/all_dissertations/2948

Richman, E. L., Rademacher, K. N., & Maitland, T. L. (2014). Coaching and college success. *Journal of Postsecondary Education and Disability*, *27*(1), 33–50.

Robinson, C., & Gahagan, J. (2010). In practice: Coaching students to academic success and engagement on campus. *About Campus*, *15*(4), 26–29.

RTI International. (2019). *First year experience, persistence, and attainment of first-generation college students*. NASPA. https://firstgen.naspa.org/files/dmfile/FactSheet-02.pdf

Sanders, M. A., & Killian, J. B. (2017). Advising in higher education. *Radiologic Science & Education*, *22*(1), 15–21.

Strayhorn, T. L. (2010). When race and gender collide: The impact of social and cultural capital on academic achievement of African American and Latino males. *The Review of Higher Education*, *33*(3), 307–332.

Strayhorn, T. L. (2012). *College students' sense of belonging: A key to educational success for all students* (1st ed.). Routledge.

Strayhorn, T. L. (2015). Factors influencing Black males' preparation for college and success in STEM majors: A mixed methods study. *Western Journal of Black Studies*, *39*(1), 45–63.

Thomas, D. E., & Stevenson, H. (2009). Gender risks and education: The particular classroom challenges for urban low-income African American boys. *Review of Research in Education*, *33*(1), 160–180.

Tollinchi, M. (2015). *Academic achievement among Latina undergraduates: An examination of psychosociocultural factors associated with academic achievement and persistence among Dominican and Puerto Rican students*. Fordham University.

Williams, I. L., Glenn, P. W., & Wider, F. (2008). Nurtured advising: An essential approach to advising students at historically black colleges and universities. *Academic Advising Today*, *31*(1), 17.

Winston, R. B., Jr., Ender, S. C., & Miller, T. K. (Eds.). (1982). *Developmental approaches to academic advising*. Jossey-Bass.

CHAPTER 13

LIVING, LEARNING (AND LEGACY) COMMUNITY: A NEW LIVING AND LEARNING COMMUNITY MODEL FOR BLACK MALES

Monique N. Golden, Paul Singleton II, Dakota W. Cintron, Michael Reid Jr. and Erik M. Hines

ABSTRACT

A Legacy Community is a living and learning community supported by broader institutional departments (e.g., student affairs, academic affairs, foundation, and alumni affairs) that dedicate resources, opportunities, and supports intended to: (a) undo legacies of educational disparities that Black/ African American males have historically witnessed and (b) build capacity for students engaged in these communities (i.e., Black/African American males) to create and leave positive legacies on their terms. In this qualitative study of Black and African American undergraduate male living and learning community (LLC) participants at a primarily white institution (Legacy House), we investigate the LLC program elements that impact participants' educational and social experiences, and foster pathways for student legacy building. Legacy house participants describe brotherhood, sense of belonging, and leaving a legacy as elements that enable positive student academic and social outcomes, campus involvement, and career readiness.

Keywords: Black males; living and learning community; brotherhood; academic outcomes; legacy; educational and social experiences

Black Males in Secondary and Postsecondary Education
Advances in Race and Ethnicity in Education, Volume 9, 235–254
Copyright © 2024 Monique N. Golden, Paul Singleton II, Dakota W. Cintron, Michael Reid Jr. and Erik M. Hines
Published under exclusive licence by Emerald Publishing Limited
ISSN: 2051-2317/doi:10.1108/S2051-231720230000009013

The American dream claims equal opportunity, meritocracy, and prosperity for individuals who work hard and follow the rules (Delgado, 2007; Woods-Wells, 2016). Yet, in America, the economic, health, and education gaps between racial/ethnic groups continue to widen (Tucker, 2014; Wildeman & Wang, 2017). According to achievement, segregation, and funding data, Black males are overwhelmingly receiving unequal professional and educational opportunities (Black, 2018; Bohrnstedt et al., 2015; Couch & Fairlie, 2010; Orfield et al., 2016; Quillian et al., 2017; Ushomirsky & Williams, 2015). At the center of this American endemic are Black males where stark disparities in completion rates from higher education institutions and inequality in employment contribute vastly to the myth of equal opportunity and upward mobility.

Compared with Asian, white, and Hispanic students, Black students, particularly Black males, are more likely to end their educational careers without obtaining a bachelor's degree and less likely to be employed (National Center for Educational Statistics, 2019). For example, according to the National Center for Educational Statistics (2019), for the 2009 starting cohort, only 40% of Blacks, compared to 73% of Asians, 63% of whites, and 54% of Hispanics, graduated from a four-year post-secondary institution within six years. For Black males compared to Black women, 43% for Black women compared to 34% for Black men graduated from a four-year postsecondary institution within six years (National Center for Educational Statistics, 2019). When education is held constant, Blacks are still less likely to be employed. Baum et al. (2016), using The United States Census Bureau data from 2015, report a 4.0% unemployment rate for Blacks with a four-year college degree that was roughly 67% higher than the 2.4% unemployment rate for white four-year college degree holders. The same employment gap for high school diploma holders was 110% (i.e., 9.7% vs 4.6%, respectively for Black and white high school diploma holders). Moreover, using 2020 annual averages from the US Bureau of Labor Statistics Current Population Survey, the unemployment rates in the civilian noninstitutional population for those with a bachelor's degree or higher by race were 4.3, 4.6, 6.6, and 5.9 for white, Asian, Hispanic, and Black men, respectively (US Bureau of Labor Statistics, 2020).

In the past, Black and minoritized students' educational trajectories were far more likely than white students to end before high school graduation. Now, these educational disparities have shifted to later stages in Black males' educational careers. In 1990, racial disparities in high school graduation rates were quite substantial (i.e., 81% for white, 66% for Black, and 50% for Hispanic students (Merolla, 2018). However, by 2012, the disparities in high school graduation rates had narrowed considerably (i.e., 93% for white, 87% for Black, and 65% for Hispanic students) (Merolla, 2018). During this same time, disparities in college completion rates between Black and white Americans remained nearly identical, albeit widening slightly (i.e., in 1990, 23% of whites and 11% of Blacks held bachelor's degrees, and in 2012, 35% of whites and 21% of Blacks held bachelor's degrees) (Merolla, 2018). Williams and Swail (2005) suggested that "if high school graduation rates were equalized, the gap in college going and college completion rates would be reduced significantly for all groups, especially for Blacks," (Williams & Swail, 2005, p. vi). Unfortunately, this equality has yet to manifest in reality.

Uncovering why Black males forgo their pursuit of higher education is critical to understanding why racial disparities in bachelor's degree attainment persist, for promoting the well-being of Black males, and for the economy. Higher education is not only good for the individual but also advances their communities and the United States as a whole (Hout, 2012). Research suggests that postsecondary degree holders have increased life expectancy and better general health, improved quality of life for themselves and their children, and increased social status (Hout, 2012; Williams & Swail, 2005). Furthermore, at the societal level, postsecondary degree holders have lower rates of incarceration, higher volunteer rates, and higher voter participation rates (Hout, 2012; Williams & Swail, 2005).

The reasons why Black males may choose to end their educational careers early are multifaceted but often center on the challenges and barriers that they experience in higher education. Black males face several challenges in higher education. Research suggests that Black males often "(re)position them[selves] as outsiders on campus primary because of the continued anti-Blackness that they face" (Brooms, 2018, p. 60) and that their "Blackmaleness" (Brooms, 2018; James & Lewis, 2014; Mutua, 2006) (e.g., the intersection of their race and gender identity) arouses gendered racism that manifests in stereotype threat, profiling, denigration, and disparities in policing (Brooms, 2018); these effects are often more pronounced at historically white institutions (Brooms, 2017; Johnson-Ahorlu, 2013; Smith et al., 2007; Wood & Palmer, 2015).

For Black males, LLCs are high-impact interventions for academic, social, professional, and personal development (Cintron et al., 2020; Hines et al., 2021). Cintron et al. (2020) found, using a quasi-experimental design, evidence that Black male LLC participants had higher short-term gains in retention and grade point average (GPA) compared to similarly matched non-LCC participant Black males at a primarily white institution. Related research has also found that Black students have more to gain than white students when they participate in academic-related and learning community activities at primarily white universities (DeSousa & Kuh, 1996; Hotchkiss et al., 2006; MacKay & Kuh, 1994). What is likely contributing to the success of the LLCs is the model (design) which blends traditional and best practices program elements, and what we have coined as legacy elements: (a) the undoing of legacies of educational disparities that Black males have historically witnessed and (b) building capacity for students engaged in these communities (i.e., Black males) to create and leave positive legacies on their terms.

BENEFITS OF LLC PARTICIPATION

Beginning college and living on-campus can be a difficult transition for many Black male students. For most students, it is the first time they have lived away from home, and now they have been exposed to a new community where they likely do not know anyone (Potts, 2021; Schauer et al., 2020). Regardless of what major a student pursues or what environment a student comes from, LLCs can help alleviate the struggles of that transition. By fostering a community of like-minded individuals, students that participate in an LLC experience a smoother transition during their first year of college (Schauer et al., 2020). Activities like brotherhood meetings, bonding activities, group study sessions, and community meetings with faculty are positive indicators of a student's successful academic and social transition (Inkelas et al., 2007).

LLCs foundationally promote peer-to-peer and student-faculty interaction while providing students with considerable resources and access: transformative opportunities (internships, study abroad, exploratory trips), collaborative learning activities (e.g., First-Year Experience (FYE) courses, students coenrolling in courses), and involvement in complementary academic and social activities that extend beyond the classroom (e.g., students meet weekly in a life, soft and academic, skills course and/or with a success coach) (Everett & Zobel, 2012).

In addition, LLCs are designed to provide students with social and academic benefits. Through their shared living space, most LLC participants ultimately live, eat, learn, socialize, and study with a common group of people. Pope et al. (2019) highlighted the importance of students being able to interact with their peers due to it being an important factor in student development. LLCs help alleviate anxiety or stress from finding study groups, or asking for additional support due to having peers in the same major who live with one another (Schauer et al., 2020). LLC participants study more in groups than non-participants, and thus feel more supported in their living environments than students who live in traditional on-campus housing (Shushok & Sriram, 2010).

A common component of students' social and academic integration is their sense of belonging, which is based on perceived social support, connectedness, being seen and mattering (Xu et al., 2018). Sense of belonging is positively linked to students' motivation, engagement, and achievement (Murphy & Zirkel, 2015; Wilson et al., 2015). How sense of belonging is associated with persistence have become increasingly apparent, with researchers like Zea et al. (1997) showing that both academic and social integration experiences impacted student persistence in college. It has become clear that the living learning communities further students' sense of belonging which is one of the defining benefits of LLCs.

HIGHER ACADEMIC ACHIEVEMENT, PERSISTENCE, AND INVOLVEMENT

The curriculum created by the faculty director in a LLC (which will be discussed later in this chapter) allows students to develop the ability to build relationships with peers within the same community. This is particularly important for Black males who may require additional support to navigate the college environment (Palm & Thomas, 2015). Relatedly, a study conducted by Hurtado et al. (2020) found that LLC residents were two to three times more likely to attend a class, meet with a faculty member, meet an academic advisor, or use academic support services where they lived. Further, students who participated in LLCs also are substantially more likely to study with other students, attend social or cocurricular activities, diversity-related activities, and health and wellness activities in their place of residence (Hurtado et al., 2020).

Additionally, it is shown that LLC students on average had a stronger sense of community, increased peer interaction particularly as it relates to academics and involvement within the community, more access to academic advising, tutoring, and other programing catered to their academic and career interests/achievement (Davis & Laster, 2019; Inkelas et al., 2018). This boost in faculty and peer interaction in combination with having access to resources and support in their first year's positions LLC participations to build the social capital within their community while also being set up for academic success while at their institution (Solanki et al., 2019).

Another benefit to the academic and social transition to college that LLC provides includes the first-year experience classes participants are enrolled in. For first-year students the curriculum is designed to help students identify university resources (finding the math lab and writing center), cultivate their soft skills (e.g., time management, study skills, etc.), and nurture their career development. The second-year students engage in a curriculum focused on exposure to graduate/professional school activities. For example, Legacy House includes a research series where professors come to the course and discuss their research agenda along with their personal experiences of attending graduate/professional school.

FYE classes allow students the ability to build relationships with peers assigned to the same community. This is particularly important for first-year college students who may require additional support to navigate the college environment (Palm & Thomas, 2015). This can be fostered through a sense of belonging a community environment offers, particularly for students of color in higher education (Banks et al., 2021). Students participating in LLCs have been shown to have higher GPAs and graduation rates than those who do not participate (Palm & Thomas, 2015).

Adding to students' academic success and social transition, many LLCs have upperclassmen residents to serve as mentors and tutors as they also provide advice on how to be successful in their classes and at the university (Phipps, 2020). Every LLC is structured differently. However, nearly all of them have systems in place that help participants foster a relationship with the larger institution community. For example Legacy House's mission focuses on encouraging involvement with the larger university community to foster peer and mentor relationships and will actively engage students in inclusion efforts at Gemini University. Additionally, LLCs often include a faculty-in-residence, where a faculty member and possibly their family live in the residence halls with students, or they are able to place a faculty member's office within the residential college. It has also been found that students who live in LLCs report more meaningful interactions with faculty (Inkelas et al., 2008).

LLCS AS A HIGHIMPACT PRACTICE

LLCs are proven high-impact practices that offer students opportunities to investigate areas of interest, based on their major or an interdisciplinary topic, through guided courses and cocurricular activities. LLCs develop knowledgeable, responsible, and engaged citizens in a culture of inquiry within a learner-centered university. While assisting students with their social and academic transition, they offer a small college feel and a sense of place on a large campus; they promote meaningful and sustained interactions with faculty, staff, and student leaders; and they provide an effective structure for curricular coherence, deeper learning, student success, persistence, and engagement. Therefore, LLCs can be a critical intervention that can lead to improved student satisfaction, retention, and persistence rates for historically underserved communities.

There are several models that describe how LLC program elements enhance student learning and development, and improve retention and persistence. One leading model, the best practices model (BPM) (which the Legacy House follows) – outlines four levels of residential learning community (RLC) structure, including: (a) infrastructure, (b) academic environment, (c) cocurricular environment, and (d) what they call the "pinnacle" – the integration of the previous three (Inkelas et al., 2018). As indicated through the BPM, RLCs differ from other on-campus housing options because of the intentionality behind their structures and programmatic efforts. Although many students have access to multiple enriching educational experiences, the RLC is often highly recognized because it "explicitly seeks to support and augment student learning and development" (Inkelas et al., 2018, p. 142). These elements help facilitate learning and development among students.

Living, Learning and Legacy Communities (LLLC) are differentiated from other LLCs/RLCs because their purpose is to undo legacies of educational disparities that Black/African American males have historically witnessed and build capacity for students engaged in these communities to leave positive legacies on their terms. Thus, we argue there are additional critical elements that are required in order for LLCs like the Legacy House to effectively serve its students.

LEGACY HOUSE

Legacy House was created due to the low graduation rates of Black males at Gemini University (pseudonym). The Assistant Vice Provost for Academic Affairs initiated the process of starting a LLC as a pilot program to see if it will help improve graduation rates. We use the term legacy as this was a finding in the current study which we will describe later in this chapter. The Assistant Vice Provost selected a faculty director who was an assistant professor with a school counseling background and a research agenda focused on the academic and career outcomes of Black males.

The eligibility process for the Legacy House included freshman or sophomore males who were interested in supporting Black males in the area of academic success. The Legacy House can house up to 50 students on half of a floor shared by another RLC.

The mission and vision of Legacy House are to increase the retention rate of Black males and persistence of students using educational and social experiences to enhance their academic success at Gemini University and beyond graduate and professional school placement. Legacy House will encourage involvement with the larger university community to foster peer and mentor relationships and will actively engage students in inclusion efforts at Gemini University. The vision of this initiative is to ensure that Black men in this program will change the narrative of being underrepresented in careers and educational pursuits beyond an undergraduate degree.

To meet students' diverse needs, the infrastructure of a Legacy Scholar Community requires a broader scope of on-campus partnerships that provide a portfolio of programs, resources, and services to scholars. To illustrate, the Legacy House works with academic and nonacademic departments (e.g., academic affairs, student affairs, alumni affairs, the University Foundation, study abroad, tutoring services, career development, to name a few).

The Legacy House supports the scholastic efforts of its students through academic and social and emotional support, access to research opportunities, study abroad, and professional development. Legacy House enables involvement with the larger university community to foster peer and mentor relationships and actively engage students in inclusion efforts at Gemini University.

WHAT MAKES THE LEGACY HOUSE A PREFERRED MODEL FOR BLACK MALE LEGACY COMMUNITIES?

The Legacy House is a preferred model for Black Male Legacy Communities due to its influence on student outcomes such as motivation and receptivity to support (Markle & Stelzriede, 2020), sense of belonging (Spanierman et al., 2013; Strayhorn, 2018), academic excellence (Millea et al., 2018), and student involvement (Astin, 1984). However it is the combination of the LLC's leadership structure, institutional partnerships, and commitment to positive student outcomes that create an academic and cocurricular environment that cultivates leaders and scholars.

The Legacy House Leadership Team comprises the following roles during the academic year: a faculty director, four graduate assistants (who also serve as success coaches), an assistant residence hall director and resident assistant, three floor mentors, and two first-year experience mentors (mentor roles are reserved for LLC participants).

The full-time faculty director is in charge of leading the program, providing office hours, informal academic advising and counseling for its members, as well as a full-time Associate Director (i.e., Graduate Assistant) focused on operations and meets with students to discuss academic and social aspects of college including transition goals and resources (Maltby et al., 2016). Two of the graduate assistants ("GAs") were responsible for cofacilitating aspects of the LLC curriculum; the other two assistants were responsible for program research and evaluation. Students are required to meet with their GA success coach once per week via email, text, or face-to-face meetings. Weekly meetings help ensure students are presented with all options should a problem arise. Opportunities to engage with a coach in college have been shown to increase persistence for students (Banks et al., 2021). Participants receive support from a success coach who will provide structured advising, mentorship, and assist them with skill development in areas of time management, advocacy, wrap-around services, as well as career development with respect to their individual strengths. Ultimately, by meeting with success coaches, on a weekly basis, students begin to build self-efficacy and adjust to college-life (Banks et al., 2021).

Students also have peer mentors who support them in their transition to Gemini and the LLC model. For example, floor mentors conduct check-ins and manage study halls, distribute pertinent community updates, such as invitations to special events and programs, and lead bonding experiences with the residents. In the FYE course, peer mentors cofacilitate activities in efforts to promote persistence, academic success, and student development (Maltby et al., 2016). As students may have a difficult time navigating the university environment, LLC models that prioritize having access to staff while working in collaboration with them, which can increase persistence and retention among participants in the LLC (Banks & Dohy, 2019; Banks et al., 2021; Brooms, 2018).

LEGACY HOUSE STUDENT ACADEMIC AND POSTSECONDARY OUTCOMES

Prior research suggests Black and African American male LLC participants have higher GPAs than their peers (Hines et al., 2018), are retained at a greater rate than their peers and are more likely to persist through graduation than non-participants (Cintron et al., 2020). These findings indicate that Black males are successful when provided a space where they can navigate the college transition and flourish. In this section, we briefly highlight some of the academic and postsecondary outcomes of the Legacy House inaugural cohort.

Legacy House alumni go on to pursue full-time jobs and advanced degree programs (master's and PhDs) in fields such as civil engineering, biomedical engineering, business administration, computer science and engineering, entrepreneurship, and education/education policy. In 2020, retention and persistence rates among LLC students surpassed historical institutional rates for Black and African American males (first- and second-year retention rates among LLC participants were 96% and 93%, respectively). At this time, the share of students involved in and/or off campus leadership roles (74%), and research and internship positions (31%) flourished. The average GPA for the first graduating cohort (May, 2020) was 3.244 (Cintron et al., 2020; Hines et al., 2021, 2023).

PURPOSE OF STUDY

In this qualitative study of Black and African American undergraduate male LLC participants at a primarily white institution (Legacy House), we explored the program elements that impact participants' educational and social experiences, and foster pathways for student legacy building. We sought to identify the additional structural design elements for similar LLCs serving Black/African American males who historically witnessed low retention and persistence at primarily white institutions.

METHODS

Procedures

The first author received institutional review board (IRB) approval to conduct this research study, and then proceeded to recruit participants for a focus group interview. Participants were recruited from a Black male residential learning community at a historically white institution (HWI), in the northeastern part of the United States. Of the 25 Black male students targeted for participation in the study, seven (28%) met the study's participation requirements and consented to participate in a focus group interview. The interview protocol was developed and grounded in cultural capital theory (Bourdieu, 1986), college and career readiness literature, and research on Black male students (Hines et al., 2020; Hines et al., 2021; Hines & Owen, 2022). Follow up prompts in a group format (i.e., a focus group) were also used to solicit participant responses (Breakwell, 1995). All participants were given pseudonyms, and the group interviews were recorded and transcribed.

Participants

The participants in this study were seven first-year students from the inaugural cohort of this LLC. Each Black male participant was asked to complete a

Table 13.1. Study Participants.

Participant Pseudonym	Classification	Age	Major
Lebron James	Freshmen	18	Sport Management
Randy Moss	Freshmen	18	Sport Management
Russell Wilson	Freshmen	18	Economics
Demase Thomas	Freshmen	18	Sport Management
Ezekiel Eliot	Freshmen	18	Communications
Clyde Bennett	Freshmen	18	Communications
Leonard	Freshmen	18	Communications

demographic questionnaire through Qualtrics (e.g., major, age, name, etc.). The questionnaire was a way to ascertain information on the participants' academic and personal experiences. A subset of participant information is presented in Table 13.1.

Data Analysis

The researchers used deductive and inductive approaches in the data analysis process, and the conceptualization of themes were created using literature on Black males and salient strands from the literature. The technique of in vivo coding was employed as a method of code identification to cite participants' exact words in addition to participants' responses presenting emergent concepts because of inductive analysis (Ryan & Bernard, 2000).

A five-step process: raw data codes, first-order clusters, second-order clusters, general dimensions, and emergent themes/comparative clusters were the result of using a blended content analysis and grounded theory analytical procedure. Identified codes were quantized to identify the level of salience of identified clusters across multiple participants at each phase of the coding process (Tashakkori & Teddlie, 1998). An auditor was used to ensure the trustworthiness and quality of the data as well as participant member checks; detailed memos; the documentation of an audit trail; and methodological, data, and multiple investigators/analysts (various forms of triangulation) (Patton, 2002).

Limitations

The study focuses on the experiences and views of inaugural participants belonging to a niche learning community and cannot be generalized to all Black males, or Black male LLCs. Moreover, the authors interviewed freshmen about their experiences, and not sophomores who may have different perspectives on the program. Last, we did not interview all freshman students in the Legacy community, just a subset.

Positionality

Positionality entails the authors who were involved with the data analysis portion of this research study. The first author is a Black woman who assisted in analyzing the data. She holds a PhD in leadership and education policy and has experience working with the Legacy House as a graduate researcher and student success coach. The second author is a Black man who is a PhD candidate and served on the data analysis team. His research interests are Black males' college and career readiness as well as mental health counseling for Black males. He has served as a GA for the Legacy House and has a background in school counseling. Also, he has a background in P-12 education.

The third author is a white male with Puerto Rican heritage who served on the data analysis team. Also, he served as the research assistant for Legacy House. His research interest includes public health in underserved communities as well as program evaluation and quantitative methods. Currently, he is working as a postdoctoral researcher. The fourth author is a Black male, who is pursuing his PhD in educational leadership and policy. He was a previous Legacy House participant and peer mentor.

Last, the fifth author is a Black male, who is an associate professor in school counseling, with a research agenda focused on understanding Black male academic and career outcomes. He has experience working with Black males in P-12 and in higher education settings. He identifies as a Black male who is committed to helping Black males and boys based on his own experiences within both private and public schools.

FINDINGS

Study participants discussed their decisions to join and their experiences in Legacy House. We find that students attribute their decisions to join and positive experiences based on three factors: brotherhood, a community of belonging, and legacy building. Thus, the name of this LLC is based on this group of Black men wanting to embrace changing the status quo, honor, and preserve the purpose of this LLC, and leave a powerful legacy for other young Black men who would join this program in the future.

Brotherhood

The theme of brotherhood emerged as participants described their experiences in Legacy House. Brotherhood was interpreted as the cultivation of a positive, supportive, and meaningful space to bond with Black male peers. Additionally, brotherhood provides nurturing of supportive and meaningful relationships with other Black males in the legacy community. Being a part of a brotherhood that provides resources, counsel, guidance, motivation, and support builds confidence and optimism in Black males to excel socially and academically at Gemini University. This was also a theme by Taffe (2022) where she conducted a similar study on the same Black male learning community.

Participants described the Legacy House as a brotherhood that motivates and supports them academically. For example, participants describe the impacts of brotherhood on their study hall behaviors:

> I believe that *Legacy House is like another brotherhood.* Like, we all got each other's back. Even some things like study hall, we all help each other out when there's homework or there's regular studying. We always help each other out.

> Just sitting in a room for two hours a week with people that are related to you, or not related to you major-wise, is really helpful. You get help with your schoolwork. You also get to ask [the Leadership team] for an opinion or help with something. And there's just people around you that are geared towards their education, and want to help you succeed, and want to see you succeed.

> In the study hall room, everybody is just working, so like when you're part of that environment, it makes you feel like – it makes you tell yourself, it's time to really work and just be a part of that. And, sometimes, we need that. You need that space to just tune yourself out, and just do what you need to do for that time.

Another participant attributes their growth in study and time management skills to the inaugural cohort's collective determination to leave a positive legacy on the Legacy House LLC:

> It definitely impacted my academics in a positive way because being here in Legacy House, we're able to go to the academic achievement center, we learn about new study skills..I really had to take the time to learn new study skills, whether that be making notecards or stuff like that... And being [at Legacy House], it definitely makes you want to succeed in your academics more because we all – especially us being the first to leave [Gemini University], *we want to put our stamp down on this learning community that it does, in fact, help us.* And they provide us with the resources here, and I definitely see the growth in study skills and time management.

At Legacy House, cocurricular programmatic experiences, such as cultural and professional development trips, and community building activities like "breaking bread" and the ropes course, help cultivate a brotherhood that lends itself to increased comfort and student engagement in broader campus activities among participants:

> The D.C. trip and smaller things like the ropes course, and even breaking bread, help build our bonds, and be there for each other. That definitely was a helpful thing just to make us all like even more – much more comfortable with each other.

> We went to D.C. I think that was helpful because, you know, not only did we get to go to the museum, but we also got to bond with each other. It created a brotherhood. And in terms of activities, we did like intramurals and things like that. So we did at ScHOLA²RS House, intramural flag football team. We did a basketball team. And it was just a good experience.

> Legacy House has basically influenced me to do certain things like the intramural flag football and basketball. I probably would have never done that. So it's like we just influenced the group just from being around each other.

Participants of Legacy House described brotherhood as a critical element to increasing their social and cultural capital on campus. This fosters an enhanced sense of self-confidence and optimism which motivates participants to perform better academically and be more engaged in student activities.

A Community of Belonging

The theme of "having a community to belong to/comfort/black boy joy" was prevalent throughout the interview with the LLC participants. The community of belonging extends from their motivation to join the LLC to their beliefs about why the LLC was valuable to them. The participants built a community in which they were invested in the success and developing of relationships with each other. This community of belonging was forged in common bonds and interests and not needing validation from anyone but themselves. For instance, multiple participants described their desire to join the LLC with regards to a community of belonging:

> I joined Legacy House because it gave me an opportunity to be myself as a Black African-American male on a predominantly White campus.

> I joined Legacy House because I just heard that it's like a community full of people who might understand my culture a bit more and I might connect with them on a different level than I would someone who isn't necessarily from the same background as me.

> I knew I was gonna be on the floor with all the Black guys, so I just knew it was gonna be something I was gonna be comfortable with and something that I wasn't gonna have to necessarily get used to. It was just gonna be natural.

The LLC provided participants a space to form a community in which they could be themselves as Black males on a historically white campus. In this space, they were able to express themselves because they felt that those in the LLC understood their culture and that they could connect with them because of their shared lived experiences as Black men.

Moreover, the community of belonging was further represented in the participants' descriptions of their experiences in the LLC. For instance, having the living aspect of the LLC was critical to one participant. As one participant noted,

> I could walk down the hall and I could be myself. You know, I don't have to change how I act. Like I don't have to put a mask on what I do or say...If I lived somewhere else, and it was like my hall was predominately White, I probably wouldn't do some of the things I do now.

Likewise, the breaking bread component of the LLC, that actively aimed to bring Black leaders and faculty from around the campus and community, also contributed to the participants' sense of community belonging and beliefs about their capability to be successful. As one participant explicated during the interview,

> I would also say that breaking bread has also helped us due to the fact that we have a lot of African-American speakers around the university coming to talk about their experiences in college and growing up, and seeing all the different challenges that they faced, and seeing how far that they made it. And it makes us say to ourselves like if they can make it, why can't I? And it just allows us to see further down the road, how great we can possibly be.

The participants also attributed their feelings of having a community of belonging to the successes that Black men have experienced at a primarily white university. As one participant so saliently described,

> I think the number one reason why Black males probably drop out of college is not because they're not smart. It's because they don't see other Black males that are smart. Because when we go around and we look around just walking around every day, we don't see too many Black males, like probably two per block wherever you walk. So it's kind of like it's hard to have somebody to look up to, hard to have somebody you want to follow or try to follow the leader. So I feel like the more leaders we have, maybe just expand the LegacyHouse and make us greater. Then other Black males coming out of high school, other freshmen, are gonna look up to us and start building upon that, and we're gonna start seeing more and more Black males graduate and then fix the retention rate.

Legacy House participants recognized a community of belonging as an essential factor to their comfort at a primary white institution. The Legacy House was a place where the participants could be themselves, be understood, and not need to change the way they were. Further, the participants reported that the Legacy House was a place where the participants' feeling of sense of community also translated to their motivation to continue their pursuit of higher education and strive for success.

Legacy Building

Within Legacy House, loyalty and commitment to the mission: the collective goal of students was to empower themselves to excel academically and socially, and leave a positive impact on the LLC. Also, shared accountability rather than formal or administrative accountability ignites commitment to the mission of scholarly excellence and positive legacies. LLCs like Legacy House have been purposefully and intentionally establishing innovative practices focused on meaningful and transformative experiences in college. Shared vision and responsibility/accountability emerged as a main component of Legacy House due to students' ongoing learning and engagement they have in the LLC daily. Legacy House participants noted that the community possesses a strong and supportive culture, which creates a standard that members must meet. The participants described having a shared responsibility for the development and sustainability of this community:

> Before arriving on campus, I saw in the media about how much scrutiny this particular learning community was getting. So like I thought we'd constantly be watchful, which I still think we are, but like we'll always be under a microscope to watch what we're doing, like make sure we're always on track and stuff like that. So I knew that coming here, like being the first wave of this, we had to put our stamp here, and make sure that this learning community could stay on for years.

> Since being in the Legacy House, I realized that our individual actions impact the whole group. So if one of us does something that makes us look bad, it's gonna affect the whole group. So we just have to be conscious and aware of what we do to make sure that we represent.

Legacy House provides support, personal and professional development, and creates an environment where every participant can contribute to embodying the mission. Moreover, participants reported that Legacy House participants have each other's back, while also holding each other accountable when it comes to homework, studying, and being an active member of the community. Legacy House participants feel that activities like breaking bread and/or community meetings give them the space to model to each other how they should conduct themselves in the community.

DISCUSSION

The findings support prior research that Black males seek social connections with their male peers as a means of building social support and developing a micro-community on campus (Brooms et al., 2018). The brotherhood Legacy House participants described reflects a micro-community, "where Black male students can meet with and develop friendships with students that are like them, students and advisors who understand the unique challenges they face, and a safe environment where they can recount their experiences, gain affirmation, and receive guidance" (Taffe, 2022, p. 154). Brotherhood is foundational to the LLC experience, and facilitates increased academic and social engagement, and more importantly, students desire to leave a positive legacy on their campus so that future participants may enjoy similar LLC benefits. Brotherhood is a critical source of social and cultural capital for Black males attending predominantly white intitutions (PWIs), and the LLC enhances this through its programs, study halls, and curricular and cocurricular experiences. Overall, participants reported feeling more confident, optimistic, and embraced their scholar identities (and shared responsibility) to excel in college and beyond.

Having a community to belong to is a critical aspect of the efficacy of the Legacy House to participants. The Legacy House was a place where participants felt that they could be themselves and that they felt they could be understood, especially around their culture and Blackmaleness. The community of belonging made participants feel that they did not have to change who they were to belong on campus. Further, participants in the Legacy House reported that having a community of belonging, or experiences with individuals like themselves, contributed to their motivation to pursue and succeed in higher education. These findings are consistent with prior research on Black males' experiences in higher education (Brooms, 2019; Hines et al., 2021; Strayhorn, 2009). Prior research indicates that one reason that Black males may leave college, especially at a primarily white university, is that they do not belong or "fit in" (Strayhorn, 2009). Brooms (2019), in a multisite qualitative study of Black male initiatives (BMIs), found that BMIs served "...as important enclaves and communities for Black men's persistence and success efforts in college" (p. 763). BMIs like the Legacy House contribute to the students' belief that they belong on campus (i.e., affirmation) as well as helping them realize the potential within themselves (i.e., feel valued). The Legacy House is an "important buffer" (Brooms, 2019, p. 763) at a primarily white university, which in the absence of the Legacy House, may make students feel isolated and alienated. Furthermore, the Legacy House participants themselves believed that being in a community of belonging contributed to their motivation to succeed. Such aspirations derived from belonging are aligned with prior research on the value of community. Specifically, a sense of belonging is associated with educational outcomes such as academic achievement, retention, and persistence to degree attainment (Rhee, 2008; Strayhorn, 2009). Consequently, the findings of this study suggest that primarily white universities may contribute to Black male success by offering those spaces (i.e., enclaves or places of respite) where they can be themselves and connect with other scholars with similar backgrounds and experiences as young Black males.

The foundation that legacy communities should be built upon includes: shared knowledge in achieving brotherhood, a sense of belonging, and shared respon-sibility (Tinto, 2003). Together, these three pillars form the foundation of a holistic educational and developmental experience for Legacy House partici-pants. Further, participants in the Legacy House had increased involvement with programs and activities because of their commitment to their fellow brothers which assisted in their social and academic integration. The aspect of shared responsibility within a LLC has been connected to higher retention and Black male participation (Hines et al., 2021; Taffe, 2022). It allows students to become more engaged in the classroom and active community members, increasing involvement drastically (Stier, 2014). Having legacy communities that have students engage in seminars, retreats, and intertwining curriculum is one way to support Black males in a new exciting way, while creating a community of belonging, fostering brotherhood, and shared responsibility that students seek in a legacy community. They feel more connected and responsible for each other but identify with the curriculum on a deeper level, influencing their involvement, as well as their retention (Stier, 2014).

RECOMMENDATIONS

The authors noted that interviews of these participants should be longitudinal to see how the legacy community continues to impact their willingness to persist in college all the way to graduation. Also, researchers should continue to compare the GPAs of those in the community with Black males who are not in the program. Moreover, research should be conducted on why students in Legacy House choose their majors so the institution can understand how to best serve Black males when it comes to career development.

Colleges and universities have resources at their disposal that can begin preparing and implementing LLLCs on their campuses. Disaggregating student success, enrollment, involvement, and attainment data provides university administration with knowledge of which historically underserved student groups, like Black males, are facing barriers to access, struggling academically, or having unknown needs. Universities may also recruit and retain faculty from diverse backgrounds whose research focus includes the persistence, academic and career outcomes, and postsecondary attainment for minoritized student populations.

CONCLUSION

Creating a LLLC for Black males takes institutional support (financially and with social capital) for this endeavor to be successful. A LLLC impacts the retention and graduation of Black males and addresses a grand challenge that most postsecondary institutions have, retaining Black males. For institutions to implement this model of programing for Black males will truly leave a transformational legacy for both Black males and colleges/universities.

AUTHOR NOTE

The authors received no financial support for the research, authorship, and/or publication of this article.

REFERENCES

Astin, A. W. (1984). Student involvement: A developmental theory for higher education. *Journal of College Student Personnel*, *25*(4), 297–308.

Banks, T., & Dohy, J. (2019). Mitigating barriers to persistence: A review of efforts to improve retention and graduation rates for students of color in higher education. *Higher Education Studies*, *9*(1), 118–131.

Banks, T., Dohy, J., Petty, N., Moore, J., Fish, C., Mukenge, M., Hawkins, J., & Grill, L. (2021). Persistence and opportunity: Leveraging living learning communities to ensure equitable access for all students. *Multicultural Learning and Teaching*, *16*(2), 129–144. https://doi.org/10.1515/mlt-2020-0007

Baum, S., Ma, J., & Payea, K. (2016). Education pays, 2016: The benefits of higher education for individuals and society. Trends in Higher Education Series. College Board.

Black, D. W. (2018). The fundamental right to education. *The Notre Dame Law Review*, *94*, 1059.

Bohrnstedt, G., Kitmitto, S., Ogut, B., Sherman, D., & Chan, D. (2015). School composition and the black-white achievement gap. National Center for Education Statistics. NCES 2015-018.

Bourdieu, P. (1986). The forms of capital. In J. C. Richardson (Ed.), *Handbook of theory and research for the sociology of education*. Greenwood.

Breakwell, G. M. (1995). Interviewing. In G. M. Breakwell, S. Hammond, & C. Fife-Shaw (Eds.), *Research methods in psychology* (pp. 239–251). Sage Publications.

Brooms, D. R. (2017). *Being Black, being male on campus: Understanding and confronting Black male collegiate experiences*. State University of New York Press.

Brooms, D. R. (2018). 'Building us up': Supporting black male college students in a black male initiative program. *Critical Sociology*, *44*(1), 141–155. https://doi.org/10.1177/0896920516658940

Brooms, D. R. (2019). Not in this alone: Black men's bonding, learning, and sense of belonging in Black male initiative programs. *The Urban Review*, *51*(5), 748–767.

Brooms, D. R., Clark, J., & Smith, M. (2018). Being and becoming men of character: Exploring latino and black males' brotherhood and masculinity through leadership in college. *Journal of Hispanic Higher Education*, *17*(4), 317–331. https://doi.org/10.1177/1538192717699048

Cintron, D. W., Hines, E. M., Singleton, P., II, & Golden, M. N. (2020). Improving the retention and GPAs of Black males at a primarily white institution: A living and learning community approach. *Journal of African American Males in Education (JAAME)*, *11*(1), 37–57.

Couch, K. A., & Fairlie, R. (2010). Last hired, first fired? Black-white unemployment and the business cycle. *Demography*, *47*(1), 227–247.

Davis, M., & Laster, B. B. (2019). Acquiring social capital: Conclusions from a social science summer bridge community. *Learning Communities: Research & Practice*, *7*(2). Article 4.

Delgado, R. (2007). The myth of upward mobility. *University of Pittsburgh Law Review*, *68*(4), 879.

DeSousa, D. J., & Kuh, G. D. (1996). Does institutional racial composition make a difference in what Black students gain from college? *Journal of College Student Development*, *37*(3), 257–267.

Everett, J. W., & Zobel, P. D. (2012). Promoting student connections and retention through an on-campus residential learning community for first-year underrepresented and low-income students. In *2012 ASEE Annual Conference & Exposition* (pp. 25–1088).

Hines, E., Cintron, D., & Singleton, P. (2018). *Legacy house living and learning community report to the Legacy (pseudonym) Foundation*.

Hines, E. M., Harris, P. C., Mayes, R. D., & Moore, J. L., III. (2020). I think of college as setting a good foundation for my future: Black males navigating the college decision making process. *Journal for Multicultural Education*, *14*(2) 129-147. https://doi.org/10.1108/JME-09-2019-0064

Hines, E. M., Mayes, R. D., Hines, M. R., Singleton, P., II, Cintron, D., Henderson, J. A., Wright, C. G., Wathen, B., Golden, M., & Vega, D. (2021). "You are going to school": Exploring the pre-college experiences of first year Black males in higher education. *Professional School Counseling*, *25*(1). https://doi.org/10.1177/2156759X211040044

Hines, E. M., Moore, III, J. L., Cintron, D. W., Singleton, II, P., Golden, M. N., Fletcher Jr., E. C., Henderson, J. A., Slack, T., Moore, W. C., Ouimette, D. T., Reid Jr., M., & Ford, D. Y. (2023). A bridge over troubled water: Designing and implementing a living and learning community to produce optimal outcomes for Black males. *Journal of College and University Student Housing, 49*(2), 66–85.

Hines, E. M., & Owen, L. (Eds.). (2022). *Equity-based career development and postsecondary transitions: An American imperative.* Information Age Publishing.

Hotchkiss, J. L., Moore, R. E., & Pitts, M. M. (2006). Freshman learning communities, college performance, and retention. *Education Economics, 14*(2), 197–210.

Hout, M. (2012). Social and economic returns to college education in the United States. *Annual Review of Sociology, 38*(1), 379–400.

Hurtado, S. S., Gonyea, R. M., Graham, P. A., & Fosnacht, K. (2020). The relationship between residential learning communities and student engagement. *Learning Communities: Research & Practice, 8*(1), 5.

Inkelas, K. K., Jessup-Anger, J. E., Benjamin, M., & Wawrzynski, M. R. (2018). *Living–learning communities that work: A research-based model for design, delivery, and assessment* (1st ed.). Routledge. https://doi.org/10.4324/9781003445777

Inkelas, K. K., Daver, Z. E., Vogt, K. E., & Leonard, J. B. (2007). Living–learning programs and first-generation college students' academic and social transition to college. *Research in Higher Education, 48*(4), 403–434.

Inkelas, K. K., Soldner, M., Longerbeam, S. D., & Leonard, J. B. (2008). Differences in student outcomes by types of living—Learning programs: The development of an empirical typology. *Research in Higher Education, 49*(6), 495–512. http://www.jstor.org/stable/25704579

James, M., & Lewis, C. W. (2014). Villains or virtuosos: An inquiry into Blackmaleness. *Journal of African American Males in Education (JAAME), 5*(2), 105–110.

Johnson-Ahorlu, R. N. (2013). "Our biggest challenge is stereotypes": Understanding stereotype threat and the academic experiences of African American undergraduates. *The Journal of Negro Education, 82*, 382–392.

MacKay, K. A., & Kuh, G. D. (1994). A comparison of student effort and educational gains of Caucasian and African American students at predominantly white colleges and universities. *Journal of College Student Development, 35*(3), 217–223.

Maltby, J. L., Brooks, C., Horton, M., & Morgan, H. (2016). Long term benefits for women in a science, technology, engineering, and mathematics living-learning community. *Learning Communities Research and Practice, 4*(1). Article 2.

Markle, G., & Stelzriede, D. D. (2020). Comparing first-generation students to continuing-generation students and the impact of a first-generation learning community. *Innovative Higher Education, 45*(4), 285–298.

Merolla, D. M. (2018). Completing the educational career: High school graduation, four-year college enrollment, and bachelor's degree completion among Black, Hispanic, and White students. *Sociology of Race and Ethnicity, 4*(2), 281–297.

Millea, M., Wills, R., Elder, A., & Molina, D. (2018). What matters in college student success? Determinants of college retention and graduation rates. *Education, 138*(4), 309–322.

Murphy, M. C., & Zirkel, S. (2015). Race and belonging in school: How anticipated and experienced belonging affect choice, persistence, and performance. *Teachers College Record, 117*(12), 1–40.

Mutua, A. D. (Ed.). (2006). *Progressive black masculinities?* (1st ed.). Routledge. https://doi.org/10.4324/9780203961438

National Center for Education Statistics. (2019, February). *Indicator 23: Postsecondary graduation rates.* National Center for Education Statistics. https://nces.ed.gov/programs/raceindicators/indicator_red.asp#info

Orfield, G., Ee, J., Frankenberg, E., & Siegel-Hawley, G. (2016). "Brown" at 62: School segregation by race, poverty, and state. Civil Rights Project-Proyecto Derechos Civiles.

Palm, W. J., & Thomas, C. R. (2015). Living-learning communities improve first-year engineering student academic performance and retention at a small private university. In *Proceedings of the ASEE Annual Conference & Exposition* (pp. 1–23). http://proxy.ulib.csuohio.edu:2066/login.aspx?direct=true&db=a9h&AN=116025900&site=ehost-live

Patton, M. Q. (2002). *Qualitative research and evaluation methods* (3rd ed.). Sage.

Phipps, S. S. (2020). *The relationship between college interventions and first-generation students' academic success at a large urban tier-i institution.* Doctoral dissertation, University of Houston.

Pope, R. L., Reynolds, A. L., & Mueller, J. A. (2019). *Multicultural competence in student affairs: Advancing social justice and inclusion*. John Wiley & Sons.

Potts, C. (2021). Seen and unseen: First-year college students' sense of belonging during the Covid-19 pandemic. *College Student Affairs Journal, 39*(2), 214–224.

Quillian, L., Pager, D., Hexel, O., & Midtbøen, A. H. (2017). Meta-analysis of field experiments shows no change in racial discrimination in hiring over time. *Proceedings of the National Academy of Sciences, 114*(41), 10870–10875.

Rhee, B. (2008). Institutional climate and student departure: A multinomial multilevel modeling approach. *The Review of Higher Education, 31*(2), 161–183.

Ryan, G. W., & Bernard, H. R. (2000). Data management and analysis methods. In N. K. Denzin & Y. S. Lincoln (Eds.), *Handbook of qualitative research* (2nd ed., pp. 769–802). Sage.

Schauer, S., Pakala, K., & Tucker, K. (2020). Review of living learning communities and their impact on first year engineering college students. https://www.semanticscholar.org/paper/Review-of-Living-Learning-Communities-and-Their-on-Schauer-Pakala/a65f71f6e9791861da3175231fa9a6de37622786

Shushok, F., & Sriram, R. (2009). Exploring the effect of a residential academic affairs-student affairs partnership: The first year of an engineering and computer science living-learning center. *The Journal of College and University Student Housing, 36*(2).

Smith, W. A., Allen, W. R., & Danley, L. L. (2007). "Assume the position... you fit the description": Psychosocial experiences and racial battle fatigue among African American male college students. *American Behavioral Scientist, 51*(4), 551–578.

Solanki, S., McPartlan, P., Xu, D., & Sato, B. K. (2019). Success with EASE: Who benefits from a STEM learning community? *PLoS One, 14*(3), e0213827.

Spanierman, L. B., Soble, J. R., Mayfield, J. B., Neville, H. A., Aber, M., Khuri, L., & De La Rosa, B. (2013). Living learning communities and students' sense of community and belonging. *Journal of Student Affairs Research and Practice, 50*(3), 308–325.

STATISTICS, U. B. O. L. (2020, November). *Labor force characteristics by race and ethnicity, 2020*. US Bureau of Labor Statistics. https://www.bls.gov/opub/reports/race-and-ethnicity/2020/home.htm

Stier, M. M. (2014). *The relationship between living learning communities and student success on first-year and second-year students at the university of south Florida*. Graduate Theses and Dissertations.

Strayhorn, T. L. (2009). Fittin' in: Do diverse interactions with peers affect sense of belonging for Black men at predominantly White institutions? *Journal of Student Affairs Research and Practice, 45*(4), 953-979.

Strayhorn, T. L. (2018). *College students' sense of belonging: A key to educational success for all students* (2nd ed.). Routledge. https://doi.org/10.4324/9781315297293

Taffe, N. (2022). He needs to be in a learning community – Learning community, a place of respite and brotherhood while persisting in college. *Journal of College Access, 7*(1). https://scholarworks.wmich.edu/jca/vol7/iss1/11

Tashakkori, A., & Teddlie, C. (1998). *Mixed methodology: Combining qualitative and quantitative approaches*. Sage Publications.

Tinto, V. (2003). Learning better together: The impact of learning communities on student success. *Journal of Institutional Research, 9*(1), 48–53.

Tucker, R. B. Sr. (2014). The color of mass incarceration. *Ethnic Studies Review, 37*(1), 135–149.

Ushomirsky, N., & Williams, D. (2015). *Funding gaps 2015: Too many states still spend less on educating students who need the most*. Education Trust.

Wildeman, C., & Wang, E. A. (2017). Mass incarceration, public health, and widening inequality in the USA. *The Lancet, 389*(10077), 1464–1474.

Williams, A., & Swail, W. S. (2005). Is more better? The impact of postsecondary education on the economic and social well-being of American society. In *American higher education report series*. Educational Policy Institute. https://files.eric.ed.gov/fulltext/ED499855.pdf. Accessed on June 7, 2022.

Wilson, D., Jones, D., Bocell, F., Crawford, J., Kim, M. J., Veilleux, N., Floyd-Smith, T., Bates, R., & Plett, M. (2015). Belonging and academic engagement among undergraduate STEM students: A multi-institutional study. *Research in Higher Education, 56*(7), 750–776. http://www.jstor.org/stable/24572053

Wood, J. L., & Palmer, R. T. (2015). *Black men in higher education: A guide to ensuring student success.* Routledge.

Woods-Wells, T. M. (2016). *Applying a cognitive lens to the exploration of social mobility for African American men: A phenomenological study.* Doctoral dissertation, Virginia Tech.

Xu, D., Solanki, S., McPartlan, P., & Sato, B. (2018). EASEing students into college: The impact of multidimensional support for underprepared students. *Educational Researcher, 47*(7), 435–450.

Zea, M. C., Reisen, C. A., Beil, C., & Caplan, R. D. (1997). Predicting intention to remain in college among ethnic minority and nonminority students. *The Journal of Social Psychology, 137*(2), 149–160.

CHAPTER 14

COLLEGE SPORTS TEAMS: AN INCUBATOR FOR BLACK MEN STUDENT LEADERSHIP IDENTITY DEVELOPMENT

Jesse R. Ford, Brittany N. Brewster and Jordan Farmer

ABSTRACT

This conceptual work synthesizes the experiences of Black men who are collegiate athletes and introduces new theoretical considerations on the formation of their leadership identities in predominantly white institutions. This scholarship focuses on historical understandings of how race and gender influenced the creation of the current Black man in collegiate identity. This work expands on Du Bois' (1903) concept of double consciousness, Fanon's (1952) views on Blackness, and Bertrand Jones and colleagues' culturally responsive leadership learning model (2016). Collectively, the three frameworks highlight the significance of leadership in the development of Black men who are student-athletes. The conclusion includes implications and recommendations for future research as we work to support and develop Black men beyond their athletic identity.

Keywords: Black men; sports; leadership; identity formation; collegiate athletes; cultural responsive leadership

A VIGNETTE INTO THE LIFE OF A BLACK MAN STUDENT ATHLETE

In high school, Jay enjoyed a decorated football career. Jay was one of the captains on a team that went all the way to the state championship game his

Black Males in Secondary and Postsecondary Education
Advances in Race and Ethnicity in Education, Volume 9, 255–271
Copyright © 2024 Jesse R. Ford, Brittany N. Brewster and Jordan Farmer
Published under exclusive licence by Emerald Publishing Limited
ISSN: 2051-2317/doi:10.1108/S2051-231720230000009014

senior year. This success led to college coaches coming to campus to recruit him to play football for their programs. These coaches would come and give their recruiting pitch on why their particular school and program was best for him to attend. Almost always, these recruiting spills would be one size fits all and consist of ways in which the program would develop Jay into what they considered a "man" should be. The college coaches often promised success and upward mobility after time in the program and completion of his degree. As a 17-year-old Black student-athlete, this all sounded promising to him. All the leaders in Jay's community that he looked up to were former college football players that he had watched growing up. His high school coaches would always talk about playing college football as if it was the ultimate prize and would reiterate that it was a privilege to have the opportunity to play at the next level. The coach would treat the players who were being recruited with favoritism, often calling them out of class or weightlifting to have them come to talk with recruiters for extended periods of time. Players took note of this and many of them began to do anything to assimilate and try to show that they too could go to college to play football. Jay and his teammates wanted to be looked at in the eyes of those in the community as a leader.

In 2011, Jay got an opportunity to become a college football player when he committed to attend and play at a small college in North Carolina. During his four years of being a college student-athlete, Jay began to develop most of his views on leadership and increase his leadership capacity. The head coach was new and full of energy. He sold Jay on the potential to get a great education and build a legacy at a program that was coming off a winless season. During Jay's time in the program, the coaching staff would reiterate how student-athletes, particularly football players, were under a microscope. They were expected to be role models and leaders on campus. These expectations carried over to the field with the coaches pushing the power of the team and everyone doing their job in order to be successful. Jay and his teammates took pride in doing their part to the fullest and modeling the standards of the program in the weight room and during practice, games, and film study. They saw the fruits of their labor in real time as they began winning more than anytime in program history. In Jay's four years on the team, the program went from 0-10 to 8-2. His senior year, their team finished the season nationally ranked. This was due in large part to the leadership skills that they developed through programs and opportunities provided by the coaching staff.

One such program that the team participated in was what the coaches called the Off-Season Team Leadership program (OTL). The OTL program was an offseason program meant to boost the team members' leadership capacity and hold themselves and their teammates accountable for academic, athletic, and social success. This program helped Jay transition to becoming a college student-athlete. Before this program started his first year, Jay was contemplating transferring and quitting football after being injured his entire first season and not feeling as if he had enough time to juggle the demands of being both a student and an athlete simultaneously. Jay's parents persuaded him to finish out the year, and the second semester he started the OTL program. During the OTL, captains were decided by the coaching staff, and they drafted the teams' players that were broken into. Every person would gain or lose points weekly based on our contributions to academic, athletic, social, and community service categories. Each week the coach would post the scores. There were team winners and individual winners. Each player would then be grouped into tiers. Each tier correlates to student-athletes leadership abilities and their accountability to the team. The coaches would make it known that any team member who finished below the third tier was not a leader or a teammate that the program could count on. Coach would often say that those who finish that low do not care about the success of the team. He would even go as far as predicting that those students who finished lower in the tiers wouldn't make it all four years in the program. Coach even allowed team captains to cut players from their OTL teams and make that player compete by themselves. This almost guaranteed that the cut player was not going to be successful in OTL. During his time at in the program, Jay never finished below tier one and was never less than third overall on the team in OTL points. Jay took pride in the skill sets that he was learning and the new opportunities he was being exposed to. In fact, it was during his time as a student-athlete that Jay was introduced to meaningful service and its reciprocal relationship with leadership. In 2013, the team completed over 1,000 hours of service for the academic year.

Another leadership opportunity offered in the program was Leadership Team Council (LTC). LTC was a leadership committee made up of coaching staff appointed leaders on the team. During sophomore year, Jay was appointed to the council and served on it for three of his four years. As a member of the LTC, you would meet weekly to give input on various program-related subjects. The goal of the LTC was to provide a bridge between players and coaches. Players also advocated for their peers. Through being a member of the LTC, Jay was able to find out about the Student Athlete Advisory Committee (SAAC) and joined his junior year. SAAC is a national student-athlete organization that provides a voice for student-athletes and even holds a National Collegiate Athletic Association (NCAA) rules committee vote. SAAC was a great opportunity to work with other student-athletes outside of his teammates and was Jay's first time working as part of a committee.

By the time he graduated in 2015, Jay was awarded a football team award named the Jay Leadership Award. This was monumental for him as it showed his dedication to modeling the way for others. Fast forward to present day and Jay still uses the leadership skills and lessons learned during his time as a student-athlete. Working as part of a team, persisting through adversity, and learning the power of accountability and discipline has been huge for him professionally. The leader Jay is today, is a testament to the lessons learned through countless reps in the weight room and field in addition to the interactions with his diverse teammates and the access to privileged experiences of being a student-athlete.

HISTORICAL AND GENERATIONAL TIES TO BLACK MEN'S EXPERIENCES

Jay's story, while not an uncommon story, is one that is connected to the historical and generational structures of oppression and white supremacy that are well documented in American history (Ahmed, 2012; Harris, 1993). The permeation of racial injustice has influenced all systematic practices, organizations, and environments. From an American viewpoint, racial inequities directly impact Black Americans' trajectory as a community and have delayed their forward mobility and communal leadership for generations (Majors & Gordon, 1994). Majors and Gordon (1994) state, "Blacks have been miseducated by the educational system, mishandled by the criminal justice system, mislabeled by the mental health system, and mistreated by the social welfare system" (p. 31). As a result of disruptions within these systems, Black men on college campuses have encountered many racial challenges on historically white college campuses (Brooms, 2016; Harper, 2012).

In addition, these systematic historical challenges have become standards that impact all aspects of Black American life, including entertainment, professional, and collegiate athletics, and educational pathways (Beatty et al., 2010; Beatty & Salinas, 2016; Brooms, 2016; Harper, 2012; Majors & Gordon, 1994). These obstacles, often seen as isolated occurrences, are systematically and generationally linked and stem from racial microaggressions, discrimination, and segregation. More specifically, the hurdles faced by Black men in educational systems often include navigating stressful environments (Smith et al., 2012), isolated leadership identity experiences within cultural and identity-based student groups to address challenges facing Black students (Harper & Quaye, 2007), and a lack of mentorship (Brooms, 2016; Harper, 2006). Moreover, leadership, according to Dugan (2017), is socially constructed and bound by time, context, and culture, as well as principles and multidisciplinary approaches. While these issues impact all Black students, the purpose of this chapter is to explore the historical and contemporary exclusion of a hyper-visible subpopulation, Black men who are student-athletes, and their leadership identity development. While the literature on the experiences of college athletes has grown considerably (Gaston-Gayles, 2004; Harper, 2006), a dearth exists in the literature highlighting the experiences of Black men in college athletics (Harper, 2009). Historically, these stories have been left out of the history books and traditionally are not positioned to expose the issues around their academic preparation, social integration, and leadership identity development.

HISTORICAL CONTEXT AND EXCLUSION OF BLACK MEN AS STUDENT-ATHLETES FROM HISTORICALLY WHITE INSTITUTIONS

The experiences of Black men who are student-athletes are a direct reflection of the lived experiences of Black men in the United States. Historic events and political movements such as colonization, slavery, and exploitation have spawned a need to reflect on history, communities of color, and challenges within American society (Ahmed, 2012; Bordas, 2007; Harris, 1993; Majors & Gordon, 1994). Moreover, the lives of Black men are often documented by living in poverty and encountering more political, social, and racial hurdles due to legal overt and covert acts of oppression (Harris, 1993; Majors & Gordon, 1994; Smith et al., 2011). Leadership identity development for Black Americans in a greater United States context was established in many cases due to a response to injustice and oppression within their local communities (Bordas, 2007). As a result, Black Americans' macro and micro challenges were mirrored in excluding Black college students and, more specifically, Black men who are student-athletes.

Before the Civil Rights movement, many Black men were denied access to predominantly white higher learning institutions due to political, economic, educational, and societal challenges due to segregation in the United States (Anderson, 1988). Before the early 1900s, the Second Morrill Act of 1890 established "separate, but equal" Historically Black Colleges and Universities (HBCUs) to maintain segregation of white and Black students (Albritton, 2012; Allen et al., 2007; Cantey et al., 2013; Dixon & Spears, 2022). Within HBCU environments, student life and athletics contributed to a distinct culture and became a prominent part of the Black student experience. However, a few Black students were able to branch out of the HBCU athletic environment into dominant white college and professional sports teams, including athletes such as Paul Robeson, Jesse Owens, John Carlos, Tommie Smith, Ralph Metcalfe, and Jackie Robinson (Agyemang et al., 2010; Siegel, 1994; Smith et al., 2014). Robeson, for example, challenged dominant ideologies around racism and fascism in the United States. His criticism of the American government resulted in his passport being revoked and becoming a target of multiple FBI investigations (Agyemang et al., 2010). The actions of Robeson and other athletes are early signs of how athletes use their public platforms to push for activism and change, but also showed the power of interest convergence (Harris, 1993; Yosso, 2005). Moreover, these athletes became successful within their respective sports, leaders within their communities, and staples in the fight for Civil Rights. To overcome racial discrimination and segregation, these Black men were propelled to be perceived as leaders within the Black community.

HBCUs After "Separate, But Equal"

The landscape of Black student life on college campuses changed drastically in 1954. *Brown v Board of Education*, a prominent Civil Rights court case in 1954 stated "separate, but equal" was unconstitutional and the desegregation of colleges and universities should occur at an "all deliberate speed" (Albritton, 2012; Allen et al., 2007; Cantey et al., 2013). Though questionable if this process was done consciously and intentionally, desegregation significantly impacted Black student-athletes' experiences on college campuses. While the integration process for Black students was slow, it happened faster for college athletics. The last significant integration of a collegiate athletic conference took place in 1966, over

10 years after the *Brown v Board of Education* decision when the University of Tennessee signed its first Black football player (Hodge et al., 2008). Black student-athletes became pioneers in the desegregation of colleges and universities (Hodge et al., 2008). Many of the first degrees awarded to Black students after the integration of colleges and universities were awarded to Black student-athletes who became instrumental in the success of many athletic programs at historically white institutions (Hodge et al., 2008).

College athletic opportunities are viewed as a catalyst for upward mobility by many Black men to uplift their communities and serve as fuel for a better life through education (Hodge et al., 2008; Simiyu, 2012). Also, the opportunity to attend historically white institutions is perceived as invaluable and often connected to messages of a successful life that Black men who were student-athletes received within sports as young boys (Hodge et al., 2008; Simiyu, 2012). The media's overrepresentation of Black men in professional sports creates a narrative that Black men and boys in professional athletic careers will have lucrative futures (Simiyu, 2012). Despite the academic opportunities awarded to Black Americans due to their athletic abilities, many Black students still face academic, leadership, and athletic identity development issues on college campuses as these identities are not always cultivated.

CURRENT LANDSCAPE OF BLACK MEN WHO ARE STUDENT-ATHLETES

Today and historically, Black men are underrepresented across all racial and gender academic sectors of education (Beatty & Ford, 2023; Ford et al., 2023; Harper, 2006, 2012; Jackson et al., 2020). Additionally, retaining and graduating Black boys and men remain a struggle among educators, scholars, and policymakers (Jackson et al., 2021a). Contemporary literature reveals academic challenges facing Black men can be seen as early as primary school and can be linked to a lack of role models, mentors, academic preparation, leadership identity development, and educational engagement (Beatty, 2014; Cooper et al., 2019; Donnor, 2005; Harper, 2006; Harper, 2012; Jackson et al., 2020, 2021b; Sims et al., 2021; Simiyu, 2012; Smith et al., 2014). Consequently, in many Black communities, societal messages to Black boys convey that athletics is their ticket to success and upward mobility in life (Harper, 2016; Hodge et al., 2008; Simiyu, 2012). Young Black boys are encouraged to become leaders on sports teams, but often do not receive the same encouragement to become leaders in academic environments (Simiyu, 2012). These early messages of becoming leaders within sports environments, coupled with misguided beliefs that athletics is the key to social, political, and economic success, follow Black men throughout their collegiate careers and have potential long-lasting adverse effects on their leadership identity development.

While these messages are influential in their development, Black men only represent a small number of the current undergraduate population in the United States. However, the voices and lived experiences of Black student-athletes have been mainly ignored in higher education literature (Hodge et al., 2008; Singer, 2008). Harper (2016) states, "Perhaps nowhere in higher education is the disenfranchisement of Black male students more insidious than in college athletics" (p. 3). For example, in the 2014–2015 academic year, Black men represented 2.5% of all undergraduate students (Harper, 2016). This number, while daunting to some, highlights a larger problem within higher education. Higher education institutions have done a poor job of recruiting Black men into colleges and universities on academic merit yet have done an excellent job recruiting Black men into athletic programs. Black men account for less than 10 % of the student body at Division I colleges and universities in the United States (Cooper et al., 2017; Ingraham, 2020). The highest numbers of Black men who are athletes in collegiate environments are basketball and football players, at nearly 60% (Ingraham, 2020). Nevertheless, on average, 68.5% of Black collegiate men graduate, however this number drops to 56.3% when the Black men are student-athletes (Harper, 2016). Black men are recruited at these rates to meet the needs of college sports teams; however, little attention is dedicated to their holistic development as students and people. In response, it is necessary to explore the challenges that contribute to how colleges address the need to cultivate their academic, leadership, and social identities.

Unfortunately, beyond their collegiate experiences, the athletic careers of most Black men end after college, as the NFL and NBA recruit only 2.3% and 2.5% of college athletes into professional organizations and often are not rewarded equally for their performance (Simiyu, 2012). The likelihood of Black men being drafted into professional leagues after their collegiate athletic careers is very low. These numbers emphasize the significance of improving Black men's leadership development to boost their postcollege professional and academic careers (Bimper et al., 2013). When Black men who are student-athletes arrive on historically white campuses, they see, on average, 7% of the total student body, 3% of the total faculty, and less than 5% of the top athletic administration and coaches who look like them (Simiyu, 2012). At the Division I level, less than 6% of the 119 leading football coaches in collegiate sports are Black (Hodge et al., 2008). With limited role models, mentors, and interactions with Black men, which have been documented as having an impact on Black boy's and men's experiences (Brooms, 2016; Brooms et al., 2015; Spencer, 2018, 2019), this population's experiences are often reduced to non-Black coaching and academic staff at these institutions (Hodge et al., 2008). As a result, Black men's limited interactions with Black mentors, role models, and staff members could heavily influence how they view, understand, and make meaning of their leadership capacity.

In addition to the representation of role models, and mentors, student-athletes often socialized with other student-athletes. In most cases, these students are in similar majors, attend the same classes, study halls, dining halls, workouts, and practices together (Simiyu, 2012). The dearth of exposure to other students with diverse backgrounds limits the growth these students may experience. Interaction with students who are not athletes and are engaged in other areas of campus life creates opportunities for this isolated population to interact with students outside of their comfort zone (Beatty et al., 2010; Bimper et al., 2013; Guthrie & Jenkins,

2018; Komives et al., 2006). Furthermore, these students' rigorous athletic schedules leave little time for social integration (Bimper et al., 2013). The absence of social integration with other students creates a barrier between the general student population and Black student-athletes. This disconnect contributes to the creation of negative stereotypes, including: "all Black men are athletes," hyper-visibility, racialized experiences, being an athlete, and tokenism (Bimper et al., 2013; Ferguson & Davis, 2019; Hodge et al., 2008; Lawrence, 2005; Smith et al., 2014). Furthermore, many colleges and universities recognize and value winning sports teams and actively recruit the "best athletes," which in some cases are not the most academically prepared (Bimper et al., 2013; Hodge et al., 2008). Despite their academic readiness, students who perform well in their sport are encouraged to be leaders among their peers and serve as peer role models for each other (Bimper et al., 2013).

BLACK MEN STUDENT LEADERSHIP EXPERIENCES

Black men's experiences are often described as a monolithic experience in higher education (Beatty et al., 2010; Bimper et al., 2013; Harper, 2006; Harper & Quaye, 2007; Sims et al., 2021). While we have limited scholarship that detangles Black men experiences beyond being students of color (Brooms et al., 2020; Harper, 2006), research is still vastly missing on their higher education leadership experiences. Northouse (2019) positions "leadership is a highly sought-after and highly valued commodity" (p. 1). In addition, scholars and researchers have outlined the importance of leadership identity development and training to enhance college students' holistic development and student success (Beatty et al., 2020; Bertrand Jones et al., 2016; Bordas, 2007), yet have failed to provide substantial literature for determining what makes this development so impactful for Black men in higher education systems.

Even though research on the leadership experiences of Black men is limited (Beatty et al., 2010), contemporary literature does highlight feelings of being undervalued (Smith et al., 2012), experiencing microaggressions (Harper, 2012; Sims et al., 2021; Smith et al., 2012), and a sense of belonging (Harper, 2016; Hodge et al., 2008) are everyday realities of Black men college students. Research shows that for Black men, low expectations of belonging within the collegiate environment combined with limited academic opportunities establishes and maintains disadvantages before and after college (Brooms, 2016; Hodge et al., 2008). For Black men who are student-athletes, the stronger their athletic identity, the more deflated their academic identity becomes (Singer, 2008). Additionally, they are often not encouraged by campus administrators to serve as leaders within the broader campus community as it impacts their performance within their sport (Bimper et al., 2013). Furthermore, these students are socialized to focus on their sports opportunities and engagement at the expense of other engagement opportunities, which could include academic and leadership experiences (Bimper et al., 2013). Despite the lack of encouragement, Black men who are student-athletes often describe an obligation or duty to give back to their local communities. As a result, for Black men, most of their collegiate clubs and organizations are based on racial and gender identities, which are often tied to their most salient identities (Beatty, 2014; Harper & Quaye, 2007; Spencer, 2018). While these experiences provide the necessary training for establishing leadership capacity, efficacy, and identity, higher education does not prepare these student-athletes to be leaders after their collegiate experience.

CULTURALLY RELEVANT LEADERSHIP LEARNING MODEL AS METHOD FOR DEVELOPING BLACK MEN LEADERS

Bertrand Jones et al. (2016) introduce the culturally relevant leadership learning (CRLL) model, which was inspired by Gloria Ladson-Billings' culturally relevant pedagogy, in order to reshape and redefine how students engage with, make sense of, and conceptualize the leadership process. Bertrand Jones et al. (2016) assert that by refocusing components of culturally relevant pedagogy, "cultural competence becomes students' own identity development and their acknowledgement of others' identities; and sociopolitical consciousness becomes students' efficacy, or belief in their capacity to enact leadership in a variety of settings" (p. 12). Identity, capacity, and efficacy are all interconnected within the CRLL framework and serve as lenses through which students conceptualize themselves as individuals in the leadership process. Additionally, Bertrand Jones et al. (2016) assert that "the synthesis combination of identity, capacity, and efficacy describes a student's way of understanding self as a change agent through interpersonal and intrapersonal development" (p. 12).

In addition to the interconnectedness of identity, capacity, and efficacy, campus climate is also an integral part of the CRLL model. The influence of campus climate is reflected in the CRLL model's five domains which include the historical legacy of inclusion/exclusion, compositional diversity, psychological climate, behavioral climate, and organizational/structural aspects. Campus climate challenges leadership educators and stakeholders to consider how environmental, historical, and societal factors impact engagement within leadership learning. This introductory text will concentrate on the CRLL model's identity and historical legacy, as well as its exclusionary elements.

Identity

Identity formation is a process of constant reconstruction of one's self and perception of one's identities. For many students, how they make sense of their identities is influenced by prior experiences, learned values, and generational histories. Additionally, Bertrand Jones et al. (2016) state, as a socially constructed concept, it is grounded in historical, political, and cultural norms (Jones & Abes, 2013) and results from one's navigation and meaning making of self, context, and relationships (Abes et al., 2007). In addition to social identities, such as race, class, and gender, leader identity is one of the multiple layers of one's identity (Hogg, 2001; Lord & Hall, 2005).

The formation of a leadership identity in the context of students' experiences is frequently a critical component of how students make sense of their social identities such as race, gender, and class. Different celebrations, rituals, relationships, mentoring, self-assessment, reflection, and new experiences all contribute to the development of a leader's identity (Bertrand Jones et al., 2016; Guthrie et al., 2013; Komives et al., 2006). The impact of these methods on an often overly visible population has the potential to have a long-term positive effect on communities of color. Student athletes' leadership identities are inextricably linked to their identities as Black men, leaders, and student-athletes, all of which are directly related to this population's generational and historical exclusion.

Historical Legacy of Inclusion/Exclusion Within CRLL

While each of the CRLL model's campus climate components is significant, this article focuses on the historical legacy of inclusion and exclusion. Due to a variety of historical and generational factors, including leadership, a heteropatriarchal white/Eurocentric lens was generated. This has resulted in dominant leadership narratives being individualistic rather than communal, positional, and rooted in power absorption. As a result, students from marginalized backgrounds do not always view themselves as leaders (Bertrand Jones et al., 2016). Beatty et al. (2021) discovered in an alumni study of undergraduate leadership learning that students must understand that leadership transcends segmented curricular and co-curricular experiences and contributes to their holistic development of knowledge, skills, and values.

Leadership, as a concept, is often understood as acts of service or activism in Black communities (Bordas, 2007; Ford & Propst, 2022). Consequently, Black students, while often agents of change, do not see themselves as leaders. Moreover, Bordas' (2007) highlights the significance of exploring how history excluded minoritized populations and how their leadership identity development evolved. Additionally, Bordas (2007) states, "multicultural leadership brings a commitment to advance people who reflect the vitality, values, and voice of our diversity to all levels of organizations and society ...multicultural leadership encourages synergy, innovation, and resourcefulness" (p. 8). Specifically, for Black men who are athletes on college campuses, the impact of being excluded due to multiple identities such as being black, male, a leader, and student-athletes may have long-lasting implications on their leadership identity development.

CREATING A CASE FOR CULTURALLY RELEVANT LEADERSHIP LEARNING EXPERIENCES FOR BLACK MEN STUDENT ATHLETES

In 1903, W. E. B. Du Bois asserted that African Americans have a double consciousness or a sense of their identity being divided into multiple parts. These multiple identities make forming, maintaining, or establishing a unified identity genuinely impossible. He states in his 1903 work *The Souls of Black Folk*:

> It is a peculiar sensation, this double-consciousness, this sense of always looking at oneself through the eyes of others, of measuring one's soul by the tape of a world that looks on in amused contempt and pity. One ever feels his two-ness, an American, a Negro; two souls, two thoughts, two unreconciled strivings; two warring ideals in one dark body, whose dogged strength alone keeps it from being torn asunder... He simply wishes to make it possible for a man to be both a Negro and an American without being cursed and spit upon by his fellows, without having the doors of opportunity closed roughly in his face. (Du Bois, 1903, pp. 2–3)

Du Bois reminds us in this statement that the most pressing social issue of his generation was race. Unfortunately, race, as a social construct continues to be a problem for Black men today. Additionally, Fanon (1952) states, "When they like me, they tell me my color has nothing to do with it. When they hate me, they add that it's not because of my color. Either way, I am a prisoner of the vicious circle" (p. 96). Fanon calls attention to the hyper-visible experiences that are often salient in Black men's daily lives, which are further exposed for Black men who identify as student-athletes. The burden of a racialized identity, as Fanon describes it, is comparable to the lived experiences of Black men on college campuses as student-athletes. Both Fanon and Du Bois's messages emphasize a double consciousness about how Black men are treated in the United States and how that treatment may be directly related to how identity is viewed in the context of the historical legacy of exclusion, as demonstrated by the CRLL model. Fanon and Du Bois do not incorporate the impact of developing a leadership identity in a higher education context as a student-athlete into their understanding of being both Black and a man. As we emphasize, this "quadruple consciousness" or belief that one can learn to balance being Black, a man, a leader, and a student-athlete is the reason for leadership educators, scholars, and practitioners to reconsider how we develop Black men who are student-athletes. This term refers to Black men who are student-athletes who must juggle multiple identities. It encompasses the ongoing identification and issues surrounding identity politics that this highly visible population faces.

Connecting Intersecting Identities Through Multiple Dimensions of Identity

Intersecting identities have been a long-standing issue for Black Americans. In the context of Black men student-athletes' experiences, their multiple identities (Black, a man, a leader, a student-athlete, etc.) around community, political, cultural, and social support on college campuses impact their trajectory at historically white institutions. More specifically, drawing on the work of Jones and McEwen (2000), a Black man who is a student-athlete's core or "inside self" or "inner identity" are personal attributes, characteristics, and identity. This "inner identity" is influenced by socially constructed identities (race, gender, culture, etc.) within the context of the individual (Jones & McEwen, 2000). For Black men who are student-athletes, navigating the complexities of establishing, managing, and maintaining identities in spaces that were historically not designed to be inclusive of them and expose them to racialized microaggressions may be difficult (Beatty, 2014; Smith et al., 2011). As a result, the issues confronting Black men who are student-athletes, who are frequently hyper-visible and juggle multiple identities in spaces not designed for them, include numerous roadblocks related to leadership identity development, stereotypes, persistence, and academic success.

The research on the experiences of Black men who are student-athletes reveals a plethora of issues centered on and surrounding their identities (Simiyu, 2012). The prevalent narrative in the media about Black student-athletes portrays athletics as the key to assisting poor and academically underdeveloped students of color (Simiyu, 2012). Singer (2008) noted, however, that these students are socialized to think of themselves as athletes first and students second, allowing institutions to capitalize on their athletic abilities at the expense of their academic and social development. This message, which is similar to what Black boys receive as children, reflects directly on how these students view themselves as college student-athletes (Hodge et al., 2008; Simiyu, 2012; Singer, 2008). Additionally, these students' collegiate experiences are frequently marred by exploitation and stereotypes. Negative stereotypes and widespread misunderstanding in the dominant culture label these students as "dumb jocks," reinforcing societal messages that they are academically unprepared for college work through interactions with peers, faculty, and campus administrators (Bimper et al., 2013; Engstrom et al., 1995). Additionally, the social construction of masculinity exacerbates and reinforces the problems that this population faces (Martin & Harris, 2007).

Hyatt (2003) identified four common barriers to academic success for Black men who are student-athletes: academic readiness and integration, self-motivation and personal accountability, career maturity, and institutional social integration. Understanding the complex identities developed by Black man student-athletes during their collegiate careers is critical to their development. According to Bimper and colleagues (2013), professionals and educators working with this population should adopt a culturally relevant pedagogical framework that considers the social and cultural identities held by Black men student-athletes. Bimper and colleagues (2013) hypothesize that developing Black men student-athletes holistically would benefit from a culturally responsive approach. Using the CRLL model developed by Bertrand Jones et al. (2016), Bimper and colleagues (2013) believed that emphasizing culturally relevant development would not only aid in academic, personal, and social aspects of their experiences, but would also help them develop their leadership identity.

The model developed in this article considers the three prominent identities discussed in the literature in relation to the experiences of Black men who are student-athletes. The outer circle in Fig. 14.1 emphasizes the CRLL model's

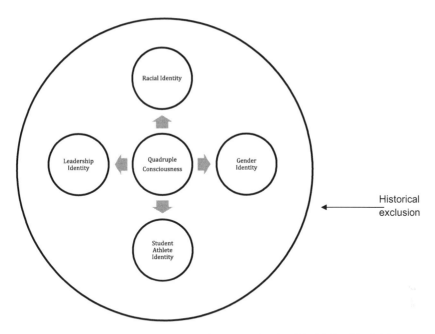

Fig. 14.1.   The Quadruple Consciousness Identity Model for Black Male
Student Athletes.

importance of historical inclusion and exclusion (Bertrand Jones et al., 2016). The four internal circles within this outer circle illustrate how we conceptualize Black student-athletes with an emphasis on leadership within their identity. Internal and external messages about the coexistence of these identities (Black, men, leadership identity, and student-athlete) provide quadruple consciousness for Black men student-athletes.

FUTURE RESEARCH

Further research should be conducted to examine student-athletes' experiences and leadership through a variety of racial, ethnic, gender, and socioeconomic lenses. Along with racial, ethnic, gender, and socioeconomic barriers, how does this look for student-athletes who have additional unexplored identities, such as disabilities or sexual orientation, or who are affected by COVID-19? Cultural diversity and sensitivity training must be expanded to include Black men who are student-athletes as a distinct subpopulation facing unique challenges. This scholarship is a first step toward bridging the divide between student-athletes, Black men, and how their leadership identity is conceptualized. Leadership educators must reconsider how they have been socialized to view Black men who are student-athletes and look for ways to support and develop the leadership identities of this highly visible minority on our campuses. Additionally, CRLL encourages leadership educators to consider students' identity, capacity, and efficacy as they engage in the leadership process (Bertrand Jones et al., 2016).

CONCLUSION

As previously stated, few connections have been made between leadership and Black men in colleges. We need to begin reshaping the conversation about Black men in college. According to Davis and Museus (2019), "an anti-deficit perspective would suggest that Black men are not 'at-risk,' but educational institutions are." Scholars and researchers frequently lament the absence of Black men student leaders as a result of the low enrollment of Black men in colleges and universities. While it is well-established that Black men participate in college sports, little is known about how institutions cultivate their leadership identities and experiences. While we acknowledge their existence, we must also consider how these students' leadership identities are defined. The narratives of Black men student leaders focus on the scarcity of Black men academically prepared to handle academic work and subsequently enrolled in colleges and universities. Despite the difficulty of recruiting high-achieving Black men for academic programs, colleges and universities have been successful in recruiting Black men student-athletes. We must work to develop Black men student-athletes into leaders as we work to create a more inclusive community.

Additionally, because of the influx of Black men into athletic programs, colleges and universities can serve as incubators for the development of Black men's leadership identities as student-athletes. Historically, marginalized group leaders have led their communities through collaborative leadership practices that emphasize shared power and greater change movements. Cultivating leaders through athletic programs has the potential to have a long-lasting impact on the advancement of Black communities. The complexities of juggling multiple identities, such as those described by Jones and McEwen (2000) for Black men student-athletes (being Black, a man, a leader, a student-athlete, etc.) who face numerous oppressions, necessitate educators utilizing culturally relevant leadership learning to develop these students as campus community leaders. To summarize, Wiborg (2020) states "definitions of leadership serve as an anchor for leadership theory, perpetuating specific assumptions about leadership; therefore, it is important for leadership learning to define its purpose in higher education (p. 13)" and how it can be used to better support Black men on college athletic teams.

REFERENCES

Abes, E. S., Jones, S. R., & McEwen, M. K. (2007). Reconceptualizing the model of multiple dimensions of identity: The role of meaning-making capacity in the construction of multiple identities. *Journal of College Student Development, 48*(1), 1–22.

Agyemang, K., Singer, J. N., & DeLorme, J. (2010). An exploratory study of black male college athletes' perceptions on race and athlete activism. *International Review for the Sociology of Sport*, *45*(4), 419–435.

Ahmed, S. (2012). *On being included: Racism and diversity in institutional life*. Duke University Press.

Albritton, T. J. (2012). Educating our own: The historical legacy of HBCUs and their relevance for educating a new generation of leaders. *The Urban Review: Issues and Ideas in Public Education*, *44*(3), 311–331.

Allen, W., Jewell, J., Griffin, K., & Wolf, D. (2007). Historically Black colleges and universities: Honoring the past, engaging the present, touching the future. *The Journal of Negro Education*, *76*(3), 263–280.

Anderson, J. D. (1988). *The education of Blacks in the South, 1860–1935*. University of North Carolina Press.

Beatty, C. C. (2014). *Exploring the leadership identity development of students of color at a selective liberal arts college*. Graduate Theses and Dissertations.

Beatty, C. C., Bush, A. A., Erxleben, E. E., Ferguson, T. L., Harrell, A. T., & Sahachartsiri, W. K. (2010). Black student leaders: The influence of social climate in student organizations. *Journal of the Student Personnel Association at Indiana University*, 48–63.

Beatty, C. C., & Ford, J. R. (2023). *Engaging Black college men engaging in leadership learning*. Information Age Publishing.

Beatty, C. C., & Salinas, C. (2016). Providing spaces on college campuses and through social media for men of color to offer counterstories. *Leadership Studies Publication*, *13*(4), 6.

Beatty, C. C., Tevis, T., Acker, L., Blockett, R., & Parker, E. (2020). Addressing anti-Black racism in higher education. *Journal Committed to Social Change on Race and Ethnicity (JCSCORE)*, *6*(1), 7–27.

Beatty, C. C., Wiborg, E. R., Brewster, B., & LeBlanc, J. B. (2021). Alumni applied leadership learning: The influence of an undergraduate academic leadership program. *Journal of Leadership Education*, *20*(1), 128–138.

Bertrand Jones, T., Guthrie, K. L., & Osteen, L. (2016). Critical domains of culturally relevant leadership learning: A call to transform leadership programs. *New Directions for Student Leadership*, (152), 9–21.

Bimper, A. Y., Harrison, L., & Clark, L. (2013). Diamonds in the rough: Examining a case of successful Black male student-athletes in college sport. *Journal of Black Psychology*, *39*(2), 107–130.

Bordas, J. (2007). *Salsa, soul, and spirit: Leadership for a multicultural age*. Berrett-Koehler Publishers.

Brooms, D. R. (2016). *Being Black, being male on campus: Understanding and confronting Black male collegiate experiences*. SUNY Press.

Brooms, D. R., Clark, J. S., & Druery, J. E. (2020). "We can redefine ourselves": Enhancing Black college men's persistence through counterspaces. *Journal of Black Studies*. https://doi.org/10.1177/0021934720976410

Brooms, D. R., Goodman, J., & Clark, J. (2015). "We need more of this": Engaging Black men on college campuses. *College Student Affairs Journal*, *33*(1), 105–123.

Cantey, N., Bland, R., Mack, L., & Joy-Davis, D. (2013). Historically Black colleges and universities: Sustaining a culture of excellence in the twenty-first century. *Journal of African American Studies*, *17*(2), 142–153.

Cooper, J. N., Corral, M. D., Macaulay, C. D. T., Cooper, M. S., Nwadike, A., & Mallery, M. J. (2019). Collective uplift: The impact of a holistic development support program on black male former college athletes' experiences and outcomes. *International Journal of Qualitative Studies in Education*, *32*(1), 21–46. https://doi.org/10.1080/09518398.2018.1522011

Cooper, J. N., Davis, T. J., & Dougherty, S. (2017). Not so Black and White: A multi-divisional exploratory analysis of male student-athletes' experiences at National Collegiate Athletic Association (NCAA) Institutions. *Sociology of Sport Journal*, *34*(1), 59–78. https://doi-org.libproxy.uncg.edu/10.1123/ssj.2016-0015

Davis, L. P., & Museus, S. D. (2019, July 26). *Identifying and disrupting deficit thinking*. https://medium.com/national-center-for-institutional-diversity/identifying-and-disrupting-deficitthinking. Accessed on February 07, 2021.

Dixon, K. M., & Spears, B. (2022). Student affairs assessment: Historically black college and university perspective. *New Directions for Student Services, 2022*(178–179), 77–86. https://doi.org/10.1002/ss.20430

Donnor, J. K. (2005). Towards an interest-convergence in the education of African-American football student-athletes in major college sports. *Race, Ethnicity and Education, 8*(1), 45–67.

Du Bois, W. E. B. (1903). *The souls of Black folk*. Dover Publications.

Dugan, J. P. (2017). *Leadership theory: Cultivating critical perspectives*. John Wiley & Sons.

Engstrom, C. M., Sedlacek, W. E., & McEwen, M. K. (1995). Faculty attitudes toward male revenue and non revenue student-athletes. *Journal of College Student Development, 36*(3), 217–227.

Fanon, F. (1952). *Black skin, white masks*. Grove Press.

Ferguson, T. L., & Davis, C. H., III. (2019). Labor, resources, and interest convergence in the organized resistance of Black male student-athletes. *Student Activism, Politics, and Campus Climate in Higher Education*, 77–96.

Ford, J. R., Matthews, D. Y., Woodard, D. M., & Kepple, C. R. (2023). "Not every advisor is for me, but some are": Black men's academic advising experiences during COVID-19. *Education Sciences, 13*(6), 543–558.

Ford, J. R., & Propst, B. (2022). From #BlackLivesMatter to critical hope: Reflecting on leadership practices in higher education. In K. L. Guthrie & K. L. Priest (Eds.), *Navigating complexities in leadership: Moving toward critical hope* (pp. 143–152). Information Age Publishing.

Gaston-Gayles, J. (2004). Examining academic and athletic motivation among student-athletes at a division I university. *Journal of College Student Development, 45*(1), 75–83.

Guthrie, K. L., & Jenkins, D. M. (2018). *The role of leadership educators: Transforming learning*. Information Age Publishing.

Guthrie, K. L., Jones, T. B., Osteen, L., & Hu, S. (2013). *Cultivating leader identity and capacity in students from diverse backgrounds: ASHE higher education report* (Vol. 39, p. 4). John Wiley & Sons.

Harper, S. R. (2006). *Black male students at public flagship universities in the U.S.: Status, trends and implications for policy and practice*. Joint Center for Political and Economic Studies.

Harper, S. R. (2009). Race, interest convergence, and transfer outcomes for Black male student-athletes. *New Directions for Community Colleges, 2009*(147), 29–37.

Harper, S. R. (2012). *Black male student success in higher education: A report from the National Black Male College Achievement Study*. University of Pennsylvania, Center for the Study of Race and Equity in Education.

Harper, S. R. (2016). *Black male student-athletes and racial inequities in NCAA Division I college sports* (2016 ed.). University of Pennsylvania, Center for the Study of Race & Equity in Education.

Harper, S. R., & Quaye, S. J. (2007). Student organizations as venues for Black identity expression and development among African American male student leaders. *Journal of College Student Development, 48*(2), 127–144.

Harris, C. I. (1993). Whiteness as property. *Harvard Law Review, 106*, 1721.

Hodge, S., Burden, J., Robinson, L., & Bennett, R. (2008). Theorizing on the stereotyping of Black male student-athletes: Issues and implications. *Journal for the Study of Sports and Athletes in Education, 2*(2), 203–226.

Hogg, M. A. (2001). A social identity theory of leadership. *Personality and Social Psychology Review, 5*(3), 184–200.

Hyatt, R. (2003). Barriers to persistence among African American intercollegiate athletes: A literature review of non-cognitive variables. *College Student Journal, 37*(2), 260–276.

Ingraham, C. (2020, September 8). NCAA rules allow white students and coaches to profit off labor of Black ones, study finds. *Washington Post*. https://www.washingtonpost.com/business/2020/09/07/ncaa-student-athletes-pay-equity/. Accessed on January 12, 2023.

Jackson, L., Ford, J. R., James, B. A., Schleiden, C. A., Harris-McKoy, D., & Holcomb, J. (2020). Expect the best; not the worst: How parent's expectations can moderate Black males' educational expectancy. *Journal of Black Studies, 51*(8), 767–789.

Jackson, L., Ford, J. R., Randolph, C., Schleiden, C., Harris-McKoy, D., & McWey, L. (2021a). School climate as a link between high school Black males' math identity and outcomes. *Education and Urban Society, 52*(7), 1–19.

Jackson, L., Ford, J., Randolph, C., Schleiden, C., Harris-McKoy, D., & McWey, L. (2021b). School climate as a link between high school Black males' math identity and outcomes. *Education and Urban Society, 53*(4), 469–487.

Jones, S. R., & Abes, E. S. (2013). *Identity development of college students.* Jossey-Bass.

Jones, S. R., & McEwen, M. K. (2000). A conceptual model of multiple dimensions of identity. *Journal of College Student Development, 41*(4), 405–414.

Komives, S. R., Longerbeam, S. D., Owen, J. E., Mainella, F. C., & Osteen, L. (2006). A leadership identity development model: Applications from a grounded theory. *Journal of College Student Development, 47*(4), 401–418.

Lawrence, S. M. (2005). African American athletes' experiences of race in sport. *International Review for the Sociology of Sport, 40*(1), 99–110.

Lord, R. G., & Hall, R. J. (2005). Identity, deep structure and the development of leadership skill. *The Leadership Quarterly, 16*(4), 591–615.

Majors, R. G., & Gordon, J. U. (1994). *The American black male: His present status and his future.* Nelson-Hall.

Martin, B. E., & Harris, F., III. (2007). Examining productive conceptions of masculinities: Lessons learned from academically driven African American male student-athletes. *The Journal of Men's Studies, 14*(3), 359–378.

Northouse, P. G. (2019). *Introduction to leadership: Concepts and practice.* Sage Publications.

Siegel, D. (1994). Higher education and the plight of the black male athlete. *Journal of Sport & Social Issues, 18*(3), 207–223.

Simiyu, W. N. (2012). Challenges of being a Black student-athlete on U.S. college campuses. *Journal of Issues in Intercollegiate Athletics, 1*(5), 40–63.

Sims, C. M., Carter, A. D., Sparkman, T. E., Morris, L. R., & Durojaiye, A. (2021). On black male leadership: A study of leadership efficacy, servant leadership, and engagement mediated by microaggressions. *Advances in Developing Human Resources.* https://doi.org/10.1177/15234223211037753

Singer, J. N. (2008). Benefits and detriments of African American male athletes' participation in a big-time college football program. *International Review for the Sociology of Sport, 43*(4), 399–408.

Smith, M. P., Clark, L. D., & Harrison, L. (2014). The historical hypocrisy of the Black student-athlete. *Race, Gender & Class, 21*(1), 220–235.

Smith, W. A., Hung, M., & Franklin, J. D. (2011). Racial battle fatigue and the miseducation of black men: Racial microaggressions, societal problems, and environmental stress. *The Journal of Negro Education, 69*(1), 63–82.

Smith, W. A., Hung, M., & Franklin, J. D. (2012). Between hope and racial battle fatigue: African American men and race-related stress. *Journal of Black Masculinity, 2*(1), 35–58.

Spencer, D. (2018). The world is yours: Cultivating Black male leadership learning. In Chunoo, V. S. & Guthrie, K. L. (Eds.), *Changing the narrative: Socially just leadership education.* Information Age Publishing.

Spencer, D. (2019). *Like a unicorn: A narrative inquiry exploring the leadership experiences of undergraduate Black men.* Doctoral dissertation. http://diginole.lib.fsu.edu

Wiborg, E. R. (2020). *A critical discourse analysis of leadership learning.* Doctoral dissertation. http://diginole.lib.fsu.edu

Yosso, T. J. (2005). Whose culture has capital? A critical race theory discussion of community cultural wealth. *Race Ethnicity and Education, 8*(1), 69–91.

CHAPTER 15

ADVISING AND ENGAGING BLACK MALE VETERANS FOR POSTSECONDARY SUCCESS

Louis L. Dilbert

ABSTRACT

Black male student veterans enter postsecondary education with three intersecting identities that should be acknowledged through the academic and student support services provided by the institution they attend. The academic guidance provided by competent and compassionate advisors coupled with student affairs engagement contribute to the graduation of this unique population.

The purpose of this literature is twofold: (a) identify and highlight effective academic support methods that contribute to Black male veteran graduation and (b) identify and highlight effective Student Affairs engagement strategies that contribute to Black male veteran graduation. The literature will further inform higher education professionals in both Academic Affairs spaces and Student Affairs spaces of collaborative partnerships that can be formed to increase the graduation rates of Black male veterans. Black male student veterans are not a monolithic population nor are the institutions they are attending. Therefore, it is also important to examine how the literature addresses advising and engagement of Black male veterans at diverse types of postsecondary institutions.

Keywords: Black males; veterans; student affairs; higher education; academic support; retention and graduation

High school students have five primary choices immediately after earning their high school diploma. They can (a) enter the workforce (in conjunction with their

Black Males in Secondary and Postsecondary Education
Advances in Race and Ethnicity in Education, Volume 9, 273–284
Copyright © 2024 Louis L. Dilbert
Published under exclusive licence by Emerald Publishing Limited
ISSN: 2051-2317/doi:10.1108/S2051-231720230000009015

postsecondary education pursuit), (b) attend community college, (c) attend a trade school, (d) attend a 4-year institution, and (e) enlist in the military (Britton, 2011). Several factors contribute to postsecondary choices such as (a) cost, (b) academic aptitude, (c) family support, and (d) level of motivation, just to name a few. Once the decision has been made to pursue a postsecondary education, the next decision is for the individual to decide the type of postsecondary institution to which they will apply. The most common options are a (a) 4-year public or private institution, (b) 2-year public or private institution (community/state college or technical school), or (c) a vocational program that leads to certification (Lee, Leon, & Youn, 2013). If the individual persists past the first two stages of college choice (the decisions to attend and type of institution), they will then focus on more specific criteria such as size, location, academic offerings, financial incentives (scholarships), and/or whether or not the institution is categorized as a Historically Black College or University (HBCU), Predominantly White Institution (PWI), Hispanic-Serving Institution (HSI), or Minority-Serving Institution (MSI).

The aforementioned factors are typical considerations for your average 18–22 who is not a veteran. Veterans that are medically or honorably discharged or retired may have additional factors to consider prior to enrolling in a postsecondary education program after their service in the military. Such factors for consideration are family, accommodations for physical and/or mental health, use of military education benefits, and the veteran support services provided by postsecondary institution(s) under consideration (Miles, 2014).

The purpose of this literature is twofold: (a) identify and highlight effective academic support methods that contribute to Black male veteran graduation and (b) identify and highlight effective Student Affairs engagement strategies that contribute to Black male veteran graduation. The literature will further inform higher education professionals in both Academic Affairs spaces and Student Affairs spaces of collaborative partnerships that can be formed to increase the graduate rates of Black male veterans. Although the literature is limited and relatively unexplored regarding this specific population, Black male veterans make up 7.1% of the Black male collegian populations. This veteran student population, particularly those that experienced recent combat, experience challenges with acclimating to campus culture, financial struggles due to GI Bill limits and health complications that stem from combat (Wood et al., 2014).

ROUTES TO SERVICE – ENLISTMENT VERSUS COMMISSIONING

The US Department of Education policy 38 USC § 101(2) provides: The term *veteran* means a person who served in the active military, naval, or air service and who was discharged or released from there under conditions other than dishonorable (United States Department of Veteran Affairs, 2019). This term is applied to an individual who took an oath to serve in the US Armed Forces regardless of the individual's length of service. The two primary methods of entering military service are enlistment and commissioning.

Veterans that enlisted chose to begin their military service at the lowest rank of their branch as opposed to those that commissioned through a postsecondary training program such as ROTC. Student veterans who enlisted chose to enter military service first and then attend a postsecondary institution as opposed to those who chose to commission after they earn a degree from a 4-year college or university. Individuals who enter the military through commissioning enter at a higher rank, which gives this method greater appeal. For example, if an individual enlists in the Army, they will start as a Private, but the highest rank they can attain is Sergeant Major. If an individual enters the Army as a commissioned officer, they begin their service as a second Lieutenant and can ascend to the rank of Army Chief Staff General (Hollings, 2021). Most student veterans at the undergraduate level enrolled at postsecondary institutions enlisted then chose to go to college because you must earn a bachelor's degree and complete an accredited ROTC program at a 4-year postsecondary institution to be eligible for commissioning into military service (Durden & Kim, 2012).

THE IMPACT OF LEGISLATIVE ACTION

In the United States, males have always had the privilege of serving in the military. In fact, until the end of the military draft that required men to serve if called to duty (regardless of interest), it was expected that males be prepared to serve regardless of race or ethnicity. For Black males, this meant they were required to serve in the Revolutionary War and Civil War even if they were enslaved. The Continental Army and Navy had to include slaves and formerly enslaved people because of the need for laborers. Black males were also segregated from their fellow service members who were White. Although the Civil War ended slavery, Jim Crow laws that emerged still made the Black male service member a second-class citizen despite his equal sacrifice to protect the country (MacGregor, 2020).

After World War II, Congress passed the Servicemen's Readjustment Act of 1944, known as the GI Bill of Rights. The 1944 GI Bill was the first legislative act to provide allowances to veterans for living expenses, education tuition, and home purchases. The GI Bill of Rights was controversial because it impacted the United States socially, economically, and politically (Cole-Morton, 2013; U.S. Department of Veteran Affairs, 2012). The passing of the Servicemen's Readjustment Act of 1944 changed the relationship between high education institution and the armed services (Hammond, 2017). Scores of service members began pursuing postsecondary degrees, which changed the landscape of postsecondary institutions across the country. However, this benefit was simply transactional and did not come with any other requirements outside of funding. From the time this legislative was passed until the post-9/11 legislation was enacted, G.I. Bill funding was limited to the service member and could not be transferred to a spouse or dependent. These funds also had a time limit to be used, so millions of dollars would go unclaimed because of service members who did not have the ability or the desire to pursue a postsecondary education (Humes, 2014).

Brown Versus Board of Education

Brown versus the Board of Education of Topeka, Kansas was a consolidated group of five cases that challenged the constitutionality of the "separate but equal" that stemmed from the landmark Supreme Court ruling in Plessy versus Ferguson that concluded that Black citizens and White citizens were "equal" but must use separate facilities. Therefore, public facilities and educational institutions were segregated. This included the military (Van Delinder, 2004; www.history.com editors, 2022).

Post-9/11 GI Bill

In 2009, the post-9/11 GI bill went into effect, broadly expanding higher education benefits to military service members and veterans in proportion to their time served since September 10, 2001 (Eliott, 2014). The post-9/11 GI Bill provides the most generous educational benefits since the original GI Bill following World War II (Vacchi & Berger, 2014). This, coupled with new laws that require state institutions to offer in-state tuition to all service members and veterans, as well as Yellow Ribbon benefits that help offset the total cost of attendance for veterans at public and private institutions, means that veterans have more opportunity to pursue higher education than at any time since the late 1940s and 1950s (Brawner et al., 2019; Fulton & Sponsler, 2015). To add to this extensive package of benefits, active-duty service members have the option of passing their education benefits on to their spouse or children, should they elect to do so prior to being honorably discharged from service.

BLACK MALE MILITARY SERVICE

A recent report from the Brookings Institute revealed a stark difference in the military service by race gender. The summation was that the overrepresentation of Black men and women in the military can be seen as a double-edged sword. On the one hand, the military has served as a means for Black males to gain social mobility. On the other hand, the dominance of Black Americans in military service – and therefore among these most likely to be put in harm's way on behalf of the nation – is striking, especially considering broader current conversations about race, justice, and equity (Reeves & Nzau, 2020).

BLACK MALE VETERANS

Recruiting Black Male Veterans

One of the biggest challenges veterans face when they leave active military service is the process of adapting to civilian life (Jones, 2013). Engaging Black male veterans begins with a college or university's efforts to recruit veterans. A strategic recruitment plan that includes goals for recruiting veterans demonstrates a commitment to providing educational access for veterans. The expansion of high tuition/high-aid financial models continues to increase the need for higher education institutions to accept students that can pay full tuition and fees (Grawe, 2018). Veterans with military education funds (post-9/11 G.I. Bill, Veteran Readiness and Employment etc.) are a partial resolution to a growing problem because they are attached to funding. A higher education institution that wishes to engage veterans for the purpose of recruitment should have a representative from the institution that is designated to recruit veterans specifically. Military installations across the United States host education fairs that allow education and training organizations to recruit active-duty service members who are preparing to end their full-time military service or remain active-duty while enrolled in an online program. Opportunities to attend military education fairs are limited, so recruiters must diversify their efforts to increase veteran enrollment. Practical recommendations for postsecondary institutions are:

- Provide veteran support information that can be attained within one or two clicks on the institution's website (and the information posted is updated and accurate).
- Distribute veteran support information among other university recruiters to increase the reach of information (brochures, handouts, etc.).
- Advertise military-affiliated publications and websites on the institution website.
- Utilize alumni veterans of the institution within their spheres of professional influence and for financial support for student veteran services.
- Four-year colleges and universities should target veterans at two-year colleges that desire to transfer to four-year institution by visiting the two-year postsecondary institutions or hosting virtual information sessions for that specific population.
- Utilize currently enrolled student veterans as ambassadors for recruitment of veterans to the institution.

Postsecondary institutions that do not have online degree or training programs are at a disadvantage to institutions that do have online programs because it limits the pool of qualified applicants they can recruit, specifically active-duty service members who need to attend a postsecondary institution virtually.

The level of diversity of the student body of a postsecondary institution correlates with its efforts to recruit and retain students of color, students from varying socioeconomic backgrounds, students with disabilities, and student veterans (Palmer et al., 2014). Blacknall and Johnson (2011) studied the college choice decisions of high-achieving African American males and found that some were predisposed to attend HBCUs based on the family legacy and explored HBCUs exclusively within their college search. If such high achieving scholars also desire to build relationships with their peers or recover from an isolated military experience, then such caveats are ripe ground for HBCU recruitment. Most notably, achievement-oriented men exhibit better academic adjustment, better academic performance, and higher educational and occupational aspirations (Johnson & McGowan, 2017).

Advising Black Male Veterans

Veterans are classified as nontraditional students by the mere fact that, if they choose to attend a postsecondary institution, it will be at an age that differs from their traditional-aged classmates (17–19 years old). Therefore, there may be heightened focus on taking courses that fall in line with the requirements of their major and no time for elective courses. At the secondary level, a supportive and trustworthy relationship with a guidance counselor can positively impact a Black male's college predisposition at a level similar to parental support (Muhammad, 2008). Conversely, on the postsecondary level, academic advisors should help Black male veterans envision a positive future regardless of their socioeconomic status and then assist them with moving toward that future (Farmers-Hinton & Adams, 2006; Toldson et al., 2009).

A study on racial, veteran, and academic major identities among Black Male Veterans revealed that being a Black male was core to the identities of 70% of the respondents, some of whom also acknowledged their veteran status as part of their core identity (Brawner et al., 2019). Nelson et al. (2020) provided some important notes for advising Black males:

- Work to build a positive relationship with Black male students by establishing rapport with them. Advisors should learn developmental theory (Aydin et al., 2018).
- Be intentional, empathetic, strategic, and patient when providing guidance, development, and support for Black male students to help them develop a healthy work/school/life balance.
- Purposefully engage in conversations on thoughts and feelings about the traumatic events that have occurred and continue to occur regarding racial discrimination and police brutality against Black men in society.
- Actively participate in professional development centered on cultural competence and awareness.
- Remind Black males to not feel compelled to explain or teach about race, racial discrimination, and/or police brutality against Black men to their white counterparts.
- Aim to become a co-conspirator willing and ready for action rather than just becoming an ally by only showing empathy to their plight.
- Understand the stigma associated with mental health in the Black community.
- Encourage Black males to join affinity groups with other Black males that meet regularly to discuss issues of racial discrimination and other experiences on campus.
- Be conscious that Black males may experience re-traumatization of past experiences of racial discrimination because of the latest racialized events in our country.
- Apprise Black males that power lies in completing their education.

Orientation

The vast majority of postsecondary institutions in the United States have a new student orientation. Depending on the size of the institution, new student orientations could have less than 100 attendees or as many as 500 in attendance. For a nontraditional student, this can be an intimidating experience. Therefore, having a separate orientation session for military-affiliated students allows them to feel valued. The amenity of having a private orientation session allows Veteran Services professionals to answer important questions that may not get answered in a larger session with the general student population that has competing concerns and interests. Understanding that some institutions have limited human resources to devote a significant amount of time to commit to a separate veteran orientation, any institution can provide literature with information pertinent to the military-affiliated population and specifically address military-affiliated student concerns during the New Student Orientation program.

Engaging Black Male Veterans

The transition from the close camaraderie of military service and into the civilian world represents a challenging and serious investment for student veterans (Abel et al., 2013). Once a veteran has enrolled at the institution, advising and programming that targets the military-affiliated student population demonstrates a commitment to retaining and graduating veterans. When students engage in college activities, they build relationships, which can lead to significant social impact on the veterans who choose to immerse themselves in college culture (Duncan & Raudenbush, 1999; Semke & Sheridan, 2011; Vianden et al., 2012).

Intersectionality of Student Veteran Engagement (Multiple Identities)

Although it is obvious that Veterans may share values, "Veterans Identity" is an underdeveloped concept in the social science literature, at least partially because Veterans as a class differ from racial minorities, women, and sexual minorities in that there is little to no pervasive discrimination against them (Gade & Wilkins, 2013). When a student enters postsecondary education, they come with multiple identities. It is the responsibility of the institution to provide academic support that connects with varying student identities. For example, a student could racially identify as Black, ethnically identify as Hispanic or Latinx, and have a sexual orientation affiliated with the LGBT+ community. Kimberlé Crenshaw, a legal scholar, created a term to describe our multiple identities: *intersectionality*. Crenshaw explains that our identities are like traffic flowing at an *intersection* – one identity may flow in one direction while another identity is flowing in a different direction (Flowers, 2019).

Black male veterans automatically come to postsecondary institutions with at least three primary identities – male, Black, and veteran. However, each value may differ in importance to an individual. Race, gender, and military status could take a back seat to a disability, age, or religious affiliation. Successful recruitment, retention, and graduation of Black male veterans will not necessarily come from targeted support for Black male veterans, but from an institution having sufficient support systems for advising and engagement of other intersecting populations that Black male veterans are connected to.

Programming

Reverting to the intersectionality of the Black male veteran identity, a post-secondary institution does not have to provide programming and support focused solely on Black male veterans to demonstrate support for the academic and emotional wellness of this population. The demonstration and support of Black male veterans comes from support in other key areas that impact another identity of the veteran. For example, providing support programs for:

- *Students of African descent such as cultural clubs and organizations, scholarships, and career development workshops* – Recognizing that the veteran identity is multidimensional, campus activities serve as a vehicle for student veterans to develop a new normal and reintegrate into society after their military service. Engagement through participation in campus activities, organizations, and with other students is an important part of the college experience. Additionally, social and academic engagement in an unfamiliar environment contributes to a sense of purpose and self-awareness for student veterans as they adjust to civilian life (Kirchner et al., 2014).
- *Peer mentoring programs* – Miami-Dade College has the Student Veteran Peer Mentor Program which is designed to connect newly enrolled MDC Student Veterans with current Student Veterans to provide support, resources, and increase campus and community engagement. The mentors use their leadership skills to guide mentees toward academic success by providing comradery and a supportive environment during the transition to college life. Mentors also receive a $75 for participation per semester (mdc.edu).
- *Emotional support groups* – Beyond physical wounds, which may obviously alter lives, mental wounds such as post-traumatic stress disorder (PTSD) and other negative mental health consequences are well-documented and all too common (Gade & Wenger, 2011).
- *Student veteran organizations*
- *Academic organizations such as honor societies*
- *Veteran-specific scholarships and career development workshops* – young veterans experience unemployment at a higher rate than their civilian counterparts (Kleykamp, 2013).

In summary, successful recruitment, retention, and graduation of Black males require an institutional commitment that is shared by all parts of the institutional community – senior administration, trustees, faculty, staff, and policymakers. Without a serious commitment, efforts to diversify and improve success rates for Black males, particularly student veterans, will not be as effective (Harper, 2013).

RECOMMENDATIONS

Research

There is minimal academic literature on successful engagement and retention of Black male veterans specifically. There are research opportunities to explore the following areas that pertain to Black male veterans and postsecondary achievement:

- Examine Black male postsecondary attainment by comparing the number of Black male veterans that choose college/university enrollment versus military enlistment directly after high school graduation. Where are Black male veterans that chose to enlist coming from? Moreover, is there a difference between the academic achievement of Black male student veterans who enlisted and the academic achievement of Black males who choose to commission into military service?
- Examine Black male veteran postsecondary recruitment by comparing strategies utilized by the US Armed Forces and higher education institutions.
- Explore factors that influence college enrollment and retention of Black male veterans by conducting an analysis of the impact of family, socioeconomic status, peer support, and academic success on college choice and retention within the institution.

Kirchner et al. (2014) offer several strategies to successfully engage student veterans. Although it is not specific to Black male veterans, it provides practical recommendations that can positively impact Black male veterans due to their veteran status. Some recommendations are as follows:

- Build support through partnerships with student veterans, faculty, staff, and senior-level administration at the institution.
- Develop an outreach and marketing plan that provides a continuous presence and visibility through campus events, displays, and social media.
- Identify needs by developing an assessment that offers an incentive to student veterans who participate, but explain the importance of the assessment.
- Partner with campus departments, student groups, and community organizations to provide military and veteran-specific programming.
- Establish an organization for student veterans with an advisor who is invested in the organization's success.
- Establish a veterans resource center that is open during normal business hours or longer and has staffing with expert knowledge of veterans' issues.

Faculty and Staff Training

The engagement of faculty and staff related to student veteran proficiencies, transition concerns, and military cultural competence is a recommended best practice to establish a military-friendly institution (Albright & Bryan, 2018; Davis, 2020). Not all faculty and staff understand the experiences of special populations, particularly student veterans. There are misconceptions of veterans that can be mitigated through *Green Zone Training* that educates the faculty, staff, and students on strategies to best support student veterans. For example, there is a presumption that most veterans have PTSD. In one major study of 60,000 Iraq and Afghanistan veterans, 13.5% of deployed and nondeployed veterans screened positive for PTSD (Reisman, 2016).

Policy

- Provide an admissions application fee waiver and exempt veterans from college entrance exam requirements (it is acceptable to limit this benefit to veterans with a minimum designated GPA.
- Grant priority registration to student veterans and assign academic advisors to work solely or primarily with military-connected students.
- Have accounting policies and procedures that align with the US Department of Veteran Affairs and the state department of Veteran Affairs. The process of certification of benefits and the distribution of funds should take no more than 2–3 weeks to ensure that the veteran gets the education financial support they need to pay tuition and fees, housing, class materials, etc. The institution should also seek additional financial resources to support student veteran success through corporate and community partnerships. It is highly recommended that an account is established through the institution's charitable foundation, so that donors can receive tax incentives for their contributions toward student veteran support.

CONCLUSION

There is still much research to be done as it pertains to advisement, engagement, and graduation of Black male veterans. The limited literature relevant to this small subsection of a key student demographic is evidence of unique opportunities to increase the amount of scholarly research pertaining that could impact the academic outcomes for Black male veterans. However, postsecondary institutions can use the limited research to review recruitment and retention strategies for Black male veterans and other underrepresented student populations and then enact changes that positively impact the academic achievement and matriculation of Black male veterans.

REFERENCES

Abel, S. G., Bright, R. J., & Cooper, R. M. (2013). Offices of veterans and military services. In F. A. Hamrick & C. B. Rumann (Eds.), *Called to serve. A handbook on student veterans and higher education*. Jossey-Bass.

Albright, G., & Bryan, C. J. (2018). *Are faculty and staff ready to support student veterans: A survey of 14,673 faculty and staff at 20 colleges and universities*. National Center for Veterans Studies: The University of Utah. [White paper]. https://go.kognito.com/Student_Veterans_Whitepaper. html?utm_source=PR&utm_campaign=StudentVeteranWP

Aydin, Y., Güneri, O., Eret, E., & Yildirim, F. (2018). The views of undergraduate students and academic advisors on the academic advising process. *Journal of Higher Education, 9*(2), 139–148. https://doi.org/10.2399/yod.18.042

Blacknall, T., & Johnson, J. M. (2011). Selective HBCUs: A competitive option. *Conference Paper Presented at 2011 ASHE Annual Conference.* http://files.eric.ed.gov/fulltext/ED530945.pdf

Brawner, C., Lord, S., Mobley, C., Camacho, M., & Main, J. (2019). *Race, veteran, and engineering identities among Black male student veterans.* American Society for Engineering Education. *ID# 25003.*

Britton, P. L. (2011). *Postsecondary aspirations of rural high school seniors.* Capella University. Pro-Quest database (876194756).

Cole-Morton, G. (2013). *Experiences and expectations of an African American male veteran student in higher education.* Electronic Theses and Dissertations. Paper 2301. https://dc.etsu.edu/etd/2301

Davis, C. (2020). *A phenomenological case study of faculty and staff experiences in green zone training to support student veteran transition into higher education.* UNC Charlotte Electronic Theses and Dissertations.

Duncan, G. J., & Raudenbush, S. W. (1999). Assessing the effects of context in studies of child and youth development. *Educational Psychologist, 34*(1), 29–41.

Durden, N., & Kim, Y. (2012). Understanding patterns of college outcomes among student veterans. *Journal of Studies in Education, 2*(2), 109–129.

Eliott, M. (2014). Predicting problems on campus: An analysis of college student veterans. *Analyses of Social Issues and Public Policy, 00*(0), 1–22.

Farmer-Hinton, R., & Adams, T. L. (2006). Social capital and college preparation: Exploring the role of counselors in a college prep school for black students. *Negro Educational Review, 57*(1/2), 101–116.

Flowers, H. (2019, July). *Intersectionality part one: Intersectionality defined.* National Institutes of Health. (online).

Fulton, M., & Sponsler, B. (2015). *In-state tuition policies under the veterans access, choice and accountability Act.* Education Commission of the States.

Gade, D. M., & Wenger, J. B. (2011). Combat exposure and mental health: The long-term effects among US Vietnam and Gulf War veterans. *Health Economics, 20*, 401–416.

Gade, D. M., & Wilkins, V. M. (2013). Where did you serve? Veteran identity, representative bureaucracy, and vocational rehabilitation. *Journal of Public Administration Research and Theory, 23*(2), 267–288.

Grawe, N. D. (2018). *Demographics and the demand for higher education.* JHU Press.

Hammond, S. (2017). Student veterans in higher education: A conversation six decades in the making. *New Directions for Institutional Research, 2016*(171), 11–21.

Harper, S. R. (2013). *Five things student affairs administrators can due to improve success among college of men of color.* NASPA Research and Policy Institute Issue Brief. https://www.naspa.org/images/uploads/main/5THINGS-MOC.pdf

Hollings, A. (2021). The complete list of military ranks (in order). https://www.sandboxx.us/blog/the-complete-list-of-us-military-ranks-in-order/

Humes, E. (2014). *Over here: How the G.I. Bill transformed the American dream.* Diversion Books.

Johnson, J., & McGowan, B. (2017). Untold stories: The gendered experiences of high- achieving African American male alumni of historically Black colleges and universities. *Journal of African American Males in Education, 8*(1).

Jones, K. C. (2013). Understanding student veterans in transition. *Qualitative Report, 18*(74).

Kirchner, M. J., Coryell, L., & Yelich Biniecki, S. M. (2014). Promising practices for engaging student veterans. *Quality Approaches in Higher Education, 5*(1), 12–18.

Kleykamp, M. (2013). Unemployment, earnings, and enrollment among post 9/11 veterans. *Social Science Research, 42*(3), 836–885.

Lee, K. A., Leon Jara Almonte, J., & Youn, M. J. (2013). What to do next: An exploratory study of the post-secondary decisions of American students. *Higher Education, 66*.

MacGregor, M. (2020). *Integration of the armed forces, 1940–1965: An investigation into race Relations in united states army.*

Miami-Dade College. (n.d.). Student veteran mentoring program. https://www.mdc.edu/media/mdc/veterans-amp-ilitaryservices/docs/MentorHandbookMDC.pdf

Miles, R. A. (2014). Career counseling strategies and challenges for transitioning veterans. *Career Planning and Adult Development Journal, 30*(3), 123–135.

Muhammad, C. (2008). African American students and college choice: A consideration of the role of school counselors. *NASSP Bulletin, 92*(2), 81–94. http://bul.sagepub.com

Nelson, M. S., Knibbs, L., Alexander, Q. R., Cherry, D. C., Johnson, B., & Johnson, J. (2020, September). Advising black male students in 2020 and beyond. *Academic Advising Today, 43*(3).

Palmer, R. T., Wood, J. L., Dancy, T. E., & Strayhorn, T. L. (2014). *Black male collegians: Increasing access, retention, and persistence in higher education: Ashe higher education report 40:3.* John Wiley & Sons.

Reeves, R., & Nzau, S. (2020). Black Americans are much more likely to serve the nation, in military and civilian roles. Brookings Institution (online).

Reisman, M. (2016). PTSD treatment for veterans: What's working, what's new, and what's next. *P & T: A Peer-Reviewed Journal for Formulary Management, 41*(10), 623–634.

Semke, C. A., & Sheridan, S. M. (2011). *Family-school connections in rural Educational settings: a systematic review of the empirical literature.* R2Ed Working Paper No. 2011-1.

Toldson, I. A., Braithwaite, R. L., & Renti, R. J. (2009). Promoting college access for school-age Black American males. In *Black American Males in Higher Education: Research, Programs and Academe Diversity in Higher Education, 7,* 117–137.

US Department of Veteran Affairs. (2019). *Verification assistance brief.*

U.S. Department of Veteran Affairs. (2012). *Born of controversy: The GI bill of rights.* http://www.gibill.va.gov/benefits/history_timeline/index.html

Vacchi, D. T., & Berger, J. (2014). Student veterans in higher education. In *Higher education: Handbook of theory and research* (Vol. 29, pp. 93–151).

Van Delinder, J. (2004). Brown v. Board of Education of Topeka: A landmark case unresolved fifty years later. *Prologue Magazine* (online).

Vianden, J., Kuykendall, J., Mock, R., & Korb, R. (2012). Exploring messages African-American men receive about attending PWIs. *CSPA-NYS Journal of Student Affairs, 12*(2).

Wood, J. L., & Harrison, J. D. (2014). College choice for Black males in community college: Factors that influence institutional selection. *The Negro Educational Review, 65*(1–4). http://interwork.sdsu.edu/sp/m2c3/files/2012/10/ARTICLE-UPLOAD.pdf

CHAPTER 16

CALLING ALL BROTHAS: RECRUITING AND RETAINING BLACK MALES WITHIN TEACHER PREPARATION PROGRAMS

Mia R. Hines

ABSTRACT

There is a national shortage of teachers of color; only 21% of teachers are from an underrepresented group (16% Black and/or Latinx), while 79% are White (National Center for Educational Statistics [NCES], 2019). While there are not a lot of teachers of color in today's classrooms, there is an even lower number of Black male teachers (approximately 2%) (NCES, 2022). These percentages do not mirror the K-12 student population, with 52% identifying as a student of color (NCES, 2019). Research informs us that having teachers of color, such as a Black male yields academic success, decreases suspension rates, increases college matriculation, and provides representation of positive role models for the K-12 students of color as well as White students (AACTE, 2019; Carter-Andrews et al., 2019). Teacher Preparation Programs must implement culturally responsive strategies to recruit and retain Black males into teaching. This chapter will share effective practices for recruiting, retaining, and advising Black male preservice teachers.

Keywords: Teachers of color; Black male teachers; recruitment; retention; advising; preservice teachers

Black Males in Secondary and Postsecondary Education
Advances in Race and Ethnicity in Education, Volume 9, 285–294
Copyright © 2024 Mia R. Hines
Published under exclusive licence by Emerald Publishing Limited
ISSN: 2051-2317/doi:10.1108/S2051-231720230000009016

INTRODUCTION

There is a national shortage of teachers of color; only 21% of teachers are from an underrepresented group (16% Black and/or Latinx), while 79% are White (National Center for Educational Statistics [NCES], 2022). While there are not a lot of teachers of color in today's classrooms, there is an even lower number of Black male teachers (approximately 2%) (NCES, 2022). The shortage of teachers of color began after the 1954 Brown vs. Board of Education decision to desegregate schools, where Black teachers were pushed out of classrooms due to Black students integrating into White schools who would not hire them (Carter-Andrews et al., 2019). Almost half of Black teachers (45%) were no longer employed in schools by 1964 (Kohli, 2021). As described by hooks (1996) in Kohli (2021):

> School changed utterly with racial integration. Gone was the messianic zeal to transform our minds and beings that had characterized teachers and their pedagogical practices in our all-black schools. Now we were mainly taught by white teachers whose lessons reinforced racist stereotypes. For black children, education was no longer about the practice of freedom. (p. 9)

The lack of culturally responsive teaching that was taken out of the classroom after desegregation that hooks (1996) in Kohli (2021) describes continues to perpetuate itself in education through teacher preparation programs and is one of the reasons why Black males are not entering the teaching profession at the same rate as their White peers. Other contributions to the shortage of Black male teachers include teacher preparation admission requirements and state certification testing policies, which will be discussed in this chapter (Carter-Andrews et al., 2019).

In response to this shortage, teacher preparation programs, individual state departments of education, and educational organizations are working to implement effective strategies for recruiting and retaining Black male teachers. The American Association for Colleges of Teacher Education [AACTE] (2019) suggests that "increasing the number of teachers of color in schools provides students of color with role models, offers opportunities to culturally connect, sets high expectations, and reduces implicit bias" (p. 3). Moreover, the percentage of teachers of color in today's classrooms does not mirror the K-12 student population, with 52% identifying as a student of color (NCES, 2019). Research informs us that having teachers of color, such as a Black male yields academic success, decreases suspension rates, increases college matriculation, and provides representation of positive role models for the K-12 students of color as well as White students (AACTE, 2019; Carter-Andrews et al., 2019). This chapter will share effective practices for recruiting, retaining, and advising Black male preservice teachers.

BARRIERS FOR RECRUITING BLACK MALES INTO TEACHER PREPARATION PROGRAMS

There are many barriers to recruiting Black males into teacher preparation programs, such as individual university admission requirements, negative experiences in their K-12 schooling journey, and the notion that teaching is not a profession that can provide financial stability. Teacher preparation programs typically accept students into their programs once they have completed two years of undergraduate coursework, meaning they begin as a junior in college. Unfortunately, this means before Black males apply to a teacher preparation program, they first must meet the admissions requirements of the university to be accepted. Furthermore, according to the National Center for Education Statistics (NCES) (2022), the college enrollment rate of 18- to 24-year-old Black males have decreased from 2010 to 2020 (35%–31%). These statistics and processes make it difficult for teacher preparation programs to recruit Black males into teacher preparation program. However, one of the largest roadblocks is teacher entrance exams, which is typically a requirement to enter a teacher preparation program. These requirements are often connected to mandates that individual states require for teacher certification and involve entry and exit tests (Boyd et al., 2007).

The inception of teacher certification exams dates back as far as 1636 when Virginia implemented oral certification exams that evaluated teachers on academic skills, "their capacity to govern a school, moral character" and their ability to keep things in order (Haney et al., 1987, p. 172). Teacher certification exams continued to evolve year after year as the number of students who begin to attend public schools grew with the goal of setting high academic standards (Haney et al., 1987). In 1940, the National Teacher Examination (NTE) was birthed because there was an influx in the amount of people who wanted to become teachers and school officials needed assistant in narrowing down candidates (Haney et al., 1987). "The original NTE was 8 hours long and covered general quality of intellectual performance, knowledge of general culture and contemporary affairs, and professional information" (Haney et al., 1987, p. 179). Moving forward to 1983, the A Nation at Risk report scared educators into thinking that students in the United States were failing and would not be able to compete with their international peers unless they implemented substantial changes (National Commission on Excellence in Education, 1983). Recommendations were made to implement school reforms in course content, expectations of students, the amount of time students spend in the classroom, and the quality of teaching (National Commission on Excellence in Education, 1983). Based on these recommendations, most states put in more rigorous standards for teacher certification, which included additional and more difficult certification exams (Ballou & Podgursky, 1997). In addition, the No Child Left Behind Act of 2001 created test-based accountability systems in which students were evaluated annually in reading, mathematics, and science and introduced the concept of "highly qualified" teachers, initiating states to alter certification exam requirements even more (Boyd et al., 2007; Ryan, 2010).

Praxis is the most common group of tests used in the United States with two-third of states using it as certification requirement (Carver-Thomas, 2018). State and national testing policies are barriers to increasing the number of Black males within teacher preparation programs. Reports from the Educational testing Center dating back to 1985 have shown Black and Latino students scoring lower on these standardized tests (Carver-Thomas, 2018), while Bennett et al. (2006) found that a disproportionately higher percentage of Black and Hispanic/Latino teachers who applied to educator preparation programs did not pass one or more of their basic skill exams in order to gain admission to teacher preparation programs. Carver-Thomas (2018) stated that research consistently shows that students of color are failing these tests at a higher rate than their White peers, however there is no data to prove the tests "predict their effectiveness as a teacher" (Carver-Thomas, 2018, p. 13). To recruit more Black males into teaching, teacher preparation programs must offer instructional and financial support to assist students with passing the tests. The author developed workshops for their students that included content knowledge for each subject area within the test, test taking strategies, as well as time to complete practice questions and get feedback from the facilitator(s). Additionally, funding was secured through the teacher preparation program and processes were developed to provide students access to exam study guides and scholarships for exam fees.

The overall decrease in Black male college enrollment, rigorous university, and state mandated teacher preparation admission requirements can be a barrier to recruiting Black males into the teaching profession. Nonetheless, teacher preparation programs can work to alleviate these problems by being intentional about their recruitment and retention initiatives as well as creating a space for teacher educators to become involved in educational policy related to preparing a diverse population of teachers, such as Black males. The next few sections will discuss best practices for recruiting and retaining Black males into teacher preparation programs and will provide recommendations for policy, creating Grow Your Own Programs, which we will discuss later in this chapter.

BEST PRACTICES FOR RECRUITING BLACK MALES INTO TEACHER PREPARATION PROGRAMS

Prior to Teacher Educators and K-12 school leaders beginning the process of recruiting Black males into teaching careers, all faculty and staff must be firmly committed to diversifying the teacher workforce. This commitment should be outlined within a detailed recruitment and retention plan for diversifying the teacher preparation program that addresses recruiting Black males that are currently at the university, community college students, and K-12 students.

Teacher preparation programs have a better chance of recruiting Black males who are currently enrolled at the university into their programs. First steps should include forging relationships with cultural centers, advisors, and Trio and/ or bridge programs on campus that implement programming that is specifically tailored toward Black males. Once the relationship is established, teacher preparation programs should facilitate information sessions specific to this population of students. Information sessions should include information about debunking myths of teaching. These myths can look different depending on the state and location of the teacher preparation program. However, the universal myth about teaching is that teachers do not make enough money to sustain a comfortable lifestyle. While it is true, teachers should receive higher salaries, some states are doing a good job at compensating their teachers. According to the National Education Association (2022), "14.6% of schools pay beginning teachers a salary of at least $50,000" with New Jersey being the highest, paying their beginning teachers $54,053. This salary is not far from the 2022 average salary of Black college graduates, which was $57,984 (McGurran, 2022). Additionally, in most collective bargaining states, teachers' salaries operate on a step scale, in which teachers receive an increase in their salary every year. School districts also compensate teachers for additional duties outside of contractual hours, such as after school tutoring and extracurricular activities. Further practices that teacher preparation programs can implement include providing a course for Black male freshman and sophomore students who are interested in applying to the teacher preparation program. This course can be focused on teaching diverse populations and include topics such as race/ethnicity, social identity, culturally responsive teaching strategies, working with K-12 students who have disabilities or are undocumented, and discussing the need for Black male teachers and the impact they can have on K-12 students.

Teacher preparation programs often forget about their local community colleges when thinking about strategies to recruit Black males into the teaching profession. It is imperative for teacher preparation programs to connect with Black males that are enrolled in community colleges a few semesters before they transfer to a 4-year institution. Black male transfer students may be aware of the admission requirements to transfer to a particular institution, but they are often not well-versed in the admission requirements to enter a teacher preparation program. Teacher preparation programs should make sure they attend community college transfer fairs, provide students with a program of study that outlines course requirements for university and teacher preparation admissions, offer in person and virtual support for teacher entrance exams, and invite students to university-wide events that focus on recruiting Black males into the teaching profession. This can be achieved through building relationships with faculty and staff at their university's feeder community colleges.

Additionally, Teacher preparation programs should build partnerships with their local school districts to develop a Grow Your Own Program for Black males, which is simply a teacher preparation precollegiate pipeline for students interested in becoming a teacher (Valenzuela, 2017). This program should include dual enrollment courses, mentorship, and programming that acclimate students to the teaching profession and university. Programming should include information on university admission requirements, financial aid, academic and social supports for Black males on campus, and discussions with Black male preservice and current teachers, examining the importance for having more Black males pursue a career in teaching. Moreover, teacher preparation programs can establish a bridge program for Black males, like the University of Connecticut's Leadership, Equity, and Diversity (LEAD) Program through the Neag School of Education (University of Connecticut, 2021). Students who are admitted to the program "are connected to the Neag School of Education during their first two years of study at the university through courses, seminars, research opportunities, and mentorship, all aimed at supporting the achievement of curricular and career goals" (University of Connecticut, 2021). Upon completion of this program, students are admitted directly into one of their teacher preparation programs.

Lastly, in addition to recruiting at the university, community college, and K-12 level, teacher preparation programs should work with their marketing and communications staff to complete an audit on all their marketing materials. All recruitment materials should be culturally appropriate for attracting Black males into the teaching profession. The brochures should specifically have pictures of Black males in the classroom, and testimonials from current Black males enrolled in the teacher preparation program, and Black male alumni. This will allow Black males to see themselves as a future student within the college and teacher preparation program.

STRATEGIES FOR RETAINING BLACK MALES WITHIN TEACHER PREPARATION PROGRAMS

Teacher preparation programs not only need to put their efforts into recruiting Black males into their programs, but they also must make sure they retain these students once they are admitted. An important part of retention at universities is this notion that students need to feel as though they belong and are a part of a community. In order for teacher preparation programs to build a community for Black male preservice teachers to thrive in, they must be a culturally sustaining program. This can be achieved by providing faculty and staff with professional development on culturally responsive strategies to use in the classroom and while supporting Black male preservice teachers. Gloria Ladson-Billings implemented a groundbreaking study in 1995 that was able to align the academic success of K-12 African American students to the cultural competence of their teachers. This concept can also be applied to faculty and staff who work with African American preservice teachers within teacher preparation programs. Gay (2014) defines culturally responsiveness as using the "cultural orientations, heritages, and background experiences of students of color as referents and resources to improve their school achievement" as well as providing opportunities for them to gain social capital (p. 357). Teacher preparation faculty and staff should engage in the following behaviors to become culturally responsive:

• Explore social and personal identities. Faculty and staff should understand how their identity contributes to who they are as a person and how they enter professional and personal spaces. Having a strong foundation in their own identity will allow them to understand how their students' identity shows up in the classroom.

- Build relationships with Black male preservice teachers through actively caring for their well-being.
- Communicate high expectations to Black male preservice teachers. This allows faculty and staff to build students' capacity to be academically and professionally successful.
- Act as cultural brokers. Cultural brokers give students the tools to build cultural capital so they can have the skillset to navigate multiple systems (i.e., education, government, economic, and health care). Faculty and staff should be prepared to advocate for and negotiate on behalf of Black male preservice teachers.

Other important factors for retaining Black male preservice teachers are academic advisors who have a professional background in education. These academic advisors should use an intrusive advising approach to assist Black preservice males in obtaining their personal, academic, and career goals. Upcraft and Kramer (1995), as cited in Varney (2007), define intrusive advising as an "active concern for students' academic preparation and willingness to assist students in exploring services and programs to improve skills and increase academic motivation" (p. 11). The intent with this approach is to make sure all students feel they are a part of a community that cares about their personal well-being as well as their ultimate academic goal of obtaining a college degree. Advisors within teacher preparation programs should actively build relationships with Black males by setting up daily meetings, fostering an open-door policy, and by various modes of communication, email, text messaging, and phone calls. This advising approach walks students through how to access resources on campus, such as tutoring and mental health services. In addition, it is imperative for academic advisors within teacher preparation programs to provide Black males with information on local and statewide scholarships that are specifically for students of color enrolled in teacher preparation programs. For example, in the state of Florida, students of color admitted to teacher preparation programs are able to apply to the Florida Fund for Minority Teachers (FFMT). FFMT's mission is to increase the number of minority teachers in Florida to better reflect the state's diverse population, to provide financial awards, and extensive pre-professional development (FFMT, 2022). Black male preservice teachers are more likely to apply to these scholarships if they are being guided on requirements and deadlines, which in the end will help to decrease their student loan debt upon graduation.

Also, teacher preparation programs can create mentoring programs that are specifically for Black male preservice teachers. For example, The Call Me Mister Program was created at Clemson University for Black males interested in becoming teachers and is now located at 22 institutions (Carver Thomas, 2018; Clemson University, 2021). This program offers mentoring, financial aid support, academic, peer and career counseling as well as support with licensure exams (Carver Thomas, 2018). In addition, The Neag School of Education at the University of Connecticut created a mentoring program, Diverse Educators

Making and Outstanding Change (D.E.M.O.). This program aims to provide academic, personal, and career support to 10 students annually enrolled in their integrated bachelors/masters teacher preparation program (Jones, 2019). Students are paired with a current teacher or administrator of color who is either an alumnus, or community partner in which both parties are given a stipend to participate in the program (Jones, 2019). In conjunction with mentoring, teacher preparation programs can develop an affinity group for Black males interested in becoming a teacher. To create this group, teacher preparation programs should assign a Black faculty or staff member to work with Black males who are currently enrolled in the teacher preparation program. The mission of this group should be to support, encourage confidence and success in Black male preservice teachers. This will allow Black males to have a safe space to discuss concerns they may have with being one of few in their teacher preparation program as well as how to solve issues they may encounter when becoming a classroom teacher.

RECOMMENDATIONS FOR POLICY

Teacher preparation programs are subject to implement state and local policies, which they usually have not had any input on, which is why it is vital for teacher educators to participate on national and statewide committees that are committed to recruiting students of color into the teaching workforce. This will allow them to provide insight on ways outside stakeholders can assist universities with recruiting Black males into the teaching workforce and eliminate policies that create barriers for admissions and completion. Advocating to eliminate policies centered around state mandated entry tests can be a game changer for the number of Black males a teacher preparation program can admit (AACTE, 2019). For example, in Connecticut, state institutions worked with state legislators to eliminate a testing barrier for not only Black males but all students of color. Beginning in the 2016–2017 school year, students in the state of Connecticut no longer had to pass the Praxis Core Academic Skills for Educators test to enter a teacher preparation program (CT Public Act 16-41, 2016). In addition, the Florida Department of Education eliminated their teacher entrance exam, the General Knowledge Test for any student earning a graduate degree upon completion of their teacher preparation program (FL Publ. L. No. 1004.04, 2019).

In conclusion, it is imperative that teacher preparation programs used the aforementioned strategies to recruit and retain Black males into the teaching profession. Research states that having more teachers of color in the classroom yields academic success, decreases suspension rates, increases college matriculation, and provides the representation of positive role models for students of color (AACTE, 2019; Carter-Andrews et al., 2019). Additionally, Gershenson et al. (2021) in *Teacher Diversity and Student Success: Why Racial Representation Matters in the Classroom*, highlight research studies in Tennessee, North Carolina, Texas, and Florida, which found that matching teachers' race/ethnicity to that of their students increases standardized mathematics and reading test scores for students of color. Furthermore, by having teachers of color in the classroom, White students can see people of color in positions of power, which increases their cultural awareness and positive attitudes toward people of color (Gershenson et al., 2021).

REFERENCES

American Association of Colleges for Teacher Education. (2019). *The Black and Latinx/Latino male teacher networked improvement community: Promising practices to recruit and retain male teacher of color.* https://aacte.org/programs-and-services/nic/

An Act Concerning the Recommendations of the Minority Teacher Recruitment Task Force, CT Public Act 16-41. (2016). https://www.cga.ct.gov/2016/act/pa/pdf/2016PA-00041-R00SB-00379-PA.pdf

Ballou, D., & Podgursky, M. (1997). *Teacher pay and teacher quality.* W.E. Upjohn Institute for Employment Research.

Bennett, C. I., McWhorter, L. M., & Kuykendall, J. A. (2006). Will I ever teach?: Latino and African American students perspectives on praxis I. *American Educational Research Journal, 43*(3), 531–574.

Boyd, D., Goldhaber, D., Lankford, H., & Wyckoff, J. (2007). The effect of certification and preparation and teacher quality. *The Future of Children, 17*(1), 45–68.

Carter-Andrews, D. J., Castro, E., Cho, C. L., Petchaur, E., Richmond, G., & Floden, R. (2019). Changing the narrative on diversifying the teacher workforce: A look at historical and contemporary factors that inform recruitment and retention of teachers of color. *Journal of Teacher Education, 70*(1), 6–12.

Carver-Thomas, D. (2018). *Diversifying the teaching profession: How to recruit and retain teachers of color.* Learning Policy Institute.

Clemson University. (2021, May 24). *Call me mister.* Clemson University College of Education. https://www.clemson.edu/education/programs/programs/call-me-mister.html

Florida Fund for Minority Teachers. (2022, November 10). https://www.ffmt.org/

Florida Statue Public Accountability and State Approval for Teacher Preparation Programs, Publ. L. No. 1004.04. (2019). http://www.leg.state.fl.us/statutes/index.cfm?App_mode=Display_Statute&Search_String=&URL=1000-1099/1004/Sections/1004.04.html

Gay, G. (2014). Culturally responsive teaching principles, practices, and effects. In H. R. Milner & K. Lomotey (Eds.), *Handbook of urban education* (pp. 353–372). Routledge.

Gershenson, S., Hansen, M., & Lindsay, C. A. (2021). *Teacher diversity and student success: Why racial representation matters in the classroom.* Harvard Education Press.

Haney, W., Madaus, G., & Kreitzer, A. (1987). Charms talismanic: Testing teachers for the improvement of American education. *Review of Research in Education, 14*(1), 169–238.

Jones, S. (2019, February 12). *$240 grant to advance ongoing neag school student diversity efforts.* University of Connecticut Neag School of Education. https://education.uconn.edu/2019/02/12/240k-grant-to-advance-ongoing-neag-school-student-diversity-efforts/

Kohli, R. (2021). *Teachers of color: Resisting racism and reclaiming education.* Harvard Education Press.

Ladson-Billings, G. (1995). Toward a theory of culturally relevant pedagogy. *American Educational Research Journal, 32*(3), 465–491.

McGurran, B. (2022, July 28). *Average salaries of college graduates 2022.* Forbes. https://www.forbes.com/advisor/student-loans/average-salary-college-graduates/

National Center for Educational Statistics. (2019). *Spotlight a: Characteristics of public school teachers by race/ethnicity [Data set].* National Center for Educational Statistics. https://nces.ed.gov/programs/raceindicators/spotlight_a.asp

National Center for Education Statistics. (2022). *Characteristics of public school teachers [Data set].* U.S. Department of Education, Institute of Education Sciences. https://nces.ed.gov/programs/coe/indicator/clr

National Education Association. (2022). *Teacher salary benchmarks.* https://www.nea.org/resource-library/teacher-salary-benchmarks

Ryan, J. E. (2010). *Five miles away, a world apart: One city, two schools, and the story of educational opportunity in modern America.* Oxford University Press.

The National Commission on Excellence in Education. (1983). A nation at risk: The imperative for educational reform. *The Elementary School Journal, 84*(2), 113–130.

University of Connecticut. (2021, May 28). *Special program in education.* University of Connecticut Undergraduate Admissions. https://admissions.uconn.edu/apply/first-year/special-programs/education

Valenzuela, A. (2017). *Grow your own educator programs: A review of the literature with an emphasis on equity-based approaches.* Intercultural Development Research Association.

Varney, J. (2007). Intrusive advising. *National Academic Advising Association Academic Advising Today, 30*(3), 11–12.

CHAPTER 17

HOW BLACK MALES IN UNDERGRADUATE ENGINEERING PROGRAMS EXPERIENCE ACADEMIC ADVISING

Brandon Ash, Ivory Berry, Tyron Slack, Le Shorn Benjamin and Jerrod A. Henderson

ABSTRACT

It is well-known and documented that despite a plethora of efforts by institutions to broaden participation in engineering, the representation, retention, and degree completion of Black males in engineering continues to lag. Coupled with a lack of representation, there is also a dearth of research that has sought to understand the experiences of Black males in engineering. In this chapter, through the lens of Hildegard Peplau's (1991) interpersonal relations theory, we sought to explore the experiences of nine undergraduate Black male engineering majors with academic advisors. Academic advisors are strategically positioned in higher education settings as guides to help students navigate college culture, policies, and procedures. Using thematic analysis, three salient themes emerged: "spots are limited," building their own "advising team," and prescriptive perceptions. As institutions imagine routes for broadening participation in engineering, they might also consider how they support advisors and encourage relationship development between students and advisors.

Keywords: Black males; academic advising; engineering; retention; representation; degree completion

Black Males in Secondary and Postsecondary Education
Advances in Race and Ethnicity in Education, Volume 9, 295–313
Copyright © 2024 Brandon Ash, Ivory Berry, Tyron Slack, Le Shorn Benjamin and Jerrod A. Henderson
Published under exclusive licence by Emerald Publishing Limited
ISSN: 2051-2317/doi:10.1108/S2051-231720230000009017

Waze, Google Maps, and Apple Maps are wildly popular apps to aid in satellite navigation from one location to another. Key features such as estimated time of arrival, route comparisons, "avoid tolls" option, "you're on the fastest route" acknowledgment, or "reported crash ahead" real-time alerts make for a more enjoyable, less stressful, anxiety-reducing driving experience with minimal "bumps" and surprises.

Every morning before I [second author] start my typical 25-minute commute to campus, I plug in the campus address into one of the navigation apps to determine which route is best for that day since it varies. Sure, I have my favorite route – the most scenic one – and it will get me to my destination (campus). However, I have quickly come to know that it is not always the best route, given that traffic is unpredictable due to construction, crashes, or street closures, and who really wants to sit in traffic for countless minutes and even hours? Thus, I like the assurance of knowing that I have done my due diligence to explore and select the best route, which is often the route that requires the least amount of time to get to my destination, although, at times, greater in distance (i.e., mileage), especially in large metropolitan cities.

At this point, I cannot imagine life without the use of a navigation app to get me to campus or other spaces around the city because I have concluded that anytime I decide to simply go the way I know (or think I know), I am always met with some surprises or bumps that could have been easily avoided if I would have taken the time to use a navigation app, a guided resource designed, in part, to allow me to have a more positive, less stressful driving experience to reach my destination.

In many ways, the navigation app can be likened to *academic advisors* and how they are strategically positioned in higher education settings to help acclimate students to college culture, policies and procedures, and university resources, as well as guide students from orientation to graduation and even acceptance into graduate or professional school or job placement. Academic advising may not always be a service that students are required to tap into to make it to their destination (i.e., graduation). However, as stated by Travis, a Black male electrical engineering major in this chapter, "I definitely would have graduated no matter what, but with her [academic advisor], it did make the journey a lot easier."

Research suggests that Black students earned 7% of science, technology, engineering, and mathematics (STEM) bachelor's degrees in 2018 (Fry et al., 2021). Between 1996 and 2016, the percentage of engineering degrees attained by Blacks declined from 5% to less than 4% (National Science Foundation, National Center for Science and Engineering Statistics, 2019). Additionally, recent reports indicate that Black males, the focus of this chapter, only represented 4% of bachelor's degrees awarded in engineering in 2019 (American Society for Engineering Education, 2020).

Considering the need to diversify the workforce in the United States, especially in STEM fields, to remain globally competitive and be on the cutting edge of new, diverse, and inclusive technologies and innovations (Jones et al., 2018; National Academies of Sciences, Engineering, and Medicine, 2018), efforts to improve educational outcomes and pathways to careers in STEM fields have blossomed. Such efforts have included funded research opportunities to learn more about Black students' experiences in STEM majors; cocurricular initiatives; and mentoring and shadowing programs to name a few (Maton et al., 2000). This chapter explicitly explores academic advising as a resource, or mechanism, to improve educational outcomes for Black males in engineering.

Prior research has shown the importance of academic advisors developing trusting relationships with Black male college students by getting to know them and understanding their needs and wants (Museus & Ravello, 2010). Research has also highlighted how Black males may benefit from a combination of advising approaches when advisors present themselves as accessible and customize the student experience (Museus & Ravello, 2021; Strayhorn, 2008). Lastly, research has revealed the importance of Black males building a network of formal and informal advisors to get the support they want and need to achieve desired outcomes successfully (Johnson et al., 2019).

This study builds upon this body of scholarship by continuing to explore academic advising as a signature resource to aid in Black male student retention and persistence to graduation. More specifically, this [qualitative] study explores nine Black male students' experiences with academic advising in engineering at their university – a designated Hispanic-Serving Institution (HSI) and Asian American Native American Pacific Islander-Serving Institution (AANAPISI). Our findings suggest that Black males in engineering have varied experiences with academic advising that may be shaped by their perceptions of academic advising and their access and proximity to academic advisors. Further, findings illustrate how students may seek out peers, faculty mentors, or leaders of student organizations to supplement or substitute perceived ineffective academic advising, essentially rendering academic advisors purposeless. Lastly, findings suggest that students mainly perceive the role of (use of) academic advisors as solely prescriptive (course selection). Thus, they rarely experience other approaches to academic advising, such as developmental or proactive (intrusive) that have proven effective in yielding positive educational outcomes for students.

We elaborate on these themes in this chapter and make a case for improvements to advising structures and mechanics and students' awareness of the roles of academic advisors to improve outcomes, particularly for Black male undergraduates majoring in engineering.

LITERATURE REVIEW

For this study, we sought to uncover Black male engineering students' experiences with academic advising. Considering the limited work conducted on the academic advising experiences of Black male engineering students, we expanded our review of the literature to include the academic advising experiences of minority students. In our exploration of the literature, three themes were prevalent.

Culturally Competent Advising

Research stresses the importance of being culturally competent when working with minoritized populations. An essential part of that cultural competency is understanding that cultural and ethnic groups are not a monolith; they come from diverse backgrounds and have varied cultural experiences (Gordon et al., 2008). Specifically, "Black students who have not spent a significant amount of time around their peer group may have different social adjustment issues than students from predominantly African American environments" (Gordon et al., 2008, p. 207). Additionally, research illustrates that their identity impacts their sense of belonging to the campus environment and major (Gordon et al., 2008; Weir, 2017; Williams et al., 2019). It is imperative that academic advisors dispel all cultural biases when advising this population and avoid misadvising based on cultural prejudices.

Developmental Advising

The positive advising experiences outlined in the literature provided examples of developmental advising. The research expressed that students appreciated academic advising experiences when the conversations went beyond scheduling classes (Fleming et al., 2013; Fries-Britt & White-Lewis, 2020; Gordon et al., 2008; Johnson et al., 2019; Weir, 2017). Research stated that students expressed favorable interactions with their advisors when discussing academic challenges, and advisors provide recommendations for academic support (Fleming et al., 2013; Weir, 2017; Williams et al., 2019). Moreover, they can have the opportunity to discuss study strategies and time management techniques (Fleming et al., 2013; Weir, 2017). Furthermore, research states that students appreciated discussing economic and financial concerns with their advisors (Gordon et al., 2008; Weir, 2017). The analysis also indicated that Black students valued the ability to discuss career opportunities (Fleming et al., 2013).

Barriers to Academic Advising

Research has also indicated that Black students encounter barriers in their academic advising experience. Black students expressed frustration due to the inability to schedule an appointment with advisors (Johnson et al., 2019). Advisors displayed disinterest in meeting with students or needed more availability to meet with students (Fries-Britt & White-Lewis, 2020; Johnson et al., 2019; Williamson, 2010). When students could meet with an advisor, their interactions were short and, at times, felt rushed (Johnson et al., 2019; Lancaster & Xu, 2017; Williamson, 2010). Moreover, Black students experienced misadvising due to advisors' limited meeting times with students, which negatively impacted their graduation date (Johnson et al., 2019; Lancaster & Xu, 2017).

GUIDING FRAMEWORK

We used Hildegard Peplau's (1991) interpersonal relations theory to examine Black male engineering undergraduates' experiences with academic advising. Though initially conceptualized based on experiences in health care settings, specifically nursing, as noted by Elizabeth Higgins (2017), Peplau's interpersonal relations theory offers a pathway for understanding the building blocks of relationship formation (and termination) between advisor and advisee. Interpersonal relations theory highlights the importance of listening, trust, dialogue, communication, and engagement as essential to quickly develop relationships. Four crucial phases of the interpersonal process are articulated: orientation, identification, exploitation, and resolution (Peplau, 1991). In an academic advising context, during the first phase, orientation, the advisor gets to know the student, including their interests, goals, challenges, and questions. Together, the advisor and advisee establish expectations for the partnership. During the second phase, identification, the student concludes they can rely on the advisor for support. In this phase, the advisor must reassure the student that they are there to help and guide them through any situations they encounter. In the third phase, exploitation, the student and advisor develop a success plan for addressing a particular challenge. However, the student expresses concern for their ability to carry out the plan to which the advisor emphasizes the importance of the student executing the success plan independently. In the final phase, resolution, the student exhibits comfort with their ability to execute the success plan, and the advisor addresses aspects of the plan that are unclear to the student.

When all phases are correctly executed, the experience is more favorable for both the student and advisor. However, the experience can be harmful and strain the relationship when the advisor or student fails to meet expectations during a particular phase.

THE ROLE OF THE FRAMEWORK

The role of theory in this study was to hone our sensitivity (Huff et al., 2021). We used the framework to inform our approach to data analysis; however, we did not use it to develop the interview protocol. We sought to see what we would authentically learn from participants' experiences. Therefore, we used an inductive data analysis approach. The guiding framework also served as an anchoring point for communicative validation (Walther et al., 2013) between research team members. For example, the framework helped give researchers additional words or language to help describe participants' experiences.

METHODOLOGY

In this qualitative study, we explored how Black male engineering students made meaning of their engineering advising experiences while pursuing their degrees. We approached this study from a constructivist epistemological perspective

(Charmaz, 2014) which posits that individuals construct meaning of the world based on their lived experiences (Creswell & Poth, 2018; Maxwell, 2013).

Institutional Context

This study occurred at a large Southwestern public university, Latimer University (pseudonym). Latimer University is designated as an HSI and AANAPISI with very high research activity (Carnegie Classification of Institutions of Higher Education, 2021). The overall undergraduate population is comprised of 10.2% Black students, 23.0% Asian students, 36.5% Hispanic students, 3.8% international students, 21.2% white students, and 5.3% Other. The college of engineering, specifically, is comprised of 5.66% Black students, 24.84% Asian students, 35.85% Hispanic students, 21.69 white students, 7.05% international students, and 4.91% Other. For a closer look at the institutional context of this study, Table 17.1 further illustrates the engineering enrollment and four and six-year graduation rates by race, ethnicity, and gender.

Advising Structure

Each engineering discipline at Latimer University has different advising structures, and the number of professional advisors varies. Table 17.2 briefly describes the number and type of advisors available to students and the advising ratio.

Table 17.1. Enrollment, Four and Six-Year Graduation Percentages for Latimer University.

Race/Ethnicity	Enrollment Number (Percentage)	Four-Year Graduation %	Six-Year Graduation %
Black	167 (5.66)	*34*	*59*
Men	120 (4.07)	33	52
Women	47 (1.60)	36	73
Asian	733 (24.84)	*30*	*69*
Men	517 (17.52)	26	65
Women	216 (7.32)	41	79
Hispanic	1058 (35.85)	*34*	*65*
Men	777 (26.33)	32	63
Women	281 (9.52)	39	71
White	640 (21.69)	*29*	*57*
Men	469 (15.89)	28	55
Women	171 (5.80)	30	63
International	208 (7.05)	*27*	*67*
Men	135 (4.57)	23	58
Women	73 (2.47)	41	94
Other	145 (4.91)	*42*	*71*
Men	100 (3.39)	33	67
Women	45 (1.52)	54	77

Table 17.2. The Number of Advisors and Enrollment Number by Engineering Department.

Engineering Major	Number and Type of Advisors Available	Undergraduate Enrollment (Advising Ratio)
Biomedical	Two professional advisors	280 (1:140)
Chemical	One professional advisor plus supplemental faculty advising support	488 (1:488)
Civil	One professional advisor	328 (1:328)
Electrical and Computer	One professional advisor	651 (1:651)
Industrial	One professional advisor	117 (1:117)
Mechanical	Two professional advisors plus supplemental faculty advising support	943 (1:471.5)
Petroleum	Two professional advisors	92 (1:46)

Participants

Participants were undergraduate sophomores, juniors, and seniors at Latimer University. We recruited students through a purposive snowball sampling procedure, word of mouth approach to identify students who met a specific set of criteria (Patton, 2002). We sent our study recruitment email to an institutional gatekeeper with extensive contact with engineering students. The gatekeeper sent the IRB-approved recruitment email to eligible participants. Participants had to be enrolled in sophomore-level engineering courses or higher at the time of the study. The sampling technique yielded nine Black male engineering students who selected their own pseudonyms (See Table 17.3). Table 17.3 also provides selected demographics of those participants.

Table 17.3. Selected Demographics of Participants.

Pseudonym	Engineering Major	Year	First Generation College Status (Yes or No)
Barry	Mechanical	Senior	Yes
Conner	Mechanical	Sophomore	No
Huey	Mechanical	Junior	Yes
Isaac	Electrical	Junior	No
Josh	Petroleum	Senior	Yes
Joshua	Industrial	Junior	Yes
Michelangelo	Chemical	Sophomore	No
Travis	Electrical	Senior	Yes
Xavier	Mechanical	Junior	Yes

Data Source

We collected data via semi-structured interviews. The semi-structured protocol development involved a series of collaborative and iterative steps, the first of which required the corresponding author to produce an initial protocol draft for critique. All authors then contributed to the refinement of each item by providing suggestions for language, sequence, and conceptual changes. The final version of the protocol consisted of 19 open-ended questions that we piloted on an undergraduate research team member and a graduate student team member. The interviews were recorded and later transcribed verbatim by an external transcription service. The participants gave informed consent to participate in this IRB-approved study.

Data Analysis

To ensure the reliability of the interview transcription, we reviewed each transcript and corrected any errors (Creswell & Poth, 2018). The third and fifth authors then used an iterative inductive process to code the transcripts. Thematic analysis (Braun & Clarke, 2019) guided our data analysis procedure. As such, we read through the transcripts and met periodically to confirm, interrogate, and critique each other's analyses. After each read of the transcripts, we discussed our reflections and instances of disagreement until all of our codes aligned. Our analysis was iteratively guided by the following six phases of thematic analysis, which include (1) data familiarization, (2) generating codes, (3) constructing themes, (4) reviewing themes, (5) defining themes, and (6) writing-up the results (Braun & Clarke, 2006). During the data analysis process, we routinely returned to the transcripts to ensure that the emerging themes aligned with participants' narratives. To confirm what we saw in the data, we assembled the team members for what we previously coined as "times of calibration" (Henderson et al., 2022, p. 10). During these convenings, all authors contributed to the process of interrogation and discussion of findings. From these discussions, we created a matrix in Microsoft Excel to illustrate findings and a preliminary Microsoft PowerPoint presentation to brainstorm the structure of the final report.

QUALITY FRAMEWORK

To ensure quality throughout this project, we engaged tenants of the "quality in qualitative interpretive research" framework (Walther et al., 2013). This framework is a recognized quality measure in engineering education (Martin et al., 2020). By engaging this framework, we were attuned to theoretical, procedural, communicative, and pragmatic validation, as well as process reliability during both "making data" and "handling data" (Walther et al., 2013, 2015) in an ongoing way. In making data, for example, though we used interpersonal relations as a guiding framework, we were careful not to use jargon in the interview so that participants could construct their own meaning (i.e., use their own words). An essential part of protocol development included ensuring it could be easily understood by the audience for which it was developed (e.g., we piloted the protocol on a Black male undergraduate engineering student before implementation). Protocol development was iterative, and all team members interrogated it at each stage. In "handling the data," first, a professional transcription service was used to transcribe the audio recording of the interview verbatim. The corresponding author updated the interview transcription to remove apparent mistakes (procedural and communicative validation). The researchers engaged in frequent peer debriefs throughout the process. Midway through data analysis, the lead researcher shared emergent findings with research team members for preliminary feedback and interrogation. As an additional layer of quality in handling data, our research team ideographically focused on the nuances of individual cases before engaging with cross-case levels of abstraction (Smith et al., 2009). In a final team meeting, two additional team members (not involved in data collection) met with the corresponding author to learn about, challenge, and pose questions related to emergent findings. Research team members reached a consensus as to the final themes. Finally, in writing the findings, the authors used examples from different participants (communicative validation).

LIMITATIONS

The researchers made some experimental design and analysis decisions that could have limited the study. For example, since the goal of the study was not to obtain generalizable results, the sample size was small. Researchers caution against assuming that participants' experiences represent all Black males in engineering. In addition, participants were from one single institution. Lastly, the study did not include students from all engineering majors offered at the institution.

POSITIONALITY

We collectively situated ourselves in this research via a positionality statement and epistemological underpinnings influencing the research process (Jones et al., 2013). For example, the positionalities of the first and corresponding authors spurred the impetus for this study. The first author is a Black male and an exploratory advising professional at a doctoral university with very high research activity. He advises students interested in declaring engineering as a major and those who have been terminated from their respective engineering programs due to low academic performance. This author contributed to the development of the manuscript. The second author is a Black male higher education and student affairs senior administrator and scholar. He provides leadership for academic advising and student services for engineering programs at his institution. This author contributed to the development of the manuscript. The third author is a Black male, third-year doctoral candidate with interests focused on the impact of racial microaggressions on Black and other underrepresented students.

This author contributed to the data analysis by identifying themes salient to the participants with the corresponding author. The fourth author is a higher education researcher of Afro-Caribbean immigrant identity whose research agenda explores the experiences of minoritized learners in various settings and the concept of quality in PhD programs. This author contributed to the theme and manuscript development. The corresponding author is a Black male who has pursued and earned engineering degrees and teaches engineering students. He is an Assistant Professor in engineering. His research interests include Black and Latino male engineering identity development and their persistence in engineering. He assisted with data collection, analysis, project guidance, and dissemination of results.

FINDINGS

This section highlights three of the most salient themes which offer insights into Black males' experiences with academic advising in engineering and their perceptions of the role of academic advisors. Those themes include "spots are limited," building their own "advising teams," and prescriptive perceptions. Table 17.4 provides a summary of those themes.

"Spots Are Limited"

Data from this chapter suggest that Black males in engineering have varied academic advising experiences shaped by their perceived or experienced access, interactions, and proximity to academic advisors. Participants often described their academic advisors as too busy and inaccessible, given the number of students they are responsible for advising. For example, Isaac, a junior electrical engineering major, said

> It's like there are so many students in ECE, so many engineering students trying to talk to this one person. They believe it's super hard for her to even talk with anybody, you know what I mean? To even schedule anything with anybody because she has so many students. I think it's more of a – it's one person against an army of students, so it's hard for her to take care of everybody.

Isaac highlights inaccessibility and even believes that inaccessibility inhibits any level of care that the advisor could have. He did not blame the advisor but

Table 17.4. Table of Themes and Descriptions.

Theme	Description
"Spots are limited"	Describes the limited access to advisors that participants experienced
Building their own "advising team"	Participants approach to satisfying their advisory needs by engaging peers, faculty mentors, or student organizations
Prescriptive perceptions	Describes the prescriptive approach to advising that participants rejected

noticed that the workload seemed too much for one person. The illustration of "one person against an army" indicates the perceived difficulty in accessing advisors. This imagery of "one person against an army" may be why students avoid advisors altogether. For Black male students like Isaac, hearing about the inaccessibility of advisors or terminology like one person against an army also communicates an adversarial relationship between advisors and students, when, actually, students and advisors are on the same team.

Another student, Xavier, a junior mechanical engineering major, said, "Spots are limited. If you want to meet with them that week, it's very rare and limited. ...." Xavier also points out that the workload of the advisors seems to be the rate-limiting factor. The opportunity to meet with someone who is supposed to support them being described as rare might also lead students to stop attempting. This could be extremely detrimental for a first-generation student like Xavier.

Like Issac, Xavier highlights the limited availability of the advisor, which may constitute a barrier to receiving advice from an official advisor from the institution. Some participants also commented on their response to this perceived inaccessibility. For example, Isaac said

> Even if I try, I don't really think I'd be able to get a hold of her. I don't know if like she's so swamped or busy or she just doesn't check. I don't know, but I'm not going to waste my time trying to contact someone I know I'm not going to get a response from... I'll just go off the course map.

Isaac once again reiterates his academic advisor's perceived or actual lack of availability. This may create another barrier to students taking the necessary classes toward graduation or an official guiding them to that path. Issac also shared that he gave up on trying to reach his academic advisor. This apparent inaccessibility has caused him to be apathetic toward advising and his academic advisor. Inaccessibility is likely impacting his and other students' sense of belonging. In addition, the inaccessibility of advisors suggests that students never make it to or through the identification phase of interpersonal relations with their advisors and never get through the orientation phase. Thus, growth with advising is hampered, rendering advising useless.

From a different perspective, several participants felt that advising challenges were not necessarily an issue of inaccessibility but rather that reaching advisors required more initiative.

Conner said, "we have to put in the effort to get to the advisor. They're not going to just come to find us, but it's more about me reaching out to ask them the questions that I need to be answered." Right or wrong, this idea of receiving advising being interpreted as something that requires more effort may hinder some students from reaching out to their advisor. Another student, Josh, said

> They're not really going to hold your hand, so you have to take the initiative to go to the advisors or email the advisors if you have any questions. They're always willing to answer and help us out, but sometimes you have to take that initiative.

Josh believes that the onus was on him to be proactive in reaching out to his academic advisor rather than waiting on his advisor to reach out to them.

Students like this highlight the additional persistence needed in contacting an advisor via email or in person, which may be off-putting to some students, resulting in them avoiding communicating with their official academic advisor.

Building Their "Advising Team"

Findings also illustrate how students sought out peers, faculty, or leaders of student organizations to supplement or substitute inaccessible or ineffective academic advisors. For example, Xavier, a junior mechanical engineering major, described the relationships he built with multiple social supports with the words "my advising team." One of his advising team members was Mr Brown (pseudonym), an adult Black male who oversaw the engineering advising center where Xavier works as a student worker. He shared that Mr Brown "gave me all the sauce to get to where the opportunity." Though Mr Brown was not an official academic advisor, Mr Brown was able to provide not only academic support and advice but also life support. Xavier even referred to Mr Brown as "an older brother who was always looking out for him." This level of support exhibits a deeper level of support, an almost fictive kin (Yosso, 2005). When thinking about how to advise Black men in engineering this – the idea of building family – like trust relationships might be a cultural capital aspect to lean into. Xavier's comments about Mr Brown exhibited that he has traversed through multiple phases of interpersonal relations with Mr Brown, perhaps orientation, identification, exploitation, and resolution (Peplau, 1991). One would hope that relationships between Black males and advisors would reach these heights.

Travis also distinguished between when he felt comfortable reaching out to his formal versus informal advisor. "...if it's for academic advising, I'd definitely go to my advisor, but if it's just like I need to rant about something or just talk about how stressed I am, Dr. Vause (pseudonym for Black professor)!" Travis indicates that his informal mentor can go places with him that his formal mentor cannot. As he put it, ranting exhibits a level of comfort with this informal mentor that he may not have with his academic advisor. We believe it is okay, and it might be essential that Black men in engineering find more knowledgeable mentors with whom they feel comfortable ranting.

In addition to turning to informal mentors, students also turned to peers to become a part of their advising teams. For example, Issac discussed how he connected with a student officer in the student National Society of Black Engineers (NSBE) chapter after being unable to reach his academic advisor. He stated,

> I really couldn't get a hold of my academic advisor, so this person gave me a lot of pointers and things of that nature...he kind of drew me up like a makeshift course map of how I should be taking my classes for my semester. That's kind of what I follow, in a way.

In drawing up the course map, this more experienced peer exhibited a level of care that Isaac needed to understand how to navigate his academic career.

Similarly, Conner (a sophomore mechanical engineering student) shared that he, too, tapped into classmates or NSBE peers for advising support.

The first people that I usually reach out to are just other classmates in general about academic advising. Then if I don't get anything from - if I don't get what I necessarily need from my peers or classmates or professors, then I'll usually go to an advisor, but it's usually my classmates' peers or my engineering society which, of course, is NSBE. That's who I usually talk with about pretty much everything in general.

Not only does he tap into his peers as a resource, but he indicated that they are who he turns to first. In addition, Huey, a junior mechanical engineering student, noted the types of advice students receive from their peers. He stated

That's why I'm minoring in Math now because I didn't know how close I was to a math minor. That information did not come from an advisor. It came from a peer about what classes I needed to take

Through the illustrations used in this theme, the Black males in our study discussed their challenges with academic advisors and demonstrated how they navigated finding the resources they needed. They emphasize an "all hands on deck" approach (i.e., the multiple supports they tap into to navigate their engineering academic experience, including advisors, professors, and fellow peers).

Prescriptive Perceptions

Last, findings suggest that students mainly perceive the role of (use of) academic advisors as solely prescriptive (course selection). Thus, they rarely experience other approaches to academic advising, such as developmental or proactive (intrusive), that have proven effective in yielding positive educational outcomes for students. Consistent across all interviews was participants' acknowledgment that academic advisors provide information on course selections and track degree progress. For example, Conner said, "I'm not too familiar with it [the role of academic advisors], but I have gone and talked to a few just in general about course advising and graduation degree planning, pretty much." Michelangelo, a sophomore chemical engineering major, also said, "I meet with her once a year, and she just looked at my degree plan to see how I was doing, like how far along I was, and it's basically made sure I was on track to graduate." Michelangelo's experiences reveal that students believe that they may not need an advisor once they have figured out how to develop a personalized degree plan. He shared, "I don't really have a use for an advisor. Like they're good to have, I appreciate them for being there, but for me personally, I don't really have a use for them."

Data reveal students' likely narrow perspectives on the utility of academic advising. Michelangelo went on to share

Okay, so I'm a very organized person, so honestly, I'm kind of like my own academic advisor. In my view, those meetings are just kind of like formalities, so I don't get a hold on my account because I'm always been a very organized person from the first day I started school. I had my own spreadsheet, and I constantly check up on the degree plan to just make sure there were no edits or revisions I need to worry about or like new requirements, so I do meet with them, but honestly, all they do is look at my spreadsheet, and they're like yes, you're good.

Barry offered a slightly different perspective acknowledging that some students may not feel as comfortable as he is with reaching out to his academic advisor:

> I would definitely advise them to be patient with students. There's a lot of students who are confused, or this is their first experience or first semester straight out of high school. Me, I don't have that problem. I'm a very social person, and I love talking to people, but other students don't, so they probably are more closed to asking. I would say they're more welcoming and more helpful in understanding.

In addition, though many students in our study had not experienced them, there were instances in which participants indicated that their academic advisors went beyond discussing course selections and degree requirements or proactively checked in on them. These instances were common for participants enrolled in smaller programs or connected to informal advisors. Joshua (junior, industrial engineering) expressed:

> Outside of academic help and academic advice, my advisor always gives me personal advice on how to go about my life, or how to go about classes, or studying habits, or things like that that have helped me become a better person... My academic advisor supports me in any way that she can. She's always reaching out to those who need help. Anybody needs help. She always makes herself available. I would say she's very available and always reaches out and makes herself available to help others.

We see how participants' narrow range of advising expectations was shaped by their limited experience interacting with an academic advisor (i.e., expecting and receiving, to a large degree, prescriptive advising). In those instances where participants were able to move beyond prescriptive experiences, they were able to access additional levels of interpersonal relationships with their advisors.

DISCUSSION

This chapter examined how Black male undergraduate engineering students experience academic advising at their institution and, more specifically, within their respective academic units. Additionally, we sought to uncover students' perceptions of academic advisors' roles and how they support their success. Our work is unique in that we specifically center the voices of Black male engineering students at an HSI and Asian American and Pacific Islander-Serving Institution.

The findings revealed that participants' understanding of the role of academic advisors and their actual experiences with academic advising depended mainly on their proximity, relationship, and access to their assigned academic advisor. Participants who had closer relationships with their academic advisor had greater access to their advisor and were more likely to consider the role of an academic advisor as extending beyond the person who simply provides them with guidance about course selection (i.e., prescriptive advising). Their overall experience with academic advising was overwhelmingly positive. The opposite can be described for participants who were more distant from their academic advisors. In many ways, in this chapter, the distance or inability to access quality academic advising can be attributed to the caseloads for academic advisors. Considering interpersonal relations theory, this chapter reveals that students rarely made it through the first (i.e., orientation) of the four phases for solidifying a strong interpersonal relationship with their advisor.

Although NACADA does not endorse a specific advisor-to-advisee ratio due to varying advising duties, institutional type, and other factors (Robbins, 2013), results from the 2011 NACADA National Survey (Carlstrom & Miller, 2013) indicate that the median advisor caseload based on participating institutions was 1:296. This ratio is often used informally in higher education settings as the benchmark for determining the time needed to deliver adequate quality academic advising to students. However, other factors must be considered, given that academic advising positions are shaped differently based on context. In this chapter, programs such as electrical engineering and mechanical engineering at Latimer University have an advisor (1 FTE)-to-advisee ratio of 1:651 and 1:471, respectively. Advisors who are assigned large caseloads may be unable to consistently deliver high-quality advising, including building meaningful, interpersonal relationships with students, responding to inquiries promptly, and customizing the student experience to tailor it to their needs and goals.

The role of academic advisors is critical to student learning, retention, and degree attainment (Drake, 2011). This is no secret to students, as they are made aware of this at every turn during the recruiting, admissions, and onboarding processes. Universities often promote to students and their families the importance of getting to know their academic advisor, as the student's academic advisor is their "go-to person" who is strategically positioned to support them with understanding and navigating their academic program and unique circumstances, answering questions, identifying resources and services, and providing them with career guidance (i.e., developmental advising). However, large caseloads may leave academic advisors overstretched and unable to facilitate an engaged partnership (Peplau, 1997) or proper orientation with their students. As revealed in this chapter, it is to be expected, then, that students will have more negative experiences of academic advising when the opportunity to develop interpersonal relationships with their advisor are constrained.

Although some participants in this chapter could not forge relationships with their assigned or formal academic advisor, many revealed their use of informal advisors for support. Informal advisors included departmental faculty, staff, and peers who were accessible and presented themselves as knowledgeable, caring, trusting, and experienced. The reliance on formal and informal advisors has also surfaced in prior research (Johnson et al., 2019). However, in this chapter, informal advisors were often replacements, rather than complements, for formal academic advisors, given advisor caseloads and participants' inability to receive timely responses to inquiries, schedule appointments, and have meaningful conversations. Though common for Black male students to develop a network of support to navigate higher education settings successfully (Harper, 2005; Strayhorn, 2012), there is also a danger with students not being able to tap into consistent, quality formal academic advising. A couple of sayings are often echoed in academic advising spaces: "friends don't let friends self-advise" and "your story may be different from another person's story." Both sayings are laced with a warning that relying on self or others to navigate sophisticated degree programs could result in extended time to degree attainment, unused credits, missed information or opportunities, and unnecessary financial penalties. Academic advisors are groomed to be competent in university systems, resources, and student development theory to facilitate a positive student experience. Findings from this chapter suggest that Black male engineering students can benefit from having quality formal and informal academic advisors to achieve desired educational and professional outcomes.

RECOMMENDATIONS FOR FUTURE RESEARCH

Though this work contributes to the knowledge based on the experiences of Black males with academic advising, future research can further clarify the nuances of those experiences. For example, our study included students between sophomore and senior years. The experiences of participants who were further along in their degree program are likely different from sophomore-level students. We also only offer a snapshot; future longitudinal studies may give additional insights into the experiences of Black men with academic advising and how they change over time. We also did not analyze data to understand the discipline-specific differences. Additional studies might be aimed at understanding those differences. In addition, future studies which lean into what students would like to experience or their conceptualizations of "better" advising might offer institutions more specific or contextual recommendations for supporting students that are important to them.

IMPLICATIONS FOR PRACTICE AND POLICY

Quality academic advising is an essential and effective resource for facilitating student retention, persistence, and degree attainment. Thus, inadequate academic advising cannot be tolerated. This chapter highlights the need for proper advisor caseloads to ensure advisors are accessible, able to employ multiple approaches to advising, and nurture an engaged partnership with their students. Expanding the number of advisors is one obvious method to balancing the advisor caseload. If increasing advising personnel is not feasible, other methods, such as executing well-designed advising campaigns during nonpeak periods, using on-demand online modules, success blogs, or social media channels to respond to frequently asked questions that arise at specific points in a semester, may help improve advising services. Additionally, planned "speed advising," "ask an advisor," chat sessions, or open walk-in advising hours can assist with responding to inquiries in a more organized fashion rather than wading through a mountain of emails daily. Lastly, advisors can teach first-year experience (FYE) courses to help acclimate students to campus and the department and use the space for ongoing group advising.

Additionally, this chapter reemphasized the importance of connecting with informal advisors for academic, professional, and personal support and campus navigation. Universities or individual academic units can lean into what we like to call the "Starting 5" concept for advising support. We strongly recommend that students identify and nurture relationships with at least five individuals who can serve as trusted advisors or cultural navigators (Strayhorn, 2015) in aiding their academic, professional, and personal success in college. The "Starting 5" may take some time to form, but at a minimum, the student's academic advisor should be in that number. For most students, the academic advisor is one of the first persons they will encounter upon enrollment. The "Starting 5" should round out with a faculty mentor, a university or department administrator or coach, a peer (e.g., student leader or upper level student), and an administrative assistant or seasoned staffer. The "Starting 5" should know how to get things done, and it should be evident that they have the student's best interest in mind. The "Starting 5" concept fully embraces the adage "it takes a village to raise a child," or, in this context, a college student (Palmer & Gasman, 2008).

CONCLUSION

In conclusion, in this chapter, we illuminate the experiences that nine Black male engineering majors have had with academic advising. Their myriad experiences highlight that this group is not monolithic. However, because of the dearth of research that has centered their voices, this chapter will hopefully encourage additional studies along these lines. Our participants exhibited a tremendous amount of capital that should continue to be highlighted in future studies. In addition, as institutions imagine new routes to broaden participation in engineering, which have often been focused on recruitment, they should also think about ways to support students once they have been recruited. With all the questions about retaining engineering students, and since most campuses already have some advising structure, institutions like Latimer University should look within and better support their academic advisors.

REFERENCES

American Society for Engineering Education. (2020). *Engineering and engineering technology by the numbers 2019.*

Braun, V., & Clarke, V. (2006). Using thematic analysis in psychology. *Qualitative Research in Psychology, 3*(2), 77–101. https://doi.org/10.1191/1478088706qp063oa

Braun, V., & Clarke, V. (2019). Reflecting on reflexive thematic analysis. *Qualitative Research in Sport, Exercise and Health, 11,* 589–597. https://doi.org/10.1080/2159676X.2019.1628806

Carlstrom, A. H., & Miller, M. A. (Eds.). (2013). *2011 NACADA national survey of academic advising.* National Academic Advising Association. Monograph No. 25. https://nacada.ksu.edu/Resources/Clearinghouse/View-Articles/2011-NACADA-National-Survey.aspx

Carnegie Classification of Institutions of Higher Education. (2021). *Basic classification description.* https://carnegieclassifications.iu.edu/classification_descriptions/basic.php

Charmaz, K. (2014). *Constructing grounded theory* (2nd ed.). SAGE Publications Ltd.

Creswell, J. W., & Poth, C. N. (2018). *Qualitative inquiry and research design choosing among five approaches* (4th ed.). SAGE Publications, Inc.

Drake, J. K. (2011). The role of academic advising in student retention and persistence. *About Campus, 16*(3), 8–12. https://doi.org/10.1002/abc.20062

Fleming, L., Moore, I., Williams, D., Bliss, L., & Smith, K. (2013). Social support: How hispanic and Black engineering students perceive the support of peers, family, and faculty. In *2013 ASEE Annual Conference & Exposition Proceedings*, Atlanta, GA, United States. https://doi.org/10.18260/1-2-22458

Fries-Britt, S., & White-Lewis, D. (2020). In pursuit of meaningful relationships: How black males perceive faculty interactions in STEM. *The Urban Review, 52*(3), 521–540. https://doi.org/10.1007/s11256-020-00559-x

Fry, R., Kennedy, B., & Funk, C. (2021, April). *STEM jobs see uneven progress in increasing gender, racial and ethnic diversity higher education pipeline suggests long path ahead for increasing diversity, especially in fields like computing and engineering.* Pew Research Center. https://www.pewresearch.org/science/2021/04/01/stem-jobs-see-uneven-progress-in-increasing-gender-racial-and-ethnic-diversity/

National Academic Advising Association (U.S.). (2008). In V. N. Gordon, W. R. Habley, & T. J. Grites (Eds.), *Academic advising: A comprehensive handbook* (2nd ed.). Jossey-Bass.

Harper, S. R. (2005). Leading the way: Inside the experiences of high-achieving African American male students. *About Campus, 10*(1), 8–15.

Henderson, J. A., Hines, E. M., Boyce, A., Golden, M., Singleton, P., II, Davis, J. L., & Junqueira, W. (2022). Factors impacting engineering advanced degree pursuit and attainment among black males. *Journal of Women and Minorities in Science and Engineering, 28*(4).

Higgins, E. M. (2017, May 25). *The advising relationship is at the core of academic advising.* Academic Advising Today. https://nacada.ksu.edu/Resources/Academic-Advising-Today/View-Articles/The-Advising-Relationship-is-at-the-Core-of-Academic-Advising.aspx

Huff, J. L., Okai, B., Shanachilubwa, K., Sochacka, N. W., & Walther, J. (2021). Unpacking professional shame: Patterns of white male engineering students living in and out of threats to their identities. *Journal of Engineering Education, 110*(2), 414–436.

Johnson, R. M., Strayhorn, T. L., & Travers, C. S. (2019). *Examining the academic advising experiences of Black males at an Urban University: An exploratory case study.* Urban Education. https://doi.org/10.1177/0042085919894048

Jones, S. R., Torres, V., & Arminio, J. (2013). *Negotiating the complexities of qualitative research in higher education: Fundamental elements and issues* (2nd ed.). Routledge. https://doi.org/10.4324/9780203123836

Jones, J., Williams, A., Whitaker, S., Yingling, S., Inkelas, K., & Gates, J. (2018). Call to action: Data, diversity, and STEM education. *Change: The Magazine of Higher Learning, 50*(2), 40–47. https://doi.org/10.1080/00091383.2018.1483176

Lancaster, C., & Xu, Y. J. (2017). Challenges and supports for African American STEM student persistence: A case study at a racially diverse four-year institution. *The Journal of Negro Education, 86*(2), 176–189. https://doi.org/10.7709/jnegroeducation.86.2.0176

Martin, J. P., Stefl, S. K., Cain, L. W., & Pfirman, A. L. (2020). Understanding first-generation undergraduate engineering students' entry and persistence through social capital theory. *International Journal of STEM Education, 7*(37), 1–22. https://doi.org/10.1186/s40594-020-00237-0

Maton, K. I., Hrabowski, F. A., & Schmitt, C. L. (2000). African American college students excelling in the sciences: College and postcollege outcomes in the Meyerhoff Scholars Program. *Journal of Research in Science Teaching, 37*(7), 629–654. https://doi.org/10.1002/1098-2736(200009)37:7<629::AID-TEA2>3.0.CO;2-8

Maxwell, J. A. (2013). *Qualitative research design: An interactive approach* (3rd ed.). SAGE Publications, Inc.

Museus, S. D., & Ravello, J. N. (2010). Characteristics of academic advising that contribute to racial and ethnic minority student success at predominantly White institutions. *NACADA Journal, 30*(1), 47–58.

Museus, S. D., & Ravello, J. N. (2021). Characteristics of academic advising that contribute to racial and ethnic minority student success at predominantly White institutions. *NACADA Journal*, *41*(1), 13–25.

National Academies of Sciences. (2018). Engineering, and medicine. In *Indicators for monitoring undergraduate STEM education*. The National Academies Press. https://doi.org/10.17226/24943

National Science Foundation, National Center for Science and Engineering Statistics. (2019). *Women, minorities, and persons with disabilities in science and engineering: 2019*. Special Report NSF 19-304. Alexandria, VA. https://www.nsf.gov/statistics/wmpd

Palmer, R., & Gasman, M. (2008). "It takes a village to raise a child": The role of social capital in promoting academic success for African American men at a Black college. *Journal of College Student Development*, *49*(1), 52–70.

Patton, M. Q. (2002). Two decades of developments in qualitative inquiry: A personal, experiential perspective. *Qualitative Social Work: Research and Practice*, *1*(3), 261–283. https://doi.org/10.1177/1473325002001003636

Peplau, H. E. (1991). *Interpersonal relations in nursing: A conceptual frame of reference for psychodynamic nursing*. Springer Publishing Company.

Peplau, H. E. (1997). Peplau's theory of interpersonal relations. *Nursing Science Quarterly, 10*, 162–167.

Robbins, R. (2013). Implications of advising load. In A. Carlstrom (Ed.), *2011 national survey of academic advising*. National Academic Advising Association. Monograph No. 25. https://nacada.ksu.edu/Resources/Clearinghouse/View-Articles/Advisor-Load.aspx

Smith, J. A., Flowers, P., & Larkin, M. (2009). *Interpretative phenomenological analysis*. SAGE.

Strayhorn, T. L. (2008). Academic advising needs of high-achieving Black collegians at predominately White institutions: A mixed methods investigation. *The Mentor: An Academic Advising Journal*, *10*. https://doi.org/10.26209/MJ1061558

Strayhorn, T. L. (2012). *College students' sense of belonging: A key to educational success for all students*. Routledge.

Strayhorn, T. L. (2015). Reframing academic advising for student success: From advisor to cultural navigator. *NACADA Journal*, *35*(1), 56–63.

Walther, J., Pawley, A. L., & Sochacka, N. W. (2015). Exploring ethical validation as a key consideration in interpretive research quality. In *Paper presented at the 2015 ASEE Annual Conference & Exposition*. https://peer.asee.org/24063. https://doi.org/10.18260/p.24063

Walther, J., Sochacka, N. W., & Kellam, N. N. (2013). Quality in interpretive engineering education research: Reflections on an example study. *Journal of Engineering Education*, *102*(4), 626–659.

Weir, M. J. (2017). *A study of the influence of advising on underrepresented minority undergraduate student persistence in STEM*. Doctor of Education, Drexel University. https://doi.org/10.17918/etd-7488

Williams, M. J., George-Jones, J., & Hebl, M. (2019). The face of STEM: Racial phenotypic stereotypicality predicts STEM persistence by—And ability attributions about—Students of color. *Journal of Personality and Social Psychology*, *116*(3), 416–443. https://doi.org/10.1037/pspi0000153

Williamson, S. Y. (2010). Within-group ethnic differences of black male STEM majors and factors affecting their persistence in college. *Journal of International and Global Studies*, *1*(2), 45–73. Gale Academic OneFile. https://link.gale.com/apps/doc/A360120088/AONE?u=googlescholar&sid=googleScholar&xid=1bedfa4b

Yosso, T. J. (2005). Whose culture has capital? A critical race theory discussion of community cultural wealth. *Race, Ethnicity and Education*, *8*(1), 69–91. https://doi.org/10.1080/1361332052000341006

CHAPTER 18

CAREER DEVELOPMENT AND BLACK MEN

Guy J. Beauduy Jr., Ryan Wright, David Julius Ford Jr., Clifford H. Mack Jr. and Marcus Folkes

ABSTRACT

Many psychological, cultural, and social barriers exist that impact Black male participation in the workforce. In this chapter, authors discuss the impact that mentorship, racism, society, culture, economics, and other pertinent factors have on the career development of Black men. This chapter examines programs and strategies that effectively address the career development needs of Black men. A review of counseling interventions and their applicability to career counseling with Black men are presented. Emerging trends in career development for Black men are also discussed. In addition, provided in this chapter are personal narratives given by the authors who contextualize their career development experiences through culturally-specific career development theoretical frameworks. Lastly, implications for research, counseling, counselor education, and policy, as well as recommendations for professional development are offered.

Keywords: Black men; career development; counseling; interventions; culturally responsive; professional development

Black men in the United States have historically suffered from prejudice, systemic racism, discrimination, and other impediments to career advancement and economic opportunity, which has led them to being disproportionately represented in the labor force. According to the Bureau of Labor Statistics (2021), Black men have the lowest rates of labor force participation and employment among men, as

Black Males in Secondary and Postsecondary Education

Advances in Race and Ethnicity in Education, Volume 9, 315–339

Copyright © 2024 Guy J. Beauduy Jr., Ryan Wright, David Julius Ford Jr., Clifford H. Mack Jr. and Marcus Folkes

Published under exclusive licence by Emerald Publishing Limited

ISSN: 2051-2317/doi:10.1108/S2051-231720230000009018

well as the greatest unemployment rates of any race or gender. However, it is important to note that despite the negative impact that systemic barriers have had on the career development of Black men in the United States, there are myriad examples of highly successful Black men in various fields.

This chapter intends to shed light on the necessity of culturally sensitive career development techniques that promote the success of Black men in the workforce by looking at recent research, existing literature, and case studies. The specific difficulties and experiences that Black men have at work are examined in this chapter, along with the significance of acknowledging and resolving these problems in the context of professional growth.

BARRIERS TO GAINFUL EMPLOYMENT FOR BLACK MEN

While typically choosing careers based on vocational interests, talents, and financial gain, Black men often contend with racial stress (Chung et al., 1999; Pitcan et al., 2018) and a paucity of role models and social support in the workforce (Chung et al., 1999). Black men endure a variety of unique and difficult employment issues, as both hidden and overt hurdles prevent them from achieving professional success and job satisfaction. Racial microaggressions are a particularly damaging obstacle that Black men frequently face. Racial microaggressions are covert but ubiquitous acts of prejudice and discrimination committed against members of vulnerable racial groups (Smith et al., 2011). Persistent microaggressions are one type of racial discrimination that has been associated with poor mental health outcomes, such as anxiety, sadness, and psychological discomfort (Paradies, 2006).

In order to effectively promote the success of Black men in the workforce, career development practitioners must comprehend the dynamics of racial microaggressions, which can include verbal or nonverbal slights, micro-invalidations, and micro-assaults – all of which can have a significant negative effect on Black men's psychological health and ability to develop in their careers. Pitcan et al. (2018) qualitatively examined how Black men experience and cope with racial microaggressions within predominantly white organizations (PWOs). Thematically, they uncovered Black men being assailed cognitively and affectively with feelings of alienation and invalidation. Furthermore, they noted how the stress of coping often precipitates psychological distress, an outcome also covered in a separate but similar study that helped shine light on precarious situations that Black men face working in predominantly white spaces (Abdullah et al., 2021).

In his book entitled *The Souls of Black Folk: Essays and Sketches* (1905), famed historian and civil rights activist W. E. B. Du Bois introduced the idea of double consciousness. The term signifies the notion that Black people in the United States need to always have two visual fields: making sense of their unique dual identities of being both Black and American; and being aware of both how they see themselves and how the rest of the world sees them. For racial minorities, including Black men, making sense of one's identity while acculturating to work environments that are typically white-dominated can lead to higher work stress (Reid et al., 2014). Carrying a double consciousness combined with facing workplace discrimination and oppression (Alleyne, 2004), the work environment can, at times, prove to be detrimental to Black men for a number of reasons including negative impact on their psychological well-being (Fila et al., 2022).

Black men may struggle with assimilating into a work culture not reflective or supportive of their identity, culture, and worldviews. In response, Black men may wrestle with the following questions: Do I address this subtle but hurtful assault on my work ethic, ability, and identity? or do I compartmentalize and work through the stress for the sake of my job? This is a stark reality that Black men face in their careers.

Another barrier impacting the career development of Black men are a dearth of Black role models and social support (Chung et al., 1999). In their analysis of six case studies, Chung et al. (1999) extrapolated that the men with present and supportive fathers benefited from financial support and encouragement. They argued that Black men may feel more empowered with such support and aspire to careers that may otherwise seem unattainable, thus allowing them to choose careers to satisfy higher order needs (self-esteem, and self-actualization) in place of survival needs (security and safety).

In sum, many Black men are forced to navigate the treacherous waters of racism and a lack of social support when choosing careers. Their career journey may be compounded by their intersecting marginalized identities such as race and social-class, which can restrict their upward mobility in careers where their representation is limited.

BLACK MEN IN SCIENCE, TECHNOLOGY, ENGINEERING, AND MATHEMATICS (STEM)

The fields of Science, Technology, Engineering, and Mathematics (STEM) are woefully underrepresented by persons of color at 9% (Parker & Funk, 2018). Black men represent only 4% of students enrolled in engineering programs and African Americans as a whole are the least likely racial group to complete a college degree in STEM (National Science Board, 2022). Historically, the STEM workforce has been largely comprised of white men (Babco, 2003). These statistics are daunting especially considering the annual wages for occupations in STEM are nearly double that of non-STEM occupations (US Bureau of Labor Statistics, 2023).

The lack of representation of persons of color in STEM, particularly Black men, calls to attention the need to mentor and nurture interest in STEM fields. Doing so can help to reflect the creativity and intelligence embedded within Black men. In a brief commentary on Black boys and men in STEM, Davis (2020) raised awareness of the need to ground STEM education and pedagogy in culturally relevant experiences for Black boys and youth. The idea that STEM is a nonblack or unattainable career field can be challenged through mentoring and exposure to a diversity of STEM careers. In his study analyzing both quantitative and qualitative data, Strayhorn (2015) was able to identify several factors that influence the preparation of Black men for college and prepare them for success in the STEM fields. He cited precollege self-efficacy, concerted cultivation of initial interest, and sense of belonging as factors that influence Black male's college readiness and success in STEM.

Initiatives created to increase minority participation can be modeled in effort to increase the numbers of Black men in the field of STEM. One such initiative is The Verizon Minority Male Maker Program ("Minority Male Makers," 2015), which seeks to increase STEM accessibility to minority middle school males. To further increase access to STEM, select historically Black universities partner with Verizon to provide an immersive curriculum related to STEM. Students can learn STEM related concepts via innovation and real-world problem solving. For example, scholars in the Verizon Male Maker program takes classes related to design thinking, augmented and virtual reality, three dimensional printing, and entrepreneurship ("Minority Male Makers," 2015). Such classes foster creative thinking, problem-solving, and oratory and presentation skills. In addition the yearlong program deepens the engagement with STEM through monthly mentorship by Black male STEM scholars and guest speakers. Housed in select Historically Black Colleges across America, the Verizon Program actively promotes STEM learning while providing direct access to mentorship.

Culturally programs such as these expose often overlooked Black youth to the immersive world of STEM. Exposure can stimulate curiosity, wonder, and confidence which are key personality traits needed to thwart self-doubt and a lack of representation during their journey toward STEM careers. Myron Rolle MD who is a Black male of Bahamian ancestry, completed a Rhodes Scholarship at Oxford University en route to his current career as a neurosurgeon. As a highly sought after football recruit he attended Florida State University where he played football. While there Dr Rolle applied for and was accepted into the Rhodes Scholar program at the prestigious Oxford University. Dr. Rolle attempted to pursue a career in the National Football League (NFL) after being drafted by the Tennessee Titans. Dr. Rolle's NFL dream was cut short which lead to a brief period of aimlessness. Social support from his mother and an awareness of his penchant for science oriented him to pursue his calling as a medical doctor ("It's Never Too Late," 2022). In reflection Dr. Rolle discussed how racism and xenophobia from classmates was transformed into the pursuit and accomplishment of dreams to be a doctor and professional football player. The unyielding social support of his brother and mother sustained his interest in realizing his goal. Dr. Rolle mentioned how a football coach instilled the importance of small incremental progress toward a goal ("It's Never Too Late," 2015) helps to sustain motivation. Dr. Rolle further credited his social support network as protective against self-doubt.

Several themes can be gleaned from Dr. Rolle's career development relevant to Black men in STEM. First, Black men of all walks of life will experience forms of oppression that aim to deter and detract away from a positive sense of self. Dr. Rolle was teased for his Caribbean ancestry leading to anger and facts in school.

He made the choice to reappropriate his anger into his passion for science through reading. Try to reframe and externalize such comments as issues with others and not reflective of your ability. Put another way "Don't let anyone steal your shine." Similarly, reframe setbacks as an opportunity to learn a skill, lesson, or to seize an unexplored opportunity. Dr. Rolle was able to view the ending of his NFL career as an opportunity to return to his passion for medicine. It is never too late to return to a passion, but it does require sustained and focused effort to achieve one's goal.

Black men pursuing a career in STEM should expect internal and external challenges on their path to greatness. You may be labeled as "acting white" or criticized for high career aspirations in comparison to your peers. Such responses often reflect internalized oppression and negative view of self on the part of those making such statements (Taylor et al., 2019). Further, it is prudent to find and nurture relationships that both validate and reinforce positive qualities about your academic ability. Fries-Brit and White-Lewis (2020) qualitatively explored how Black males in undergraduate STEM majors appraise their relationships with faculty members. They noted that Black males majoring in STEM experience relationships with faculty more rewarding and affirming of their abilities, when defined by emotional validation and an interest in their personal life. Such relationship can allow Black men to sustain renewable resilience (Gazley & Campbell, 2020) defined by the ability to continually utilize resources to manage stressful situations. It is such resources that have allowed Black scholar of the past to contribute to the world of STEM.

George Washington Carver made significant contributions for the use of peanuts (Sandborn, 2019), Alan Emtage invented the first internet search engine called Archie (Samuel, 2017), and Gerald Lawson invented the first video game with interchangeable cartridges (Smith & Bowman, 2021). These great men are examples of the possibilities of what can be achieved by Black men in STEM.

CAREER DEVELOPMENT FOR FORMERLY INCARCERATED BLACK MEN

According to a report by the Sentencing Project in District of Columbia, an advocacy group supporting social justice reform in prisons, Black men are six times more likely to be incarcerated compared to their white and Latinx counterparts ("Trends in US Corrections," 2019) due to racial bias in policing. Furthermore, the advocacy group noted that of United States residents born in 2001, Black men had a 33% or one in three chance of being imprisoned during their lifetime. Sadly, these data have become synonymous with the Black male experience in the United States and impacts their ability of successful reentry in mainstream society (LaCourse et al., 2019; Williams et al., 2019).

In their quest for meaningful work and professional advancement, formerly incarcerated Black men face a number of obstacles including prejudice in the hiring process, limited access to job training and educational programs, and a criminal record (Williams et al., 2019). For Black men with criminal records, obtaining jobs with self-sustaining pay is often a struggle due to the stigma associated with having a history of incarceration (DeVeaux, 2022). These factors taint the image of formerly incarcerated Black being viewed as employable (Pager et al., 2009) while reducing and objectifying them as criminals; a belief reflective of biased and systemically racist policing policies (Klein & Lopez, 2021).

Extant literature highlights the oppressive and pervasive impact that imprisonment has on the employability of Black men in the United States. Most often marked with a criminal record for the rest of their lives (Ispa-Landa & Loeffler, 2016), Black men face the double jeopardy of being a minority and an ex-offender (Pager, 2003; Williams et al., 2019). Employers may often be reluctant to gainfully employ and seriously consider such job applicants. In an exploration of the daily experiences of formerly incarcerated Black men, Williams et al. (2019) highlighted their struggle to secure gainful employment. Participants cited being reduced to their criminal record while struggling to generate an appreciable income. An inability to work can attenuate a positive view of self and ability to meaningfully contribute to society.

For Black men, incarceration history has been positively associated with psychological distress, perceived discrimination, and depressive symptoms (Assari et al., 2018). For this reason, an important area of consideration for formerly incarcerated Black men relative to career development is self-perception; a belief that they have worth, value, and meaning. This belief is reflected in the construct of somebodiness (Johnson, 2016), which denotes that Black men have worth because they exist. This concept is applicable to Black men as they grapple with reconstructing a new identity devoid of internalized negative stereotypes about their identity. Bell (2018) eloquently depicted how the key assumptions of existential therapy help to conceptualize career counseling for formerly incarcerated Black men. When viewed existentially, work can be reframed as an opportunity to generate meaning and purpose in one's life. For Black men, work can be an avenue to contribute and provide for family. In this way, the ability to provide financial security and stability cements his role and identity as a provider and protector. These salient themes both motivate and drive behavior to acquire gainful employment.

In supporting formerly incarcerated Black men in their efforts to re-enter larger American society and its workforce, the concerns of death, meaning, freedom, and isolation can be utilized as a guide for career choice. Though all concerns are impactful, the concern of meaning may serve as a nexus for career decision making and powerful motivation for career exploration. In helping formerly incarcerated Black men generate a strong sense of "why," they can be aided in reconstructing a new way of being that affirms their self-worth. By linking career choice to salient values, a greater degree of purpose can be reinforced. Thus, their identity and sense of self can be expanded.

Social Cognitive Career Theory (SCCT) Social Cognitive Career Theory (SCCT) is one of the few approaches developed to conceptualize career development from a culturally-sensitive perspective. SCCT is a unifying framework that brings together elements identified by the previous theorists in career development, such as Bandura (1986). The developers of SCCT acknowledge the effect of environmental conditions and genetic factors on the career decisions made by individuals. Also, they recognize the significance of learning experiences on career decisions. Flores and O'Brien (2002) noted that SCCT focuses on the specific cognitive mediators that affect learning experiences in career decision-making behavior.

SCCT focuses on how abilities, interests, and other variables relevant to career development interrelate and the specific way in which environmental and personal factors impact career decisions. According to Lent et al. (1994), SCCT is a culturally sensitive approach. In particular, the theory provides a cultural context vital in understanding career development. The theory helps to conceptualize career development by making meaning of the interaction between social cognitive mechanisms such as beliefs, personal background variables such as ethnicity, and environmental mechanisms such as discrimination (Kantamneni et al., 2018).

Contrary to the traditional career development theories that address cultural variables in a cursory way, SCCT describes how cultural learning experiences directly affect an individual's agency. According to Lent et al. (1994), personal agency reflects outcome expectations, self-efficacy beliefs, and the development of career goals and interests. Hence, from Kameny et al.'s (2014) argument, cultural learning experiences have a positive but indirect influence on career development as it influences self-efficacy, thus impacting career goals and interests. Lent et al. (1994) hypothesized that differences in learning experience due to gender and or racial socialization can directly influence the sources of outcome expectations and self-efficacy beliefs. Findings of a research study by Evans & Herr (1991) suggest that culture influences career development. The study showed that African Americans often change their career goals to deal with the dual impacts of real and perceived racism in the workplace. Also, the study showed that African women and men avoided career fields to avoid the impacts of racism in the workplace.

Lent and Brown (1996) noted that SCCT views contextual variables such as ethnicity, race, and gender as relevant to opportunity structure. The researchers framed ethnicity and gender as socially constructed aspects of experiences. They also identified that social-cultural processes and conditions mold the learning opportunities individuals are exposed to, the reactions they receive from performing different activities, and the anticipated outcomes. In addition, SCCT suggests that outcome expectations regarding tasks and activities influence career decisions.

According to Hall and Post-Kammer (1987), outcome expectations encompass numerous types of values, including expectations of having social interactions, helping others, and receiving money. The authors noted that individuals seek career paths consistent with their values. SCCT helps explain how expectations for receiving valued outcomes relate to developing interests and career goals. In this vein, Carter and Cook (1992) identified that the traditional over-representation of African Americans pursuing careers in social sciences and education could have resulted from the values socialized within the context of their community or families.

Tang et al. (1999) utilized SCCT in describing the career development of Asian Americans. The study revealed that self-efficacy was a major mediating factor in career choice. In the study, the research found that career choice was predicted by self-efficacy, acculturation, and family involvement. Other studies employing the SCCT framework that have revealed the influence of culture on career development include Fouad and Kantamneni (2013) and Poon (2014).

To summarize, SCCT is a theory that helps to explain career outcomes through formed relationships based on an individual's behaviors, lived experiences, and contextual influences. SCCT can help to conceptualize Black men's career development by reviewing pertinent variables such as a lack of privilege in career choice and the dearth of diversity in specific career fields.

INSTRUCTIONAL BARRIERS

Instructional barriers such as standardized testing, gatekeeping, limited resources, and a lack of qualified educators are noted consistently throughout career development literature (Bryan et al., 2020), thus illuminating the gaps that exist between minority students and their white counterparts. A research study conducted by Khan and Siriwardhane (2021) investigated the barriers to career progression in higher education and it revealed that instructional barriers negatively affected career progression. The researchers found that promotions in the academic system are merit-based, and one must have adequate performance and research output to qualify for promotion. Results from their study found that people of color faced resource constraints due to their gender and color. The researchers noted that a lack of resources limited adjunct professors from career advancement, resources that would've been vital for the publishing of research. Consistently, Wanelik et al.'s (2020) study investigated barriers in the disciplines of STEM and found that ethnic minority groups were highly likely to experience instructional barriers to career progression. In particular, the study established that ethnic minority groups had fewer publications upon completing their Ph.D. than their white peers due to a lack of institutional resources and access.

Instructional barriers in the workplace include underrepresentation in management, overrepresentation in under-resourced departments, and a lack of access to skills and knowledge-related programs (Rutledge & Gnilka, 2022). Kameny et al. (2014) revealed that the underrepresentation of minority groups in management hampered the career growth of aspiring employees. The participants in this study noted that they lacked a role model, and this affected their interests and goals. In addition, career progression can be restrained by gatekeeping conducted by white counterparts. Consistently, Abelson et al. (2018) established that ethnic minorities in the academic system are highly likely to lack role models, which limits their promotion opportunities.

Research by Lewis (2007) revealed that Black men working in the higher education administration experienced instructional barriers in their career advancement. The study revealed that respondents had limited opportunities for career growth compared to their white male colleagues. More specifically, the findings unearthed that regardless of their experiences and degrees, Black male administrators were placed in designated positions, such as entry level teaching positions. Also, the study established inequality in the allocation of resources and funds by the higher education institutions favoring the white administrators. Consistently, a study by Sparkman (2021) involving Black male executives in higher education in predominantly white institutions revealed how institutional barriers affected the trajectory of their careers. The respondents noted that their departments were underfinanced and had limited skills development opportunities. On the contrary, their white counterparts' departments were well-financed, and these colleagues were allowed to advance their skills. A lack of advanced skills and knowledge resulted in a limited number of Black male executives advancing into the top leadership level in the institutions.

CONSTRUCTING AND CRAFTING A CAREER CALLING

As Black men journey from preschool to graduate and professional schooling in a chosen career path(s), they must do so by navigating many significant individual, systemic, and generational obstacles (Bell, 2018; Owens et al., 2010). One way Black men can help their career growth is by developing a philosophy and strategies for crafting their career calling. Dik et al. (2009, p. 625) defined calling as (a) "a transcendent summons, experienced as originating beyond the self," (b) "to approach a particular life role in a manner oriented toward demonstrating or deriving a sense of purpose or meaningfulness," (c) "that holds other-oriented values and goals as primary sources of motivation." Shackelford and Denzel (2021) defined calling as special activities to perform in the world – a fulfillment based intentional design which naturally results in service or benefits the global society, community, next generation, and addresses overall generosity. A calling is described as a sense of passion for a particular line or type of work, along with the belief that this work is meaningful and purposeful (Ehrhardt & Ensher, 2021).

How Can Black Men Find a Career Calling?

Black men can journey in finding a career calling by engaging in experiences such as career exposure that will foster self-discovery. The journey in identifying a career calling requires walking through process and plan – not in step by step (linear process) but an intentional assessment, evaluation, and reflection on vital components that provide data to make decisions. This journey is a lifelong journey – a marathon, not a sprint.

One component for Black men to engage in during P-12 schooling and postsecondary education is to access age appropriate career assessments. This is encouraged throughout schooling for the betterment of understanding self throughout the changes of development. Engaging in career assessments allows individuals to participate in self-discovery and obtain insight about themselves. The assessment reports will provide self-discovery perspectives about their own interests, strengths (area of strengths and weaknesses), values, and personality.

Career assessments such as Interest Profilers and Career Profiles can enable assessment takers to obtain data driven self-awareness that will provide an essential component of navigating the career calling journey (Hines & Owen, 2022).

Another key component to engaging in career exposure and experiences is for Black men to learn about potential career paths in various vocations and industries by participating in intentional experiential learning opportunities. These opportunities may include internship or volunteer opportunities provided by community leaders (businesses, organizations, or civic groups) that link with the student's interests, skills, abilities, and talents will provide an environment that cultivates and provides clarity for a career calling.

Benefits of Black Men Constructing a Career Calling

Literature supports the rationale that individuals are increasingly seeking a sense of purpose and seek to identify meaning in their work (Adams, 2012). The by-product of finding meaning in work will contribute to a better understanding of self, skill set development, psychological health, and healthier well-being (Steger et al., 2006). From a communal viewpoint, an individual who gains self-awareness is better able to discern their skills and aptitudes for different kinds of work, and is thus more capable of contributing to the development of the community as a whole, which includes their colleagues and the individuals they serve. When a person recognizes their career calling, and displays and applies their skill set in the community, it benefits the community as a whole. Others in the community can learn from this individual's career journey, and become better themselves as a result (Keller, 2012).

Practical Steps Black Men Can Take to Construct a Career Calling

From a philosophical perspective, Black men can benefit by operating from a mindset that constructing and crafting a career calling is a journey and a process of self-discovery, evaluation, and decision-making. As young Black men mature into manhood, the constant evaluation and engagement of one's identity as a worker and skill set acquisition is ongoing (Hines & Owen, 2022; Keller, 2012; Shackelford & Denzel, 2021). From a practical perspective, Shackelford and Denzel (2021) frame the career calling process by encouraging one to define (look at your current context and define the desired outcome), discover (engage in self-discovery exercises and evaluation of the positive and negative of work experiences), decide (consider constraints and course of action), and do (experiment with expectation, dedicate to projects and embrace uncertainty). Hines and Owen (2022) structure the career calling conversation by proposing individuals to construct (engage in activities permit understanding of self), confirm (engage in activities that validate skillset), clarify (engage in activities that give understanding about your next possible course of action), and correct (engage in activities that will challenge your mindset and course of action).

PSYCHOLOGICAL BARRIERS TO SUCCESS AND BELONGING

Black men may face psychological barriers that impede their success in their respective careers, which can impact their sense of belonging in the workplace. This section deals with barriers like "imposter syndrome" and "stereotype threat" and how to address them.

Imposter Syndrome

Imposter syndrome refers to the psychological condition that occurs when a person has self-doubt about their skills and the feeling that their achievements are fake. Because Black men may already be subjected to racism and discrimination in the workplace, this can be especially damaging to their ability to advance in their careers. Because of this additional self-doubt, which is induced by impostor syndrome, the person may begin to question their own capabilities, undervalue their efforts, and be less willing to advocate for themselves or look for opportunities to progress their careers. Furthermore, the additional stress that is brought on by impostor syndrome can have a detrimental effect on a person's mental health as well as their overall well-being. Imposter syndrome is a condition that can be exacerbated when a person feels they are under pressure to overcompensate or prove oneself in the workplace. This is especially prevalent among Black men.

Individuals with the imposter syndrome experience feelings of self-doubt (Chrousos & Mentis, 2020). These individuals believe they are a fraud individually and/or professionally; they believe they are not good enough, do not belong, and they will soon be discovered to be a fraud (Carver-Madalon, 2020). Imposter syndrome threatens diversity and hits harder when you're Black (Chrousos & Mentis, 2020; Doggett, 2019). The imposter syndrome has a higher prevalence among racial and ethnic minority individuals and for college students from racially minoritized identities, imposter feelings are a better predictor of mental health problems than minority stress. Imposter syndrome may explain the attrition of racially minoritized people from STEM and if institutions and departments do not address those fears, STEM (as well as other disciplines) will suffer (Chrousos & Mentis, 2020).

Doggett (2019) stated that no matter how qualified you believe you are, how much experience you have, and how much reassurance and positive feedback you receive, you still believe you are not as capable as others may believe and you are doomed for failure. Microaggressions that minoritized individuals face cause them to become their own aggressors and they fill themselves with negative internal dialog. As a result, minoritized individuals experience poor physical and mental health outcomes and they too easily believe the false information they received from society and their own brains. Solutions to imposter syndrome include racial and ethnic minoritized individuals merely showing up (especially in predominately white spaces), more research that examines the roles that race, gender, age, and socioeconomic status play in mental health outcomes (especially those stemming from the imposter syndrome), more medical and mental health professionals from minoritized identities, and medical professionals must close the research gap and examine the influence racism and discrimination have on mental health outcomes, especially the imposter syndrome (Doggett, 2019).

Stereotype Threat

Imposter syndrome is not the only way a person's own negative beliefs can have an impact on their career development. Being reminded of your identity – i.e., race – and the stereotypes associated with that identity can also impact one's career (Locke, 2020). The risk of confirming unfavorable stereotypes about one's group, which can lead to poor performance and self-esteem, is referred to as stereotype threat (Steele & Aronson, 1995). In the workplace, stereotype threat can emerge for Black men as a concern of confirming unfavorable preconceptions about their IQ, work ethic, or ability. This can result in diminished confidence and motivation, which can have a negative effect on their career progress. In addition, they may always feel the need to prove themselves, which can lead to increased stress and burnout. This can result in a lack of self-advocacy for promotion and restrict their access to professional development and advancement chances. Further, those that experience stereotype threat tend to underperform in threatening intellectual environments, thus, validating those negative stereotypes. One example occurs when Black people are stressed while taking standardized tests because they fear their performance will be judged based on the stereotype that associates being Black with poor academic and intellectual ability. The stress about validating this stereotype can interfere with their performance and produce a stereotype-consistent outcome – low test performance (Johns et al., 2008). Solutions to stereotype threat include practicing tasks in safer environments, a focus on a different part of your identity, and focusing on a positive stereotype (Locke, 2020).

DYNAMICS OF EDUCATION ON CAREER DEVELOPMENT AND VOCATIONAL PLANNING FOR BLACK MEN

When considering socially responsible approaches to career development for Black men, it is critically important to understand the plight of the Black man in the United States from childhood to adulthood. We posit that the formation of Black men's conceptualization of their own career development starts many years before they begin career exploration and may be impacted by early childhood development.

Early childhood development is shaped by the type of "nature and nurture" received in a child's first years of life (Music, 2016). Childhood experiences with family, in daycare, at school, and in society help young children shape their foundational worldview. Unfortunately for many young Black boys, especially those born in inner-city communities, their views on the world are shaped through the lens of a child in low socioeconomic status. With poverty typically comes a combination of other risk factors such as single parenthood, a lack of parental education, and parental unemployment (Masten et al., 1995). Research suggests that father involvement with children during infancy and toddlerhood plays a vital role in scholastic preparation and success (Baker, 2017). Fatherhood and role modeling has also been shown to play an integral role in the career development of young Black men (Allen, 1978).

Throughout childhood, Black boys are disproportionately impacted by adverse experiences like abuse and household dysfunction due to systemic oppression and a mix of personal and intergenerational trauma exposure (Hampton-Anderson et al., 2021). Many young Black boys will go on to encounter poor academic and social outcomes in grade-school education (Cramer, 2015). These issues make for Black men who, by the time they reach high school, are tasked with considering their career choices despite facing a myriad number of systemic and oppressive obstacles. Once the teenage years are reached, the saliency of career development becomes paramount and holds steady up to and throughout adulthood (Stringer et al., 2012).

Education and the Workforce

Aside from inter-community, cultural, and familial dynamics that help shape the minds of Black men in their early years of development, there are historic and current systemic barriers that circumscribe the career development of Black men that may impact their educational attainment and vocational choices. Proctor and Johnston (1978) described the educational system and the economic system as two main forces that largely impact the career development of Black men. This rings true today as, from an economic standpoint, Black men face less favorable labor market outcomes than their white male counterparts (Daly et al., 2017). Not only are unemployment rates consistently higher for Black men than white men, but lifetime earnings by Black men are drastically affected by myriad factors such as incarceration, poor health, unemployment, and economic segregation (Sakamoto et al., 2018). Veering into education, Black students receive far less quality of education in grade school than their white counterparts (Griffin & Allen, 2006). Racial inequities affecting Black men are further evidenced by lower postsecondary enrollment and lower educational attainment (Harper, 2012). Contributing factors such as institutional and experienced racism and a lack of academic integration play a key role in the undermining of Black male collegiate success (Maiden et al., 2020; Patitu, 2000; Hamilton & Toure, 1992).

Despite the disparities present in educational attainment among Black men, contemporary data show that Black students are prioritizing education. This is evidenced by an exponential increase in Black student college enrollment over the last few decades (Nichols & Evans-Bell, 2017). High school graduation and college enrollment rates among Black students have also increased dramatically in recent years (DePaoli et al., 2015; Hussar & Bailey, 2013). With Black men having ever more opportunities at obtaining higher education, it is crucial that resources and support are prioritized to help them in materializing their career and vocational pursuits.

Once reaching the workforce, Black men are faced with additional obstacles. In her dissertation study examining the impact of racism on the career development of Black men, Cornileus (2010) found that repressive and facilitative structures can impact Black male career development. She concluded, among other findings, that racism and disparate treatment inflicted on Black men in the workforce impact their career development "in ways not experienced by White men or African American women" (Cornileus, 2010). Black women's college enrollment outnumber Black men's enrollment by a margin of 2:1 and they outpace Black men in all levels of degree attainment (Scott & Sharp, 2019). These numbers impact the number of available opportunities for Black men to represent themselves in the workforce after college, especially in higher paying careers in STEM.

A push for Black men in college to view themselves as viable in any future workspace and efforts to help increase their self-concept is crucial in increasing the representation of Black men in higher-paying careers. In their study of constructivism and career decision self-efficacy, Grier-Reed and Ganuza (2011) found that implementing a constructivist career course could help improve the career decision self-efficacy of Black college students. The course incorporated activities that focused on the four tools of narrative, action, construction, and interpretation. The course afforded students the opportunity to explore the origins of their ideas about careers, construct their identities, and overcome barriers to career decision self-efficacy.

Mentoring for Positive Career Development

According to Kameny et al. (2014), mentors are crucial in career progression. Mentors provide guidance on career building, helping the employees acquire relevant skills and knowledge. It is our contention that programs designed to help Black men in the areas of career and vocational planning should consider the incorporation of mentorship. Literature supports the notion that mentoring plays an integral role in the success of Black men in education and the workforce (Brown et al., 1999; Oliver et al., 2020). Research has shown that mentoring has a positive impact on the career development of Black men in STEM and other areas of work and education (Alston et al., 2017). Similar to research mentorship in academia, where pretenured Black male faculty are offered instructional and relational support toward improved professional development (Briggs & Pehrsson, 2008), occupational mentorship in the workplace can benefit Black men by increasing their likelihood of career advancement, promotions, and organizational commitment (Ivey & Dupré, 2022).

PERSONAL NARRATIVES

We are honored to be invited by the editors of this text to contribute an autobiographical account of the events, forces, and people that influenced and shaped our career journeys. Considering lived experience is tantamount to understanding the unique needs of Black men as it relates to career development. Each author of this chapter has chosen a specific career development theory that helps explain their lived experiences and career journeys. What follows are their narratives that have been grounded in those career development theories.

Folkes' Narrative

Theory of career choice, defined by John Holland (1987), maintains the notion that in choosing a career choice, people would rather have employment where they are surrounded by individuals similar to them. Individuals seek out environments that allow them to utilize skill and abilities while expressing their values and attitudes, while taking on roles and problems that they enjoy. Holland's (1987) theory suggests that individuals fit into one of the six personality types, which are realistic, investigative, artistic, social, enterprising, and conventional.

Often, my friends and colleagues ask me what motivated me to become a counselor and counselor educator. They consider this professional career intensely challenging and wonder what attracted me to it. In a sense the career chose me. Personal experiences throughout childhood significantly contributed to my choice to become a therapist. I grew up in a Jamaican spiritual home where compassion, empathy, and caring were highly valued. My mother always reminded us of the importance of listening and having empathy toward other people who are suffering, sometimes stating "that could be us." Friends often came to me to share their secrets and unburden their wounds. I would sit them down, and together we puzzle on the best way to address their struggles.

At age 15, I became aware of my ability to empathize with others and my ability to listen to others. Holland's theory of career choice maintains that in career choice, individuals prefer jobs where they would be around others who are like them (Holland, 1987). In particular, individuals search for an environment that allows them to use their abilities and skills and express their values and attitudes while talking in enjoyable roles. I fit in the social and investigator personality type of Holland's six personality types. Individuals with this personality type like doing things to help others, such as counseling, teaching, and nursing. They value helping others and solving social problems (Ramadhani et al., 2020). Hence, when choosing my career, I was looking for a job that would allow me to fully utilize my abilities and express my values and attitudes. I looked forward to working with others who value helping and empathizing with those suffering.

Wright's Narrative

My earliest inclinations of being a helper were becoming aware of and accepting that I was an emotionally sensitive male with an aversion to conflict. My temperament contrasted the expectations of young Black males growing up in Washington, DC. As a result, I was often teased and ridiculed by both family and peers. Was there really something wrong with me or was I in an environment that did not suit me? This question was answered as I traveled and lived abroad.

I realized that men being sensitive and verbally expressing their emotions was the norm rather than the exception. Seeing masculinity exist juxtaposed to emotional expression allowed me to redefine and honor my strength of being acutely aware of my emotions. Ironically, the more I accepted my sensitive nature, the more inner consent I gave myself to take jobs where I could excel as an empathic healer.

Conceptually, Trait and Factor Theory best accounts for my journey as a counselor, due to its focus on person and environmental fit (Chartrand, 1991). As I chose careers that aligned with therapeutic relationships, I began to have more intrinsic satisfaction. The journey from a dedicated aide serving children with special needs to a burgeoning doctoral student has been sustained by choosing jobs correlated with supporting others in distress. My proclivity for such jobs is reflected in a stable assessment score on the Meyers-Briggs and Strong Interest Inventory. These assessments measuring personality and career interest (Sharf, 2013), consistently support my personality type as an Introverted iNtuitive Feeling Perceiver (INFP) and work value preference for social investigative and artistic professions. Jobs that afforded me the opportunity to work with people coupled with autonomy and creativity yield the greatest satisfaction.

Pursuing a career as a counselor is the amalgamation of my personality, values, and passion for helping and empowering others. Working as a mental health counselor was confirmation that my personality and values were in alignment with the right profession. I find that my work is more impactful and appreciated as I am empowering others while utilizing my strengths. As black male I have been able to make contact with my emotional self and assist other black males in doing the same. This has been the most rewarding part of my career journey; turning a perceived weakness into a strength to share and empower others.

In practical terms, I encourage men of color to strongly self-reflect and explore how to best blend intrinsic motivation with jobs that allow for sustainable pay. One's interest may not be financially lucrative in the beginning and may require relegation to being a hobby. While one's interest is a hobby, financial stability can be achieved while the hobby is sustained. Practicing mindfulness interventions such as self-reflection can reinforce primal values that authentically reflect your interests.

Lastly, explore what type of environments caters to and allow for full expression of such values. This is akin to what Robert Greene (2012) refers to as discovering your calling. When we connect to our calling it can guide us toward more life fulfillment and a stronger sense of purpose. Heeding our calling may denote existing in white spaces or challenging narrow minded cultural or gender-based expectations. No matter your calling, give full expression to interests that authentically reflect your life purpose. This is your gift to the world as it adds value and inspiration to the lives of those you encounter.

Beauduy's Narrative

As a kid, becoming a licensed therapist and a professor in counselor education was not in my canon of career development and consciousness. In high school, I attended a magnet program for broadcasting and was geared to become a news reporter. My secondary dream job was to become a maestro or band director, as I had excelled for many years in my school's band program. Being a young Black man who conceptualized my career possibilities didn't come by chance. Throughout my teenage years, I attended my local Boys & Girls Club where I received an immeasurable amount of mentorship. While at "the club" I was able to take on leadership roles, travel the country attending leadership conferences, provide mentorship and support to younger kids, and develop my identity as a future leader. Despite graduating near the top of my class, life circumstances (similar to many young Black men in America) forced a halt in my pursuit of higher education. But after a four-year hiatus from school, I decided to attend college at the age of 22.

While in community college, I majored in economics and received my associate's degree. I then transferred to a university to major in accounting. But midway through my junior year, I decided that I wanted to pursue a career that would allow me to use my lived experience to help others. Hence, after switching my major to liberal studies, I graduated with my bachelor's degree.

When contemplating what to study at the graduate level, a proverbial light bulb went off in my head. What dawned on me was the many times throughout adulthood I had switched jobs while in school: In my early 20s, I worked as a technical support agent and did late night shifts as a cashier at my local 7–11; in my mid-20s I worked as an account manager for a large bank and as a certified personal finance counselor. In both roles, I found no personal fulfillment. I reflected on my teenage years and remembered the impact that my therapist had on me as I struggled with personal issues in the ninth grade. I thought to myself, "What if I join a career field where my work not only makes me money but allows me to give back to my community?" Moreover, I asked myself, "What role could I play where I'd be passionate about my work and uplift young Black men who've had similar struggles as I?" When deciding upon a master's-level field of study, enrolling in a graduate-level counseling program proved to be the answer, and ultimately, my calling!

While in graduate school, I studied to become a licensed mental health counselor and specialized in clinical rehabilitation counseling where most students go on to have careers in vocational rehabilitation. During my practicum and internship experiences, I enjoyed making a difference in the lives of persons with disabilities and other mental health needs. I would eventually graduate from my master's program and go on to pursue doctoral study to be trained as a counselor educator. My current work includes working as a therapist, teaching as an adjunct professor in counseling programs, various roles in vocational rehabilitation, and as a mentor. Looking back, it was the seeking of personal and outward satisfaction through my vocational choice that ultimately led me to more fulfilling work as a counselor and professor. The Minnesota Theory of Work Adjustment (TWA), often referred to as the Person-Environment Correspondence Theory, best conceptualizes how I previously adapted to short-term work environments and how I was led to find a career that is a good fit between myself and the organizations for which I'd work.

TWA evolves from trait-and-factor counseling (Chartrand, 1991) and is conceptually grounded by person-environment (P-E) psychology (England et al., 2014). TWA focuses on an individual's work adjustment and predictability of their satisfaction *in* the work environment. TWA is conceptualized as having two models: predictive and process, whereby the predictive model seeks to explain whether the worker is both satisfied with and satisfies the work environment, and the process model focuses on the relationship between both the worker, their work environment, and the fit between the two (Swanson & Schneider, 2013). TWA can be used as a point of reference in an effort to help Black men in career development. Increased emphasis can be placed on Black male satisfaction with their possible or current work environments and how adjustment and the gaining of work skills can help to increase such satisfaction. Based on TWA, Black men will seek to satisfy six key values while adjusting to the work environment: achievement, comfort, status, altruism, safety, and autonomy (Dawes, 1994). My suggestion to Black men when developing their careers is to seek a balance between their passion, their work, and the environments in which they spend their time. TWA helps to address this.

Mack's Narrative

A theory that has resonated with my journey to being a School Counseling and Counselor Educator is Career Constructive Theory (CCT) by Savickas (2002). The essence of CCT contends that individuals construct their careers by gleaning meaning from their vocational behavior and occupational experiences (Savickas, 2012). As counselors may use this theory, they will use this framework to listen to clients' narratives for the storylines of vocational personality type, career adaptability, and life theme.

Career construction counseling (Savickas, 2011) begins with a career story interview, with four to six questions about how clients construct theirselves and careers. Next, counselors examine these stories and develop them into life patterns. Then the client and counselor use those concepts learned to construct intentions and actions that begin the next steps in the client's occupational journey. Demonstrations of career construction counseling enable counselors to evaluate the use and usefulness of this life design intervention (Savickas, 2012).

Starting in High school, the opportunity to serve in my church as a youth leader led to my understanding and enjoyment of counseling and proving an empathic ear. While serving, working in a variety of food and sales positions provided experiences, learning opportunities educated me on the construction of my skill and life design being best suited for serving in the area of counseling services domain.

My journey through undergraduate and graduate school, engaging with internships, career conversations with persons in school counseling scaffolded and constructed my journey to being a school counselor. For a sizable portion of my educational career – this author considered marriage counseling. The education and experience via school counseling constructed a foundation to serve in the school counseling industry.

Ford's Narrative

Krumbholtz's Happenstance Learning Theory (HLT) directs career professionals to help clients make the most out of chance events (Dugger, 2016). Chance has a major impact on career development and career professionals must help clients maximize the likelihood of potentially beneficial chance events and help them capitalize on those opportunities. Learning occurs from two perspectives. First, people behave the way they do due to instrumental and associative learning experiences occurring in the context of their environment and genetic makeup. Second, learning is the overall goal for career counseling and career assessment. Krumboltz also criticized trait-factor theories because they pathologized indecision. He viewed indecision – or open-mindedness – as an asset, not a problem to be solved. People who have settled on one career goal may be limiting themselves regarding chance events and taking risks and changing directions. Those who have not settled on one direction may be more open-minded to a range of possibilities, more flexible regarding their direction, more optimistic about potential options, and more willing to take risks required to capitalize on unplanned opportunities (Dugger, 2016).

As I reflect upon my own career development, HLT explains my journey. I have several instances where chance events have influenced my career choices. My first full-time job after college was working as a certified nursing assistant (CNA). I was open to trying something new and did not have any issues with where I would be placed once I finished my training course. I epitomized open-mindedness. By chance, I was attending the same church as the head nurse of the neurology unit at the local hospital and someone who worked as a CNA on that unit. She informed me that she had an opening, and I could have it if I wanted it. I had no experience with neurology but was open to the opportunity. Another aspect of HLT is where learning occurs and the neurology environment taught me so much about empathy, working in a crisis situation, and about how the brain works. I continue to use this knowledge as a counselor and a counselor educator. I want to capitalize on that knowledge and get my degree in Nursing, which will enhance my work as a counselor and counselor educator.

Another chance event occurred when I applied for a hall director position at a small, state-supported historically Black college/university (HBCU). At the time, I was unemployed and about to lose my housing. From my experience, I assumed that hall director positions were live-in, but unfortunately, this position was not. I ended up not getting the job. When I interviewed, I saw that the director of housing and residence life was someone that I had known almost all my life. I had no clue that she was in that role. A day later, I received a call from the university offering me an assistant hall director position that was live-in. While I had no student affairs experience, I was open-minded to the possibility and took the offer. This position taught me about working with college students, student development theory, Maslow's hierarchy of needs, career, and academic advising, and how to deal with a crisis situation. It also influenced my decision to get my master's degree in Counseling and my Ph.D. in Counselor Education and Supervision.

Because of my work in residence life, my career trajectory was to be a Vice-President for Student Life. I did not want to provide therapy at all. I knew that I had to get my doctorate but had little information about that process. Krumboltz would tell me that I should not be too settled on one career goal but be open-minded about my career trajectory. Looking back on my career, I would agree with him. I was, however, open-minded about what degree to pursue (Ed.D. versus Ph.D.), and in what discipline would get my doctorate (Higher Education Administration or Counselor Education and Supervision). I was open to either but decided to pursue my Ph.D. in Counselor Education and Supervision, which would open more possibilities for me. I also decided to pursue licensure. My doctoral program opened my eyes to more possibilities, which included teaching, providing therapy, and providing clinical supervision. As such, I became open to academic positions instead of administrative positions. Currently, I am a tenure-track Assistant Professor in a counseling program and even though I decided not to go the administrative route full-time, I will serve as our Ph.D. program co-coordinator once it launches.

Chance events and open-mindedness have led me to where I am in my career. I have learned to embrace these unplanned opportunities influenced by my environment and my personal relationships. I have learned to embrace being open-minded in my career journey. I have internalized what I have learned in all my positions to be successful in my current career. I do not know where my career will take me next, but I am open to the possibilities. Thanks Dr. John D. Krumboltz.

RECOMMENDATIONS FOR RESEARCH, PRACTICE, AND POLICY

The content provided in this chapter is helpful but limited. This underscores the importance of more research needed about ways to increase career and vocational development for Black men. Future studies should look to help inform practice, policy, and education around career development for this population. Recommendations for future studies would include exploring inclusivity and representation in roles that affect policy change which could help to increase the presence of Black males in various professions. In addition, future studies should seek to understand the dynamics of occupational mentorship and diversity support and how it impacts the success of Black men in early stages of career development.

Relative to practice and policy, decision-makers should be intentional about increasing efforts toward the recruitment and retention of Black men. To do this, there must be a developed understanding of the myriad socioeconomic and sociocultural factors that influence the Black male's perception of their career development. Additionally, to reduce the negative self-concept, negative outlook on career development and exploration, and instances of imposter syndrome, there should be the establishment of critical relationships to help support Black men in their educational and career pursuits. This can be accomplished by incorporating culturally responsive mentoring initiatives with career development programs and planning.

CONCLUSION

In summary, the purpose of this chapter was to shed light on the myriad of mental, cultural, and social obstacles that prevent Black men from actively participating in the labor force. We were able to gain a deeper understanding of the obstacles that Black men experience in the course of their professional development by reviewing research on mentorship, racism, society, culture, economics, and other elements that are pertinent to Black men's career development. Counseling interventions and their applicability to career counseling with Black men were also discussed, along with programs and strategies that effectively address the career-development needs of Black men. In addition, we talked about how to effectively address the career development needs of Black men.

Lastly, this chapter looked at growing patterns in the professional development of Black men and provided helpful insights through the use of case studies that were described by the writers. The importance of research, counseling, counselor education, policy, and recommendations for professional development were also covered in this chapter. These topics were reviewed with the goal of enhancing the career development outcomes for Black men.

It is essential that we keep working toward removing the obstacles that prevent Black men from participating in the workforce and that we give them the support they need to realize their full potential and achieve their professional goals.

REFERENCES

Abdullah, T., Graham-LoPresti, J. R., Tahirkheli, N. N., Hughley, S. M., & Watson, L. T. J. (2021). Microaggressions and posttraumatic stress disorder symptom score among Black Americans: Exploring the link. *Traumatology, 27*(3), 244–253. https://doi.org/10.1037/trm0000259

Abelson, J. S., Wong, N. Z., Symer, M., Eckenrode, G., Watkins, A., & Yeo, H. L. (2018). Racial and ethnic disparities in promotion and retention of academic surgeons. *The American Journal of Surgery, 216*, 678–682. https://doi.org/10.1016/j.amjsurg.2018.07.020

Adams, C. M. (2012). Calling and career counseling with college students: Finding meaning in work and life. *Journal of College Counseling, 15*(1), 65–80.

Allen, W. R. (1978). Race, family setting, and adolescent achievement orientation. *The Journal of Negro Education, 47*(3) 230–243.

Alleyne, A. (2004). Black identity and workplace oppression. *Counselling and Psychotherapy Research, 4*(1), 4–8.

Alston, G. D., Guy, B. S., & Campbell, C. D. (2017). Ready for the professoriate? The influence of mentoring on career development for Black male graduate students in STEM. *Journal of African American Males in Education, 8*(1), 45–66.

Assari, S., Miller, R. J., Taylor, R. J., Mouzon, D., Keith, V., & Chatters, L. M. (2018). Discrimination fully mediates the effects of incarceration history on depressive symptoms and psychological distress among African American men. *Journal of Racial and Ethnic Health Disparities, 5*(2), 243–252.

Babco, E. L. (2003). Trends in African American and Native American participation in STEM higher education. In *Commission on professionals in science and technology.*

Baker, C. E. (2017). *Father involvement and early childhood development in African American families: Implications for research, practice, and policy.*

Bandura, A. (1986). *Social foundations of thought and action: A social cognitive theory.* Prentice Hall.

Bell, T. J. (2018). Career counseling with Black men: Applying principles of existential psychotherapy. *The Career Development Quarterly, 66*(2), 162–175. https://doi.org/10.1002/cdq.12130

Brown II, M. C., Davis, G. L., & McClendon, S. A. (1999). Mentoring graduate students of color: Myths, models, and modes. *Peabody Journal of Education, 74*(2), 105–118.

Briggs, C. A., & Pehrsson, D. E. (2008). Research mentorship in counselor education. *Counselor Education and Supervision, 48*(2), 101–113.

Bryan, J., Williams, J. M., & Griffin, D. (2020). Fostering educational resilience and opportunities in urban schools through equity-focused school–family–community partnerships. *Professional School Counseling, 23*(1_part_2). https://doi.org/10.1177/2156759X19899179

Carter, R. T., & Cook, D. A. (1992). A culturally relevant perspective for understanding the career paths of visible racial/ethnic group people. In Z. Leibowitz & D. Lea (Eds.), *Adult career development* (2nd ed., pp. 192–217). AACD, The National Career Development Association.

Carver-Madalon, L. (2020). How one can thrive despite experiencing imposter syndrome. *Authority Magazine.* https://medium.com/authority-magazine/dr-leilani-carver-madalon-how-one-can-thrive-despite-experiencing-impostor-syndrome-f46f61132c12. Accessed on June 9, 2022.

Chartrand, J. M. (1991). The evolution of trait-and-factor career counseling: A person × environment fit approach. *Journal of Counseling & Development, 69*(6), 518–524.

Chrousos, G. P., & Mentis, A. A. (2020). Imposter syndrome threatens diversity. *Science, 367*(6479), 749–750.

Chung, Y. B., Baskin, M. L., & Case, A. B. (1999). Career development of black males: Case studies. *Journal of Career Development, 25*(3), 161.

Cornileus, T. H. (2010). *A critical examination of the impact of racism on the career development of African American professional men in corporate America.* Doctoral dissertation, uga.

Cramer, L. (2015). Inequities of intervention among culturally and linguistically diverse students. *Penn GSE Perspectives on Urban Education, 12*(1), n1.

Daly, M., Hobijn, B., & Pedtke, J. H. (2017). Disappointing facts about the black-white wage gap. *FRBSF Economic Letter, 26,* 1–5.

Davis, J. E. (2020). Commentary on black boys and men in STEM. *Journal of African American Males in Education, 11*(2), 7-11.

Dawes, R. V. (1994). The theory of work adjustment as convergent theory. In M. L. Savikas & R. W. Lent (Eds.), *Convergence in career development theories: Implications for science and practice* (pp. 33–43). CPP Books.

DePaoli, J. L., Fox, J. H., Ingram, E. S., Maushard, M., Bridgeland, J. M., & Balfanz, R. (2015). *Building a grad nation: Progress and challenge in ending the high school dropout epidemic.* America's Promise Alliance. Annual update, 2015.

DeVeaux, M. (2022). Not just by rates of recidivism: How NYC black men define success after prison. *Journal of Offender Rehabilitation, 61*(5), 233–244. https://doi.org/10.1080/10509674.2022. 2081648

Dik, B. J., Duffy, R. D., & Eldridge, B. M. (2009). Calling and vocation in career counseling: Recommendations for promoting meaningful work. *Professional Psychology: Research and Practice, 40*(6), 625.

Doggett, J. A. (2019). Imposter syndrome hits harder when you're Black. *HuffPost.* https://www.huffpost.com/entry/imposter-syndrome-racism-discrimination_l_5d9f2c00e4b06ddfc514ec5c. Accessed on June 9, 2022.

Dubois, W. E. B. (1905). *The souls of black folk: Essays and sketches.* Archivald Consabel & Co.

Dugger, S. Z. (2016). *Foundations of career counseling: A case-based approach.* Pearson.

Ehrhardt, K., & Ensher, E. (2021). Perceiving a calling, living a calling, and calling outcomes: How mentoring matters. *Journal of Counseling Psychology, 68*(2), 168–181.

England, G. W., Dawis, R. V., & Lofquist, L. H. (2014). *A theory of work adjustment.* Reprinted by permission of publisher and authors from A Theory of Work Adjustment, Minnesota Studies in Vocational Rehabilitation, January 1964, Bulletin 38.

Evans, K. M., & Herr, E. L. (1991). The influence of racism and sexism in the career development of African American women. *Journal of Multicultural Counseling and Development*, *19*, 130–135.

Fila, M. J., Purl, J., & Jang, S. R. (2022). Demands, resources, well-being and strain: Meta-analyzing moderator effects of workforce racial composition. *Applied Research in Quality of Life*, 1–28.

Flores, L. Y., & O'Brien, K. M. (2002). The career development of Mexican American adolescent women: A test of social cognitive career theory. *Journal of Counseling Psychology*, *49*(1), 14–27. https://doi.org/10.1037/0022-0167.49.1.14

Fouad, N. A., & Kantamneni, N. E. E. T. A. (2013). The role of race and ethnicity in career choice, development, and adjustment. In *Career development and counseling: Putting theory and research to work* (Vol. 2, 215–243).

Fries-Brit, S., & White-Lewis, D. (2020). In pursuit of meaningful relationships: How black males perceive faculty interactions in STEM. *The Urban Review*, *52*(3), 521–540. https://doi.org/10.1007/s11256-020-00559-x

Gazley, J. L., & Campbell, B. P. (2020). The role of resilience in Black men's success in STEM graduate programs. *The Journal of Negro Education*, *89*(3), 360–372.

Greene, R. (2012). *Mastery*. Penguin.

Grier-Reed, T., & Ganuza, Z. M. (2011). Constructivism and career decision self-efficacy for Asian Americans and African Americans. *Journal of Counseling and Development*, *89*(2), 200–205.

Griffin, K., & Allen, W. (2006). Mo'money, mo'problems? High-achieving Black high school students' experiences with resources, racial climate, and resilience. *The Journal of Negro Education*, 478–494.

Hall, E. R., & Post-Kammer, P. (1987). Black mathematics and science majors: Why so few? *The Career Development Quarterly*, 206–219.

Hamilton, C. V., & Ture, K. (1992). *Black power: Politics of liberation in America*. Vintage.

Hampton-Anderson, J. N., Carter, S., Fani, N., Gillespie, C. F., Henry, T. L., Holmes, E., Lamis, D. A., LoParo, D., Maples-Keller, J. L., Powers, A., Sonu, S., & Kaslow, N. J. (2021). Adverse childhood experiences in African Americans: Framework, practice, and policy. *American Psychologist*, *76*(2), 314–325.

Harper, S. R. (2012). *Black male student success in higher education: A report from the National Black Male College Achievement Study*. Center for the Study of Race and Equity in Education, University of Pennsylvania Graduate School of Education.

Hines, E., & Owen, L. (2022). *Equity – Based career development and post secondary transitions: An American imperative*. Information Age Publishing, Inc.

Holland, J. L. (1987). Current status of Holland's theory of careers: Another perspective. *The Career Development Quarterly*, *36*(1), 24–30. https://doi.org/10.1002/j.2161-0045.1987.tb00478.x.

Hussar, W. J., & Bailey, T. M. (2013). *Projections of education statistics to 2022 (NCES 2014-051)*. National Center for Education Statistics.

Ispa-Landa, S., & Loeffler, C. E. (2016). Indefinite punishment and the criminal record: Stigma reports among expungement-seekers in Illinois. *Criminology*, *54*(3), 387–412.

Ivey, G. W., & Dupré, K. E. (2022). Workplace mentorship: A critical review. *Journal of Career Development*, *49*(3), 714–729.

Johns, M., Inzlight, M., & Schmader, T. (2008). Stereotype threat and executive resource depletion: Examining the influence of emotion regulation. *Journal of Experimental Psychology*, *137*(4), 691–705.

Johnson, P. D. (2016). Somebodiness and its meaning to African American men. *Journal of Counseling and Development*, *94*(3), 333–343. https://doi.org/10.1002/jcad.12089

Kameny, R. R., DeRosier, M. E., Taylor, L. C., Sturtz McMillen, J., Knowles, M. M., & Pifer, K. (2014). Barriers to career success for minority researchers in the behavioral sciences. *Journal of Career Development*, *41*, 43–61.

Kantamneni, N., Dharmalingam, K., Orley, G., & Kanagasingam, S. K. (2018). Cultural factors, perceived barriers, and Asian American career development: An application of social cognitive career theory. *Journal of Career Assessment*, *26*(4), 649–665.

Keller, T. (2012). *Every good endeavor: Connecting your work to God's work*. Penguin.

Khan, T., & Siriwardhane, P. (2021). Barriers to career progression in the higher education sector: Perceptions of Australian academics. *Sustainability*, *13*(11), 6255.

Klein, J. E., & Lopez, D. W. (2021). Trauma and police violence. Issues and implications for mental health professionals. *Culture, Medicine, and Psychiatry, 46*, 212–220. https://doi.org/10.1007/s11013-020-09707-0

LaCourse, A., Listwan, S. J., Reid, S., & Hartman, J. L. (2019). Recidivism and reentry: The role of individual coping styles. *Crime & Delinquency, 65*(1), 46–68.

Lent, R. W., & Brown, S. D. (1996). Social cognitive approach to career development: An overview. *The Career Development Quarterly, 44*, 310–321.

Lent, R. W., Brown, S. D., & Hackett, G. (1994). Toward a unified social cognitive theory of career/academic interest, choice, and performance. *Journal of Vocational Behavior, 45*, 79–122.

Lewis, O. (2007). *Navigating barriers of African American male administrators: Manifesting mechanisms for career advancement in mainstream institutions of higher education.*

Locke, C. (2020). How we undermine ourselves: Overcoming imposter syndrome and stereotype threat. *Forbes.* https://www.forbes.com/sites/londonschoolofeconomics/2020/03/19/how-we-undermine-ourselves-overcoming-impostor-syndrome-and-stereotype-threat/?sh=129eca28cd5b. Accessed on June 9, 2022.

Maiden, J. L., Stewart, D. O., Mizelle, N., & Thorne, D. (2020). Examining factors that promote doctoral degree attainment for African American males in counselor education programs. *Journal of African American Males in Education, 12*(1). Males in Education, *11*(2), 7–11.

Masten, A. S., Coatsworth, J. D., Neemann, J., Gest, S. D., Tellegen, A., & Garmezy, N. (1995). The structure and coherence of competence from childhood through adolescence. *Child Development, 66*, 1635–1659.

Music, G. (2016). *Nurturing natures: Attachment and children's emotional, sociocultural and brain development.* Routledge.

National Science Board. (2022). *Science and engineering indicators 2022.* National Science Foundation.

Nichols, A. H., & Evans-Bell, D. (2017). A look at Black student success: Identifying top-and bottom-performing institutions. *Journal of Counseling and Development, 73*(3), 279.

Oliver, K. B., Jr., Nadamuni, M. V., Ahn, C., Nivet, M., Cryer, B., & Okorodudu, D. O. (2020). Mentoring black men in medicine. *Academic Medicine, 95*(12S), S77–S81.

Owens, D., Lacey, K., Rawls, G., & Holbert- Quince, J. (2010). First-generation African American male college students: Implications for career counselors. *The Career Development Quarterly, 58*(4), 291–300.

Pager, D. (2003). The mark of a criminal record. *American Journal of Sociology, 108*(5), 937–975. https://doi.org/10.1086/374403

Pager, D., Western, B., & Sugie, N. (2009). Sequencing disadvantage: Barriers to employment facing young black and white men with criminal records. *The Annals of the American Academy of Political and Social Science, 623*(1), 195–213.

Paradies, Y. (2006). A systematic review of empirical research on self-reported racism and health. *International Journal of Epidemiology, 35*, 888–901. https://doi.org/10.1093/ije/dyl056

Parker, K., & Funk, C. (2018, January 1). *Women and men in stem often at odds over workplace equity: Perceived inequities are especially common among women in science, technology, engineering, and math jobs who work mostly men.* http://hdl.handle.net/10919/92671

Patitu, C. L. (2000). College choice and satisfaction level of African American male college students. *Journal of African American Men*, 71–92.

Pitcan, M., Park-Taylor, J., & Hayslett, J. (2018). Black men and racial microaggressions work. *The Career Development Quarterly, 66*(4), 300-314. https://doi.org/10.1002/cdq.12152

Poon, O. (2014). "The land of opportunity doesn't apply to everyone": The immigrant experience, race, and Asian American career choices. *Journal of College Student Development, 55*(6), 499–514.

Proctor, S. D., & Johnston, G. S. (1978). The significance of education for Blacks. In *Beyond desegregation: Urgent issues in the education of minorities* (pp. 64–67). College Entrance Examination Board. Psychology. *The Career Development Quarterly, 66*(2), 162–175.

Ramadhani, E., Jannah, A. T., & Putri, R. D. (2020). Analysis of Holland theory career guidance in student career planning. *ENLIGHTEN: Jurnal Bimbingan Konseling Islam, 3*(1), 19–25. https://www.canr.msu.edu/news/george-washington-carvers-

Reid, J. A., Romans, J. S., & Koch, J. M. (2014). Job stress and acculturation strategies in African-American professionals. *Western Journal of Black Studies, 38*(1), 24–34.

Rutledge, M. L., & Gnilka, P. B. (2022). Breaking down barriers: A culturally responsive career development intervention with racially minoritized girls of color. *Journal of College Access*, *7*(1), 7.

Sakamoto, A., Tamborini, C. R., & Kim, C. (2018). Long-term earnings differentials between African American and white men by educational level. *Population Research and Policy Review*, *37*(1), 91–116.

Samuel, A. (2017, February 21). Meet Alan Emtage, the Black technologist who invented ARCHIE, the first internet search engine. https://daily.jstor.org/alan-emtage-first-internet-search-engine/

Sandborn, D. (2019, February 19). *George Washington Carver's contributions to agriculture in the US*. https://www.canr.msu.edu/news/george-washington-carvers-contributions-to-agriculture-in-the-us

Savickas, M. L. (2002). Career construction. A developmental theory. In D. Brown & Associates (Eds.), *Career choice and development* (4th ed., pp. 149–206). Jossey-Bass.

Savickas, M. L. (2011). *Career counseling*. American Psychological Association.

Savickas. (2012). Life design: A paradigm for career intervention in the 21st century. *Journal of Counseling and Development*, *90*(1), 13–19.

Scott, L., & Sharp, L. A. (2019). Black males who hold advanced degrees: Critical factors that preclude and promote success. *The Journal of Negro Education*, *88*(1), 44–61.

Shackelford, S., & Denzel, B. (2021). *You on purpose: Discover your calling and create the life you were meant to live*. Baker Books.

Sharf, R. S. (2013). *Applying career development theory to counseling*. Cengage.

Smith, L., & Bowman, E. (2021, September 17). *Their dad transformed video games in the 1970s – And passed on his pioneering spirit*. NPR. https://www.npr.org/2021/09/17/1037911107/jerry-lawson-video-game-fairchild-channel-f-black-engineer

Smith, W. A., Hung, M., & Franklin, J. D. (2011). Racial battle fatigue and the miseducation of Black men: Racial microaggressions, societal problems, and environmental stress. *The Journal of Negro Education*, 63–82.

Sparkman, T. E. (2021). Black male executives in higher education: The experience of ascending the academic leadership ladder. *Advances in Developing Human Resources*, *23*(4), 277–299.

Steele, C. M., & Aronson, J. (1995). Stereotype threat and intellectual test performance of African Americans. *Journal of Personality and Social Psychology*, *69*(5), 797–811.

Steger, M. F., Frazier, P., Oishi, S., & Kaler, M. (2006). The meaning in life questionnaire: Assessing the presence of and search for meaning in life. *Journal of Counseling Psychology*, *53*.

Strayhorn, T. L. (2015). Factors influencing Black males' preparation for college and success in STEM majors: A mixed methods study. *Western Journal of Black Studies*, *39*(1), 45.

Stringer, K., Kerpelman, J., & Skorikov, V. (2012). A longitudinal examination of career preparation and adjustment during the transition from high school. *Developmental Psychology*, *48*, 1343–1354.

Swanson, J. L., & Schneider, M. (2013). Minnesota theory of work adjustment. In *Career development and counseling: Putting theory and research to work* (pp. 29–53).

Tang, M., Fouad, N. A., & Smith, P. L. (1999). Asian Americans' career choices: A path model to examine factors influencing their career choices. *Journal of Vocational Behavior*, *54*, 142–157.

Taylor, E., Guy-Walls, P., Wilkerson, P., & Addae, R. (2019). The historical perspectives of stereotypes on African-American males. *Journal of Human Rights and Social Work*, *4*, 213–225.

U.S. Bureau of Labor Statistics. (2023, January 1). *Composition of the labor force*. U.S. Bureau of Labor Statistics. https://www.bls.gov/opub/reports/race-and-ethnicity/2021/home.htm. Accessed on January 14, 2023.

Wanelik, K. M., Griffin, J. S., Head, M. L., Ingleby, F. C., & Lewis, Z. (2020). Breaking barriers? Ethnicity and socioeconomic background impact on early career progression in the fields of ecology and evolution. *Ecology and Evolution*, *10*(14), 6870–6880.

Williams, J. M., Wilson, S. K., & Bergeson, C. (2019). "It's hard out here if you are a black Felon". A critical examination of black male reentry. *The Prison Journal*, *99*(4), 437–458. https://10.1177/0032885519852088

CHAPTER 19

ENGAGING BLACK COLLEGE MEN'S LEADERSHIP IDENTITY, CAPACITY, AND EFFICACY THROUGH LIBERATORY PEDAGOGY

Darius A. Robinson, Johnnie Allen Jr. and Cameron C. Beatty

ABSTRACT

This chapter will highlight the process of engaging Black college men in leadership learning by centering their intersecting identities. We employed liberatory pedagogy through an anti-deficit achievement framework for course design and delivery. The chapter addresses the importance and implications of understanding how engaging with same-race and same-gendered peers in formal leadership curricula can support Black men in continuing to develop their leadership identity, capacity, and efficacy. This chapter will end with key course outcomes, pedagogical methods to center identity and build leadership capacity, and key takeaways for leadership educators developing courses that engage Black college men. This chapter concludes with recommendations for research, policy, and practice and offers reflection questions for educators, advisors, and mentors to consider when designing curricula that center on Black men and their leadership learning.

Keywords: Black men; college; liberatory pedagogy; race; identity; leadership

Black Males in Secondary and Postsecondary Education
Advances in Race and Ethnicity in Education, Volume 9, 341–354
Copyright © 2024 Darius A. Robinson, Johnnie Allen Jr. and Cameron C. Beatty
Published under exclusive licence by Emerald Publishing Limited
ISSN: 2051-2317/doi:10.1108/S2051-231720230000009019

Within leadership education and curriculum, Black male leadership (BML) continues to be an under-discussed topic. One critical component that Black males need to engage in the leadership process is their sense of belongingness in higher education institutions. Strayhorn (2008) notes that supportive relationships with peers, faculty, and staff are critical to this sense of belonging and overall satisfaction at college. These supportive relationships help Black male leaders examine their leadership identity, capacity, and efficacy in constructed environments that validate their experiences (Beatty et al., 2010; Guthrie et al., 2021). However, at predominantly white institutions (PWI), Black males who engage in the leadership process have shown the inability to fully express themselves and have their abilities challenged regularly, which is not seen in their majoritarian peers (Harper et al., 2011). If these environments are not supportive and see their experiences reflected equitably, Black males may feel less inclined to engage. Ultimately, to fully understand and engage in the leadership process, consideration must be given to the social environment and how conducive it is to their values and the impact that they want to make on campus (Beatty et al., 2010; Beatty & Ford, 2023).

This chapter will highlight the process of engaging Black college men in leadership learning by centering their identity. We employed an anti deficit framework (Harper, 2006) within pedagogy and course design. This chapter will address the importance and implications of understanding how engaging with same-race and same-gendered peers in formal leadership curricula can support Black men in continuing to develop their leadership identity, capacity, and efficacy. This chapter highlights key course outcomes and pedagogical methods to center identity and build leadership capacity and efficacy and shares key takeaways for leadership educators developing courses that engage Black college men.

CULTURALLY RELEVANT LEADERSHIP LEARNING (CRLL)

A possible framework to engage Black college men that can be a tool for leadership educators is the CRLL model (Bertrand Jones et al., 2016). CRLL transforms leadership programs to consider how difference creates advantages and disadvantages through two dimensions. First, it recognizes that current leadership learning practices and theories reinforce majoritarian ideals and do not recognize the lived experiences of marginalized individuals. By recognizing this, CRLL centers on the lived experiences of all individuals and how these individuals utilize their experience to understand their leadership identity, capacity, and efficacy (Bertrand Jones et al., 2016; Guthrie et al., 2021). The framework is grounded in culturally relevant pedagogy, which calls for educators to utilize an asset-based approach to empower students in the classroom (Ladson-Billings, 2014).

The CRLL model examines how leadership identity, capacity, and efficacy support students when engaging in the leadership process. Leadership identity recognizes that students discover their identities through cultural contexts, addressing the question "Who am I?" (Guthrie et al., 2021). Capacity recognizes students' ability to the activity of leadership and "the knowledge, skills, and attitudes" developed in leadership learning (Guthrie et al., 2021, p. 33). Lastly, efficacy is the belief that students have in their ability to compete within the leadership process. Within the leadership learning process, CRLL examines their intersections through five critical domains: the historical legacy of inclusion/exclusion, compositional diversity, and behavioral, organizational/structural, and psychological dimensions (Bertrand Jones et al., 2016, p. 16).

FIVE CRITICAL DIMENSIONS TO CONSIDER

Within organizational culture (whatever organization you might be a part of), CRLL takes into consideration five critical dimensions which include: (a) historical legacy of inclusion and exclusion, (b) compositional diversity, (c) psychological climate, (d) behavioral climate, and (e) organizational/structural aspects (Bertrand Jones et al., 2016). The historical legacy of inclusion and exclusion forces us to think about who has traditionally participated in your organization and how they have engaged in the leadership process. What does the history of your organization tell you? Compositional diversity represents the proportion of various populations represented in your organization, as leaders and followers. Who shows up to engage in your organization? The psychological dimension emphasizes attitudes about difference, perceptions of discrimination, and individual views of group relations in your organization. What do individuals (both leaders and followers) think about the health of the group overall? Interactions and the quality of interaction across differences in your organization is the behavioral dimension. How do people act in your organization, especially while engaging in the leadership process? Finally, the organizational/structural dimension focuses on what processes guide the operation of your organization. What do your policies and overall structure reveal about your organization?

Our development, learning, and growth are all directly impacted by the environments and cultures we are a part of. CRLL recognizes how outside factors affect the conditions for developing leadership. The five categories of culturally relevant leadership learning are intended to inspire and equip each of us on our leadership learning journey to think critically about the value of our unique experiences and our participation in the leadership learning environment. Approaching CRLL through a liberatory pedagogy lens allows educators to critically interrogate the environment learning is happening to disrupt and dismantle oppressive learning spaces.

WHAT IS LIBERATORY PEDAGOGY?

The goal of liberatory pedagogy is to provide a lens through which educators are more capable of examining, interacting with, and critiquing the politics of education (Sayles-Hannon, 2007). Liberatory pedagogy, which has roots in critical pedagogy (Freire, 1970; Giroux, 2006), refers to "educational theories and practices intended to raise learners' critical consciousness concerning oppressive social conditions" (Sayles-Hannon, 2007, p. 34). In critical pedagogy, students and educators reflect on structures of power and use the classroom as a place for the exchange of knowledge, in contrast to the "banking" style of teaching (Freire, 1998, p. 33). Freire's critical pedagogy continues to ask questions about the relationships between theory/practice and reflection/action as we consider power in our social institutions.

Liberatory pedagogy challenges educators, students, and administrators to recognize, engage, and critically examine undemocratic practices and institutions that maintain inequality and oppressive identities (Sayles-Hannon, 2007). This method promotes the development of educational practices that encourage educators and students to critically examine and identify relationships of power, ideology, and culture, and then how this critical investigation can then inform praxis. To examine the diverse histories and perceptions of race, class, gender, ethnicity, sexuality, and nationality, it is intrinsic that both the students' and educators' voices be heard. By engaging both the students' and faculty members' voices in classroom discussions, educators can unchain themselves from traditional relationship restraints with students. By centering multiple voices and deconstructing the power dynamics in the classroom, new relationships are forged through engaging dialog that moves toward liberation (Sayles-Hannon, 2007).

ANTI-DEFICIT FRAMEWORK AS A PEDAGOGICAL PRACTICE

At all levels of the educational system, Black males are the subject of deficit models and negative narratives (Ingram, 2013; Warren, 2016). Black boys are disproportionately overrepresented in dropout rates, expulsion, suspension, and remedial education in K–12 schooling (Zilanawala et al., 2017). The literature demonstrates how racial and gender stereotypes about anger and violence frequently affect Black males in primary school (Carter Andrews, 2016; Griffin, 2002; Irving & Hudley, 2008). As these students struggle with seeming menacing in unwelcoming school contexts, these misconceptions frequently result in racial prejudice at a young age. Racial battle fatigue in K–12 education is a problem for many Black men because of the unfavorable messages connected to feeling alone by educators, peers, and administrators (Griffin, 2002; Irving & Hudley, 2008). These emotions are frequently duplicated in racially charged interactions, and they persist into postsecondary and graduate study for students (Harper et al., 2011; Ingram, 2013; Warren, 2016). Additionally, research on Black males in the K–12 education that is deficit-informed contributes to the narrative about subpar academic achievement and risky behaviors (Hines & Holcomb-McCoy, 2013; Warren, 2016). The experiences of Black men historically "lag behind every other demographic in academic achievement and success" (Cuyjet, 2006, p. viii). As a result, we educators, mentors, and advisors must reframe this thinking from a deficit lens to an anti-deficit lens (Harper, 2009). We acknowledge and appreciate the foundational work of Black scholarship on Black men in higher education, like Dr Cuyjet (2006), but we urge educators, mentors, and advisors to reframe the discourse regarding how Black men enter, engage, and construct leadership identities in college (Beatty & Ford, 2023). Cuyjet (2006) recognized the popularity of Black student research and the growing desire to make the "campus environment more comfortable and nurturing for students" (p. ix). However, engaging Black men is essential to disrupting the inequities that plague historically white postsecondary institutions. Black men's experiences are continuously changing, evolving, and repositioning. Leadership learning and education is one avenue to disrupt deficit thinking and center Black men's identity, experiences, and efficacies for engaging in the leadership process (Beatty & Ford, 2023).

A BLACK MALE LEADERSHIP (BML) COURSE EXAMPLE

The development of the BML conceptual framework roots back to curricular engagement of Black males. One of the most powerful ways to engage Black men is through the use of identity-based courses. Spencer (2018) advocates for these types of courses to allow Black men communal spaces to investigate their identities, capacities, and efficacies while also incorporating the CRLL framework. For educators, it also provides them a space to engage in critical leadership pedagogy, teaching leadership from a critical lens of Western society (Pendakur & Furr, 2016). It is through the use of courses that the Black male experience is both provided a voice in academia and given room to learn leadership with other Black males.

A course that follows Spencer's (2018) push for the actualization of identity-based courses is one taught at Florida State University called "Black Male Leadership.". The course is housed within the Leadership Learning Research Center's (LLRC) undergraduate leadership certificate program. The course is an elective that students can take for three credits toward the program. Class sizes are limited to no more than 18 students to make sure that an intentional community of leaders is being developed while maintaining high engagement between instructors and students. While the class is not exclusively for Black males due to Florida Board of Education limitations, this group of students makes up the majority of the participants.

Course Description

The course introduces the study of Black males and their enactment of leadership from historical and contemporary perspectives. The course itself is divided into themes based on content and built to scaffold from the previous theme. For the first 4 weeks, students engage with their own leadership identity, capacity, and efficacy. During the 4 weeks, students build up a sense of Black identity by learning about US history concerning Blackness, especially from a Black male perspective. The third set of weeks focuses on bringing in what is masculinity and how Black males think about it from personal and professional contexts. The final segment weaves the three previous themes together to show how Black males enact leadership today and what this leadership means in today's society. Throughout the entirety of the course, the various Black male perspectives – perceptions, images, realities, myths, and narratives – are weaved in and critically examined to heighten their awareness to students. In addition to the themes, topics addressed in the course include allyship, LGB+, feminism, corporate America, and inclusive leadership theories.

Learning Outcomes

As a result of engaging in the class, students should be able to:

(1) Discuss personal leadership development through active reflection, critical self-evaluation, and leadership theory analysis;
(2) Identify, interpret, present, and analyze empirical theories concerning leadership and Black male issues in the United States;
(3) Demonstrate awareness and sensitivity to the sociopolitical nature of American society, as it relates to Black men, and how leadership influences it;
(4) Identify the impact of social, political, educational, religious, and civic institutions and their subsequent impact on Black males in the United States, especially BML;
(5) Analyze the human experience of Black males from multiple lenses, specifically in the framework of leadership;
(6) Explore one's own cultural norms or values of BML with those of a different cultural group.

Assignments and Learning Assessments

Built upon culturally relevant pedagogy, critical leadership pedagogy, and socially just leadership learning, the assignments in the BML course are developed to maximize student reflection on their thoughts about BML in the world today. The courses scaffold the themes and the student engagement, each building off the work of previous assignments. Students not only get a chance to learn more about themselves in relation to BML but also get to show their class community how Black male leadership is integral in making a diverse, equitable, and inclusive world.

Reading Journals. Done throughout the semester, the reading journals provide students an opportunity to reflect on what they are learning in class. Each journal has a different prompt where students provide a 250-word response. This prompt pushes students to reflect, tie their learning into their cocurricular experiences, and engage with the instructor on an informal level.

Reflection Paper. In the leadership identity-capacity-efficacy-themed section of the course, students engage in a true colors in-class activity facilitated by the instructor. After discovering their color and actionizing it through activities, students create a 3-page paper discussing their views on leadership. The paper needs to discuss the student's understanding of leadership, how they have developed their leadership in college, and provide examples to showcase both.

Personal Leadership Philosophy. Within the second section of the course, students will have an opportunity to expand further on their leadership philosophy from the first paper. Within the 5-page paper, students discuss their own leadership ideology and flow, including stating their philosophy and the influences behind it. They also need to provide examples to support their philosophy.

Black Male Leader Book Club. Students are introduced to four different books that focus specifically on a Black male to connect their knowledge of leadership identity, capacity, and efficacy as it relates to BML. Students rank their book preferences and are placed evenly into four groups to complete the assignment. By this phase of the semester, students have gained enough knowledge to engage critically in the book club assignment. The book club assignment has two major parts: Firstly, the group 45- to 50-minute class facilitation, including core insights from the book, course materials and theories, and class engagement activities. Secondly, the book club ends with a 1- to 2-page reflection paper. Each book hones in on a variety of different course topics, such as masculinity, BML, leadership identity, capacity and efficacy, and Black identity development.

Black Male Leader Interview Podcast. The concluding assignment is a developmental opportunity for students to showcase their knowledge from the semester in a creative and personalized format. Students are tasked with completing a podcast interview with a Black male leader. Their interpretation of a Black male leader stems from course readings, class discussions, and assignments to build a definition that guides their choice of who to interview. The podcast should be between 15- to 20-minutes long and follow a list of interview questions that get to the essence of Black male leadership and how conceptually it looks different based on the individual. Prior to the interview, students are required to send a list of interview questions to the professor and current teaching assistant(s) to receive approval. After completing the interview, students present to the entire class no longer than a 5-minute clip of their podcast highlighting a key conversation during the interview or a specific connection to topics covered throughout the semester. Lastly, students listen to their peer's podcasts in small groups and provide feedback and complete a final 1- to 2-page reflection paper about their experience.

Leadership Identity Course Outcomes

Students enrolled in the BML course are provided opportunities to discover their leadership identity. This happens by using course reflection papers, assignments, and personal leadership philosophy to unpack the multiple layers of one's own identity and how their identity(ies) influences their leadership engagement. Guthrie et al. (2021) offer leadership educators and learners with knowledge on how to begin the process of leadership identity discovery. Through the BML course, students can analyze and evaluate how they come to understand leader, leadership, and leadership identity. Critical self-reflection is embedded in course assignments to encourage new ways of thinking about individual social identities because social identities influence leadership. Each reflection paper offers guiding questions that position students to gauge their leadership identity development over the course of the semester. The overall outcome of the reflection papers is to ensure that each student leaves the class with a deeper understanding of BML and how an increased awareness of BML can guide their leadership identity journey. Additionally, leadership identity is important as the hope is that students' leadership philosophy is constantly evaluated as new knowledge can enhance beliefs, values, personality, and assumptions of leadership. The BML course is a space and opportunity to engage in reflection that is often overlooked in other courses throughout the student's college experience. Therefore, the BML class is an environment that offers liberation to promote leadership identity development and discovery.

Leadership Capacity Course Outcomes

Within the course, the leadership capacity of the students is built upon strongly. There are various opportunities for them to engage with their leadership capacity within multiple assignments, such as the reflection assignment. However, more rigorous assignments push both individual and collective leadership capacities of the students. The knowledge, skills, and attitudes of individual students get impacted through various contexts (Beatty & Guthrie, 2021). These two capacities reflect an interrelated nature that connects back with the intention of leadership education to develop collectivist, collaborative environments.

One of the rigorous assignments of the course was a course book club. For the assignment, the students are organized into groups to provide a discussion on an autobiographical book written by a Black male leader. In the present, discussion leads are expected to discuss their book, focusing on book themes and their connection to course content. They are also expected to discuss their own sense of leadership identity, capacity, and efficacy in relation to the book material.

Throughout multiple points in the assignment, the course pushes students to engage strongly in their individual and collective capacity. By situating the book club in a group format, students are provided reflective opportunities in consultation with their peers to see what skills and knowledge on how to break up the assignment. During the discussion portion of the book club, leadership capacity is also seen in how the students divide up how they will address the book at each step of the assignment. Based on their assigned portion of the discussion, the students organize themselves and utilize strategic thinking to decide who will take which portion based on their individual and collective knowledge of the book and public speaking abilities. Each portion of the assignment not only brings together the complex leader and leadership identities but also how to maximize the capacities of each person based upon their identities, knowledge, skills, and attitudes. It is through assignments such as the book club that BML develops a community where liberatory practices to engage their capacities among peers who share a similar identity to them.

Leadership Efficacy Course Outcomes

Engaging in BML courses offers students intentional opportunities to enhance their leadership efficacy through critical self-reflection and socially just leadership knowledge and practices regarding BML. Spencer et al. (2023) note the importance of including diverse voices in academic spaces that have historically and traditionally not been centered. Bringing these voices and perspectives to the front of the classroom allows students, especially Black men, Black women, and students of other racial and ethnic identities, to grow in their leadership efficacy. Learning from someone who has the same or similar salient identities shifts their perspective and belief of who and what a leader is. One key assignment of the BML course that brings diverse voices and perspectives to the classroom is the Black male leader podcast interview. The Black male leader podcast assignment provides students the opportunity to use their definition of BML in conjunction with course readings, lectures, and discussions to choose a Black male leader best fitted to complete their assignment. In the interview, students develop a range of questions focused on the course learning outcomes of identity, capacity, and efficacy, Black identity, masculinity, and BML. The overall goal of the assignment is to allow students to display their competence and knowledge of course content to critically engage in dialog with a Black male leader. The podcast interview is reflective of students' leadership efficacy, both self and collective efficacy. Guthrie et al. (2021) outline the importance of distinguishing the difference between leadership self-efficacy and self-confidence to ensure that individuals engaging in the leadership process do not confuse the two. Self-efficacy "is a personal belief in your ability to be successful with a specific task or process" (Guthrie et al., 2021, p. 51). Additionally, collective efficacy is described "as a concept and process, that provides critical hope in responding to inequitable systems and institutional practices" (Guthrie et al., 2021, p. 53). The podcast interview challenges students to rely on the knowledge gained from the course to develop a final project that highlights BML, using that experience to influence their leadership efficacy in curricular and cocurricular environments. Through the knowledge gained from the podcast assignment, students can take those experiences with them to enhance their leadership self and collective efficacy to enact social change in higher education, organizations, and communities. Understanding the complex experiences of Black men and leadership is a way to contribute to asset-based perspectives and knowledge regarding BML through liberatory pedagogy practices.

RECOMMENDATIONS FOR RESEARCH, POLICY, AND PRACTICE

In the Recommendations for Future Research , we encourage you to focus on the recommendations offered, and we challenge educators, mentors, advisors, and individuals involved in the leadership learning process to implement culturally relevant leadership and leadership learning opportunities specific to Black men in higher education. The leadership development of Black men varies due to different identities and backgrounds of Black men as their intersecting social identities, environment and institution type, functional area involvement, and unique situations all influence how leadership and leadership learning opportunities are designed. Using the CRLL model, leadership educators can integrate recommendations for research, policy, and practice to further the advancement of Black men in higher education as the model is centered on identity, capacity, efficacy, and context.

Recommendations for Future Research

Future research and conceptual frameworks could employ new anti-deficit models to better understand the experiences of Black males in college settings. One model to consider is Ford's (2020) Identity Responsive Early Career Socialization Model (IRECS). To encourage, socialize, and holistically develop Black males in their leadership development journey, we sent this model as a call to action for higher education and leadership educators. The process by which people "acquire the knowledge, abilities, and dispositions that make them more or less effective members of their society" is known as socialization (Weidman et al., 2001, p. 4). This socialization process, which differs from that of white students, ignores the identities, cultural origins, and familial upbringing that students of color had before enrolling in educational environments (McCoy & Winkle-Wagner, 2015). IRECS places identity at the core of Black men's educational experiences. While identity remains a critical part of Black men's experiences, Griffith and Ford (2022) highlight leadership as a critical part of the professional development experiences of Black students. Building on their findings, we add that as Black men continue to navigate leadership experiences on college campuses, we are assisting their professional development and, subsequently, their early career socialization and success during and beyond college. In addition, IRECS situates mentoring and academic preparation along with professional development (leadership experiences) as the central elements of their experiences.

Recommendations for Policy

Recommendations for policy and leadership learning for Black men centers on community. This form of leadership relies on the concept of Umoja, or unity, one of the core principles of Kwanzaa (Wallace & Smith, 2023). It is necessary for Black men's leadership learning to engage in community (Burt et al., 2019). Community includes blood and chosen family, as well as cultural kinship with other Black people (Yosso, 2005). On a college campus, this community may include Black students, Black faculty, Black staff and administrators, or members of the Black community which surrounds the institution. In the vignette, Darius carries leadership lessons from his grandmother and his undergraduate mentor. These "pedagogies of the home" (Delgado Bernal, 2002, p. 109) and like-identity mentorship opportunities assist people of color in navigating spaces not created with them in mind (i.e., HWIs; Tolliver & Miller, 2018). Black graduate men must reject the individualistic and competitive nature of graduate education in the UnitedStates and seek to pursue collectivism as a means of survival and leadership learning. Jerome Morris (2004) discussed Black social capital referencing the network that Black people use to traverse and survive systems of racism and discrimination. For Black men, community-oriented leadership can result in a greater sense of inclusion and purpose in graduate education (McGaskey et al., 2016). How can community policies create more opportunities for Black men to engage in the leadership process?

Community-oriented leadership may take the form of study groups/ partnerships, Black social groups, and connections with community organizations and programs (Johnson-Bailey et al., 2008; Scott & Sharp, 2019). This aspect of leadership may also provide the opportunity to resist the dominant narrative of "networking up" and elevate opportunities to network with Black peers, Black undergraduates, and Black staff members in service and administrative roles (e.g., housekeeping staff, groundskeeping staff, administrative assistants). It is these community aspects where Black graduate men can cultivate their leadership and find reprieve in predominantly white spaces. Finally, this aspect of leadership for Black men underscores the importance of interaction with Black people of other genders, namely Black women. Learning from, and being in community with, Black women are critical to the personal growth and academic persistence of Black graduate men (Grimes, 2018). How our community programs build and cultivate supportive and nonharmful spaces where Black men can learn from and interact with others, both cisgender and transgender and Black nonbinary people? Local community leaders must foster the community-oriented aspects of leadership learning for Black men and implement policies for opportunities like this to be cultivated (Wallace & Smith, 2023).

Recommendations for Practice

Emerging research demonstrates that informal and formal mentoring have significant effects on Black men (Brooms & Davis, 2017; Harper, 2006, 2012; Harper & Wood, 2016; Hines & Holcomb-McCoy, 2013). It has been established that the duration and frequency of these interactions have a significant effect on motivation, encouragement, commitment, and degree completion (Harper, 2006; McGowan, 2017). Pedagogy paired with experiential learning that centers mentoring for Black men is one recommendation for practice that we offer. In relation to Black men, mentoring remains a positively influenced method for providing the necessary assistance to overcome barriers that impede many Black men from earning a degree. Moreover, Pang and Gibson (2001) asserted, "Black educators are far more than physical role models, and they bring diverse family histories, value orientations, and experiences to students... attributes often not found in textbooks or viewpoints often omitted" (pp. 260–261), which is also valuable for understanding Black men experiences with leadership.

Mentoring is crucial to the survival and success of Black men in higher education environments (LaVant et al., 1997), but Black men experience isolation on college campuses due to the paucity of Black men (Lynn, 2006). This isolation exacerbates the difficulty of forming relationships, as Black men frequently lack individuals who can relate to and grasp their constant struggle in society. Brooms and team (2021) found that Black men being mentored and engaging in leadership practices "advanced and expanded their leadership capital, a new form of cultural capital, which can be understood as cultural knowledge developed within leadership roles and experiences" (p. 225). This scholarship creates a bridge between Black men's leadership experiences and the influence of mentoring on their development, a connection that must be further considered and investigated as we rethink and reimagine leadership for Black college men.

CONCLUSION FOR NEW DIRECTIONS FOR ENGAGING BLACK IN LIBERATORY LEARNING SPACES

Beatty and Ford (2023) offer questions to reflect on when engaging Black men in leadership learning. As a result of historical and social factors that influenced higher education and, subsequently, Black men in America, we reframe the questions offered by Beatty and Ford (2023) and offer the following questions to consider the historical and present-day contextual underpinnings of Black men in leadership learning in higher education teaching, mentoring, and advising.

Reflective Questions for Teaching, Mentoring, and Advising Black Men on Your Campus

(1) What influence has history had on your campus' perceptions of Black men?
(2) What campus politics and what campus sociocultural and historical issues continue to shape the experiences of Black men?
(3) How do Black men currently engage outside of the classroom in your context?
(4) How are Black men engaging in leadership meaning making in your context?

Self-Reflective Questions for Teaching, Mentoring, and Advising Black Men in Leadership on Campus

(1) How do you, as an educator, mentor, and advisor, foster leadership learning for Black men in your context?
(2) How do you see your own leadership experiences guiding your current leadership learning engagement with Black men?
(3) What role do you play in perpetuating barriers for engaging Black men in leadership learning in your context?

REFERENCES

Beatty, C. C., Bush, A. A., Erxleben, E. E., Ferguson, T. L., Harrell, A. T., & Sahachartsiri, W. K. (2010). Black Student Leaders: The Influence of Social Climate in Student Organizations. *Journal of the Student Personnel Association at Indiana University*, 48–63.

Beatty, C. C., & Ford, J. R. (2023). *Engaging black men in college through leadership learning.* Information Age Publishing, Inc.

Beatty, C. C., & Guthrie, K. L. (2021). *Operationalizing culturally relevant leadership learning.* Information Age Publishing, Inc.

Bernal, D. D. (2002). Critical race theory, Latino critical theory, and critical raced-gendered episte-mologies: Recognizing students of color as holders and creators of knowledge. *Qualitative inquiry, 8*(1), 105–126.

Bertrand Jones, T., Guthrie, K. L., & Osteen, L. (2016). Critical domains of culturally relevant leadership learning: A call to transform leadership programs. In K. L. Guthrie, T. Bertrand Jones, & L. Osteen (Eds.), *New Directions for Student Leadership: No. 152. Developing culturally relevant leadership learning* (pp. 9–21). Jossey-Bass.

Brooms, D. R., & Davis, A. R. (2017). Staying focused on the goal: Peer bonding and faculty mentors supporting Black males' persistence in college. *Journal of Black Studies, 48*(3), 305–326. https://doi.org/10.1177/0021934717692520

Burt, B. A., Williams, K. L., & Palmer, G. J. (2019). It takes a village: The role of emic and etic adaptive strengths in the persistence of Black men in engineering graduate programs. *American Educational Research Journal, 56*(1), 39–74.

Carter Andrews, D. J. (2016). Black boys in middle school: Toward first-class citizenship in a first-class society. In S. R. Harper & J. Luke Wood (Eds.), *Advancing Black male student success from preschool through PhD* (pp. 45–60). Stylus Publishing.

Cuyjet. (2006). *African American men in college* (1st ed.). Jossey-Bass.

Ford, J. (2020). *In the Trenches: Black men in the academy navigating racialized encounters.* Doctoral dissertation, The Florida State University.

Freire, P. (1970). *Pedagogy of the oppressed.* Continuum.

Freire, P. (1998). *Pedagogy of freedom: Ethics, democracy, and civic courage.* Rowman & Littleman Publishers, Inc.

Giroux, H. A. (2006). *The Giroux reader.* Paradigm Publishers.

Griffin, B. W. (2002). Academic disidentification, race, and high school dropouts. *The High School Journal, 85*(4), 71–81.

Griffith, T. O., & Ford, J. R. (2022). Say her name: The socialization of Black women in graduate school. *Journal of Student Affairs Research and Practice*, 1–14. https://doi.org/10.1080/19496591.2022.2042006

Grimes, J. (2018). *Motivating factors impacting Black men's pursuit of a doctoral degree in education* [Doctoral dissertation, The University of Georgia]. ProQuest Dissertation Publishing.

Guthrie, K. L., Beatty, C. C., & Wiborg, E. R. (2021). *Engaging in the leadership process: Identity, capacity, and efficacy for college students* (Ser. Contemporary Perspectives on Leadership Learning). Information Age Publishing, Incorporated.

Harper, S. R. (2006). *Black male students at public flagship universities in the U.S.: Status, trends and implications for policy and practice.* Joint Center for Political and Economic Studies.

Harper, S. R. (2009). Niggers no more: A critical race counternarrative on Black male student achievement at predominantly White colleges and universities. *International Journal of Quali-tative Studies in Education, 22*(6), 697–712.

Harper, S. R. (2012). *Black male student success in higher education: A report from the National Black Male College Achievement Study.* University of Pennsylvania, Center for the Study of Race and Equity in Education.

Harper, S. R., Davis, R. J., Jones, D. E., McGowan, B. L., Ingram, T. N., & Platt, C. S. (2011). Race and racism in the experiences of Black male resident assistants at predominantly White uni-versities. *Journal of College Student Development, 52*(2), 180–200. https://doi.org/10.1353/csd.2011.0025

Harper, S. R., & Wood. (2016). *Advancing Black male student success from preschool through Ph.D.* Stylus.

Hines, E. M., & Holcomb-McCoy, C. (2013). Parental characteristics, ecological factors and the academic achievement of African American males. *Journal of Counseling and Development, 91*(1), 68–77. https://doi.org/10.1002/j.1556-6676.2013.00073.x

Ingram, T. N. (2013). Fighting FAIR (Feelings of Alienation, Isolation, and Racism): Using critical race theory to deconstruct the experiences of African American male doctoral students. *Journal of Progressive Policy & Practice*, *1*(1), 1–18.

Irving, M. A., & Hudley, C. (2008). Cultural identification and academic achievement among African American males. *Journal of Advanced Academics*, *19*(4), 676–698.

Johnson-Bailey, J., & Cervero, R. (2008). Different worlds and divergent paths: Academic careers defined by race and gender. *Harvard Educational Review*, *78*(2), 311–332.

Ladson-Billings, G. J. (2014). *Culturally Relevant Pedagogy 2.0: A.k.a. the Remix*. https://doi.org/10.17763/HAER.84.1.P2RJ131485484751

LaVant, B. D., Anderson, J. L., & Tiggs, J. W. (1997). Retaining African American men through mentoring initiatives. *New Directions for Student Services*, *80*, 43–53.

Lynn, M. (2006). Education for the community: Exploring the culturally relevant practices of Black male teachers. *Teachers College Record*, *108*(12), 2497–2522.

McCoy, D. L., & Winkle-Wagner, R. (2015). Bridging the divide: Developing a scholarly habitus for aspiring graduate students through summer bridge programs participation. *Journal of College Student Development*, *56*(5), 423–439. https://doi.org/10.1353/csd.2015.0054

McGaskey, F. G., Freeman, S., Jr., Guyton-Middle, C., Richmond, D., & Guyton, C. W. (2016). The social support networks of Black males in higher education administration doctoral programs: An exploratory study. *Western Journal of Black Studies*, *40*(2), 141–158.

McGowan, B. L. (2017). Visualizing peer connections: The gendered realities of African American college men's interpersonal relationships. *Journal of College Student Development*, *58*(7), 983–1000.

Morris, J. (2004). Can anything good come from Nazareth? Race, class, and African-American schooling and community in the urban south and midwest. *American Educational Research Journal*, *41*(1), 69–112. https://doi.org/10.3102/00028312041001069

Pang, V. O., & Gibson, R. (2001). Concepts of democracy and citizenship: Views of African American teachers. *The Social Studies*, *92*(6), 260–266.

Pendakur, V., & Furr, S. C. (2016). Critical leadership pedagogy: Engaging power, identity, and culture in leadership education for college students of color. *New directions for higher education*, *2016*(174), 45–55.

Sayles-Hannon, S. J. (2007). Feminist and liberatory pedagogies: Journey toward synthesis. *International Journal of Diversity in Organizations, Communities, and Nations*, *7*(2), 33.

Scott, L., & Sharp, L. A. (2019). Black males who hold advanced degrees: Critical factors that preclude and promote success. *Journal of Negro Education*, *88*(1), 44–61.

Spencer, D. (2018). The world is yours: Cultivating Black male leadership learning. In K. L. Guthrie & V. S. Chunoo (Eds.), *Changing the narrative: Socially just leadership education* (Ser. Contemporary Perspectives in Leadership Learning, pp. 109–126). Information Age Publishing, Inc.

Spencer, D., Jr., Ford, J. R., & Bowden, B. (2023). Curricular leadership courses and assessments centering Black college men. In C. C. Beatty & J. R. Ford (Eds.), *Engaging Black Men in College Through Leadership Learning* (pp. 213–224). Information Age.

Strayhorn, T. L. (2008). The role of supportive relationships in facilitating African American males' success in college. *NASPA Journal*, *45*(1), 26–48.

Tolliver, D. V., & Miller, M. T. (2018). Graduation 101: Strategies for African American men college completion. *Education*, *138*(4), 301–308.

Wallace, J. K., & Smith, T (2023). Leadership beyond the undergraduate degree. In C. C. Beatty, & J. R. Ford (Eds.), *Engaging Black Men in College Through Leadership Learning* (pp. 201–210). Information Age.

Warren, C. A. (2016). Making relationships work: Elementary-age Black boys and the schools that serve them. In *Advancing Black Male Student Success From Preschool Through Ph. D.* (pp. 21–43). Routledge.

Weidman, J. C., Twale, D. J., & Stein, E. L. (2001). *Socialization of Graduate and Professional Students in Higher Education: A Perilous Passage? ASHE-ERIC Higher Education Report. Jossey-Bass Higher and Adult Education Series* (Vol. 28, Number 3). Jossey-Bass.

Yosso, T. J. (2005). Whose culture has capital? A critical race theory discussion of community cultural wealth. *Race ethnicity and education*, *8*(1), 69–91.

AFTERWORD: A CONCLUDING PERSPECTIVE

Communicated throughout the theoretical, scientific, and popular literature, the complex dynamics of Blackness and maleness are often viewed as a salient part of the educational identities and experiences of Black men and boys (Ford & Moore, 2013; Moore et al., 2021). This literature base frequently fails to examine the larger historical, systemic, and structural forces that often compromise their learning in formal and informal educational spaces. For many Black men and boys, everyday life is constrained by the American social hierarchy (Wint et al., 2022) in which whiteness and maleness are deemed as assets and superior and Blackness and maleness are synonymous with hardships, shortcomings, and liabilities. There is no denying that Black men and boys "occupy a significant space within the American psyche and imagination" (Noguera, 2008, p. xi). The negative image of Blackness and maleness – that saturate the American educational system – is bleak and widespread (Jackson & Moore, 2006, 2008; Moore et al., 2021). Regardless of socioeconomic status, there is a salient racial stigmatization assigned to Blackness and maleness that is seemingly inescapable to shake (Lacy, 2007). Negative stereotypes and images of Black men and boys are customarily emblematic of their life experiences (Moore et al., 2021), especially in formal and informal educational spaces. At various junctures of education, these deeply held negative assumptions tend to have unfavorable effects on learning and their overall scholastic experience. Simply put, Noguera (2008) asserts:

> The trouble with Black boys is that most never have a chance to be thought of as potentially smart and talented or to demonstrate talents in science, music, or literature. The trouble with Black boys is that too often they are placed in schools where their needs for nurturing, support, and loving discipline are not met. Instead, they are labeled, shunned, and treated in ways that create and reinforce an inevitable cycle of failure. (p. xxi)

With little hope for change, "the advancement of young men and boys of color is likely to remain constrained. In the worst ways, the racism, discrimination, and racial oppression that they have experienced and continue to endure are central to many of their struggles" (Moore et al., 2021, p. 2) and relevant to the unfavorable experiences they encounter (Gaylord-Harden et al., 2018). With both care and brilliance, this edited volume presents a vivid contextualization of the experiences of Black men and boys across various educational stages by underscoring those factors that commonly undermine and enhance teaching, counseling, learning, and career development for them. Thus, in many of the chapters, the authors offer a refreshing perspective on how individuals – professionals employed in K-12 and postsecondary settings – can inspire, nurture, and support Black men and boys. After reading this edited volume, I hope that the readers will become more knowledgeable and informed about the psychological resiliency and emotional capacity that Black men and boys bring to educational spaces. To this end, I really appreciate the range of topics covered in the edited volume and how the authors characterize historical and contemporary topics in education applicable to Black men and boys. I applaud the editors in pulling together these brilliant education scholars and researchers to address grand challenges that Black men and boys experience at every juncture of education. Noted by Noguera (2008), "[o]ur challenge as educators, parents, policymakers, and activists is to find ways not merely to save Black boys and others who are at risk but to create conditions so that saving is no longer necessary. How we respond to our schools and those who are not now well served there is more than merely a call to do good" (pp. xxvii–xxviii).

In America, none of us can afford to sit on the sideline and/or wait for someone else to respond to the grand challenges that Black men and boys experience across every juncture of education. Each of us can play an intricate role in supporting Black men and boys by helping to create optimal teaching, counseling, and learning experiences for them. Without question, when Black men and boys are not able to obtain a world-class education, the entire country loses. Thus, only through unwavering commitment, concentration, and effort can the country eradicate the grand challenges in education noted by the authors. In order to improve their educational experiences and, equally as important, their academic and career outcomes, there must be a strong commitment to pinpointing and changing any educational policies, processes, programs, and practices that impede optimal learning and advancement in education for Black men and boys (Jackson & Moore, 2008; Wint et al., 2022). Across a variety of educational contexts and settings, this edited volume certainly offers real solutions to real problems endured by Black men and boys. Kudos to the two editors and the contributors for putting this edited volume together.

James L. Moore, III, PhD
Distinguished Professor of Urban Education
College of Education and Human Ecology
The Ohio State University

References

Ford, D. Y., & Moore, J. L., III. (2013). Understanding and reversing underachievement and achievement gaps among high-ability African American males in urban school contexts. *Urban Review, 45*(4), 400–415.

Gaylord-Harden, N. K., Barbarin, O., Tolan, P. H., & McBride Murry, V. M. (2018). Understanding development of African American boys and young men: Moving from risks to positive youth development. *American Psychologist, 73*(6), 753–767.

Jackson, J. F. L., & Moore, J. L., III. (2006). African American males in education: Endangered or ignored? *Teachers College Record, 108,* 201–205.

Jackson, J. F. L., & Moore, J. L., III. (2008). The African American male crisis in education: A popular media infatuation or needed public policy response? *American Behavioral Scientist, 51,* 847–853.

Lacy, K. R. (2007). *Blue-chip Black: Race, class, and status in the new Black middle class.* University of California.

Moore, J. L., III, Hines, E. M., & Harris, P. C. (2021). Introduction to the special issue: Males of color and school counseling. *Professional School Counseling, 25*(1), 1–7.

Noguera, P. A. (2008). *The trouble with Black boys: And other reflections on race, equity, and the future of public education.* Jossey-Bass/Wiley.

Wint, K. M., Opara, I., Gordon, R., & Brooms, D. R. (2022). Countering educational disparities among Black boys and Black adolescent boys from Pre-k to high school: A life course-intersectional perspective. *The Urban Review, 54,* 183–206.

INDEX

9781804555798